The Rise of the Terrors

DUNDEE UNITED FC,
A COMPREHENSIVE HISTORY 1945–1979

Steve Gracie

Arabest Publishing Dundee

By the same author

A Passion for Survival: Dundee United FC, A Comprehensive History 1909–1945

© Steven F Gracie 2009

Published by Arabest Publishing

ISBN 978 0 9558341 1 0

British Library Cataloguing in Publications Data

A catalogue record for this book is available from the British Library

All photographs © D C Thomson & Co Ltd and Dundee United FC

Set in Minion Pro 11pt

Cover designed by Clare Brayshaw

Prepared by:
York Publishing Services Ltd
64 Hallfield Road
Layerthorpe
York YO31 7ZQ
Tel: 01904 431213
Website: www.yps-publishing.co.uk

Foreword by Bill Littlejohn Director 1992 – 2002

It is indeed a great privilege to write this foreword in the period leading up to Dundee United FC centenary celebrations. It is a time to celebrate as United has much to be proud of as it rose from obscurity to a leading role in Scottish football and a name to be feared in the European game. My father had a long association with the Club (almost 50 years) and I grew up as a supporter during the period this book covers so well. The story contains many memories for our family and highlights in its well researched and detailed history, the progress made by the Club.

The Fifties period highlights the goals of Peter McKay and John Coyle, the near disaster of relegation to C Division followed by the appointment of Jerry Kerr as Manager taking the Club from the doldrums of Division 2 to an established and challenging Division 1 team. The Sixties introduced the magic of the Scandinavians, Dossing, Persson, Wing, Berg, Seemann and the incredible consistency of Doug Smith who in a 10 year period missed only two league games out of 340 – and the first taste of European football. The beginning of the Seventies brought the appointment of Jim McLean, which was to bring unprecedented success to the Club. Within three years the Club had appeared in its first ever Scottish Cup Final and European football was to become a regular event at Tannadice.

All of these memories and many many more are captured and brought back to life in this exciting history of the Club. This book does not however complete the history because the story has only been partly told – the best was yet to come.

Bill Littlejohn

February 2009

Authors Notes and Acknowledgements

This is the second book in a series on the history of Dundee United FC, following the publication of *A Passion for Survival*, which covered the years from 1909 to 1945.

The same reference sources have been used, with the majority of the research carried out using the archives of local newspapers published by D C Thomson & Co Ltd. On the internet there are numerous websites available which were useful. As a result, there was less need to examine player records at the SFA in Glasgow, although a visit was undertaken to verify some details. Companies House provided most of the financial information on the Club.

As readers of the first book will know, this project began in the latter part of 2002, primarily to satisfy my own desire to find out everything I could about Dundee United FC, but it grew to become an all-consuming passion and I decided to put together a detailed history of the Club. This volume documents the rise of Dundee United from a mediocre Second Division side in the post-Second World War years, into a force within Scottish football and on the continent. A third book is planned, to chronicle the most recent years and it is intended that this final chapter will be released in late 2009.

The increased stature of Dundee United following the Second World War ensured that there was enough information to keep the fans informed. However, it also produces a dilemma for the author – what to include and what to leave out. I have tried to incorporate everything that is relevant. As before, when compiling match details, player information and statistics, all possible care has been taken to ensure accuracy.

I would again acknowledge the invaluable assistance of D C Thomson & Co Ltd., without whom it would have been impossible to complete this project. Special thanks are owed to Anne Swadel and her team for all their help. D C Thomson & Co Ltd again provided the vast majority of photographs used in this book. Other than some of the older and rarer images, most of the photographs included are good quality.

The Local Studies Department of Dundee City Libraries again provided access to their bound newspaper volumes and microfilmed archives. I would also thank Richard McBrearty and Kenny Strang at the Scottish Football Museum, for allowing me access to player registration records. The *Dundee United Who's Who* by Pat Kelly was utilised to confirm some player information. Very special thanks go to Shug Falconer of the A90 Arab Society who gave me copies of his statistics on United covering much of the period 1960-1979. Shug planted the idea for this book, and can now vaguely remember! I would also thank Mike Watson who supplied me with statistics for most of the period 1945-1960. Statistics from these two sources were used as a basis but were all checked to at least one other source. Any errors are therefore mine alone.

My close friends Denys Carnegie, Bill Greig and Tom Cairns helped enormously as test readers for this volume. Their comments and encouragement were extremely helpful and shaped the final version that went to print. I would again thank Kirstin McCarle who edited the early versions of this book. I also owe her an apology for mis-spelling her name in the first book. Thanks also to Alison Farrell who again carried out the proofreading and to Duncan Beal and his staff at York Publishing Services Ltd.

My most grateful thanks go to my wife, Carol-Anne who encouraged me through some difficult times over the last two years.

I would also thank everyone who contacted me with comments about the first book. Remarks and criticisms were gladly accepted and I am pleased to say that they were positive. Dundee United fans are a special breed and have won well deserved praise throughout Scotland and indeed all over Europe for their excellent behaviour and good humour.

To all you Arabs, I dedicate this history of Dundee United 1945-1979.

Season By Season 1945–1979

Picking Up the Pieces

The end of the Second World War marked a significant turning point in the history of several provincial clubs and Dundee United were no exception. In the previous thirty-six years, United had stumbled from one crisis to another and had almost gone out of business on at least five occasions. There had been some highlights along the way. But a few brief flirtations with life in the First Division and the final of the Emergency War Cup in 1940 had to be considered an inadequate return. The Board at Tannadice were determined to move the Club forward and the target was a permanent place in the top flight. However, that was some way off and to begin the post-war years United picked up where they left off in 1939, an ordinary Second Division side.

The late 1940s witnessed the beginning of the new Dundee United and after the post-war reorganisation of the Scottish Leagues was completed, the first signs of a youth development policy emerged at Tannadice. By the mid 1950s, an innovative Board would encourage supporter involvement through Dundee United Sportsmen's Club and gradually a firm financial base would be formed to allow managers much more latitude to improve the side. With money available, the success of the Club would be built on a continuous youth programme augmented with the purchase of experienced players.

In the immediate post-war years, a place in the First Division was foreseeable but no-one at Tannadice could honestly have imagined that United would then consolidate in the top flight, not only taking part in European football but also becoming a Club that was feared on the continent.

But first, United had to negotiate many obstacles. The journey from mediocrity to excellence would take the Club along an often difficult road, but gradually the name of Dundee United would be written in football history over and over again.

1945-46

Post-War Doldrums

It had been widely assumed that the Scottish Leagues would be back to business as usual for season 1945-46 but in June, after much discussion amongst the committee and member clubs, it was decided to continue the Southern League in a two league set up as a transitionary measure. However, no matter how it appears, it was the Scottish League in all but name. It was proposed that the top flight, League A would consist of sixteen teams and League B would be made up of twelve teams but this was later increased to fourteen. A committee of three representatives from the Southern League and three from the North Eastern League was set up to decide which clubs would occupy each league and after considerable debate, protests and compromise, a final selection was agreed. Hearts, Falkirk and Rangers, who had each operated teams in both war time leagues, were obviously reduced to one team each and were allocated to League A along with twelve of the other former Southern League sides plus Aberdeen.

Dundee United were allocated to League B along with the remaining North Eastern League sides plus Airdrieonians, Stenhousemuir, Ayr United, Albion Rovers, Alloa Athletic, Cowdenbeath, St Johnstone and Dumbarton. Others such as Brechin City, Montrose, Forfar Athletic and Stirling Albion were excluded and left to make their own arrangements.

An historic meeting of four Scottish football associations took place on 5th July 1945 at SFA headquarters in Carlton Place, Glasgow, with each convening in turn to formalise the new set up. The North Eastern League was first to meet, followed by the Scottish League, then the Southern League and finally the SFA. All unanimously agreed the new league structure and then fixed the admission prices at 1/6 (7½p) for B Division. Wages were set at a maximum of £3 and match guarantees at £50 for B Division. The final meeting of the North Eastern League took place on 25th July, presided over by George Graham of the SFA, just as he had done for the entire existence of the league. Mr Graham had been the key official who kept Scottish football going during the war years and he continued to play a highly significant part in the game in the years that followed. He was later knighted for his services to the sport.

Maintenance work was being carried out at Tannadice in preparation for the new season but there were few movements in the squad. From the final campaign of WW2, United had retained Jimmy Robertson, Norman Fraser, John Simpson, Ian Smart, John Ross, Sid Smith, Lomond Reid, Bobby Chalmers, Alf Burnett, Johnny Hutton, George 'Piper' MacKay, Sandy Elder, George Maxwell, Ronnie McWalter, Bill Shaw, David Jack, Ian Hay, Tommy Adamson, Willie Jennett, Ernie Stygal, Dave Clark, Dick Scott, Robert Walls, Bobby Ross, Bobby Moodie, Albert Simmons, Willie Wann, Jimmy Adamson and Alec Shirley. Many of these players were unlikely to play for United again but retaining the registrations might bring in transfer fees once everything returned to normal. Albert Juliussen was still with United but he was registered with Huddersfield Town. Jennett was placed on the transfer list in late June, and in July, Moodie left to join Cowdenbeath.

The season kick-off was fast approaching before United signed any new players. Hugh Young from YMCA Anchorage and William Smith from St Monance Swifts joined shortly after the trial match on 4th August but United fans were stunned to learn of the departure of Juliussen five days later. The undoubted goal scoring prowess of United's war time star striker had attracted the attention of Aberdeen initially, but it was Dundee who secured his signature for a reported fee of £2,000, despite the fact that the player had never kicked a ball in major competition for Huddersfield's first eleven!

United's opening game of the Southern League B was at Dunfermline Athletic on 11th August but Manager Charlie McGillivray had still not put together a full team. Few of the retained players were actually available to play as many were still in the armed forces and they were not stationed locally. As a result, left back John McGowan signed on a short-term deal from Thornliewood United on the morning of the match and he joined Smith and Young making debuts along with a trialist. It was a disjointed performance at East End Park and United lost 7-0. To shore up a leaky defence, centre half Willie Kelly was signed from St Mirren and went straight into the side. It seemed to make little difference, as visitors St Johnstone stormed into a 3-0 lead at Tannadice in the first home match a week later. Hay scored twice and MacKay got the other as United drew level, but the Perth side won 4-3 with a late goal.

The next signing was centre forward John 'Jacky' Hunter on loan for a month from Morton and he went into the side to face Albion Rovers at Coatbridge on 25th August. It was an improved United display with two trialists in the side but the Club suffered a third defeat, although by just a single goal. Before the next match, McGillivray signed former Middlesbrough, Notts County, Luton Town, Aberdeen and Arbroath attacker, Charlie Ferguson. He made his debut against Ayr United along with Arbroath half back Alec MacFarlane, who turned out as a trialist and after the 3-2 win, he also signed. Former Ipswich Town, Nottingham Forest, Raith Rovers and Kilmarnock full back, Frank Shufflebottom joined United in time to play in the local derby at Dens Park on 8th September. It was an even match decided by a single goal for the home side, with both defences playing well.

At home to Raith Rovers next, United suffered another 7-0 thumping. McGillivray was so angered by that result, he restored himself to the forward line a week later when Alloa Athletic were the visitors, but even with two goals to his credit he could not inspire his team as United lost 5-2. Considering the difficulty he had in getting a side together each week, it is perhaps surprising that McGillivray then allowed Shaw, Adamson and Hay to go to Brechin City. The Manager then brought Peter Cabrelli back to Tannadice on 29th September, although the player did not take part that day as United secured only the second win of the campaign, 4-2 over Airdrieonians, with John Ross netting a hat-trick.

Team selection problems brought in more trialists and three in particular stood out. Despite losing 4-2 at Cowdenbeath and 4-1 at Arbroath, keeper Bob Carrie of Dundee Violet had impressed and he turned out for a third time against Stenhousemuir on 20th October. Leslie Young from Manchester United made a scoring debut in that match as United won 7-0. The second trialist, centre forward Aitken of Croy Celtic scored a hat-trick. Carrie and Aitken were offered terms but unfortunately for United neither accepted. Carrie signed for Falkirk and Aitken later joined Hibs. Emilio Pacione of Lochee Harp was the third trialist in the match against Stenhousemuir, scoring twice. He netted again in the 5-2 home win over East Fife a week later, with Watford winger John Tivendale making his debut.

There were changes in the Boardroom around this time. William McIntosh was back as a Director and Arthur Cram, who had worked very hard for the Club during the war years and was credited with much of the success in the Emergency War Cup of 1940, resigned as Company Secretary but stayed on the Board. McGillivray was offered the post of Manager/Secretary but declined. In fact, he requested a free transfer on 17th October, although he agreed to stay on until a new Manager was found. The appointment of the new Manager/Secretary happened very quickly when Willie MacFadyen took the position on 30th October 1945. He was well known in football circles, having played with Motherwell before moving south to Huddersfield Town and then to Clapton Orient. His first signing was one for the future as he acquired Pacione on a provisional form.

Bobby Ross

There was no improvement in results, with four defeats in the month of November, starting with a 2-1 reversal at Dumbarton. The new Manager also lost Ferguson in mid November when he moved to North Shields to work, taking up the post of player/manager with the local side. MacFadyen then began a search for a replacement, first bringing in Alec Stewart from St Johnstone but he made only two appearances. The first was in a 3-0 defeat away to his former club on 10th November. Former Huddersfield Town and Bradford Park Avenue forward Willie Martin was next to join the Club but he did little better with just four appearances, beginning with the 2-1 home defeat from Dunfermline Athletic a week later. Finally, a goal scorer was found but it was a right winger, Neil McKinnon signed from Rangers on 19th November and he became a regular in the side. Two days later, Shirley left to join Halifax Town whilst Benny Yorston from Aberdeen and George Mudie from Brechin City came into the squad, but each turned out only once. McKinnon, Yorston and Mudie all made debuts on 24th November in a 3-2 home defeat by Albion Rovers. George Barron from Aberdeen Muggiemoss was also signed on a provisional form but did not make his debut until April in a friendly against a Polish Army side.

A point was gained in 1-1 draw at Ayr United in the first match of December but poor form continued with a 3-1 defeat at Alloa Athletic and a 5-0 hammering at Raith Rovers. Just one more point was collected that month in a 1-1 draw at Airdrieonians on 22nd December. Inside left Harry Smith from Clapton Orient made his debut in that match, one of four new players signed towards the end of the year. Along with right half Bill Harrow from local junior side Elmwood, inside right Ed McInally from Lanark United made his debut at home to Cowdenbeath in a 2-0 defeat a week later.

Signed on a short-term deal, Tranmere Rovers' full back Percy Steele made his debut at inside left on 1st January 1946 as United lost 3-2 in the home derby against Dundee. However, a significant change to the side going into the New Year was the inclusion of Pacione, by then at United full-time. A rearranged side had a positive impact from the next match, a 4-1 win at home to Dumbarton with new keeper Devon Reid from Brechin Victoria playing as a trialist. He was then signed and the 4-1 result was repeated against Arbroath three days later. Shortly afterwards, United had a change of trainer when Johnny Hart returned to Tannadice. He replaced Willie Cameron who moved up the road to Dens Park to cover for Willie Arbuckle who was ill. Sadly, United's war time trainer, Arbuckle died a few months later. January continued with a 2-2 draw at Stenhousemuir a week later. In the final match of a short league campaign, a 2-0 defeat at East Fife on 19th January, United fielded new signing Martin Buchan from Aberdeen, alongside teenager John Cruickshanks, on loan from the Pittodrie side until the end of the season.

There were four cup competitions to fill the remaining weeks of the season. First came the Supplementary Cup, with a tie against Raith Rovers over two legs.

The first match was at Tannadice on 26th January and the 4-1 win for the visitors was an injustice to United. Raith Rovers' keeper was inspired and kept the Black and Whites at bay whilst his outfield colleagues won the match with a fortunate three goal burst in the second half. United completely turned the tie around in the second leg in Kirkcaldy a week later. Pacione, MacKay and Buchan scored to level the aggregate at 4-4 and a play-off was arranged in midweek at Dens Park. Raith Rovers took a 2-0 lead in the third match but United fought back with goals from Pacione, Buchan and Harry Smith to lead 3-2. After the interval, Raith levelled it again. Strangely, the Scottish League had left it up to the clubs to decide whether a drawn outcome would require extra time and then a replay if necessary. Confusion reigned at the final whistle and it appears that United were caught out by the decision merely to flip a coin to decide the winner and Raith Rovers won the toss! An unsuccessful protest by United followed. Shortly after that match, Hutton left to join Millwall following his request for a transfer to a London club for personal reasons. The first round of the Forfarshire Cup was next and was played on a two leg basis. United drew the first leg match 2-2 with Arbroath at Gayfield on 16th February, with former United Juniors player Jack Wilson making his only United appearance.

The forerunner to the present day Scottish League Cup was the Southern League Cup, which had been introduced by the Southern League clubs in 1942. The draw placed United in the same four team section as Stenhousemuir, Ayr United and Dumbarton. United started with a very good 4-0 win over Stenhousemuir on 23rd February but then lost 2-0 at Ayr United. On the same day, United transferred Kelly to Morton after he had requested a move two months earlier. Frank Shufflebottom was still in the forces but was due to be demobbed, which meant he would soon leave the area. In anticipation of this, Alex Jardine was signed from Wishaw Juniors as a replacement and he made his debut on 9th March as United beat Dumbarton 3-2. A 1-1 draw at Stenhousemuir was followed by a 2-1 home win over Ayr United, with new signings Lloyd Hull from Lesmahagow Juniors and Len Rae from Inverurie Locos making debuts. In the final sectional match on 30th March, United won 2-1 at Dumbarton but once the final placings were ascertained, Dundee United and Ayr United were tied on exactly the same points with the same 12-7 goals tallies. The clubs could have spun a coin for the right to go into the hat for the next round but neither was willing to. Instead, they agreed to a play-off with extra time if needed. The deciding match took place before a crowd of 11,700 at Hampden Park on 3rd April, with outside left Bob Collins from Dundee Arnot making his debut for United. Ayr United won by a single goal in a match that never lived up to expectation.

After losing 5-3 in a friendly against the Polish Army XI, United geared up for the final tournament of the season, the Victory Cup. Queen of the South were the opponents in this two leg affair and a crowd of 15,000 saw United take a 2-1 advantage to Dumfries, with goals from McKinnon and Pacione. In the second leg, McKinnon scored in between two goals for the home side and the tie was finely balanced. Either side might have won but it was the Doonhamers who got the decisive goal to win 4-3 on aggregate, although it was hard luck on United, who hit woodwork twice.

MacFadyen's search for players had intensified following the news that the Scottish League would revert to the pre-war format, with three leagues in season 1946-47. The fourteen teams in Southern League B were to form the new Scottish League B Division and there would be two promotion places open to the B Division sides. As expected, there were a large number of free transfers handed out at the end of April, including many of the players retained during the war years. Robertson, Jack, McWalter, Cabrelli, Harry Smith, Hugh Young, William Smith, Scott, Chalmers, Fraser, Sid Smith, Maxwell, McInally, Stygal, Shufflebottom, Leslie Young and Reid were all released. The registration of Elder was more than likely cancelled around this time also. On the retained list were Clark, Jardine, Harrow, Bobby Ross, Hull, McKinnon, Buchan, Pacione, Rae, MacKay and Collins along with young goalkeeper Jimmy Adamson. MacFarlane, John Ross, Burnett, Simpson and Simmons who were in the armed services, were also retained. Cabrelli signed for Arbroath almost immediately and his influence along with that of Archie Coats (who would later become assistant manager and then trainer with United) helped the Red Lichties hammer United 6-0 on 4th May in the Tannadice leg of the Forfarshire Cup tie, with Coats helping himself to a hat-trick.

Overall the league season was a poor one. Just six wins and three draws left United in third bottom place, one point ahead of bottom pair Raith Rovers and Arbroath. Only the Southern League Cup had brought any hint of success with early exits in the other three cup tournaments. Of the 44 players and numerous trialists used over the season, MacKay was the only ever present. Keeper Clark made over thirty appearances and full backs Jack and Shufflebottom were just short of that figure. Pacione was undoubtedly the find of the season with 13 goals in his 17 league and cup outings.

1946-47

Business as Usual

Preparations for the first post-war Scottish League season were well under way at Tannadice by the end of May, with most of the retained players re-signed. The Board also took the decision to run a reserve side in the new C Division but to do so a bigger squad was needed. As a result, Ian Smart was re-signed in late May and he was quickly joined by former Celtic and Preston North End half back Alec Miller who cost a reported £400 from Motherwell. Stobswell full back Doug Berrie also signed at the end of May. The only activity at Tannadice over the next few weeks was work carried out, with the assistance of around a dozen volunteers, to improve the standing areas.

Tivendale re-signed on 29th June and a few days later former Rangers and Falkirk right half Sammy Ross was signed from Motherwell for around £350, ahead of stiff competition from several English sides. In early July, United added Jake Davidson from Dundee Violet to the squad and Burnett returned after he was demobbed from the armed forces. Johnny Hart was confirmed as trainer again. A trial match was arranged for 3rd August and 6,000 fans turned up to see a good game with seven trialists on show, in a match that ended in a 3-3 draw. Immediately afterwards, full back Robert Simpson from Lochgelly Albert and left half Jimmy Salmond from Jeanfield Swifts were added to the squad. George Brown from Bannockburn Youth Club and Dan Craig of Thornliewood United were recruited for the reserves along with Mungo Kirkland and just before the new season kicked off the welcome news that Pacione had re-signed was announced. Wann left United and was reinstated to the juniors.

Sammy Ross, Miller, Simpson and Davidson were the new faces making debuts in the opening match of the new season on 10th August at Tannadice, where a 13,000 crowd saw an encouraging United performance result in a 3-0 win over Dunfermline Athletic. In a midweek Supplementary Cup tie against Stenhousemuir, Davidson scored a memorable hat-trick and MacKay netted from a free kick in a 4-1 win. Salmond made his first and only appearance for United in the next league match at Ayr United and scored the first goal in a 3-3 draw. In the second leg of the Supplementary Cup, United drew 2-2 at Stenhousemuir to go through to the next round.

October 1946
Standing: *Simpson, Jardine, Clark, S Ross, R Ross, Miller*
Seated: *McKinnon, Buchan, Pacione, Lister, MacKay*

Saturday 24th August was derby day at Tannadice and 21,000 spectators witnessed a thrilling first half but no goals. After the interval MacKay put United ahead from the spot but the lead was short lived as former United favourite Juliussen levelled the match. It might have gone either way after that but it was Dundee who snatched a goal for a 2-1 win. The fans though were not disheartened as the opening matches held out promise for the rest of the season. This appeared to be borne out with a comfortable 4-1 home win over Dunfermline Athletic in the Supplementary Cup on 28th August. Making his debut in that match was George Jeffrey, newly signed from Hamilton Academical on a one month deal.

United lost the next league game at St Johnstone, but had chances to consolidate a half time lead before the Perth Saints took control and won 3-1. Smart scored United's goal in that game on his Scottish League debut. That was followed by a home tie against East Fife in the Supplementary Cup with keeper Peter MacKay in goal for his only game at first team level. He was not at fault for any of the goals and the 4-2 defeat was hard to take, but the side had only themselves to blame as the forwards failed to take any of a number of second half chances. The next league match on 7th September resulted in another two lost points as Albion Rovers capitalised on some poor defending to score three times in seven first half minutes. Jeffrey scored in what was his penultimate match for United, but the team could not find a way back and lost 3-1. United followed up that result with a 1-1 draw at Raith Rovers before the new Scottish League Cup competition took centre stage. Kirkland was released around this time and Salmond left to join Brechin City.

United were drawn in a League Cup section with Cowdenbeath, Dumbarton and Arbroath. In the first match on 21st September, the team secured a 2-0 victory at home to Cowdenbeath and then cantered to a 3-0 win at Dumbarton. At Arbroath on 5th October, a comfortable 3-1 win was achieved by a United side wearing numbered jerseys for the first time. Scottish teams had just recently been given permission to do this by the football authorities. Cowdenbeath exacted some revenge at Central Park with a 4-1 win but only after an even first half had ended 1-1 and United lost Smart to injury. The home fans got their first sight of United in numbered shirts on 19th October in a 2-1 win over Dumbarton with debut man Alex Lister from Third Lanark scoring an equaliser and Pacione getting the winner. Qualification for the next round of the League Cup was assured a week later but it took a last minute Pacione goal to secure the 3-2 win over Arbroath.

Back on league business on 2nd November, Airdrieonians stole the points at Tannadice with a 2-1 win, scoring two late goals when United appeared to have the match wrapped up. George Stewart, signed from New Stevenston, made a scoring debut the following week at Alloa Athletic where United lost 4-1, largely because keeper Clark was injured. Alf Burnett made his competitve debut in that match. The next two matches were at home to Dumbarton and then East Fife and both followed the same pattern to end in 2-1 wins. Stewart scored from an early penalty, the visitors equalised and United scored a winner late in the second half.

John Simpson was back at Tannadice after being demobbed from the military but he was released soon after. Collins was handed a free transfer at his own request just before United lost 3-2 at Stenhousemuir on 30th November. It was also the last appearance for McKinnon before he was transferred to Albion Rovers three weeks later. George Grant of New Stevenston made his debut against Arbroath on 7th December as the Black and Whites lost 3-1. The next two matches might have gone either way. First, with Berrie showing up well in his debut, United won 3-2 at home to Cowdenbeath thanks to a late Lister header, but in the next match United conceded twice in the final minutes at Dunfermline Athletic to lose 4-3. In the final game of 1946, United gave their best display of the season to trounce Ayr United 5-1 but in the New Year's Day derby fixture, United were beaten 2-0 at Dens Park by Dundee. Over the festive period there were rumours of a player swap with MacKay going to Blackpool in exchange for George Eastham, and Burnley were showing a keen interest in Grant. Fortunately for United fans neither player left at that time, but Craig appears to have been released then.

Angus McGillivray joined United from Arbroath but played just a few games in the reserves before he was released again. After trials in the reserves, centre half Tom Wyllie from Arbroath Victoria had signed in October 1946. He made his first team debut on 2nd January as United lost 4-2 at home to St Johnstone but Bobby Ross was back in his usual place two days later in a 2-0 win at Dumbarton. Willie Crothers from Dunipace Juniors was the next trialist to make a debut, scoring twice as Alloa Athletic were thrashed 6-2 at Tannadice on 11th January, with Pacione and Lister also getting two each. In torrential rain the visitors started the second half a man short and by the end, they had lost another two players, suffering from exhaustion. Crothers signed immediately after his fine performance against Alloa Athletic and netted again in the match at Arbroath a week later. That match was a tremendous end to end battle with United leading 3-1 at half time. Just as full-time approached, it was level at 4-4 and then the Red Lichties scored a fluke winner when the ball was punted goalwards, bounced off the keeper and the post and trickled into the net. On 25th January, the match against Queen's Park in the Scottish Cup at Hampden Park only just survived the winter freeze and despite a valiant effort, United went down 3-0.

Another good team display brought full points at Methil in a 2-1 win over East Fife on 1st February but the weather then wiped out most of the February fixtures throughout the country and it was a full month before United were in action again. It was a game well worth the wait however, as United faced Rangers at Ibrox in the first leg of the League Cup quarter final. The Black and Whites gave the Glasgow side a real fright on an icy pitch and were unlucky not to get a penalty in the first half before Waddell put Rangers in front. Lister equalised from the spot early in the second half as United gave as good as they got but with just twenty minutes left, Rangers scored a second. United were never out of it and came close to levelling again before the final whistle. Four days later the second leg was due to be played at Tannadice, but the pitch was knee deep in snow and the match had to be switched to Dens Park, where the snow had been cleared. United again took the game to their more fancied opponents but Rangers scored early with a dubious goal. Undaunted, United stuck to the task and after half time Lister levelled. United were reduced to ten men when Simpson went off injured and the side deserved more from the game but went out on a 3-2 aggregate. Signed from Bridgeton Waverly in September 1946, goalkeeper Tommy Muir made his debut in the first leg against Rangers and was on again for the second. On both occasions his performance was outstanding and reflected a worthy team effort.

There was another weather enforced delay before United played their next match, a 1-1 draw at Cowdenbeath on 29th March. Then, after torrential rain caused a friendly at Stirling Albion to be abandoned, United played the first match at Tannadice for more than three months when they met Stenhousemuir on 12th April and drew 2-2. In a rearranged league match against Raith Rovers two days later, Lou France, who had signed from St Johnstone YMCA in January, made his debut in a 3-0 win. The league season ended with defeats away to Airdrieonians and Albion Rovers and in both matches United conceded five times. Tommy Kinloch from Benburb made his competitive debut alongside John Brannan in the second of these matches on 3rd May. Mixed in with the last two league games, the Forfarshire Cup became the main focus for end of season interest and against Brechin City on 15th April, United won 2-0 at Glebe Park. They went on to cruise past Forfar Athletic two weeks later with a 6-2 win in which teenager Brannan, signed from Maryhill Hibs in January, made an impressive debut. However, in the final on 17th May, United came across a strong Dundee side with Albert Juliussen on form. The former United favourite showed no mercy to his old club as he netted four of the goals in Dundee's 5-0 win at Dens Park.

United ended the league campaign in tenth place but just four points ahead of bottom club Cowdenbeath. It was obvious that work was still required to improve the side. Top scorer Lister finished the season on 18 goals in all league and cup matches, with Pacione the closest to him with 11 to his credit. Simpson and Sammy Ross played in all but one of the 39 competitive matches and another six players made more than 25 appearances each. Muir, Jardine, Simpson, Berrie, France, Bobby Ross, Sammy Ross, Rae, Grant, Crothers, MacKay, Smart, Wyllie and Brannan all re-signed before the end of April and in May, they were joined by Kinloch, Harrow, Miller, Pacione and Lister. Adamson, MacFarlane and Simmons were still on the retained list whilst on national service. Burnett, who had been on loan at Barrow, was signed by the non league side. Surprisingly, keeper Clark was released and he was joined through the exit door by Barron (who had been on loan at Huntly), Brown, John Ross, Buchan, Tivendale and Stewart.

1947-48

Courting Relegation

The Manager brought in only a few new players, beginning with lifelong United fan Johnny Kerr from Dundee North End. Centre forward John Peters joined United reserves from Stobswell in June. Davidson refused the re-signing terms offered and was transfer listed in early July. He later joined East Fife where his brother Doug played. The annual trial match was arranged for 2nd August and after seeing several new prospects in action, MacFadyen signed only one, (William) Joe Dalling from Tulliallan Juveniles.

The new season therefore kicked off with no debutants as United faced Albion Rovers in the League Cup away on 9th August and lost 3-0. New signing Kerr came into the side in midweek against Alloa Athletic in a league match at Tannadice and although the visitors were much the better side, United had Crothers and Pacione to thank for two late goals to win 5-3. On the right wing, Dalling was then drafted in for the first of only three games for United over the season, but lowly Leith Athletic came back from two goals down to draw 2-2 for a League Cup point at Tannadice. New goalkeeper John Boyd from Dunipace Juniors also made his debut in that match, but could not be blamed for any of the goals. In the League Cup a week later, Cowdenbeath left Tannadice with both points after winning 2-0 completely against the run of play. Alec Malcolm from Jeanfield Swifts then made his debut in a 1-0 away defeat at Albion Rovers in a midweek league match. That was followed by a 2-1 League Cup win over the same team at Tannadice on 30th August, with Frank McKee from Lochgelly Albert making his first start. However, thoughts of a repeat of the previous season's League Cup quarter final had long since faded and defeats at Leith Athletic, 3-1 and Cowdenbeath, 1-0 ensured United's short League Cup campaign finished on a low.

In the last of the League Cup games, ex-Dundee player Jimmy 'Soldier' Jones had the first of only two outings for United in a match that also saw the first appearance of Peter McKay from Newburgh Juniors. Considered to be one of the best juniors in the area, McKay had netted 16 goals in just five games for the Fife junior side prior to signing for United. Although he had a quiet debut he would soon become the toast of Tannadice and write himself into the history of the Club, as United's all time top scorer. When McKay joined United on 8th September, MacFadyen only beat Jimmy Crapnell, manager of St Johnstone, to the signature of the player by a few minutes.

The poor start to the league season continued with a 3-2 defeat at home to Stirling Albion on 20th September and then Kilmarnock thumped United 5-2 at Rugby Park. On the positive side, United could take heart from the form of McKay who scored one in each game. Unfortunately, the centre was injured and missed the entire second half against Killie, becoming the latest in a string of injured players. He also missed the next match which was against a strong Arbroath side, and they took a 3-1 lead before United rallied to win 4-3. A free Saturday on 11th October gave United the opportunity to take a team north for a friendly at Elgin City and five reserves were given an outing in a hard fought 3-2 win. Left half Malcolm Sinclair signed on a free transfer from Falkirk and made his debut in the next league match, a 1-0 defeat at home to Dumbarton on 18th October. Despite the poor form of the team, the Directors then displayed their confidence in the future of the Club with a collective purchase of just over 3,800 shares by John Carnegie Jnr., William McIntosh and Ernest Robertson whilst Jimmy Littlejohn, Arthur Cram and Bill Robertson bought 200 shares each.

The trip to Cowdenbeath a week later exposed a fragile United defence that conceded five goals in the first half of a game they eventually lost 6-2. MacFadyen was on the look out for players and after losing Miller and Sammy Ross to Morton by the end of October, he added ex-Third Lanark and Queen's Park Rangers centre half John Barr in mid November. The Manager also brought in two defenders on short-term deals for the reserves, adding William Wright from Clyde and former Dundee and Arbroath player John Evans. In November, home form improved with a comfortable 4-2 win over Stenhousemuir. United then lost at Dunfermline Athletic but the side suffered injuries to Sinclair and Lister during the 5-3 defeat. Two more home wins followed as United beat Leith Athletic 2-1 and Hamilton Academical 3-2. In the last game of the month at Kirkcaldy however, Raith Rovers completely overwhelmed United to win 5-1.

United were 4-1 down to St Johnstone on 6th December but after a great fight back it ended 4-3 to the Saints with United on the attack and looking likely to level. Barr made his debut a week later at Ayr United where the Tannadice side recovered from 3-1 down to almost steal full points but had to settle for one. Boyd in goal was the star of the show in the 3-3 draw. The next match was at Alloa Athletic against a rejuvenated side, with former United and Rangers player Jimmy Simpson as their new manager. United took a one goal lead but faded after half time and lost 3-1. It was another good performance but the team was not taking the chances on offer and points were being given away. Before the next match, United fans were hit with an unexpected bombshell. On Christmas Day 1947, it was announced that Piper MacKay was moving to Dens Park in exchange for half back Jimmy Dickson plus a cash adjustment to United. The final say was left with Dickson who agreed to the move two days later and he made his debut on 27th December against Albion Rovers in a 3-0 win.

Following the loss of Miller and Sammy Ross, the departure of yet another key player had an adverse effect on the team. In the next five league matches United recorded only one win, 3-2 over East Fife at Tannadice. The other four results saw Kilmarnock leave Tannadice with full points from a 3-2 win and United lost 6-0 at Arbroath, 3-1 at Stirling Albion and 3-2 at Dumbarton. In an attempt to bolster the defence, the Manager persuaded Gibby McKenzie to sign from Airdrieonians, although he had turned United down only a month earlier. He made his debut on 31st January in the defeat at Dumbarton. The poor league form made the trip to Glasgow to face Partick Thistle in the Scottish Cup on 7th February a daunting prospect, especially as McKay and Lister were both out through injury.

Partick Thistle sat third top of Division A whilst United were third bottom of Division B. The home side opened the scoring in just two minutes and then increased the lead on the quarter hour mark. The Jags fans sat back for the expected massacre. However, the small band of United fans were making plenty of noise and increased the volume after Grant pulled one back with a low drive. The team produced a fighting rally to end the first half and were unlucky to go in 2-1 down. In the second half, Pacione grabbed the equaliser from point blank range before the home side went back in front, but United fought back again and Dickson made it 3-3. United pressed hard for a winner and Partick were grateful for the final whistle and a chance of extra time. The Jags scored the deciding goal just into the second period of time added, but United left with great credit for another battling cup performance. It later transpired that trainer Johnny Hart had used a new idea in his approach to the game. He had taken with him a tactics board and spent a long time with the players planning for the game in their Glasgow hotel, on the night before the match. It almost paid off.

That cup tie was the final appearance for McKee who was transferred to Birmingham City on 12th February. United also lost the services of Tom Wyllie at around the same time. He moved north to work and went on loan to Elgin City. Jimmy Craig from Rosslyn Juniors was brought in to replace McKee and he made a scoring debut on 14th February in a 3-3 draw with Cowdenbeath. United had the lead against the Fife side three times but the visitors levelled each time. That result and defeats at the hands of Dunfermline Athletic 4-0, Leith Athletic 1-0 and Hamilton Academical 6-0, left United perilously close to relegation. John McCormack from Stenhousemuir had been drafted into the forward line against Leith Athletic but MacFadyen needed more power up front and in a bold bid to avoid the drop he signed three players on loan just as the transfer deadline approached on 16th March. Centre forward George Henderson was brought in from Stirling Albion, centre half Ralph McKenzie from Aberdeen and outside left Jack Dewar from Hearts. United also allowed both Crothers and Malcolm to go on loan to Stirling Albion. Crothers later returned but Malcolm remained as a permanent transfer.

All three of United's loan signings made debuts on 20th March against Raith Rovers in a 3-0 home win. United won again a week later at St Johnstone, by a single goal scored from the spot by Dickson, after just six minutes. The Supplementary Cup tie at Hamilton Academical on 29th March resulted in an exit for United, beaten 3-2, but the fans were more concerned with league survival and five days later at Tannadice, it was secured. It was not achieved without putting the fans through more trauma though, as United were twice behind to Ayr United and held a precarious one goal lead before Grant scored with two minutes left to seal the 4-2 win.

On 7th April United took part in a Forfarshire Cup tie at home to Montrose but with only seven minutes remaining and United leading 3-1, the referee abandoned the match due to bad light! United felt the score should stand but common sense did not prevail and a replay was ordered. Before that could take place, United had a visit from Birmingham City on 12th April as part of the McKee transfer deal and 10,000 fans saw the English side win 5-1. McKee could not make an appearance due to injury and the full-time English side won comfortably, but only after United sustained injuries to Grant and Pacione who both missed the next league match two days later. The loss of two more players on an already weakened side was compounded when McKay was hurt early in the first half at East Fife, making the home side's job easy but not quite as easy as the 5-1 score line suggests.

Both sides fielded a number of reserves in the Forfarshire Cup replay at Montrose and it ended level at 1-1, prompting yet another replay. The final league match of the season on 24th April was at Stenhousemuir and United were beaten 3-0 with all the goals scored in the second half. Two days later, in the second Forfarshire Cup replay against Montrose at Tannadice, United came from behind twice to win comfortably 5-2. Then, with just a day to prepare for the next round of the competition, United were lucky to get a replay in a 0-0 draw at Brechin City. The rematch could not be arranged and was held over until the following season.

Chairman John Carnegie Jnr. and his Directors, brought down the curtain on 1947-48 and were very relieved to have avoided relegation. Sitting second bottom of the table just three points ahead of bottom club Leith Athletic was far from what the Board wanted and the 88 goals conceded in the league indicated where the problems lay. The forwards were not blameless either, with only McKay getting into double figures with 13 goals scored. In 37 competitive matches over the season, 35 players were used, with only Boyd and Pacione playing more than thirty times. Dewar, Henderson and McKenzie had already returned to their respective clubs when the list of players to be released was announced. There were no real surprises as Muir, France, Dalling, Sinclair, Harrow, Rae and Kerr were allowed to go.

Even before the season was over, MacFadyen was in the market for players and persuaded Jack Court of Cardiff City to return to Tannadice where he had played as a guest during WW2. The signature of Court was obtained against stiff competition from some English sides. All nineteen retained players re-signed by early May and were quickly joined by Willie Hume from Aberdeen. The left wing berth vacated by the departure of Piper MacKay had been impressively filled by Dewar whilst he was on loan and he was signed from Hearts in mid May.

1948-49

Building for the Future

No news came from Tannadice during the summer months until, after a closed doors match on 5th August, it was announced that the experienced centre half Duncan Ogilvie had been signed on a free transfer from Motherwell. He was well known to MacFadyen as the pair had played together at Motherwell and in the same Scotland team against Austria. The full public trial match took place two days later and 4,000 fans were treated to an entertaining game which included a McKay hat-trick, but the only player signed afterwards was centre half Alec Palmer from Third Lanark. Palmer though, would never make it into the first team.

Court, Ogilvie, Hume and Dewar were all in the starting line up for the opening league game of 1948-49 at Dumbarton on 14th August. United lost by the odd goal in five with McKay getting both United counters and he had a late effort ruled out. With newly signed goalkeeper Fred Watson from Renfrew Juniors making his debut, the Black and Whites were unlucky to lose 1-0 at home to Dunfermline Athletic four days later but could have no complaints after the 3-0 defeat at St Johnstone. The Forfarshire Cup replay against Brechin City, held over from the previous season, was arranged for 25th August, and United progressed to a final meeting with Arbroath after a comfortable 3-1 win in front of a mere 1,000 crowd. Poor league results continued with a 3-1 defeat at home to Airdrieonians, although United had their chances before the visitors took control in the second half. In the game at Alloa Athletic on 1st September, Frank Quinn from Celtic made his debut after some good performances in the reserves, including a hat-trick in his first game. It was a spirited showing from United who snatched the first point of the season after they came from 3-1 behind to draw level. Keeper Watson saved a penalty when United were just one goal in arrears near the end.

Junior international outside left George Cruickshank from Banks O' Dee made his debut as a trialist on 4th September as United recorded their first league win of the season, against Kilmarnock. Crothers scored to put United in front but then Hume was lost to injury. Instead of going on the defensive, United attacked and were rewarded with another two goals from Crothers to complete a hat-trick and one from Pacione made it a 4-0 half time lead. The Rugby Park side rallied after the interval but could not break down a solid defence until the dying minutes when they breached the United back line for a consolation goal. Shortly after that match, Court requested a transfer and within a few weeks he was signed by Dundee for a reported £1,000.

League football then took a break for three cup competitions. First, the League Cup campaign kicked off with a visit to Perth on 11th September with former Dundee forward Kinnaird Ouchterlonie making his league debut (although he had turned out for United during WW2). United drew 1-1 at St Johnstone in a match they should have won, such was their superiority in possession. Four days later, Airdrieonians won rather flatteringly 3-0 at their Broomfield home to knock United out of the Supplementary Cup, but the Black and Whites improved their chances of advancing in the League Cup with a well deserved 4-2 home win over Stenhousemuir. A week later Hamilton Academical were at Tannadice and with the score level at 1-1, Dickson missed from the spot. Shortly after, the visitors went 2-1 ahead and held that advantage until the end, despite enormous pressure from United. St Johnstone then came to Tannadice to find McKay on form as he collected the first of many hat-tricks in his career, to help United to a 4-2 win.

In the midst of the League Cup campaign, it was perhaps odd that United should agree to play the 1947-48 Forfarshire Cup final against Arbroath but play it they did, at Dens Park on 6th October. McKay starred again, netting another hat-trick as United won 4-1 to lift the trophy. However, an unchanged side faced Stenhousemuir away only three days later in the League Cup and lost 2-1, largely because the players tired late in the game. The League Cup challenge was already over before the visit to Hamilton Academical where United, with six changes in the side, lost 6-3. United then signed Ted Leven from Brechin Renton on a provisional form after trials in the reserves.

Then it was back to the job of gathering league points, beginning with a visit from Arbroath and it turned into another astonishing match between the teams, who had taken part in a number of high scoring matches since WW2 ended. Quinn, Dickson and McKay put United 3-1 ahead but Arbroath scored again before the break and then scored two more within the first twenty minutes of the second period, to lead 4-3. United regained the lead through Cruickshank and Grant but in the final minute Arbroath were level again and it ended 5-5. A week later United went three up before half time at Cowdenbeath but the Tannadice side almost threw it away, conceding twice for a final score of 3-2. In late October, a strange rumour surfaced in Dundee. Jack Cowan, who played his football for the University of British Columbia in Canada, announced that United were bringing him over for a signing-on fee of £2,000. MacFadyen was asked to comment but could not, as he had never heard of the player! Chairman John Carnegie Jnr. confirmed this at the Club AGM shortly afterwards. The Chairman also advised that United had made a profit of £500 in the year to 30th July 1948, despite a poor season.

McKay scored United's consolation goal in the 4-1 home defeat to a competent Raith Rovers on 6th November and he netted again as United fell 5-2 at Stirling Albion. United's next match was at home to East Stirlingshire and McKay's early goal was cancelled out by a surprise late strike by the visitors, for a 1-1 draw. McKay completed a remarkable run, scoring in ten games in a row, with a hat-trick in the 4-2 win at Hamilton Academical.

Two more players were added in December but both Jack Smith from Loanhead Mayflower and Robert Harvey from Stenhousemuir were short-term signings for the reserves. On 4th December, United lost 2-1 at home to a fortunate Ayr United but inspired again by McKay, a week later at Tannadice, Queen's Park were trounced 5-2, with the centre scoring four. Consistency was still lacking and United were undone by late goals in the matches at Stenhousemuir, where they lost 3-2 and Dunfermline Athletic, where the home side won 2-0 on Christmas Day. In the New Year's Day encounter with St Johnstone at Tannadice, an even match could have gone either way but finished 4-3 to United. A hard fought point was gained in a 1-1 draw at Airdrieonians two days later.

The Manager then dipped into the transfer market to sign George Mitchell from Aberdeen Sunnybank after he had played as a trialist against St Johnstone. Goalkeeper Alex Edmiston was signed from St Andrews United after successful trials in the reserves and went into the side against Dumbarton on 8th January. He had an excellent debut, keeping a clean sheet. Mitchell scored one of the goals and McKay recorded another hat-trick in a 4-0 win. Next came an away match

Action from the 4-3 win over Celtic

at Kilmarnock and United were leading 3-2 until a late equaliser robbed them of a point. However, the players might be forgiven for allowing their thoughts to drift towards the upcoming Scottish Cup tie. The visitors were Celtic, the match was a sell out and those present witnessed an unforgettable game.

Right from the kick-off United took the game to Celtic and McKay had a fifteenth minute goal ruled out, before he netted from the spot after a hand ball incident. Dickson made it 2-0 with a 15-yard shot before Tully pulled one back and then Mitchell had one disallowed before half time. In the second half Gallacher levelled for Celtic and then incredibly, yet another goal was disallowed, this time for Cruickshank after the referee consulted a linesman. Undeterred, United charged at the Celtic defence and went in front again through McKay. Celtic hit back almost immediately through Gallacher but with ten minutes left, the Black and Whites grabbed the winner with a Cruickshank effort. United held out against a desperate final barrage from the visitors, to record one of the most remarkable wins in the history of the Club.

In later years, the popular myth that grew around this result was that the name the 'TERRORS' was borne of the attitude of the players that day but it has to be said that the local press makes no mention of Dundee United as the Terrors until many years later. However, Celtic supremo Desmond White did comment after the match saying "McKay at centre was a terrier!" and the player was indeed referred to as Peter (The Terror) McKay, but only rarely. The nickname appears therefore to have been sometimes used in reference to McKay individually but not to the team as a whole. It was not until United were in the First Division again that the Terrors became the nickname in common use. Until then they were consistently referred to as the Black and Whites.

29th January 1949 v Alloa Athletic
Standing: Hart (Trainer), Berrie, Jardine, Edmiston, Ogilvie, R Ross, Dewar, Grant
Seated: Quinn, Dickson, McKay, Mitchell, Smart

In what ever manner the 'Terrors' nickname came into being, the same attitude was certainly evident again a week later. United hammered Alloa Athletic 5-1 in the league as the warm-up match to the next round of the Scottish Cup on 5th February. The tie against Dumbarton was settled only after a replay. In the first match, a thrilling encounter could have gone either way but ended 1-1 with a replay scheduled for the following Wednesday afternoon. Even then, a 10,000 crowd turned up hopeful of a repeat of the type of play seen against Celtic and it should be remembered that United had thrashed the Sons at Tannadice only a month earlier. An unchanged side lined up but the visitors took the initiative and an early lead. A rare Edmiston error gave Dumbarton a two goal advantage before McKay pulled one back but it was all over by half time, as United went 3-1 down. Despite an all out effort from United after the break, there was no further scoring and they went out of the tournament.

The league was all that was left but there was little to play for other than pride. Any chance of a promotion challenge had evaporated in the poor start to the campaign. Nevertheless, a 2-1 win against Cowdenbeath at Tannadice and a 3-1 victory at eventual champions Raith Rovers, were well deserved. On 21st February, United signed half back James Cameron from Blairhall Juniors and MacFadyen was also tracking his team mate, Andy Dunsmore. Cameron made an impressive debut on 26th February against promotion candidates Stirling Albion, who won by a single goal at Tannadice. By the time United travelled to meet East Stirlingshire a week later, Dunsmore had been signed in the face of competition from Blackburn Rovers and Southend United but his debut was delayed by a week. He was probably glad, as a poor display at second bottom East Stirlingshire resulted in an easy 3-0 win for the home side. Crothers was allowed to move to Alloa Athletic on loan shortly after.

With Dunsmore in for the first time against Hamilton Academical, United were fortunate to get a 2-2 draw at Tannadice. Both United goals came after the visitors had a man sent off late in the match. If luck was in for that match, it was out a week later as United travelled west. They lost one goal in thirty seconds, another two before half time and five after the break, for a win of 8-0 to a rampant Ayr United. That was the lowest point of the season. It took a huge effort on the part of the Manager and players to recover to win the next match 2-0 against Stenhousemuir in front of a 5,000 crowd, which was around half of the average attendance. United were also unlucky to lose by a single goal at Arbroath a week later.

On Forfarshire Cup business on 16th April, there was yet another hat-trick for McKay in a 4-1 win for United at home to Montrose. The last game of the league campaign was a goalless affair at Hampden Park against Queen's Park and that was followed by the second leg of the Forfarshire Cup at Montrose. United appeared to be on easy street with a three goal advantage after fifteen minutes but the home side fought back to level the match, although United won the tie on aggregate. To conclude the season, United played a friendly on 28th April at St Andrews United, which ended goalless.

The season ended with United in eighth place and far removed from the near relegation experience of twelve months before. MacFadyen's preference for bringing young players through the reserves was the first real attempt at a youth policy for Dundee United and early signs of success were evident. Not surprisingly, McKay led the scoring with 38 goals in his 37 league and cup appearances. On top of that, he had netted eight times in three Forfarshire matches! No other player even came close. With the Forfarshire Cup in the Boardroom and a memorable cup match against Celtic, the Directors must have been reasonably satisfied with the improvement in the side, brought about with a settled line up.

Gibby McKenzie had already left United to take up an SFA coaching post when the list of free transfers was announced. Boyd, Brannan, Kinloch, McCormack, MacFarlane, Simpson, Watson and Smith were released and perhaps only the names of Lister and Ouchterlonie raised a few eyebrows. All the others were retained for the next campaign, although Craig and Hume did not feature again. During the close season, Dickson was transferred to Queen of the South.

1949-50

Evidence of Progress

There was no transfer activity at Tannadice until Bob Sherry signed from Kilmarnock near the end of June. The annual trial match was arranged for 6th August, when a crowd of 7,000 witnessed nine goals and shortly afterwards the Manager signed six new players. First were Jimmy Elliot from Ayr United and Andy Donaldson from Dunfermline Athletic but neither made much impact over the season, each with just a few appearances. John Crossan from Cowdenbeath and Matt Naismith joined the Club purely as reserves and never made it into the first team. Keeper Bert Hood of Brechin City, who had played as a trialist for United ten years earlier, signed on a one month deal and ex-Partick Thistle, Airdrieonians and Bournemouth & Boscombe Athletic forward, Jimmy Colgan also arrived on the same terms. The contribution of this latter pair was restricted to a couple of games in the League Cup. It would fall largely on the players from the previous season to carry the Club through 1949-50.

Some very interesting information concerning Dundee City Athletic Company Ltd came to light just as the season got under way. A successful Petition for Liquidation to the courts in 1935 had been at a standstill but in August 1949 the old company (originally formed as Dundee Hibernian and Athletic Company Ltd in September 1909) was finally dissolved after years of inactivity. The only asset was 1,966 shares in Dundee United Football Company Ltd, and these were re-allocated and divided as appropriate amongst the shareholders of the old company. Until 1947, Dundee City Athletic Company Ltd was in fact the majority shareholder in Dundee United FC, but no-one connected with the old company took the opportunity to gain control at Tannadice as they might have.

The season opened with the League Cup and in the first match on 13th August at Airdrieonians, Hood made his competitive debut in goal only to find himself picking the ball out of the net five times before McKay scored a late double. Sherry and Colgan made debuts in the next match and Edmiston was restored between the posts as United overwhelmed Dumbarton with four goals in the first half and eventually won 5-1. At Gayfield next, United just managed to overcome Arbroath, with late goals from Dunsmore and Quinn, securing a 4-2 victory. Elliot came in for his first appearance as the team completely dumbfounded the pundits in a stunning 6-0 win over Airdrieonians at Tannadice, with McKay netting a hat-trick. Unfortunately, the good form was not repeated for the visit to Dumbarton a few days later and after playing well to keep the score level at 1-1 until half time, United fell to a 3-1 defeat. A 4-1 win at home to Arbroath made for a good end to the League Cup campaign but by then the section was already lost.

20th August 1949 v Arbroath
Standing: Berrie, Jardine, Edmiston, Mitchell, Sherry, Grant
Seated: Quinn, Colgan, McKay, Dunsmore, Cruickshank

To mark the opening of a new pavilion at Newburgh Juniors on 6th September, United sent a side made up mostly from the reserves. There were also several first team regulars in the side including McKay and back on his old stomping ground, he scored one of the goals in United's 2-0 win. Donaldson and Leven made debuts in that match and Willie Guthrie, still a Newburgh player, turned out for United.

McKay was on top form again as the league season began four days later with a visit from Alloa Athletic and the pint-sized centre was the architect of a 6-1 win, scoring one and setting up four others. By then of course, he had an intimate knowledge of the Tannadice pitch as he was employed as assistant groundsman to Walter Low! Around the same time, United provisionally signed another young player for the future, amateur full back Dave Stratton from Elmwood. Earle Downie of Dundee Violet had been attracting the attention of United for two years and finally signed on 13th September and Archie Livingstone was added to the reserves.

Donaldson made his debut in major competition in a Supplementary Cup tie on 12th September at Kilmarnock where McKay scored a hat-trick in the second half. Unfortunately, Killie had been 3-0 ahead before he did so and the Rugby Park club won the match 4-3 with a very late goal. A week later United were involved in yet another high scoring match, this time in the Forfarshire Cup at Arbroath. For the second game in succession, United went three goals down and despite a rally to pull back two goals, the Red Lichties stepped up the pace and it ended 6-3 in their favour.

Astonishingly, the opening ten matches of the season had produced an average of six goals per game. Although the scoring rate dropped very quickly, the fans were still treated to some high scoring matches as the league programme got into full swing. United continued a good run of league results with well deserved wins over St Johnstone 3-1, Kilmarnock 3-2, Hamilton Academical 4-1 and Dumbarton 5-0, with McKay getting a hat-trick in the latter match. It became six wins in a row with a 3-1 win at Dunfermline Athletic on 15th October. In that match, Downie made his debut as United turned out in new red jerseys and white shorts. Around the same time, it was announced that Tom Wyllie was going to Arbroath on loan. Bob Young was signed from Motherwell on a free transfer but he never made it out of the reserves.

McKay was in great scoring form and recorded his third hat-trick of the season in the 3-3 draw at Arbroath on 22nd October. A week later, he scored again in a 2-2 home draw with Cowdenbeath to bring his total for the season to 28 goals in just 17 games. He had failed to find the net in a match on just one occasion. No wonder then that his exploits drew admiring glances from the south with Portsmouth, in particular, watching with interest. The player however, was very happy at Tannadice and even if an offer had come in at that time it is unlikely he would have moved.

After such a whirlwind start to the league, United fans were optimistic of a promotion push, but the next four matches severely dented these aspirations as United lost 4-1 at Hamilton Academical, 2-0 at home to Forfar Athletic, 5-2 at Morton and by the same score at home to Albion Rovers. Provisional signing from Monifieth Tayside, Bob Wyllie, had an unhappy debut in goal for the game at Morton. Guthrie then made his first competitive appearance and scored against Albion Rovers in the second successive 5-2 defeat. United seemed to stop the rot with a comfortable 4-0 win at Ayr United. With a free Saturday on 10th

December, United travelled to the south coast of England to play Bournemouth & Boscombe Athletic in a friendly and found themselves out of their depth. The Black and Whites were three goals behind in just fifteen minutes and by half time the home side were five goals up. The final score of 7-2 might have been worse for United had the English side taken their chances in the second half. Just before the trip south, United had signed Charlie Campbell from Dundee North End after he played well in trials for the reserves but he would have to wait almost ten months to make his debut.

The remainder of 1949 brought a mixed bag of results, with a 3-1 win at home against Stenhousemuir followed by a 3-3 draw at Alloa Athletic on Christmas Eve and a single goal defeat at home to second placed Airdrieonians on Hogmanay. After losing heavily at St Johnstone, 5-0 on 2nd January, United were well and truly out of the promotion running. More players were signed in the early part of 1950, but the majority never broke into the first team. Ex-Cardiff player Joe Nibloe, who had been with Kilmarnock, joined United in early January and George Morrison had trials in the reserves before he signed from Thornton Hibs at the end of the month. Later, Jimmy Moore of Stirling Juveniles and Andy Comrie from Grove Academy were acquired but even their reserve appearances were few. Only Morrison of this group would make it into the first eleven.

In the next match, at home to Kilmarnock, United were just one goal up through McKay in a first half which they dominated. Crothers, who had only recently returned to Tannadice, scored twice in the second half to make it a 3-0 win and put a more accurate reflection on the play. The result was all the more impressive as Dewar was seriously injured and three other United men suffered heavy knocks during the match but played on. With teams frequently handicapped by the loss of injured players, the subject of substitutions during games was creating debate in football circles. In some international matches, substitutes were already permitted but the new rules allowed for only injured players to be replaced and some countries had been accused of abusing the rules to make tactical changes. In Scotland, opinions were divided and it was suggested that players would have to be assessed by a doctor, who would then decide whether a substitute could be used! The situation was not resolved at the time and the debate continued for years before substitutes were finally allowed in Scotland in 1966.

Nevertheless, injuries were taking a toll on United and frequent changes to the line up contributed to points dropped. In the next three matches only one point was gained in a 1-1 home draw with Dunfermline Athletic, whilst United lost 3-0 at Dumbarton, and Arbroath stole the points with a late goal in a 4-3 win at Tannadice. No doubt this had some effect on the fans generally as a crowd of only 8,000 turned out for the Scottish Cup tie at home to Ayr United on 28th January. Crothers opened the scoring early in the match and Dewar quickly added a stunning second that effectively ended the tie as a contest. Crothers and Grant scored in the second half for an excellent 4-0 win. Grant and McKay were still hitting the headlines and scouts from Burnley, Hull City, Portsmouth and Hearts, were at the match.

United had to travel to meet Partick Thistle in the next round of the Scottish Cup following a 2-1 league defeat at Cowdenbeath. The cup tie was called off on the Saturday due to snow and was rescheduled with a Tuesday afternoon kick-off. United found the Jags in top form on a day that it all went right for them and wrong for United. Two goals down at half time, United conceded three more after the break to lose 5-0 as the home side adopted a long ball approach and United tried to play a passing game unsuited to the conditions. Worse for United, Cruickshank had just returned from injury but suffered a reaction and was out for the rest of the season. His replacement was Alec Shaw signed from Lovell's Athletic and he made his debut at Forfar Athletic in a 3-0 win in the league on 18th February.

There was nothing much left to play for but the fans were treated to a great performance when league leaders Morton were the visitors a week later. Although it ended 2-2, United deserved more from a game in which they showed character and spirit. Unfortunately this form was not repeated at Albion Rovers where United lost 2-0 in a poor match, but the following week, a much improved performance brought a good 4-1 home win over Ayr United. Morrison made his long awaited debut at centre on 25th March at Stenhousemuir, scoring twice in an easy 5-1 win. However, the home side played most of the match with ten men after losing a player to an early injury.

The end of season matches in April began with a shock 3-1 home defeat at the hands of C Division Brechin City in the Forfarshire Cup. Then Airdrieonians, who had just secured promotion to the First Division, beat United 2-0 at Broomfield. The Dewar Shield was next and the Black and Whites lost over two legs to Aberdeen, who won 2-1 at Tannadice and then 1-0 at Pittodrie. The final two league matches were both against Queen's Park, with the first game at Tannadice producing the highest score of the season. The visiting amateurs actually opened the scoring in just four minutes but from that point on, it was all United, with Shaw and Quinn making it 2-1 by half time. United were rampant after the break and netted five more through Quinn, Shaw, McKay and Dunsmore, who scored two, making it 7-1. Queen's Park fielded young goalkeeper Ronnie Simpson, later to become a Celtic legend. Ronnie was the son of Jimmy Simpson who played for United, Rangers and Scotland. A week later a quieter match at Hampden Park ended in a 1-0 win for United and the goal came from McKay to bring his total of league and cup goals to 35 from 36 matches. Quinn was his nearest challenger with 20, a remarkable strike rate for a winger. United's seventh place finish was their best in the Scottish League for thirteen years. But for a series of injuries at crucial times, it might have been even better as only six points separated the teams from third to tenth. Overall, it had been a good season for United with progress definitely evident. An ever present, Berrie played in all 39 competitive matches, one of six players exceeding thirty appearances.

The annual exodus of players saw free transfers handed to Tom Wyllie, Cameron, Donaldson, Elliot, Guthrie and Leven. The latter player had been on loan at Brechin City. Several reserves were also allowed to go and Simmons appears to have left at around the same time. Pacione had been unable to get back into the side and he too was freed, whilst Ogilvie decided to retire. Of the rest of the squad, only Dewar and Jardine did not immediately re-sign for the next campaign.

1950-51

United's Famous Five

During the close season the lack of income meant that the Directors had to assist the Club financially with short-term loans. With money in short supply the Manager could therefore only bring in new signings on free transfers. Of the existing squad, Dewar re-signed at the beginning of July and he was joined by Stratton who, as an amateur, was only permitted to register for one season at a time and had to re-sign every summer. Davie Johnstone came to United from St Johnstone in early August and after the trial match on 5th August, former Rangers and Dumbarton inside right, Archie McIndewar was signed. Later that week, MacFadyen added half back Jimmy Green from Queen of the South and Tommy McCann, a forward, from Celtic. Despite good displays in the trial match, neither of these players moved beyond reserve level at Tannadice. The last of the unsigned players, Jardine, had made it clear that he wanted to leave and just after the season kicked off, he joined Millwall for a reputed bargain fee of £700, which was still a welcome addition to the coffers. Goalkeeper John Boyd returned to United in late August after a season with Albion Rovers and the Manager also brought in his own son, Ian 'Buddy' MacFadyen from Ashdale Amateurs to play in the reserves on an amateur form.

The new season opened at Tannadice with a League Cup tie against Stenhousemuir on 12th August and McIndewar was the only new face in the United line up. It took an equaliser from McKay and a late goal by Quinn to carve out a 2-1 win for United after the Warriors had taken a shock first half lead and missed a penalty. McIndewar played again and scored from the spot in an easy 5-2 midweek win at St Johnstone, but that was the last appearance for the player, other than in the reserves and he left in September. Over the next two matches, the League Cup section was almost thrown away as United could only draw 2-2 at Cowdenbeath and on the visit to Stenhousemuir, the home side won a close contest 3-2. The front five of Quinn, Grant, McKay, Dunsmore and Cruickshank were now referred to as United's 'Famous Five' and with them restored in full to the team for the last two games of the section, the Tannadice side won 4-1 at home to both St Johnstone and Cowdenbeath. With the backing of around 15,000 fans at each game, the team turned in two impressive performances to advance to the quarter finals.

Before meeting Ayr United over two legs in the quarter final of the League Cup, United had to face a tricky away league match at Dumbarton and were fortunate to come back with a point from a 1-1 draw, secured by McKay's first minute goal. It was virtually all over in the first leg of the League Cup quarter final on 16th September as Ayr United won 3-0, with the Black and Whites rarely seen as an attacking force. The line up was unchanged for the second leg in midweek and despite a 5.45 pm kick-off, another 15,000 crowd packed into Tannadice, most supporting Dundee United. Grant scored to give the fans some hope with almost an hour still to play but the visitors restored the three goal advantage early in the second half. They soon wrapped it up with another, for a 5-1 aggregate win.

Attention then turned back to the league campaign as MacFadyen prepared the players for a visit to St Johnstone on 23rd September and Campbell made his long awaited debut. United were the better side and were leading with two minutes left but the Perth Saints grabbed a late goal to level the match at 2-2. A week later Johnstone made his debut against Kilmarnock who finished a player short after losing him to injury. United won 5-3 with two early McKay goals and a Quinn hat-trick. With Stratton making his debut, the Tannadice side then lost 3-1 at home to Hamilton Academical, and at Stenhousemuir a few days later, that result was repeated. The Manager had introduced Matt McIlwain from Ayr United on a month's trial in the latter of these two matches. Then David Kinnell was brought in from St Andrews United against stiff competition from Rangers and Ipswich Town. Kinnell went into the side to face Dunfermline Athletic on 14th October and played a big part in the 5-1 home win, with a goal and assists to his credit.

It was however, just a fleeting recovery from a poor run of form as United then lost another three in a row. Against Arbroath on 21st October, it might have gone either way in a rip-roaring encounter at Tannadice with the Gayfield side 3-0 up before McKay scored either side of half time. The visitors scored again and Quinn set up a thrilling last fifteen minutes but United could not find the equaliser their play merited and lost 4-3. The following week United were hammered 6-0 at Cowdenbeath and the finger of blame was pointed in the direction of the inexperienced young players. The criticism was unfair as the whole team failed to perform to their capabilities. The next match was at home to Stirling Albion. Boyd was dropped in favour of Wyllie in goal and a couple of the young players were replaced by older heads. United lost 3-1 but it was a much better performance and United might have had a draw if the home keeper had not been in top form.

Hugh Ormond was signed on a free transfer from St Mirren in November, and made a few appearances over the next two seasons, whilst McIlwain left United in mid November after his one month deal was up. One player going nowhere was Peter McKay. There was a cheeky enquiry from Stirling Albion for the prolific scorer but United did not even indicate a price for the player, as he was still perfectly happy at Tannadice in his dual role of player/assistant groundsman.

After such a poor start to the league, few would have predicted that United would then go on a run of nine league wins in succession, established by the same eleven players, except for two matches in which there were enforced changes. Forfar Athletic were the first victims, with a controlled United display producing a 3-1 away win on 11th November. At Tannadice a week later, Queen of the South were thumped 5-0 and another five goal win would have followed at Albion Rovers if Grant had not missed a penalty in a match that ended 4-0, with a McKay hat-trick the main highlight. A good 3-1 home win over Ayr United was blighted by injuries to Smart and Cruickshank. The following week, with Ormond in for his debut and Shaw replacing Cruickshank, it looked as if the run would end with Queen's Park two goals up, but United rallied, staging a great fight back to win 3-2. Narrow wins against Alloa Athletic 2-1, Dumbarton 3-2 and Hamilton Academical 2-1 were followed by a hard fought 2-0 win over St Johnstone on New Year's Day, to complete the nine in a row. In the nine wins, McKay had netted a dozen goals and Quinn scored ten. By New Year's Day, United were clear in second place. It is also worth pointing out that the vast majority of the United squad were plucked from the junior ranks. Jimmy McMillan was another player from that source, arriving in early December from Whitburn Juniors to join the reserves. He would have a short spell in the first team two years later. The other December signings were Bob Swan on a free transfer from Alloa Athletic and John Nelson from Whitburn Juniors but the latter did not even make it into the reserve side. Stratton had by then a regular place in the side and the international selectors were keeping an eye on him. He went on to win amateur international caps against Wales, England and Northern Ireland before the end of the season, making him the first Scottish international player from Dundee United.

A midweek 2-0 defeat at Kilmarnock on 2nd January was soon forgotten as United hammered Stenhousemuir 6-0 at Tannadice the next weekend. Two weeks later at Arbroath, United won 3-1 but only after the home side had taken the lead and then lost a player through injury in the first half. Immediately after that game, United were completely focused on the next match, an eagerly awaited Scottish Cup tie against Dundee at Dens Park. With a crowd of 38,000 attending, gate receipts were around £3,000 and the fans witnessed an all action encounter. United conceded a penalty early in the first half but no-one seemed to know why and despite protests, Dundee led from the spot kick. Just before half time, the Dark Blues went two goals in front but United were giving a good account of themselves. It was no surprise that McKay got one back and when Dunsmore pulled it level to earn a replay it was no less than United deserved. Four days later at Tannadice, a crowd of 22,000 witnessed a game of two halves, with Dundee in command and scoring the only goal of the game in the first half. After the interval, United were the better side but could not engineer an equaliser and went out of the competition.

Promotion was now the primary aim and the squad was strengthened with the addition of Dicky Grieve from Wrexham in late January on a free transfer. In February, John Coyle, who had signed provisionally in September 1950 from St Joseph's, joined the reserves. Grieve made his debut on 3rd February in a home match against Cowdenbeath but finished on the wrong end of a 5-1 result. A week later, league leaders Stirling Albion stretched their advantage over second place United to ten points, with a 3-1 win. United kept up their challenge with a close fought 2-1 home win over Forfar Athletic. The Directors then announced that they were offering the players a share in the maximum allowable £500 'talent money', if promotion was achieved. This new style of bonus scheme had only recently been approved by the Scottish League.

A 3-3 draw at Palmerston Park against Queen of the South kept United three points clear in second place but both the chasing pair of Ayr United and Queen of the South had games in hand. United had to rely on these sides dropping points in the run in. The Black and Whites then recorded a rather fortunate 2-1 win at home to Albion Rovers. Following a free Saturday during which the team travelled to Swansea Town for a friendly losing by the odd goal in nine, United lost 4-2 at Queen's Park on 17th March leaving the Tannadice side requiring a miracle to take second place with just three games left. They did their best to achieve the impossible and thrashed Alloa Athletic 10-1 at Tannadice a week later. McKay scored four of the goals and made it a memorable debut for Swan. Another friendly was arranged two days later at Berwick Rangers, then an Eastern League side. Despite almost the entire regular United first eleven on the field against the English outfit, which contained several experienced players, it ended goalless. The penultimate match in the league campaign came on the following Saturday at Dunfermline Athletic where United fell to a 1-0 defeat, but by then the league race was almost over. United slipped into third place as Queen of the South played out their fixture backlog and went on to win the title. The last match of the season at Ayr United on 28th April was the third place decider. The Black and Whites had to win to finish third and therefore the 2-2 draw achieved was not enough and left them fourth.

Prior to that final match the team had travelled to London to watch Scotland win the international 3-2 against England. They then played a two match tour in Wales winning 2-1 at Swansea Town and losing by the same score at Llanelli. On returning to Scotland, the two leg Forfarshire Cup first round match at

Arbroath produced a very easy 5-0 win. After completing the league programme at Ayr, McKay scored a hat-trick in the return leg of the Forfarshire Cup against Arbroath at Tannadice on 30th April. John Coyle made his first appearance in a United shirt in that match, which resulted in a repeat of the 5-0 score line for a 10-0 aggregate. The semi final was scheduled for Friday 18th May but before that, United were off on their travels again. They had been invited to London to play Millwall in a friendly and were unfortunate to lose 2-1. On the journey back to Scotland, a stop off in Yorkshire to play Barnsley saw United crash to an 8-1 defeat.

The Forfarshire Cup semi final at Tannadice was a 6-1 a triumph for United over Brechin City, with three goals scored in twelve first half minutes, resulting in a 3-1 lead at the interval. Included in the six goals United scored, was a McKay hat-trick. The final was arranged for the following day at Dens Park and considering the lack of rest between the two matches, it was a tremendous effort from United to beat Dundee 3-2. The Dark Blues were on top in the first half after McKay opened the scoring in just two minutes and at half time it was 1-1. Dunsmore put United ahead but Dundee were level again within minutes. McKay then scored with a typical opportunist goal to win the cup, which was presented by the Earl of Selkirk.

There were changes in the Boardroom in April, with the addition of Denys Carnegie, the fourth member of the Carnegie family to sit on the Board. Denys replaced his late father John Carnegie Jnr., who had died in late March. A loss of £927 for the season was confirmed at the AGM in late June but the Board were not overly concerned. Around this time, it was also decided to improve the North Terracing by laying in concrete blocks to replace the wood and cinder banking.

Doug Berrie

The season had to be considered a success with a fourth place finish, a big improvement in twelve months and the best since 1934-35 but United were still nine points behind the top two. The Scottish Cup had been successful in terms of income and United were only just edged out by Dundee. A measure of revenge, albeit small, was gained in the Forfarshire Cup win. The improved placing was built on a regular line up and top scorer McKay, with 38 goals (plus another 10 in the Forfarshire Cup!), was an ever present in league and cup matches. Ross also played in every match, whilst Berrie, Downie, Smart, Grant, Cruickshank and Quinn made over thirty appearances each. The latter was also second top scorer with 25 goals. In total, the team bagged a century of competitive goals. Crothers appears to have left United midway through the season and at the end of the campaign, United announced that Boyd, Sherry, Shaw, Dewar and Grieve along with reserves, Green and McCann, were being released. In the latter part of the season, several players had been given trials in the reserves but only Dickie Sneddon from Lochore Welfare was signed and he would feature in the first team in the following season.

1951-52

Missed Opportunities

The retained players all re-signed in the early summer months and the only addition to the squad initially was Jimmy Knight from Dundee Violet in mid July. As the Manager appeared satisfied that the existing squad could mount a challenge for promotion, United had no new faces in the side when the season began on 25th July with the Festival Quaich. Alloa Athletic were the visitors for this match in one of the earliest starts to any season. United opened slowly and were soon a goal down but recovered to win 3-1 with Grant, McKay and Quinn scoring. The next round of the tournament brought a visit from Hamilton Academical and although Quinn put United in front, by half time it was level at 1-1. The Black and Whites then passed up several chances to increase the lead before disaster struck late in the second half, when a short pass back let the visitors in for the winner. The trial match on 31st July was, on this occasion, not open to the public and afterwards John Houston of Bayview Athletic was signed as a reserve.

There were several changes made to the side for the first League Cup match at home to Cowdenbeath on 11th August, including a debut in major competition for John Coyle. An early Dunsmore penalty was not enough as United failed to convert a huge percentage of possession into goals and the Fife side brought it back to 1-1 after the interval. Although the result was the same, the situation was reversed in the next League Cup match at Stenhousemuir, as United recovered from an early setback to earn a point, with a Grant goal. Two more away matches followed and both finished in defeat, 3-0 at Falkirk and 2-0 at Cowdenbeath, to end United's interest in the competition. On the positive side, the Cowdenbeath match on 25th August brought an improved performance and a noteworthy debut from new signing George McMillan, from Kirkmuirhill Juveniles. McMillan retained his place for the visit of Stenhousemuir and Coyle was restored to the side for his second game, netting all four goals as United won 4-2. In the final

League Cup match, Falkirk, the runaway leaders of the section, won 1-0 at Tannadice against the run of play, to maintain a 100% record in the section. In late August, MacFadyen signed Jimmy Melville from Arnot as the reserve keeper and added Tommy Dunlop from Osborne to the squad.

11th August 1951 v Cowdenbeath
Standing: Hart (Trainer), Ormond, Berrie, Edmiston, Downie, Ross, Mitchell, Stratton
Seated: Quinn, Grant, McKay, Dunsmore, Coyle

The league season began on 8th September with a visit from Alloa Athletic and United won comfortably 4-1. Shortly afterwards, John Love was signed from Hibs on a free transfer for a trial period in the reserves. On 15th September, Knight made his debut at Hampden Park where the Tannadice side beat Queen's Park 2-1, very much against the run of play. St Johnstone were the visitors at Tannadice the following week and in an all action game, McKay scored a brace to help United win 4-3. Sneddon made his debut in that match along with Neil Fleck, newly signed from Llanelli. Fleck had impressed MacFadyen when United met the Welsh side a few months earlier in the friendly there. The Manager also signed another reserve keeper, Douglas McKay from Aberdeen University, to cover for Melville who was out through injury. United continued the league campaign with a 2-2 draw at Cowdenbeath but with better luck they would have won and the Fifers' equaliser came right at the end. The improvements to the North Terracing were completed in late September and the Directors revealed plans for further changes, including a new South Stand, covered North Terracing and concrete blocked terraces behind each goal. Unfortunately, lack of money meant that these plans would not come to full fruition until very much later.

On Monday 1st October, United met Dundee at Dens Park in the first leg of their Forfarshire Cup tie. A crowd of 17,000 turned out for the match and saw Dundee win 3-1 but Berrie had been forced to go off with an injury. Even though they were beaten, United still advanced to the next round to meet Arbroath, because six weeks later Dundee quit the Forfarshire Association. It also became known that both Burnley and Portsmouth were showing interest in McKay but the Board issued a hands-off warning, stating that even an offer of £20,000 would not tempt the Club to part with their star centre.

Good league form continued with a 3-2 home win on 6th October over a solid Hamilton Academical who gave United a stern test, and after five games, the Black and Whites sat top of the league. Unfortunately, that lofty position lasted no longer than a week as United could only draw 3-3 at Forfar Athletic. Any aspirations the fans had for a quick return to the top were soon dashed as United lost the next three games. The first of these was at Ayr United where the home side gave little away in their 2-0 win and then, at Tannadice, United lost 5-3 to Clyde but the performance at least was wholehearted. The same could not be said of the 6-0 thrashing at Falkirk where United collapsed after being just one goal down at half time. For the next match, against Kilmarnock on 10th November at Tannadice, there were several changes in the side, including a debut for Dunlop at centre half. Trialist Johnny McIvor was on the left wing and he signed from Maryhill Harp immediately after the match. A crowd of only 2,500 turned up in atrocious weather conditions and after taking an early lead, United defended for much of the game to win by a single goal. The opening stages of the next match gave no hint of what was to follow as McKay levelled an early Stenhousemuir strike at Ochilview. The Stirlingshire side netted another three quick goals before half time to finish the match as a contest and at full-time, it was 6-2 to the home team. MacFadyen then signed former St Mirren half back Walter Reid and Jackie Nicolson from Brentford. Both went into the reserve side but neither stayed long at Tannadice.

In the remainder of 1951, United took ten points from six matches, starting with a 2-1 home win over Dunfermline Athletic. United had a tough time against the Pars and had Wyllie to thank for saving a spot kick. At Arbroath in the first match of December, United won 3-1 with a McKay hat-trick after the home side lost an injured player. Albion Rovers pulled off a shock 3-0 win over United on 8th December, scoring all three goals in the last twenty minutes. A week later, United played their best game of the season to win 4-1 at home to Dumbarton with McKay chalking up yet another hat-trick. Had it not been for some solid defending by the visitors, United might have doubled their tally. At Alloa Athletic, United won deservedly 3-2 and on 29th December, they hammered a makeshift Queen's Park side 5-0 at Tannadice to secure fourth place in the league and were back in the promotion hunt. Unfortunately, they did not keep the run going, losing 4-1 in Perth to a fairly ordinary St Johnstone side on New Year's Day.

The next day, the situation could not have been more different as United took Cowdenbeath apart in a 5-1 win at Tannadice. After a 1-1 draw at Hamilton Academical where the home side should really have taken full points, United notched an 8-1 win over Forfar Athletic at Tannadice. MacKay and Quinn each scored a hat-trick but the Loons had genuine cause to grumble at the margin of defeat, as they were not as bad as the score line suggests. The Black and Whites followed that up with a 2-2 draw at home to fellow promotion challengers Ayr United. The weather turned wintry the following week and that hampered United's preparation for the approaching Scottish Cup trip to meet Inverness Caledonian on 26th January. The team travelled up 24 hours early but the fans did not have that luxury. Two buses carrying them north left very early on Saturday morning taking a circuitous route via Aberdeen because of the snow. After an incident packed journey, one bus arrived just on time and another a few minutes after kick off and they witnessed a game to remember.

100 Caley fans had helped to clear the snow using school benches tied together and dragged back and forth across the pitch. It was an unorthodox way to do the job but it worked and it looked as if their efforts were to be rewarded. Caley went ahead in just twelve minutes and led 2-0 at half time after an unfortunate Ross own goal. United were on the rack until Fleck put them back in contention just after half time but it was soon 3-1 to the home side. With time running out, McKay scored with three minutes left after he beat three men and then with the last kick of the ball he levelled the tie at 3-3, with a shot from the edge of the area. The replay took place the following Wednesday afternoon and 8,000 fans turned up to see United move through to the next round. McKay scored in the first minute and Quinn had United well in control with his fourth minute strike. By half time, the same player made it 3-0 and then United cantered to the final whistle with a fourth goal from Dunsmore.

Another weather induced break meant the next match was again a Scottish Cup tie, on 9th February at Leith Athletic. The Edinburgh side took a shock first half lead but Quinn restored parity within five minutes of the restart and then McKay netted a hat-trick for a final score of 4-1. A league match at Kilmarnock followed a week later and yet another McKay hat-trick was the highlight of a well deserved 6-2 win at Rugby Park. Even then, Wyllie saved a last minute penalty to underline United's superiority.

The win at Killie was good preparation for the next round of the cup, with Aberdeen the visitors to Tannadice where a Club record domestic crowd of 26,407 saw United at their best. Cruickshank gave the Black and Whites an early lead in the first half and the Dons were fortunate to be level by half time. They were also lucky to go ahead in the second half. Dunsmore missed from the spot but United rallied and the visiting keeper made a series of top class saves before McKay made it 2-2 near the end. United had to hold off a late challenge but if the Dons had won it would have been a great injustice after such a fine display.

United could not repeat the same level of performance in the midweek replay and were a goal down after only a minute. By half time, it was 2-0 and the home side scored a third early in the second period. Only then did United show what they could do, and a goal from Dunsmore and a late penalty from Grant gave the Dons a nervy last few minutes. Nevertheless, United were out, beaten 3-2, with only the consolation of half the gate money from two bumper crowds to swell the bank balance.

After the cup exit, there was still some way to go in the league. Promotion for United was possible but they could not afford any slip ups. To comply with the rules of the Second XI Cup, United had to sign a goalkeeper very quickly to honour a semi final commitment at Ibrox and it was old wartime favourite Charlie Brownlee who was only too happy to return to Tannadice yet again.

Back on league business on 1st March, United faced a strong Dunfermline Athletic side at East End Park and came from behind to record a 2-1 win. Four days later a comfortable 3-0 home win over Stenhousemuir kept the league challenge going. That was followed by a 3-1 victory over Arbroath and although it was goalless at half time, United were always in control. After the break, two long range Dunsmore efforts and a late goal from Cruickshank gave United the win and pushed the Black and Whites into second place. Unfortunately, it all went wrong after that and just one more point was collected from the remaining four league matches. Eventual champions Clyde beat United 3-0 on 11th March and four days later, the promotion challenge was over as a tired looking side drew 0-0 at home with Albion Rovers. A visit to Dumbarton ended in a 2-1 defeat with McKay injured early in the match and a passenger thereafter.

High scoring winger
Frank Quinn

Downie scored United's goal, his only one in his Tannadice career, late in the match. United returned to Boghead to play Dumbarton again a week later in the Supplementary Cup without the injured McKay, who was replaced by newly signed John Scott from Cowdenbeath. Keeper Wyllie was the star of the show with an outstanding performance but the home side breached United's defence eventually to win 1-0. Former Dumbarton, Clyde and Kilmarnock outside left Charlie Bootland was added to the reserves around this time, as Dundee United 'A' took part in the C Division League Cup.

The third away match in a row brought a trip to Aberdeen in the first leg of the Dewar Shield and the Dons won rather easily 3-0. United looked a beaten side throughout and the disappointment of missing out on promotion was evident. The final match of the league campaign at home to Falkirk only underlined the way the season had gone. Leading 2-1 with just a few minutes left United conceded twice to lose 3-2. The season wound down with a series of local cup ties and friendlies, beginning with a 5-2 win over Cowdenbeath at Central Park on 19th April. Nothing was at stake, and United fielded a mix of regulars, fringe players and trialists, including recently signed former St Johnstone and Kilmarnock inside right, Jimmy Irving. The highlight of the match was a Grant hat-trick. After beating local side Coupar Angus 3-1 in another friendly, United then pulled off a shock result against Aberdeen in the second leg of the Dewar Shield, winning 4-1 to take the tie to a replay. The hectic programme of matches took its toll as United lost 4-3 to Arbroath in the Forfarshire Cup, despite leading 3-1 with twenty minutes left. The Dewar Shield replay took place at Tannadice on 5th May and United were five goals behind before they came to life and eventually lost 7-3. A week later Crystal Palace were the visitors and an entertaining friendly ended 1-1. United gave a debut to provisional signing Jimmy McMillan in that match. Jimmy Guy from Falkirk was one of three trialists in the side, and he joined United shortly after.

The Directors considered that the cost of running a second eleven was becoming prohibitive and was largely blamed for the loss of around £1,200 recorded by the Club. It was therefore decided that a reserve side would not be entered in C Division the following season. The recently signed reserves were all released along with Kinnell, Smart, Ormond, Downie, Dunlop, Mitchell, Knight, Houston, Scott, Fleck and Sneddon, whilst United retained Wyllie, Berrie, J McMillan, Swan, Dunsmore, Morrison, Ross, Quinn, Grant, McKay, Irving, Coyle, Guy and Cruickshank. Another three players, Edmiston, McIvor and Campbell were absent on national service but they too were retained and Stratton signed for another season. McKay was again the top scorer with 36 goals in his 40 appearances and it was no wonder other clubs were keeping him under observation. Quinn too kept up his amazing strike rate with 23 goals in his 43 outings. In the 44 game season, no player had lined up for every match. Quinn missed just one game and consistency of selection brought 35 appearances or more for another seven players.

The points dropped in the early stages of the league campaign were crucial to the final outcome but the late loss of form also cost United any chance of promotion. Despite finishing fourth in the league, the sense of disappointment around Tannadice was tangible. A settled side had not achieved what they were, without doubt, capable of and the Club missed opportunities in both the league and Scottish Cup.

1952-53

A Backward Step

During the summer, work was under way to move the boundary wall in front of the main stand several feet back to accommodate the widening of the pitch, planned for twelve months later. Season tickets for the stand went on sale at £3 each on 21st June, whilst all the retained players plus Stratton and George McMillan had all re-signed. MacFadyen arranged a public trial on 2nd August with the first team squad taking part, along with a few senior professionals and junior trialists. Sandy Stephen from Elmwood was amongst this group and although he did not sign then, he would join United two years later. The trial match entertained the 4,000 crowd who saw a team containing the first choice United front men win 4-1, with McKay getting a hat-trick.

From the outset of 1952-53, the Directors made their feelings clear. After finishing fourth two seasons running, they considered that promotion was achievable. As an incentive to the players they put the £500 'talent money' bonus on the table, to be shared amongst a promotion winning team. However, just as the season got under way the first problem arose. Bobby Ross asked for a transfer to a London club. He ran his own taxi business in Cowdenbeath and was keen to try a similar venture in a more lucrative market. As a forerunner to letting him leave, Alec Arnold was signed from Dundonald Bluebell as cover. At the same time, full back George Munro was brought in from St Johnstone. Both had played in the trial match.

United's League Cup section was a tough one and included Dumbarton, Ayr United and Stirling Albion. The opening match on 9th August saw United dumped 3-1 at Dumbarton, with Irving, Jimmy McMillan and Guy making debuts in major competition. Stirling Albion, the newly relegated side from A Division, then gave United a lesson in taking chances when they came to Tannadice and won 6-2. Short-term signing Charlie McMullen from Hamilton Academical got one of United's goals, making his debut along with Munro. By the time

United travelled to Ayr United for the next match in the section, Ross had been transferred to Millwall and Arnold came in for his debut. Despite a Quinn goal to give United a lead, which they held until half time, the Tannadice side wilted in the second half and finished on the wrong end of a 4-1 result. The section was therefore already lost before United beat Dumbarton 1-0 at Tannadice on 23rd August. Then, for the second time in as many weeks, the Black and Whites conceded six goals to Stirling Albion. United had to reshuffle before and during the game because of injuries. They got off to a bad start, missing from the spot, but they were well beaten 6-1 by the side that would eventually win the B Division flag. In the last game in the section, Ayr United were beaten 2-1 at Tannadice but there was nothing at stake as Stirling Albion had already won the group.

The league campaign kicked off on 6th September at Arbroath and the 2-1 defeat troubled the fans so much that the Supporters' Club requested a meeting with the Directors to voice their concerns at the poor start to the season. Before the meeting took place, United won 4-2 at home to Alloa Athletic with something like the previous season's fighting quality on show. The fans' representatives were reassured by the Directors at a meeting on 18th September, but a 1-1 draw at St Johnstone and a goalless draw at home to Cowdenbeath gave the supporters little comfort. The visit to league leaders Stenhousemuir on 4th October was a daunting prospect and provided another major problem. Although out of C Division, United were still committed to the Second XI Cup and had to act fast to get a team together to meet Clyde 'A' in this tournament, on the same day they were to play Stenhousemuir. There were not enough reserves and only signed players could take part in the cup. Therefore, two days before the match, Charlie Brownlee was a United player yet again along with Chic Robbie (ex-St Johnstone and Brechin City). MacFadyen then travelled to the west and returned with Jimmy Timmins from Hamilton Academical and Dick Cumming from Motherwell. The Manager also signed Eddie Beaton from Aberdeen and then added John Crichton from Montrose on 3rd October. These signings were all short-term but it was worth the effort as United 'A' beat Clyde 'A' 3-0 to advance to the next round. As to the Stenhousemuir match, United confounded everyone with a 4-0 win, in which McKay scored another hat-trick.

Timmins was about to begin a university course and did not want even part-time football but he was persuaded to make his only first team appearance when United were short handed for the visit of Stirling Albion on 11th October. United looked good for the points with a 2-1 lead thanks to two cracking Quinn goals but the visitors hit back with two of their own to win 3-2 for both points. Quinn was on the mark again with a hat-trick at Dumbarton as United won 3-1 in style. But inconsistency was exposed again with a 3-2 home defeat by league leaders Hamilton Academical. The visitors were 3-0 up before Cruickshank and McKay got United's goals late in the match. In the 2-1 home win over Queen's Park that followed, Quinn scored both goals, the second direct from a corner.

He also scored the fourth of United's goals in the 4-2 win at Albion Rovers after McKay netted another hat-trick in that match. The arrival of Sam English from Albion Rovers coincided with three defeats in a row, with the first of these a 4-0 reversal at home to Ayr United on 15th November. To make matters worse, McKay was sent off in the second half. At Tannadice against Morton, another 4-0 defeat followed as United crumbled in the first half. The visit to Alloa Athletic on 29th November produced sweeping changes to the line up, including trialist Johnny Laird from Rosyth Recreation, but United were thumped 6-2. Laird signed two days later. Strangely, with McKay suspended, his deputy John Coyle was allowed to go to Brechin City for the rest of the season and the centre forward berth was then filled by trialists until McKay returned.

Inside right Jim Temple signed from Dundonald Bluebell in time for the first match in December, which brought a fortunate 1-1 draw at Dunfermline Athletic. A week later, in atrocious weather, which reduced the attendance to a mere 2,000, both sides played surprisingly good football as United beat Forfar Athletic 4-1 at Tannadice. McKay returned from suspension to play in the home match against Arbroath on 20th December but United lost 2-1, with the Red Lichties netting the winner from the spot near the end. During the visit to Kilmarnock the following week, United's defence led a charmed life but eventually lost to a single goal. The now customary New Year's Day game with St Johnstone was won for United with Quinn's first minute goal but with better finishing, the margin might have been much bigger. The second goalless draw of the season with Cowdenbeath was followed by a good 3-1 win over Stenhousemuir. Trialist Kenny Dick of Carnoustie Panmure was in goal for that game as Wyllie had suffered a foot injury at work. The keeper, unavailable again for the next match at Stirling Albion, was replaced by Brownlee, and even though United were beaten 2-0, the emergency keeper played well. With Wyllie still injured, Brownlee was the only goalie available to play in the Scottish Cup tie at Berwick Rangers on 24th January. Dick could not play, as he was not a signed United player.

The cup tie was eagerly awaited and the Directors were hoping for a good run in the competition to boost both the bank balance and morale but it did not turn out that way. C Division Berwick Rangers had a good squad of experienced professionals, including former United wartime favourite Albert Juliussen and with his help the English side knocked United out of the competition after a replay. United started well in the first match, with Quinn scoring in two minutes but the home side were quickly level. After the interval Berwick Rangers took the lead but McKay and Laird put United back in front. It looked like they would win the tie until Houliston scored to make it 3-3 during a goalmouth scramble with just two minutes left. The midweek afternoon replay did not deter a crowd of around 10,000 and by half time the visitors were 2-1 up. They increased the lead soon after the break before Quinn scored, but try as they might, United could not get back on level terms and went out 3-2 to the better side. In the next match,

United were two goals up before losing Swan for most of the second half after he was injured. Visitors, Dumbarton took full advantage of United's handicap to win 3-2. The team were heavily criticised for lack of spirit and shortly after that defeat, the Board announced that all the players were available for transfer. This reaction was prompted by the unexpected exit from the Scottish Cup and the resultant loss of anticipated income. Other than selling players, the Directors had no other means of keeping the Club financially viable. There was no queue of clubs knocking on the Tannadice door though, not even for the high scoring McKay.

Johnny Raeburn from Lochgelly Albert was in top form, having netted 49 goals for his junior side and he did not disappoint when he turned out for United at Hamilton Academical as a trialist on 14th February. He scored the opening goal but the home side were level by half time and controlled the second half to win 3-1. That was followed by a 3-0 defeat away to Queen's Park and United had Wyllie to thank for keeping the score down! Jimmy Lovie from Peterhead made his debut in a 2-1 home win over Albion Rovers on 28th February. A week later, United lost 2-1 at Ayr United, where the defeat might have been much worse if Wyllie had not been in good form.

United then faced another cup dilemma. The Club were due to visit Morton in a league match and also Airdrieonians 'A' in a Second XI Cup replay on 14th March, but did not have enough signed players for both games. Jackie Swan was signed from Hamilton Academical for the reserve match but that still left United two men short. Consequently, two trialists from Blantyre Celtic were enlisted for the first team game and one of them, Denis Logue, scored a late second goal in the 2-1 win. The other was Jimmy Murphy who would sign for United a year later. The second string also won to progress to the Second XI Cup semi final, but were knocked out by Dundee 'A' shortly after.

A hard working United side took a point from Dunfermline Athletic in a 1-1 draw at Tannadice on 28th March and a week later, beat Forfar Athletic 3-1 away in the penultimate league match of the campaign. A strong Falkirk team came to Tannadice and won 5-2 in a friendly on 11th April but only after United tired in the later stages of the match. The last league match at home to Kilmarnock was a good advert for the game, with hat-tricks on both sides. Quinn fired United into the lead before Mays scored twice for Killie. Although McKay had one chalked off in the first half, he scored four in the second half and Mays completed his hat-trick for a final score of 5-4 to United and an eighth place finish in the league.

The season wound down with the Forfarshire Cup and in the two leg semi final United beat Montrose 3-1 at Tannadice and drew 2-2 at Links Park for a 5-3 aggregate. In the final, the cup went to Brechin City for the first time since 1909 with a controlled performance to win 2-1 at Tannadice. There was no disguising the disappointment of the season after a poor League Cup campaign, a mid table finish and a very early Scottish Cup exit. It was a backward step, proved by the scoring rate, which was well below the previous two seasons. Even the normally high scoring McKay netted just 17 times in his 31 appearances, whilst the top scorer was Quinn, with 24 goals in 37 games. It had been a reasonably settled side throughout 1952-53 with eight players making 25 appearances or more in a 38 game season. The poorer performance can only be attributed to the lack of reserve strength and some enforced changes in personnel. The fans and the Board, now with the addition of former player Duncan Hutchison, who was co-opted in mid March, would be keen to see improvements.

When the list of free transfers was made public, Berrie was perhaps the only surprise and he was released along with Brownlee, Bob Swan, Munro, Jimmy McMillan, George McMillan, Campbell, Morrison, Guy and Irving. Stratton did not re-sign for the next campaign. The rest of the players were retained and centre forward Henry Morris from East Fife was added to the squad in late May. Work to widen the pitch by three yards was under way by the end of the month and was completed in time for the new season.

1953-54

Flirting with Disaster

In the late spring of 1953, United had just twelve signed players: Wyllie, English, Grant, Arnold, Quinn, Temple, McKay, Morris, Dunsmore, Lovie, Cruickshank and Laird, although the last of this group would not feature for United again and Lovie would soon return to Peterhead. John Coyle was due to return after his season at Brechin City, and Edmiston and McIvor were on national service but still retained. However, Wyllie was subject to protracted negotiations with Blackpool and he left to join the English side in late May. The squad was therefore far short of the numbers required for the season, bearing in mind that even without a reserve side in C Division, United had still to field a side of signed players in the Second XI Cup. In June therefore, MacFadyen moved into the transfer market and signed Albert Juliussen on a free transfer from Everton, although he had been two years on loan at Berwick Rangers. Johnny Samuel joined United from Third Lanark in the latter part of the same month but no more signings were made until after the trial match on 1st August. A new trainer was then needed after Johnny Hart gave up the job due to health problems and assistant manager Archie Coats took over the role.

Stand season tickets were on sale at £3 each with ground tickets costing £1.5/- (£1.25) and 7/6 (37½ p) for juniors, and sales were going reasonably well. Former Celtic half back Phil Gormley was signed from Aldershot on a two month deal the day before the trial match, for which a further eleven players were brought in. The priority was a goalkeeper and that position was filled by former Queen's Park, Celtic, Arsenal and Airdrieonians custodian Des McLean, but his contract was for just two months. MacFadyen also signed Willie Westwater from Morton, Archie Smith of East Fife and Jimmy Forbes from Rangers. Of the eleven who played in the opening match, a League Cup tie at Morton on 8th August, only English, Grant, McKay and Cruickshank were from the previous season's squad. United were 2-1 down at half time and despite two Juliussen goals from the penalty spot, the Black and Whites lost 5-3. An unchanged side faced Motherwell at Tannadice in the next match in front of a 17,000 crowd. United were four goals down in just twenty minutes, offering little against very good opposition and it ended 5-0 to the visitors. The next port of call was Rugby Park, where United again suffered a first half barrage to go three goals down. In the end, it was 4-1 to Kilmarnock.

There were changes to the side for the return visit of Morton, including inside left Jimmy Ward, a free transfer from Blackburn Rovers newly signed on a short-term deal. Smith made his first appearance and Edmiston was restored to the goal after he returned from military service in Korea. It was a much improved showing but United had to come from behind twice to earn a 2-2 draw, with McKay scoring both goals. McLean left after this match as his contract had ended. Away to Motherwell, United lost 3-1, with the home side scoring two late goals. The last match in the League Cup section brought the visit of Kilmarnock who ran out 3-0 winners with a fighting United out of luck. That match marked the last game for Gormley and he left four weeks later. There was a break from the rigours of the national competitions when United beat a fairly tame Brechin City 2-0 in the first leg of a Forfarshire Cup tie on 2nd September. Temple scored twice in the second half but United should have scored more. Juliussen made his final appearance for United in that game and two months later, he left to join Brechin City.

17th October 1953 v Motherwell
Standing: Smith, Hamilton, Edmiston, Forbes, Arnold, Tait
Seated: Quinn, Grant, McKay, McCann, Cruickshank

The team for the opening league match showed five changes from the first of the League Cup matches and set the trend for a campaign, which saw frequent alterations to the line up. Bert McCann had signed for United as an amateur from North End and he made his debut in the opening league match at Tannadice against Dumbarton. He played an important part in the 2-1 win, but it was not a performance to inspire the fans. At Stenhousemuir a week later, McKay scored a hat-trick but still finished on the losing side as the Stirlingshire club won by the odd goal in seven. Yet another short-term signing was made when the Manager brought in James McKee from Doncaster Rovers but he lasted just one game. Along with Andy Tait from Dumbarton, McKee made his debut in the 2-1 defeat at home to St Johnstone on 19th September. Both these players missed the next game and were probably glad, as United were trounced 9-1 at Third Lanark, with six of the goals coming in the first half. United's defending was shocking but no blame was attached to Edmiston, who could do little to prevent any of the goals. A week later, the side looked disjointed again and had to come from two goals down to scrape a 2-2 draw at home to Arbroath. On Monday 5th October, United had a visit from Blackpool as part of the Wyllie transfer deal and the 14,000 crowd saw a good performance from the English side in their 5-2 win. Shortly afterwards, with Second XI Cup commitments still to meet, United signed former Alloa Athletic and Cowdenbeath defender Jimmy Hamilton, former Halifax Town, East Fife and Queen of the South player George Gilmour and half back Ernie Doig, who had been with Kilmarnock and Falkirk. Gilmour never progressed to the first team and Doig appeared just once, but Hamilton became a regular in the left back slot for the rest of the season.

The league campaign continued on 10th October at Kilmarnock where, in a game of two halves, United deservedly led 2-0 at half time but a revitalised Killie were 3-2 in front within thirteen minutes of the restart and that was how it finished. United then turned over a more fancied Motherwell 1-0 at Tannadice a week later, with Hamilton making his debut. Then at Cowdenbeath, the Black and Whites did well to keep the score level at 2-2 in the first half, but lost 4-2 after the home side scored twice in the last five minutes. A late goal was again United's undoing, as they went down 3-2 at Forfar Athletic on Halloween, with Doig making his only first team appearance for United. Following that result, the Directors, players and the Manager got together before the next match against Queen's Park on 7th November and a full and frank exchange of views took place. It was stated later that the players shouldered the responsibility for the poor results and to prove what they were capable of, they won the match 4-0 with the help of another McKay hat-trick. Even with that 4-0 win, United were still in bottom place after collecting just seven points from ten games. At home again a week later, Morton hammered United 5-1, scoring three times in the opening eleven minutes. The level of performance at Alloa Athletic on 21st November was not much better but United won 3-1, taking their chances despite having much less possession than the home side. Frank Callaghan from Paisley St Mary's played as a trialist in the match and did enough to earn a second outing three weeks later and he signed on 17th December.

It was only thanks to Edmiston that United returned from Ayr United with just a 2-1 defeat on 28th November. Had the keeper not been on form it would have been much worse. At the end of that month, two more players, Fred Pirie and Albert Henderson, both from Coupar Angus, were signed as reserves following the departure of some others. Just as Morris was leaving on a free transfer, Alec Stenhouse was signed from Auchterarder Primrose and he soon became a regular in the first eleven. The first match in December brought a welcome two points as United beat front runners Dunfermline Athletic 1-0. John Shearer was then signed from Airdrieonians in time to make his debut at Albion Rovers a week later in a match that ended 3-3. At the same time, Ward was released after his short-term deal ended. United were severely hampered by injuries at this time and had to field a side with two trialists, one of whom was Callaghan. To complete the year, United drew 2-2 at Dumbarton and 1-1 with Stenhousemuir at Tannadice. Both games should have been wins for the Black and Whites but in the first match, Forbes missed a potential match winning late penalty and in the second, the visitors scored a fortunate late equaliser.

With the news that Westwater was emigrating to Canada, 1954 began with United in a new strip of black shirts with white sleeves, white shorts and black socks, for a visit to Perth where St Johnstone won 4-1, although United were hampered by the loss of Shearer for a large part of the second half. Provisional signing Alf Scrimgeour from Stobswell scored on his debut in the 1-1 home draw with Third Lanark on 4th January but that was followed by three defeats. The first, at Arbroath was a 4-3 reversal with the home side four goals in front at half time before United fought back to almost steal a point. Stenhouse made his debut in the next match and United were left to rue missed first half chances as Kilmarnock won 2-0 at Tannadice. The next game resulted in United's record defeat in any competition. The venue was Motherwell, the date was 23rd January 1954, the result was Motherwell 12 Dundee United 1. United actually scored first with Tait netting early in the first half! Wilson Humphries (who was later to join United) scored three, Hunter two and Redpath one in the first half for Motherwell and the same players repeated the scoring after the interval. The unfortunate Joe Locherty signed from Sheffield Wednesday made his debut that day and it turned out to be his only United appearance. The post match comments from United were that the team had not played too badly. What then might the score have been if they had played badly?

Such a result was certainly not the kind of preparation needed prior to the Scottish Cup visit to Morton the following week. Not surprisingly, there were changes to the United formation. John Coyle came in and he gave United a half time lead but Morton scored twice before Coyle netted again with ten minutes left. It looked as if United would get the replay they deserved until an unfortunate own goal by English gave the home side a 3-2 win.

As the season drew to its conclusion, the fans knew that there would be no opportunity to make any late loan signings. A change in the rules meant that any player transferred after 31st December could not return to his own club for eighteen months. The only player added was Jacky Peat from Leith Athletic but he was needed only for a forthcoming Second XI Cup match against Falkirk 'A'. On February 6th, United drew 3-3 with Cowdenbeath at Tannadice in a cracking match. The Black and Whites twice came from behind to earn the point, with Callaghan getting the vital third goal. Then, with just seven games left, the prospect of relegation became more and more real with each passing week. Poor results continued with a 1-0 home defeat from Forfar Athletic who stole the points against the run of play to ease their own worries. Away to Queen's Park on 27th February, United lost 3-1 and a week later they lost 4-1 at Morton. Until then, United had been comforted by the fact that bottom club Dumbarton were also doing poorly, but that changed the following week when Alloa Athletic recorded a 1-0 win at Tannadice, while Dumbarton picked up full points in their game.

Everything hinged on the last three games but United also had to rely on Dumbarton dropping points. With the going getting tough, United had to get going. They met Ayr United on 20th March at Tannadice and after a goalless first half, the players rolled up their sleeves and won 4-0 with a battling performance. It was the first home victory for more than three months! A week later they had to defend in depth at Dunfermline Athletic, where McCann's solitary goal won the points. With one game left, United were three points ahead of Dumbarton but the Sons had two games in hand. All United could do then was keep the pressure on Dumbarton by winning their final league match. They did that in style, beating Albion Rovers 6-2 with McKay netting a hat-trick. Dumbarton had to win all of their remaining matches but crucially dropped a point in an astonishing 6-6 draw with Motherwell. When the dust settled, United survived in B Division on goal average, only because the rules did not grant promotion to the reserve sides of the many league clubs who formed the two C Divisions. Only one team was relegated after C Division (South and West) was won by Rangers 'A'. The single promotion place to B Division went to Brechin City who had won C Division (North and East).

The season ended with the Forfarshire Cup. Although United lost 3-2 at Brechin City in the second leg of their tie, the first leg 2-0 result in September secured an aggregate win. It took three attempts to settle the semi final with Montrose and only after a fortunate 1-1 draw at Links Park and then a fairly ordinary 2-2 match at home, did United advance, winning 2-0 at Tannadice. Montrose though were unlucky in the third game, losing their keeper to injury near the end of the first half. Just prior to that match United had keeper problems of their own. With Edmiston injuring a knee before the match, Arnold had to don the No. 1 jersey in the joint benefit match for George Grant and Jimmy Toner against Dundee at Dens Park on 24th April. The emergency keeper had a torrid time as United lost 9-3, but the score line flattered the Dark Blues. The Forfarshire Cup final against Arbroath, with a Saturday evening kick-off at Tannadice, brought down the curtain on 1953-54. United won 2-1, with both goals from Callaghan, the second from the penalty spot. The end of the season was greeted with a huge sigh of relief at Tannadice after flirting with the disaster that would have resulted if the Club had been relegated. The only ever present in the side was McKay who was top scorer with 26 goals in 37 games. Edmiston and Cruickshank made over 30 appearances each and four others made 25 or more. The problem throughout the season was the lack of consistency, allied to selection difficulties, due in part to the absence of some players on national service.

When the list of players to be released was announced, most observers were surprised to see three of the 'Famous Five', Quinn, Dunsmore and Cruickshank included. They were joined through the exit door by several reserves plus Smith, Shearer, Samuel and Temple. Amateurs McCann and MacFadyen did not renew their one year contracts. The players retained were Edmiston, Hamilton, Arnold, Grant, Stenhouse, McIvor, McKay, English and Tait, although the latter player never turned out for United again. Still on national service, Callaghan, Coyle and Forbes were also retained.

During the season, there had been interest in McKay from several clubs, including Burnley, Falkirk and Dundee. Hibs too were keen on the player and asked if he could join them on their forthcoming continental tour as a trialist

Alec Edmiston

but that request was turned down out of hand. With the reputation for goal scoring that he had earned, McKay had no need to prove himself in trial matches. Burnley though were perfectly satisfied that he had the necessary ability and when their offer of £3,000 came in on 11th May, the Board had little choice but to accept. It was a big gamble for the popular centre who had netted an astonishing 203 goals in 241 competitive matches but he was determined to test himself at a higher level. He soon proved that he was good enough to step up from the lower Scottish league to top class English football. Indeed his popularity with United fans was quickly matched by the same level of adulation at Burnley. His transfer also assisted the Club financially, as they had just announced a loss of £524 for the year ended 31st July 1953. The McKay fee therefore gave the Club a good start for the new financial year.

1954-55

The Reign of Reggie Smith

Rebuilding the team for the season ahead began with a closed doors match on 5th June, arranged so that the Manager could make an early assessment of several players. Workington were interested in one of those on view, the towering Hibs defender Vince 'Alpine' Halpin and their manager, Bill Shankly, advised United that he would attend. However, United were not doing this for the benefit of anyone else and Mr Shankly was firmly but politely advised that, as it was a private trial, he would not be admitted. Two days later MacFadyen signed former Celtic player Jimmy Murphy (who had been on trial with United in March 1953) and Danny Bell, a right back from Dumbarton. Ahead of stiff competition from Norwich City and Workington, Halpin was also signed and he was joined by Ian Irvine from Huddersfield Town and Dave Cross from Airdrieonians. After the public trial on 7th August, Jimmy Robertson from Plymouth Argyle and Tom McLeod from Wisbech Town were added on short-term deals to complete the pre-season signings.

Tannadice in 1954 showing the old stand and the pavilion located in the south east corner.

The new season kicked off against Ayr United in a League Cup tie at Tannadice on 14th August with four of the recent signings, Bell, Cross, Irvine and McLeod all making their first appearance for United. It was an all action opening with the visitors ahead in just twenty seconds, but by half time it was level at 2-2. United were on the rack after the interval and conceded three more to make it a 5-2 defeat and a bad start to the season. The much travelled Alex Anderson was signed on a short-term deal in time to join Robertson, making their debuts in the next match at Dunfermline Athletic. United again started well but fell away in the second half, eventually losing 3-1. At Brechin City for the third match in the section, United did not play well and the home side won 2-0 with some ease. By this time, it was all too much for MacFadyen and he resigned on 24th August. Until a new Manager could be appointed, Duncan Hutchison took temporary charge of team matters and his first action was to bring in Jimmy Brownlie to assist him.

The introduction of Coyle to the side for the visit to Ayr United resulted in an improved front line performance but it still ended in a 3-1 defeat. However, in the next match on 1st September, Coyle had the desired effect on section leaders Dunfermline Athletic. His two goals in the opening nine minutes paved the way for a 3-1 home win. But Coyle was still on national service and unavailable against Brechin City in the last of the section's six games and poor finishing did not help as United lost 1-0. Even this early in the season there were worrying signs but the Board were aware of the problems and action was planned. One Director said, "We are out to capture the old spirit at Tannadice. We can give no wild promises but every effort will be made to get the team on a sound footing. We must get the old fighting spirit back and this is where our fans can help … The 'Tannadice Howl' puts spirit into our players … We want to see those days back and with the Directors, players and supporters pulling their weight we can do it."

Around forty applications for the Manager's job arrived within a week, including one from Andy McCall. He was unsuccessful this time but would get the job a few years later. Whilst the Directors prepared a short list, Duncan Hutchison lined up the side for the first match of the league campaign on 11th September, against Stenhousemuir at Tannadice. Two trialists from Dundee Osborne were in the side that earned a 1-1 draw and free transfer Lawrie Higgins from Aberdeen was signed on a trial basis in time to make his debut also. Billy Ritchie was the trialist at centre and he scored the equaliser. The other trialist was Eddie Stewart who signed for United shortly after. Centre forward was the position causing most concern and another trialist, Billy Boyle, was wearing the No. 9 jersey in the next match at Perth where St Johnstone powered through a disjointed United and won 4-0. On 25th September, in Hutchison's last game in charge, another trialist centre, Dickie Cruickshank netted both goals in a hard earned 2-0 win over Third Lanark.

Reggie Smith was appointed as the new Manager and he took charge on 27th September. Smith had been with neighbours Dundee for six years and prior to that, had gained international honours with England during his time south of the border with top sides Crystal Palace, Spurs and Millwall. He had his own ideas on how a team should be built. His three year plan and the new Club policy would be to bring through young players from the ranks of the juniors. He also intended to take a very active role in the training, visiting Glasgow every week to coach the out-of-town players himself. His first match in charge was at Airdrieonians and he wasted no time in experimenting, playing full back Bell at centre. The match ended in a 2-1 defeat for United but the Manager was pleased with the fighting attitude of the players. Not all of them were in his plans however and he quickly released Jimmy Robertson, McLeod, Irvine and English.

The return of Peter McKay to Tannadice on 4th October drew a 10,000 crowd who witnessed the former United man in top form. He scored two of Burnley's goals in a 4-0 friendly win. Results did not improve for the new Manager and United lost at home by the odd goal in five to Brechin City, followed by a 5-1 hammering at Ayr United on 16th October. Halpin, who had been plagued with injury since he signed, made an unhappy first and only appearance in that match, scoring two own goals! Worse was to follow for United as they went out of the Scottish Cup at Tannadice, beaten 3-1 by a determined Forfar Athletic. Immediately after, there were more personnel changes. Higgins was released after his trial period ended and outside left Sandy Stephen of Elmwood came in for a trial

Reggie Smith

against Albion Rovers on 6th November and played well. Another trialist in the side for that match was Billy Dawson who scored United's equaliser in the 1-1 draw. In the week leading up to the next match, United signed Tommy Robertson from Cheltenham Town and Stephen also put pen to paper. Meanwhile, the last member of the 'Famous Five', George Grant, left United to join Falkirk and coming in the opposite direction was Willie Dunlop in a player swap deal.

Dunlop and Tommy Robertson made their debuts at Dunfermline Athletic on 13th November but they had little impact as United suffered a 3-1 defeat. Left back Alan Massie was signed from Dundee and went straight into the side to face Queen's Park a week later. Also making his first appearance in the 3-1 defeat in that match was trialist goalkeeper Sandy McLaren of Perth Celtic and he signed a few days later. Duncan McMillan was signed from Grimsby Town and made his only appearance for United on 27th November in a 5-4 win over Alloa Athletic.

The star of that game was trialist Billy Boyle who netted four of United's goals. Unfortunately, he could not be persuaded to sign for the Club.

It had taken the new Manager two months to record his first win but there was still no sign of any real improvement in the side. A week later former favourite Frank Quinn came back to haunt United, setting up a late equaliser for his side, Hamilton Academical, in a 1-1 draw at Douglas Park. Tom McGairy from Walsall made his debut in that match. Tommy Robertson was then released as yet another new player was added to the squad with the arrival of Tom Simpson from Crusaders of Belfast on a short-term deal. He made his debut as United crashed to a 5-0 defeat at Morton on 11th December. A week later, with trialist Ronnie Johnston making his first appearance, United threw away a three goal half time lead to go down 4-3 at home to Forfar Athletic. With ten minutes remaining in that match, United were still 3-1 in front but then panicked, conceding three times in as many minutes. Now bottom of the table, there was little doubt that the frequent changes to the side were having an unsettling effect, but Smith was still confident he would get it right. McMillan was released and Johnston signed after his successful trial and terms were offered to Bobby Flavell, just released by Dundee, but he went to Kilmarnock instead. Smith also tried to sign Billy Dawson but the player decided to stay with his junior side as they were on a good cup run.

On Christmas Day, United beat Stenhousemuir 4-3 away, with the aid of a McGairy hat-trick but the other two games in the festive programme ended in defeat. The first was a poor performance at Tannadice where St Johnstone won 5-1, followed by an easy 2-0 win for Third Lanark at their Cathkin Park ground. In early January, Simpson was released and Hamilton was transfer listed at his own request. John McBain was signed from Arbroath, making his debut on 8th January as United lost by the odd goal in seven against Airdrieonians. Smith kept looking for ways to improve the side and to give him more time to devote to training in the evenings a good set of floodlights was installed at Tannadice. It seemed to pay off as a solid team performance brought a 3-0 win against Ayr United and a week later at Arbroath the team again played well but lost 3-1. Archie Aikman was acquired from Falkirk and made his debut on 5th February at Brechin City and with the breaks going their way for once, the Black and Whites won 3-2, with Aikman scoring twice. At home to Cowdenbeath a week later, United should have won again but had to settle for a point in a goalless draw.

Around this time, it was announced that the Directors had given the Manager permission to go to South Africa in April for three months, to honour a coaching commitment he had there. Smith told the supporters that he would sign up the squad for the following season before he left. There would be no rush to fix up players following the public trial as he considered this a far from satisfactory way to build a team. As early as 26th February, he announced that he had already decided on the reserves. He may have had reserve players but finding games for them in the next season would prove to be a different matter.

The weather had wiped out most of the football card for two weeks and on 5th March, United's match against Dunfermline Athletic was in doubt, until the Manager led a team of volunteers at Tannadice, breaking up ice on the pitch. They managed to get the fixture played but despite a good first half, United lost 4-1. That was followed by a 1-1 draw at Queen's Park and a goalless draw at Alloa Athletic. In both these matches United were forced onto the defensive but deserved the point each time. Bob Penman was signed from Jeanfield Swifts and eighteen year old Jimmy Reid from St Joseph's was lined up to play a trial against Hamilton Academical at Tannadice. United lost the match 2-1 after two defensive errors but Reid played well and was signed immediately after.

A week later the question being asked was – Why are United bottom of the league? A 5-0 win over Morton was achieved with an impressive performance and United also hit woodwork five times. Continuing their attacking form into the next match, United beat Forfar Athletic 4-1 at Station Park and again they could have scored more. Johnston was transfer listed at his own request on 15th April. Smith made one more signing before he left for South Africa, adding left winger Maurice Milne from St Joseph's, after he had impressed in a 6-1 home win on 16th April over Arbroath, in which Aikman scored a hat-trick.

Johnston had already left United before the list of players to be released was announced on 23rd April. Leaving at the end of the season were Jimmy Hamilton, Bell, Halpin and McIvor. The retained players were Edmiston, McLaren, Massie, Cross, McBain, Callaghan, Arnold, Stewart, Murphy, Stephen, Stenhouse, Aikman and McGairy plus provisional signings Penman, Reid and Milne, along with Ian Hamilton of Harris Academy. Forbes and Coyle were retained but still on national service. Dunlop was offered terms but refused to re-sign.

On the same day, United failed to master a bumpy pitch at Cowdenbeath, losing 3-1. A few days later in a Dewar Shield match the side came back from a two goal deficit to record a 2-2 draw at St Johnstone. On 30th April in the first leg of a Forfarshire Cup tie with Montrose, the Black and Whites again drew 2-2 and had two goals disallowed. Two days later, the last match in the league programme saw a gallant United lose 3-2 to a last minute penalty at Albion Rovers. The last match of the season was a poor display at Montrose, where the home side won the second leg of the Forfarshire Cup tie 3-1 to knock United out.

It had been another season of disappointments with hardly a positive to be found, other than the emergence of a few youngsters with potential. United finished in fourth bottom place in the league, just three points ahead of bottom club Brechin City. The Club never recovered from a poor start to the season and part of the problem lay in the lack of a consistent line up. Including trialists, almost forty players were used over the season. Cross was the only ever present with 37 league and cup appearances, whilst just Arnold and Callaghan exceeded 30 outings and five others topped twenty appearances each. Goal scoring was also a major problem, with the position of centre filled by more than a dozen different players until the arrival of Aikman. His 7 goals was a creditable haul for just 11 games. Top scorer McGairy netted 11 times in 20 appearances. At the end of May, Archie Simpson and Neil McKinven were released by Dundee and United were interested in both but they turned down offers to move to Tannadice.

1955-56

Youth Takes the Stage

There were discussions at national level on the issue of substitutes, but at the time, the SFA were only in favour of allowing players to be replaced during international matches involving the four home nations. Meanwhile, another decision affecting United's future plans was made by the Scottish League. Initially there was a suggestion that the B Division would split into East and West leagues with a sixteen team A Division. This idea was not favoured by the lower league sides who instead wanted just two leagues. They got their wish in the end, with C Division scrapped and the Scottish League restructured into an eighteen team A Division and a nineteen team B Division.

This decision gave United a problem though, as the reserve side had already been accepted for a place in C Division. Now there was no league for the second eleven to compete in as they were also excluded from the re-established Scottish Alliance. In a B Division of nineteen teams there would of course always be one team inactive each Saturday. The Directors therefore considered playing Dundee United 'A' against the idle team each week but with guarantees to be paid, it would prove too costly, and the idea was dropped.

By the end of June, Dunlop had re-signed and Coyle was demobbed and available again. More significant though was the arrival of a group of players, all from St Mary's Youth Club. Smith had been tracking the players for some time and in his absence, Ally Gallacher arranged the signings. Three were signed in June including Jimmy Coyle (brother of John Coyle), Fred Grubb and Jimmy Briggs. The latter would go on to serve the Club for many years to come. In mid July, two more St Mary's players, Alex Will and Dave Sturrock were added to the squad and that completed the pre-season signings. Exactly as the Manager had said, the emphasis was firmly on youth. United lost groundsman Wattie Low who left just before the public trial match. With no-one else to do the job, Reggie Smith was seen tending to the pitch. It took until the end of August to find a replacement groundsman, Frank McCusker. For the trial match on 12th August, Smith sprang a late surprise with two experienced trialists turning out but neither impressed.

A last ditch attempt to form a B Division reserve league was thwarted when a meeting of the clubs had to be cancelled, after Third Lanark and Albion Rovers withdrew their support. Morton and St Johnstone were doubtful starters and Queen's Park decided to take their chances finding friendlies in the Glasgow area. That left only United, Dumbarton and Ayr United committed to the proposal, so the league never got off the ground. The second string were therefore left to play just friendlies against teams of varying ability. A large number of games were arranged over the season and ultimately it helped produce a stronger first team. A run in the Second XI Cup might have been beneficial too, but United 'A' were knocked out in the first round by Aberdeen 'A'.

As usual, the season got under way with the League Cup sections and without a new face in the side, United lined up for the opening fixture at home to Albion Rovers on 13th August. The visitors won 3-1 quite comfortably and a few days later, Bob Penman made his debut at Motherwell as United were thrashed 7-1, despite scoring first. Edmiston was blamed for many of the goals conceded and he was dropped in favour of McLaren for the next match, away to Forfar Athletic, where a 5-2 win flattered United. Dundee-born Frank Barclay signed from Nottingham Forest on a free transfer and made his debut in that match.

In the midst of the League Cup section, United began the league campaign with a visit to Brechin City on 24th August and Smith took a huge gamble, giving debuts to Briggs, Will and Jimmy Coyle. The team wore their new continental style shirts and the line up contained eight players under twenty years of age, along with three veterans. John Coyle scored twice and although the home side levelled the match after the interval, the performance delighted the Manager, Directors and supporters alike. Back on League Cup business in the next match, a more experienced United managed a 3-3 draw at Albion Rovers. The line up was shuffled again for the visit of Motherwell and the Lanarkshire side, who went on to win the section, won 3-0 but it was only finally decided with two late goals. The last match of the section brought Forfar Athletic to Tannadice and United took control, wrapping it up by the interval for a 3-2 win.

Meanwhile in the reserves, several players had trials, including Ian Lornie, a pupil at Harris Academy. He was due to begin studying at St Andrews University and signed as an amateur. Lornie made his first team debut in goal at Tannadice against Queen's Park on 10th September in a 2-2 draw. The league campaign continued with yet another 2-2 result, against Forfar Athletic in midweek and it took a late strike by Aikman to save a point for United. With Edmiston back between the posts, a visit to East Stirlingshire followed. A real end to end match finished in an incredible 5-5 score line, with a late Massie penalty earning the point. It was also at this time that United revealed the new Club badge, with DUNDEE UNITED in a banner above a red Scottish lion flanked by the letters FC.

The Coyle brothers scored two each in the next match, a 6-2 win over Alloa Athletic on 21st September. Then St Johnstone were the visitors to Tannadice, leaving with a fortunate point from a 1-1 draw. The same result was achieved in the match at Forfar Athletic and United had to thank their defence for a hard-earned point. On 1st October, United went to Arbroath and the Coyle double act helped the side return with two points from a 4-2 win. The October Holiday Monday brought a Dundee derby friendly at Dens Park where the Black and Whites earned a creditable 1-1 draw, in which Edmiston saved a late penalty. United's ninth game undefeated in the league came at home in a 1-0 win over Third Lanark but Edmiston had to save another spot kick to secure both points.

Duncan Young of Butterburn Youth Club was asked to sign after playing well in the reserves. He turned out for his first team debut along with Hamilton and Sturrock in a friendly at Arbroath on the evening of Wednesday 12th October. Also playing that night as a trialist was Ernie Fenton, a teenage Harris Academy pupil who then joined the reserves. Although United lost 2-0, the match was notable as it was the first time United played under floodlights. The unbeaten league record was lost a few days later in a 3-0 defeat at Hamilton Academical after which Murphy, Dunlop and McGairy were advised that they were free to find another club. Murphy soon joined Brechin City and Dunlop appears to have left in January but McGairy stayed until the end of the season.

Director William McIntosh, who had done so much for the Club in the 1930s, died suddenly on 18th October and his passing was marked by a minute's silence before the next match, a Scottish Cup tie against Dumbarton. In front of 12,000 spectators, United turned on the style and although it was 1-1 at the interval, an excellent performance in the second half brought three more goals for a 4-1 win. However, a week later, a complete reversal of fortunes saw a shot-shy United lose 4-1 at Stenhousemuir. On 5th November against Cowdenbeath, there was another first at Tannadice when a thrilling encounter that ended 4-4 was broadcast live on radio to local hospitals. A week later at Montrose the match finished 2-2 and with United fast becoming the score draw specialists, it was 3-3 at home to Ayr United seven days after that.

After earlier declining to join United, Neil McKinven had signed for Arbroath when he left Dundee. In mid November however, he was released at his own request and was then signed immediately by Smith, playing initially in the reserves. The remaining weeks of 1955 brought a mixed bag of results, starting with a 2-0 defeat at Stranraer. That was followed by a 1-1 draw at Albion Rovers, thanks to a John Coyle equaliser. Then at home to Morton, two points were gained in a comfortable 4-2 win on 10th December. Willie Penman was signed from Montrose and it was announced that Briggs had effectively ended his junior status as he had played more than the permitted number of games at senior level. Penman made his debut on 17th December in a 3-2 defeat at Berwick Rangers.

After some press speculation, Smith denied rumours of a £5,000 offer by Leeds United for John Coyle but confirmed that he expected to lose Stewart and Stephen, as both had been called up for their national service. In a friendly against a Combined Services XI on Christmas Eve, McKinven made his first team debut in a match that ended 6-5 for the visitors, with Aikman getting a hat-trick for United. Three days later United's 3-1 win at home to Brechin City was well deserved with Edmiston saving a late penalty. On New Year's Eve, with McKinven making his league debut, the points were given away cheaply in a 2-0 defeat at Dumbarton. At St Johnstone two days later, United gave a tired display as they again lost 2-0.

Jimmy Reid

On 7th January, John Coyle scored all the goals, including a penalty, in a 4-0 win over East Stirlingshire but if the team had taken all the chances on offer, the score might have been into double figures. On the same day, against Powis of Aberdeen, United fielded a reserve side with every player under eighteen years of age. Indeed, two players, Nicoll Cargill and Ernie Fenton were still not yet fifteen! Inconsistency was still a problem, and with Sturrock making his league debut, it ended 0-0 at Queen's Park on 14th January. By this time, United had used twenty-nine players. Largely because there was no competitive reserve league, the Manager had to try out new players and emerging youngsters in the first eleven. Amongst the trialists, George Grant from Arbroath made his debut against his former club on 21st January in a 2-1 win, achieved with a last gasp John Coyle goal. Massie was then added to the list of players free to leave the Club. At Third Lanark a week later, United played with ten men when Callaghan was injured after just ten minutes, making the 1-0 win all the more creditable.

For the next seven days, the city was buzzing in anticipation of the eagerly awaited Scottish Cup tie between United and Dundee at Tannadice. Five inches of snow had to be cleared to get the pitch playable and it only just survived the weather. Prices had been increased because of additional policing costs and on the day, 20,000 spectators paid a total of £2,500 to see a fascinating 2-2 draw. Milne had United a goal in front but they then succumbed to pressure from the Dark Blues to go 2-1 down. A never-say-die attitude brought the reward of a late goal from Milne to earn a second chance. Dundee's full-time training paid dividends in the midweek replay, with a 3-0 win, as United tired on a heavy Dens Park pitch.

Still smarting from the cup exit, United drew 3-3 with Hamilton Academical the following Saturday and two weeks later, despite playing against ten men for much of the game, United lost 1-0 at Alloa Athletic, with Young making his league debut. At home to Stenhousemuir a week later, United retained an unbeaten home record with a hard fought 1-0 win. They then lost 3-2 at Cowdenbeath, where former United man, Frank Quinn, turned the tables on his old club yet again. He scored twice to wipe out a 2-1 lead and United's cause was not helped when Arnold was sent off near the end.

It emerged that Notts County were checking up on John Coyle, having had him watched on several occasions. Their representative was at the match against Montrose on 17th March and he saw a United side, with Coyle and a clutch of other home bred players, take the visitors apart in a 6-3 win. A 1-0 defeat at Ayr United a week later was witnessed by scouts from both Luton Town and Cardiff City but they left unimpressed. With just a handful of league matches to go, United were safely in mid table and nothing much was at stake. A 2-2 draw with Stranraer at Tannadice was followed by a comfortable 2-0 home win over Albion Rovers. Nevertheless, crowds had been falling and the Directors announced that United were losing on average £200 each week. The Board felt that the Club's policy of nurturing young players was working but it was costly and had to be backed by cash through the turnstiles. If this did not happen then United could be forced to sell top players such as Coyle and Milne. Another of the young players, Fred Grubb made his only first team appearance in the next match, a 3-2 defeat at Morton on 18th April.

For business reasons, Grant was released at his own request during a hectic mid April. Smith was due to leave for South Africa again for a three month coaching commitment there. As a parting gift, his side thrashed Berwick Rangers 8-1 at Tannadice on 21st April. John Coyle scored four of the goals, the second of which was United's 2,000th in Scottish League matches. Two days later, a side showing just two changes lost 5-0 in the first leg of the 1953-54 Dewar Shield final at Stirling Albion, newly relegated from the top division. The match was watched by scouts from Cardiff City, Preston North End, Luton Town and Aberdeen who witnessed a very poor United display. The April programme continued with the final home league match against Dumbarton. United preserved their unbeaten league record at Tannadice with

John Coyle

a 1-1 draw, courtesy of a very late Coyle penalty. The second leg of the Dewar Shield final resulted in a 2-2 draw and the last match of the season was a 2-1 Forfarshire Cup defeat by Dundee at Dens Park.

At the end of April, United released McLaren, Bob Penman, Willie Penman, Massie, McKinven and McGairy, and it would appear that Fenton and Lornie also left at around this time. Retained were Edmiston, Callaghan, Briggs, Young, Cross, Stewart, Arnold, Will, Forbes, Stenhouse, Stephen, John Coyle, Jimmy Coyle, Reid, and Sturrock. McBain was retained although by then he had left for India where he had a new job. Provisionally signed Ian Hamilton and Nicoll Cargill were also retained but neither progressed much further than the reserves. Luton Town had wanted both John Coyle and Milne but felt United had asked too much for them. Chairman Ernest Robertson, however, considered the English side were bargain hunting and would not allow the players to leave cheaply.

The goal scoring plaudits went to John Coyle who netted an average of one per game for a Club record, 43 goals in one season that is unlikely to be beaten. He had missed just two games all season and along with Edmiston, Arnold, McBain and Aikman, formed the nucleus of the team. The eighth place league finish was a vast improvement on the previous campaign and had been achieved by a well balanced side, with several of the younger players making good progress.

1956-57

The First Key to Success

Chairman Ernest Robertson was quick to point out that whilst there was no news emanating from Tannadice over the early summer months of 1956, the Manager and the Directors were not wasting time. In late June, he said, "We have considered several experienced players and there may soon be a signing or two. However, we are not to depart from our policy of signing and coaching local boys. Our present youngsters are showing great promise and have continued training at Tannadice." A week later Smith announced that United would no longer allow training facilities for players of other clubs as had been the recent custom. On 30th June, Noel Wannan was signed on a free transfer from Montrose. In keeping with the youth policy, fifteen-year-old schoolboy John Markie was signed on a provisional form on 10th July but he would never make the breakthrough into the first eleven.

New Directors George Fox and J Johnston Grant were elected at the AGM in late July when it was also announced that a huge loss of £5,271 had been incurred for the year ended July 1955. This was attributed to the policy of bringing through young players and lack of income from transfer fees. The financial situation caused major concern for the Board but the problem was being addressed through the formation of Dundee United Sportsmen's Club. Modelled on a similar scheme at Nottingham Forest, the Sportsmen's Club would soon provide substantial cash donations, which would transform the fortunes of Dundee United and provide the first key element in the future success of the Club. The credit for introducing the scheme at United must go to Jimmy Littlejohn who witnessed it first-hand during a business trip to England.

Former Dundee outside right Sandy Evans and keeper Bobby Henderson signed on 4th August after both had taken part in the public trial. The fans were then delighted to learn that John Coyle had also re-signed. There was news that the Scottish League intended running a Second Division reserve league commencing in September. Unfortunately that never happened. A Scottish Alliance League, including United 'A' and six other reserve sides, was arranged and throughout the season, the second XI had competitive opposition to ensure a real test for the first time since 1952.

When the season opened with a League Cup tie against Ayr United on 11th August, Henderson was the only debutant in the side that hammered the Honest Men 6-1, with John Coyle scoring a hat-trick. After such a flying start, United crashed back to earth with a 3-2 midweek defeat at Stenhousemuir but then returned with a 2-1 win from Third Lanark. The Scottish League programme opened on 22nd August at Alloa Athletic where John Coyle snatched a last gasp equaliser for a 2-2 draw. It was also the debut game for Wannan and Evans. Away from home, for the fourth game in succession, as the League Cup section resumed, United drew 1-1 with Ayr United. The section seemed to have slipped away after Stenhousemuir won 4-3 at Tannadice in an enthralling match. However, a noteworthy team performance to win 2-1 against Third Lanark put United into a play-off against Arbroath for the right to meet Dundee in the quarter final.

29th August 1956 v Stenhousemuir
Standing: Young, Cross, Henderson, Will, Arnold, Forbes
Seated: Callaghan, Sturrock, John Coyle, Reid, Milne

The first leg of the play-off was at Gayfield on 3rd September and although United pounded the home goal for the entire first half, it was goalless at the interval.

The Red Lichties had all the good fortune in the second half, scoring twice after United lost Arnold to injury. Arbroath felt they had probably done enough but they did not count on a fighting display by the Black and Whites two days later, when United thumped in five goals without reply to progress on a 5-2 aggregate. With no match on the Saturday, United fielded a strong reserve side in a Second XI Cup tie at Aberdeen 'A'. That proved to be a mistake, as keeper Henderson suffered a broken leg and was unavailable for the League Cup match at Dens Park. Further injuries to players during the match on 12th September hampered United but the 7-3 defeat was attributed more to the fitness and strength of the Dark Blues, rather than to any failing in the United side. Recently signed Davie Gray made his debut for United in the second leg at Tannadice three days later. Still injury ravaged, United gave a lion-hearted display against the odds to win 2-1 and restore some respectability, but went out of the tournament on an 8-5 aggregate.

Smith had the players quickly re-focused on the league challenge. The visit of Alloa Athletic brought two points from a 4-3 win, but at St Johnstone in the next match, United lost the points when the

15th September 1956 United v Dundee

home side won 3-2 with a late penalty. An early two goal lead was thrown away a week later at home to Stranraer, who left with a point from the 2-2 draw. United then thumped Berwick Rangers 6-1, with Clive Wallace of Kirrie Thistle playing as a trialist on the left wing. An unpredictable United lost 3-1 at Stenhousemuir and followed that with a battling 2-1 win over Hamilton Academical. The pundits gave United little chance of an upset in the forthcoming Scottish Cup tie against Third Lanark on 20th October. Even the fans were lacking belief as only 7,000 attended the match but those who stayed away were the losers as United won 5-2 with some style. Coyle scored a first half double and Milne got two more after the break before Coyle completed his hat-trick. Some slackness gave the visitors two consolation goals but this did not detract from an outstanding United performance. Newly signed keeper Charlie Hutton from East Fife was the only change in the United line up a week later when Third Lanark were the visitors again, on league business, but United lost 1-0 in a dour encounter. That result ended United's unbeaten home run, the longest in Britain at the time, going back to 26th March 1955. The next two matches also ended in defeats, 4-1 away to

Morton and 4-2 at home to Clyde but two points were gained against a plucky Forfar Athletic in a 2-1 win on 17th November. Wallace again showed his worth with both United's goals. However, after one more match with United he decided not to sign as he was still at school and wanted to finish his exams. United did sign another player, amateur Don Watt from Aberdeen University and he made his debut on 24th November at Montrose in a 2-2 draw.

A week later, United hammered Albion Rovers 7-0, with John Coyle scoring four of the goals, but Albion played the entire second half with ten men, after losing a player through injury. With just one change in the side on 8th December, United faded after leading at half time and lost 3-2 at Dumbarton. The following week, former player Frank Quinn again did the damage against United with a hat-trick, as United lost 6-2 at Cowdenbeath. Worse still, attendances at Tannadice were dropping and the Club were losing around £120 at every home game. Crowds of around 3,000 were becoming the norm, whereas 7,000 were needed just to break even. One Director was quoted as saying United might have to sell players and it was not beyond the bounds of possibility that the Club would become amateur. By then, the Sportsmen's Club set up to raise money for the football club, had launched Taypools, the first local football pool competition in Scotland. Despite paying out prizes of up to £100, their income was not yet sufficient to allow any money to be donated to the football club. As if to underline the problem, only 1,200 fans attended the next match at Tannadice, a 3-1 win over East Stirlingshire.

Just before Christmas, Hutton and Wannan were released as both decided to give up the game. On Christmas Day, United hammered Berwick Rangers 6-0 away. Four days later, Ian Inglis, signed from local junior side Elmwood, made his first appearance along with Markie in a 3-2 defeat by a Dundee Junior Select. In the select side was Willie McDonald of St Joseph's and he signed for United six weeks later. On New Year's Day, nothing seemed to be going right for United. First the rope on the new flag broke when Reggie Smith tried to raise it and then the match against St Johnstone, on a muddy pitch, developed into something bordering on farce as United lost 2-1. At Brechin City the following afternoon, the score was 0-0 and three days later United concluded a hectic New Year programme with a closely fought 1-0 win over Arbroath.

Falkirk had been on the verge of making an offer for John Coyle but changed their minds. A disjointed United then lost 1-0 at Stranraer. Coyle had been off form for several weeks, but it was little wonder as he was working late almost every night in his job as a bricklayer. Falkirk may have failed to take Coyle but without much warning, they were then successful in luring Reggie Smith to Brockville! He saw United beat Stenhousemuir 2-0 on 19th January and three days later, he left. Assistant Manager, Ally Gallacher took over immediately and he was aided by Archie Coats who, by then, had been United's trainer for five years. The next day, Jimmy Reid left United to join Bury and Gallacher immediately brought in John McGuinness who had been with Dundee. An army regular with five years' service, he signed as an amateur with the permission of his commanding officer and made his debut in a 4-1 defeat at Hamilton Academical. It was also announced, that because of other business commitments, Jimmy Littlejohn was standing down from the Board after fifteen years service to the Club. After all the unwelcome events of the previous week, there was one highly significant piece of good news. Dundee United Sportsmen's Club, with a membership approaching 15,000, handed over a cheque for £300.

The Scottish Cup took centre stage next and United went to Stenhousemuir but could only manage a 1-1 draw. Just over 4,000 were at Tannadice for the replay, which United eventually won 4-0 after the regulation ninety minutes produced plenty of chances but no goals. United were fortunate to benefit from two own goals in extra time and John Coyle scored the other two. McDonald made his first appearance for United in the next game, a 2-0 league win over Stirling Albion and then he signed. It was also announced that George Bennett, formerly of Sheffield United and signed in September, was taking charge of the reserves. On 16th February, United travelled to Kirkcaldy to meet Raith Rovers in the Scottish Cup. Facing a forward line that had scored 73 goals so far that season, United were completely overwhelmed and lost 7-0. Stenhouse was then transferred to Portsmouth and the Directors intimated that the fee received would be used to bring in a replacement.

The next match at Third Lanark was abandoned at half time with the score at 1-1. That meant that the next officially recorded result was another 7-0 thrashing, at home to Morton, but this time at least there was some mitigation. During the game Cross was injured and United lost Arnold to injury early in the second half. A visit to Clyde followed and United conceded seven again as the home side won 7-1. The newest acquisition for United was Archie Coats (son of the United trainer), a goalkeeper with Elmwood. He made his debut in a 3-1 defeat at Forfar Athletic on 16th March, whilst Inglis got his first and only outing in major competition. United then announced that the financial year ended July 1956, had resulted in a loss of £1,232.

The following week, rumours of a new Manager coming to Tannadice were initially denied by official sources but soon after United drew 2-2 at home with Montrose in front of just 1,800 fans, it was announced that an appointment would be made the following week. Ally Gallacher immediately resigned, although the Directors wanted him to stay on and revert to his former scouting role. The new Manager was Tommy Gray, a former player with Dundee, who had just resigned his post as manager at Arbroath. He took the job with United on a part-time basis and suffered a 5-1 defeat at Albion Rovers in his first match in charge. Gray then began a search for players to bolster the young Tannadice side. He brought in goalkeeper Bill Lucas from Broxburn Athletic on a provisional form after a fine display, including a penalty save, in the 2-2 draw at Arbroath on 8th April.

Before the next match against Cowdenbeath, centre half Andy Hamilton was signed from Dunfermline Athletic and right winger Alex Berry joined United on trial from Preston Athletic. Both had good debuts in a 4-1 win.

A change of policy was then announced, completely contrary to Reggie Smith's ideas. It was decided that there would be no reserve side operated in 1957-58. The cost of bringing through young players and running two teams was considered prohibitive and Gray intimated that he would not give this the high priority it had previously enjoyed. Instead, he would look to sign players from any source and new signings would be of a 'suitable physique'. The Directors also publicised plans to cover the west terracing with what is now known as 'The Shed'. The cost of £2,000 for the work was funded entirely by Dundee United Sportsmen's Club, who had just donated another £500.

Apparently galvanised by the new regime, United recorded a 3-2 win at second placed Third Lanark with a performance that begged the question – Why were United so far down the league? Two days later, they beat another strong side in Dumbarton by 3-1 after which Lucas signed professional forms. A 2-1 win over Brechin City was followed by a 2-1 defeat at Stirling Albion. After that match, trialist Jimmy Brown from Glencraig Colliery, who had first played as a trialist against Brechin City, was added to the growing band of new players. At the same time, it was decided not to retain Berry after three matches on trial. The season concluded with a 3-2 defeat at East Stirlingshire with United twice losing the lead. That left United in a disappointing thirteenth place in the league. John Coyle had missed just one of the 50 competitive matches played and was top scorer again with 38 goals. Cross, Forbes and Milne all racked up over forty appearances each, with the latter also second top scorer on 19. In a season of so many changes and three Managers, it was perhaps not surprising that United had an inconsistent campaign.

Over the season, several players were signed as reserves but never made the breakthrough, including Bob Wynd (ex-Stobswell), George Wright, Morris Ross and Angus McKelvie. Barclay had left early in the season and several other players had trials at reserve and first team level but did not impress enough to have terms offered. The end of season clearout resulted in free transfers for Edmiston, Henderson, Callaghan, Arnold, Forbes, Evans, Aikman, Jimmy Coyle and Watt, whilst McBain, who had returned from India, retired through injury. As an amateur, McGuinness was also released and did not re-sign. Youngsters Markie, Inglis, Ian Hamilton and Coats also appear to have been allowed to leave. In the forces but still retained, were Stephen, Will and Stewart and the latter was on loan at Norwich City. The retained players were Lucas, Andy Hamilton, Brown, John Coyle, Young, Briggs, McDonald and Gray. Milne was also retained but he left to join Norwich City in mid May. The Manager was keen to get players fixed up well in advance of the new season and signed former Clydebank and Dundee inside right Joe Roy from Third Lanark and ex-Motherwell forward

Wilson Humphries from St Mirren on 17th May. Humphries was the first £1,000 player to join United. He was well remembered at Tannadice as the player who scored half of Motherwell's goals when they inflicted the record 12-1 defeat on United.

1957-58

Cashing in on Progress

The Manager continued his player search through the summer and at the end of June, half back Alistair Gibson was signed from Queen of the South, followed by left winger Jimmy King from Cowdenbeath. The full squad was then called to Tannadice on 22ⁿᵈ July, when they were greeted by the return of Jack Qusklay, back at Tannadice to help with training. The annual public trial match was arranged for 3ʳᵈ August and although several free transfer players and juniors took part, only former Celtic and St Mirren right winger Jim Duncan was signed afterwards.

As usual, the League Cup sectional matches were the first fixtures on the calendar and United had Humphries, Duncan and Gibson making debuts in the first match. Despite a Humphries goal in just forty-five seconds, United got off to a bad start in the competition with a 4-1 defeat at home to Clyde on 10ᵗʰ August. An away match followed and, although United lost an early goal, they kept control for a comfortable 4-2 win over Dumbarton. Three days later, Coyle netted a hat-trick in a 4-2 win at Stranraer. The next match was preceded by a presentation of a cheque for £1,000 by Dundee United Sportsmen's Club to bring the total donated to £2,000 since Taypools had started. Unfortunately, the match itself was a big disappointment as United lost 4-0 to Cowdenbeath in the first league game of the season. It was back to League Cup business again, and United hit rock bottom, thrashed 8-1 at Clyde after Coyle had scored to level the match at 1-1 in the first half. Dumbarton were the next visitors to Tannadice and only Lucas and Briggs stood between United and another big defeat. As it was, United played a shocker and lost 3-0, with King making his first appearance for the Club. That score line was reversed in the last game of the section against Stranraer, with just 1,200 at Tannadice to see United win easily.

United signed former Alloa Athletic, Leicester City and Mansfield Town winger Jimmy Wilson from Duntocher Hibs as a player/coach and also added Dundee Violet inside left Bobby McKillop, who had taken part in the public trial.

Both made debuts on 4th September at Arbroath where the home side won 3-1, despite a good United performance. McKillop never played for United again and Wilson had just one more game before being released in October. Poor results continued with a 4-3 defeat at home to Ayr United as the Black and Whites relinquished an early two goal advantage.

10th August 1957 v Clyde
Standing: Gray, Cross, Lucas, Brown, Young, Gibson
Seated: Sturrock, Humphries, Coyle, McDonald, Duncan

The first league point of the season came in a 1-1 draw at Cowdenbeath, where a Coyle first minute goal was levelled by the home side who also had a penalty saved by Lucas. United were struggling and lost the next match 2-0 at East Stirlingshire. It appears that the Manager felt that the problem lay in the half back line. He tried unsuccessfully to get Doug Alexander on loan from Dundee but the player refused a move to Tannadice. This proved to be a blessing in disguise as the Club then unearthed a star in the making in Stewart Fraser from Banks O' Dee. He made his debut in an unforgettable 5-5 draw with Arbroath, in which a Sturrock penalty five minutes from the end won the point.

By this time, the new covering for 'The Shed' was well on the way to completion, as the Sportsmen's Club handed over another £500. The fans who turned up to see United play St Johnstone on 21st September were glad of the protection in pouring rain as United won 2-1 to record their first league win

August 1957. Work in progress on the Shed

of the season. Former East Fife right half, George Fox, made his only appearance for United in that match. Joe Roy was the next player to make a debut and a lot was expected from the experienced inside forward but he did not play well, as an under strength Dumbarton won 2-0. On 5th October, an unfortunate own goal paved the way for a 2-1 defeat at home to Stenhousemuir. One stroke of good fortune occurred when Banks O' Dee were surprisingly knocked out of the Scottish Junior Cup, which allowed United to bring Fraser to Tannadice earlier than expected. He went straight into the side to face Brechin City a week later and United collected a point from the match in a well earned 1-1 draw. It then took a late Humphries equaliser to earn a 2-2 draw at Alloa Athletic.

A friendly at Dunfermline Athletic 'A' on 26th October brought a narrow one goal win and a week later the Pars first eleven scored at will, as they thumped United 6-1 at East End Park. That was the lowest ebb of the season but it proved also to be the turning point, as United began a slow climb up the table. Despite the poor form of the team, the Directors, with the backing of the Sportsmen's Club, were drawing up plans for the future, including the installation of floodlighting and a new stand, originally planned for construction behind the terracing on Sandeman Street.

After he was demobbed, Stewart returned from his loan spell at Norwich City, going straight into a re-jigged half back line for the home match against Forfar Athletic and a solid team performance earned a 5-2 win. Following that match, United announced that the Sportsmen's Club had paid over another £500, bringing the total donations received since August 1956 to £3,300. There were rumours that Clyde had lodged an offer for Coyle but the Directors advised that they had no intention of selling him and indeed were in the process of trying to arrange top English opposition for a benefit match for the player. The speculation did not affect the squad as they went to Berwick Rangers and returned with a 2-1 win. At home to eventual Second Division champions Stirling Albion a week later, United lost 2-1, playing against ten men for much of the second half. Alex Cameron from Luncarty Juniors played as a trialist in that match and signed two weeks later.

The revival in form continued with a hard fought 2-1 win at Hamilton Academical on 30th November but Coyle dropped a bombshell on the morning of the next match when he handed in a transfer request. Then, to underline his goal scoring prowess, he helped himself to a hat-trick in the 4-1 win over Morton. With left winger Alan Garvie of Perth Celtic making his debut as a trialist at Albion Rovers a week later, United went behind in just fifteen seconds, never to recover and lost 3-1.

Despite denials of a move just six weeks earlier, on 19th December, John Coyle left United to join Clyde for a transfer fee reported at £5,000. It also emerged that United had been keeping tabs on centre half Ron Yeats at Aberdeen Lads Club. After being watched in action for his junior club just twice, he had been signed on 14th December. Coyle was definitely missed in the attack as United lost 3-2 at Montrose and could only draw 0-0 with Stranraer at Tannadice. On New Year's Day, a barely deserved 3-3 draw at St Johnstone was achieved thanks to a late Garvie strike during a goal mouth scramble. The following day, Yeats made his debut but the man of the match in the 7-0 hammering of East Stirlingshire was Roy. Unfortunately, just as he was beginning to make an impact, Roy was carried off in the 1-1 draw at Ayr United two days later and the knee injury he sustained ended his playing career. His loss was considered the biggest blow to United during the entire season.

Promotion chasing Dumbarton won 2-1 at Tannadice on 11th January with United's goal coming from the recently demobbed Stephen, direct from a corner kick, but the forward line still lacked a chance-taker to replace Coyle. The Directors were more than willing to use the money received from his transfer to bring in a replacement, but they were being quoted some very high fees. For instance, United offered £1,500 for George Whitelaw of St Johnstone, but the Perth side wanted more than double that figure. The Directors also tried to reduce the playing staff and offered a free transfer to Duncan but he was not willing to leave. Hamilton accepted a similar offer and was soon courted by Highland League club, Lossiemouth.

On 18th January, United played in front of only 350 spectators at Stenhousemuir and won 6-1, with Humphries hitting a hat-trick. It was the lowest crowd for a United match in a long time. Two weeks later, United lost 1-0 to Dundee at Tannadice in a Forfarshire Cup tie. The Dark Blues were just too good for United and the score might have been worse but for some solid defending. Shortly after that, United signed George Forrester who had been released by Dundee. The weather had caused problems in the weeks preceding the Scottish Cup tie against Hibs on 15th February and it took a huge effort to get snow cleared to allow the match to proceed. A crowd

Wilson Humphries

of 15,543 witnessed a great performance (worthy of the Terrors tag, although the nickname was still not in use) and the visitors were fortunate to leave unscathed in the 0-0 draw. The replay in Edinburgh drew a crowd of 24,550 and United had as much of the play as the First Division side but two second half goals put United out. Gate receipts over the two games came to almost £4,500 and swelled the Tannadice bank balance by around £2,000. The future was beginning to look brighter.

Stewart asked for a transfer after he lost his place in the side but his request was turned down. The league campaign resumed on 22nd February with a match at home to Dunfermline Athletic, who would eventually take the second promotion slot. Forrester made his debut in that match but unfortunately for him, he netted the Pars second goal from a pass back as the visitors fought back from a two goal deficit to draw 3-3. A week later United took a well earned point in a 1-1 draw at Forfar Athletic. Shortly afterwards, the Directors revealed a profit of £3,786 for the year ended July 1957. The profit had been achieved from transfer fee income, cost cutting economies and donations from the Sportsmen's Club, which had been the salvation of Dundee United, according to Chairman, Ernest Robertson. United were cashing in on the progress made by Taypools after just two years.

There was considerable activity on the scouting front in March with several players watched. Bids for Hugh Hay of Aberdeen and George O'Brien of Leeds United failed but Ally Rae was signed on a free transfer from St Johnstone. On 15th March, league leaders Stirling Albion won 5-3 after United had taken a two goal lead, and a week later, with Rae making his debut, United beat Hamilton Academical 3-0 in style. In the next match at Morton, United again surrendered an early two goal lead and lost 3-2 but a sound team performance brought two points in a 2-1 home win over Albion Rovers on 5th April. That result was repeated against Montrose but a third home game in a row brought a horrendous 7-1 defeat from Alloa Athletic, managed at the time by Jerry Kerr. Also facing United that day was Dennis Gillespie. There was in fact little between the sides and with twenty minutes remaining it was just 2-1 to the visitors but then Kerr's side ran riot. United recovered to win 4-1 at Stranraer, with Humphries netting a hat-trick and in a lacklustre match at home to Brechin City, United lost 2-1 after the visitors established an early two goal advantage. The final match of the season brought Berwick Rangers to Tannadice and a 7-0 win was achieved against a very poor side. It also hoisted United up four places to ninth in the league; a quite remarkable finish as United had been in the bottom third of the table for most of the campaign.

Although he left early that season, Coyle had scored 20 goals but top scorer was Humphries with 27 from his 37 appearances. Lucas was the only ever present in the side, and only Gibson, McDonald and Humphries made more than thirty appearances each. An unsettled line up included a dozen players who had come and gone, making little or no impact. Added to that, around twenty trialists were used throughout the campaign. The reasons for a fairly ordinary season therefore become apparent. In addition to those who had already left, United released Cross, Will, Brown, King, Stephen, Duncan and Garvie, whilst Gray announced his retirement. Roy was retained but did not play again and later took on scouting duties. The retained players were Lucas, Yeats, Young, Fraser, Forrester, Rae, Cameron, McDonald, Sturrock, Stewart, Gibson, Humphries and Briggs, who was by then in basic training for his national service.

A swap deal involving Stewart for Frank McGrory of Dundee was denied by both camps and United failed in a bid for Dave Easson, freed by the Dens Park club. United also failed in bids for Ally Hill of Clyde and Harry Melrose of Rangers but Ian Douglas from Banks O' Dee was added to the squad. United then invited a group of eleven free transfer players to Tannadice for a closed door game against a United XI. Despite it being a private trial, officials from three other clubs arrived to watch the match but were not admitted. Following the match, Clive Wallace who had been with United as a trialist two years earlier was signed from Dundee. United also reached an agreement with Motherwell for Jackie Hunter who was transfer listed at £1,250. Just before the end of May, Gray added Hugh Hay, transfer listed at £1,000 and Jimmy Wallace, both from Aberdeen.

1958-59

A Stumble on the Road to Success

In May, work began to complete the last phase of 'The Shed' and the final section, nearest Tannadice Street, was added by the start of the season. The Club also decided to install concrete stepping on the east terracing and that work too was soon under way. There were plans to make the east terracing another covered area and the drawings for the proposed new stand behind the north terracing on Sandeman Street were made public. The Directors also revealed their intention to add a new south stand. Whilst the Sportsmen's Club would assist with the funding of the work on the east terracing, it was intended that a debenture style scheme would be used to meet the £25,000 cost of a new north stand. The Directors proposed that interest free loans of £100 would be granted by 250 members, with reserved seating for them in the centre of the new stand. The reserved seating would be available to the member as long as the loan remained unredeemed. The new north stand and the covering of the east terracing did not go ahead of course but the work to concrete the east terracing did. The new south stand would be built three years later.

United unveiled a new strip for the new season, white shirts with two broad black bands across the chest. Secretary, George Fox also advised that the Club would not put forward a team in the proposed new Second Division reserve league as it was considered uneconomic. Qusklay was again at Tannadice to assist with training. He organised a circuit-style regime, which gave equal emphasis to all aspects of skill, strength and fitness. The Manager also arranged a closed doors practice match with Dundee, which was soon followed by the public trial in which seven trialists were fielded but none was signed. Gate prices were increased to two shillings (10p) for all Second Division matches, although United voted against the increase at the Scottish League AGM.

With new signings Hunter, Hay and Jimmy Wallace making their debuts in the attack, United began their League Cup section on 9th August in Perth, recovering from a one goal deficit to win 2-1 against St Johnstone. The first home match of the section was against Cowdenbeath and despite their first half superiority, the Black and Whites fell behind, and had only a late Humphries consolation to show in a 3-1 defeat. Morton then scored three in the first seventeen minutes and ran out 4-1 winners at Tannadice in the next match. Hay was injured in that game and sidelined for a month. A reshuffled team faced the first league match of the season at home to a very ordinary East Stirlingshire and lost 5-2. Douglas made his debut in that match but bad news followed when it was revealed that a broken wrist for Yeats would keep him out of the side for months.

Former Hearts and East Fife full back Jock Adie was signed on a short-term deal in time to make his debut in the next League Cup match, against St Johnstone on 23rd August. With seven changes in the side, United won 5-3 but there were still signs of weakness at the back. That was confirmed over the next two matches as United lost 6-1 away to Cowdenbeath and then by the same score line at Morton to end a forgettable League Cup. The league campaign got under way again with a 3-2 win at home to Forfar Athletic, with Humphries netting twice from the spot, the second a fairly soft award, to give United both points. Full back Andy Young of Kirkintilloch Rob Roy appeared as a trialist and signed immediately after that game. Tommy Martin, a left winger from Forfar Athletic made his debut next, in the 4-3 win at St Johnstone. It was a remarkable result as United were 3-0 down at half time but completely turned the match around with a tremendous fight back. Nevertheless, the Directors were unhappy and planned to bring all the players in for extra training on Sundays. The suggestion had originated in the previous season when eventual champions Stirling Albion used Sunday training to great effect and won the Second Division. However, Tommy Gray vetoed that idea.

In the 1-0 defeat at Brechin City on 10th September, neither side impressed but goalkeeper Alec Brown from Lochgelly Albert did, making his debut as a trialist and he signed two weeks later. The return of Fraser after recovering from a close season cartilage operation inspired a 3-1 win when Hamilton Academical were the visitors at Tannadice three days later. It was also at that time that the Directors had a change of mind and decided to run a reserve side. They considered entering the Combined Reserve League but instead invited other teams to take part in friendlies. Over the rest of the season, several matches were arranged but not enough to give the reserve players any real opportunity to show what they could do.

Before the next match, against Forfar Athletic at Station Park on 17th September, Forrester left to join Brechin City. At Forfar, United did well to come back from a two goal deficit to earn a 2-2 draw. Then left winger, Ian Scott, signed from Brechin City and made his debut as United lost 4-3 at Dumbarton, who won with a late spot kick. With results not coming up to expectation, the Directors decided that a full-time Manager was required and initially offered the post to

Gray but he was not interested. The job was advertised but there was no rush to fill the position as Gray was happy to remain until the new man came in and the Directors asked him to stay after that to coach the reserves. United then faced the visit of Stenhousemuir, with Charlie Robertson from Osborne playing as a trialist at left back and following the match he was signed. It was a dull first half but United came out with all guns blazing after the break to win 5-2. But in a complete reversal of form, United lost their next match 5-1 at East Fife, where the home side were in control throughout.

The October Holiday brought a visit from Portadown, managed by former United player Gibby McKenzie. United were under strength but still won 5-1 with ease. During the visit of the Irish side, there was some speculation that McKenzie was in line for the empty Manager's chair at Tannadice but he quickly denied any approach. Gordon Tosh, signed on a month's loan from Forfar Athletic, made his first appearance for United in that friendly. He was in the side for his second and last game for the visit to Queen's Park where United lost 2-1. United were then dealt another blow with the news that Fraser would be unavailable as he had been called up for national service.

United won a friendly against a Scottish Command Select 5-1 on 18th October but with the uncertainty that existed at the Club, several players handed in transfer requests. Lucas wanted to leave as he had lost the No. 1 jersey to Brown. Clive Wallace wanted away as he was also unable to hold down a regular first team slot and an enquiry from Portsmouth was prompted after Sturrock asked for a free transfer. Neither of the three left at that time. The season continued with a somewhat flattering 4-1 win at home to Berwick Rangers and with the news that Yeats would be out for much longer than expected, United signed Andy Irvine from Falkirk on 28th October as cover. The following day it was announced that from a list of thirty applicants, the new Manager was Andy McCall. He had a distinguished playing career with Ayr United, St Johnstone, Huddersfield Town and Nottingham Forest before taking up a coaching position with Dundee. McCall became the third Manager in succession to arrive at Tannadice from neighbours Dundee. In fact all three, Reggie Smith, Tommy Gray and Andy McCall had worked together at Dens Park.

Andy McCall

McCall sat in the stand for Tommy Gray's last match in charge on 1st November but it was a sad end, as United lost 3-1 at Alloa Athletic with Irvine making his debut. McCall's tenure began just as badly, with a 6-2 thrashing at his home town club Ayr United. He achieved his first win a week later at home to Cowdenbeath but the 2-0 result did little to inspire, with both sides adopting a defensive approach. The 1-1 draw at Montrose the next week was a fair outcome and United were then unfortunate to lose 3-2 at home to Arbroath, but a poor display resulted in a 4-1 defeat at Stranraer on 6th December. Yeats made his long awaited comeback a week later as United lost 4-3 to Albion Rovers despite an all out attack in a final twenty minutes that saw half a dozen efforts cleared off the line. It was a good performance if nothing else. At Morton, the team again played well but lost 2-1. In a Forfarshire Cup tie on Christmas Day, United missed a penalty and overcame a two goal deficit to win 4-3 against Forfar Athletic.

Hay was injured and carried off in the first half of the match at East Stirlingshire and United had to hang on for a 1-1 draw. Injury was again the problem in the New Year's Day match against St Johnstone at Tannadice. Goalkeeper Lucas had to retire hurt after just quarter of an hour and St Johnstone then established a three goal lead. United pulled it back to 3-2 but the Perth side never really looked in any danger. Two days later United were beaten 1-0 at Hamilton Academical but neither side made much of the game in treacherous underfoot conditions.

Clive Wallace was then given a free transfer and he was soon joined by Cameron. Stewart was offered for transfer at a nominal fee but there were no takers until after he was released at the end of February. He then went to Arbroath. The season continued with a drab 1-1 draw with Dumbarton and at Stenhousemuir, the home side dominated, with Yeats the only player to earn a pass mark as United lost 1-0. After ten weeks in his new job, McCall made his first signing when he acquired Newburgh winger Andy Napier. He had played just four times for the junior side and made his first United appearance as a trialist against Hamilton Academical two weeks earlier and signed immediately after the Stenhousemuir match. United drew both the next two league matches, 1-1 at home to both East Fife and Queen's Park in the run up to the Scottish Cup tie against East Stirlingshire. The cup match was originally scheduled for 31st January but had been postponed because of the weather and as a result, the sides had to meet on Monday 9th February. The first match ended 1-1 and the replay at Tannadice the following day finished goalless after extra time. The second replay went ahead at Tynecastle a day later and United went through with a comfortable 4-0 win. Just over 6,000 watched all three matches, which meant there was very little to share out in the way of gate receipts even after Hearts generously waived their right to payment for the use of Tynecastle. It is also interesting to note that, because of a clash of colours, United did not wear their own black and white in any of the three games. On Monday, they wore St Johnstone strips. On Tuesday, they turned out wearing Dundee's change strip of white with blue trim and on Wednesday, it was St Johnstone colours again!

The rules of the Scottish Cup compelled United to play in the next round against Third Lanark at Tannadice on the following Saturday, 14th February. It is little wonder then, that a tired part-time United lost 4-0 after the three day marathon against East Stirlingshire. The game was played on "a pitch that looked like the Sahara" according to the *Sporting Post*, heavily sanded as it was, and the visitors won with quick goals at the start of each half despite a valiant effort by the Black and Whites.

Some good news came out of Tannadice in mid February with the announcement that the Club had made a profit of £10,653 in the year to July 1958, due entirely to the donation of £10,680 from the Sportsmen's Club. A deficit of £5,158 had been brought forward but United were now in the black to the extent of £5,494. The money received had gone mostly on ground improvements but it also meant that the Directors were able to fend off bids for players and in particular, prize asset Yeats who had been watched by a host of clubs. Following the Scottish Cup exit, McCall announced that he would be experimenting with the line up and the fans could expect to see trialists in the side every week. There were none in the match at Berwick Rangers on 21st February as United suffered a humiliating 8-2 defeat, with the home side recording their biggest win in the Second Division.

The first trialist lined up was Jim Stalker of Dalry Thistle and he played well in the 3-2 home defeat by league leaders Ayr United on 7th March. After being on the wrong end of a 6-0 defeat at Cowdenbeath, Stalker was given a third trial and signed immediately following United's 3-0 win over Montrose. It was the first win in fifteen matches and moved United out of second bottom place. Jimmy Wallace was then released and provisional signing from Aberdeen Lads Club, Jimmy Welsh made his debut at Arbroath, who won 2-0 with a penalty kick in each half. Bobby Norris from Rutherglen Glencairn made his first appearance on 4th April in a 1-0 win against Stranraer and after another game in the side that lost 3-1 at Albion Rovers, he was signed for £200. Another Rutherglen Glencairn player, Bobby Craig got his chance against Morton in a 4-1 win, along with Willie Dickie from Dalry Thistle. Both were signed a few days later.

On 22nd April, in a 1-1 draw with Alloa Athletic at Tannadice, Doug Smith from Aberdeen Lads Club played for the first time in United colours as a trialist, to begin a long and illustrious career with the Club. Finally, Watt Newton from Forfar Celtic played a trial in the last league match of the season, a 2-1 defeat at home to Brechin City, and he was then signed. The Angus side were also the opposition in the last match of the season, a Forfarshire Cup final at Gayfield. United went a goal down but then played most of the match with ten men after losing Douglas with an injury. They held out for a long time but finally wilted under pressure and lost 3-0.

No-one at Tannadice could find much to enthuse over in a season that saw the Club finish third bottom of the Second Division. McDonald was top scorer with 15 goals and Scott, Humphries and Hunter were all into double figures. Humphries, Robertson, Sturrock, McDonald and Andy Young topped thirty appearances each in a frequently altered line up. One positive at least was the healthy financial position, achieved with the donations from the Sportsmen's Club, by then with 54,000 members. Lucas, Duncan Young, Humphries, Irvine,

Scott, Gibson and Rae were given free transfers. McCall transfer listed Hay, Hunter and Martin and then went looking for players. Peter Collins was signed from Partick Thistle as soon as the season ended and he was soon joined by former United defender Ian MacFadyen from Motherwell and Frank McGrory from Forfar Athletic. Ernie Ewen was brought in later in the month to look after the reserves and then, with no warning, McCall tendered his resignation on 23rd May 1959! The Board accepted without much hesitation and advertised for a replacement but decided to take their time recruiting the new man for the job. In the meantime, the players were kept busy with private trial matches each weekend with Ernie Ewen in temporary charge.

1959-60

Jerry Kerr – The Second Key to Success

Jerry Kerr

Weekly private trials were going on, but the burning question was – Who will be the new Manager? Bobby Brown of St Johnstone and Bill Shankly of Huddersfield Town were approached but both turned the job down. Another front runner was Willie Moir of Stockport County but on 7th July 1959, the Board introduced Jerry Kerr as the new man in charge. He had of course been a player with United in the early years of WW2 and was in the side that played in the Emergency War Cup final in 1940. He had also played at Alloa Athletic, Motherwell, St Bernard's and Rangers. His managerial career had started at Peebles Rovers before he moved to Berwick Rangers and then Alloa Athletic. His remit in his first season was simple. All the Directors asked was that he bring the Club stability and a foundation from which to build. What Kerr delivered exceeded the expectation of everyone connected with Dundee United!

One of Kerr's first steps was to organise a place for Dundee United 'A' in the Combined Reserve League, to establish a competitive arena for the development of the young players and to keep fringe players match fit. To get to know his squad better, the new Manager arranged to attend training sessions with the out-of-town players who met up weekly in Aberdeen and in Glasgow. He also planned to set up another training meeting, personally supervised in Edinburgh. A private trial in mid July resulted in the signing of Jim Goldie from Falkirk and Peter Smith from Hearts. United then played Dundee in a closed doors match, which gave the new boss a better understanding of the capability of his side. The public trial held soon after did not attract a big crowd and the only signing that followed was Jimmy Reid, who returned to United after his spell in England with Bury and Stockport County.

United were in section 9 of the League Cup, which contained the Second Division's bottom five teams from the previous season, playing each other once for a play-off place against the winner of section 8. There was little in the way of fanfare to mark the start of another season with the visit of East Stirlingshire on 8th August. MacFadyen, Peter Smith, and McGrory made their debuts for United and Reid played his comeback match. It was Reid and Newton who scored the goals in a comfortable 2-0 win. Collins and Goldie made debuts in the next match, a 1-1 draw at Montrose. United continued a good opening run with a 2-0 win over Stranraer although it took a long time to convert pressure into goals. After signing for the Club from Whitburn Juniors and scoring twice in a reserve match, Jim Irvine was the next player to make a debut when he turned out in the 3-1 away win at East Fife, in United's first league match of the season. Then, with ten days to wait until the last match of the League Cup section, three crucial events took place.

Firstly, the Directors announced a bonus scheme for the players, which would give them each an extra £2 in their pay packets when United were in the top four in the league. In addition, they would all share in a £500 bonus if promotion was achieved. Secondly, Kerr made a trip to Aldershot to see Major Sharp, the man who would be Yeats' commanding officer while he was on national service. Sharp was a football man and agreed to allow the big centre half leave to play for United. Major Sharp was as good as his word and Yeats missed just three league matches and one League Cup game during the season. The third important event in that ten day period was the arrival of Dennis Gillespie. Kerr returned to his former club Alloa Athletic and signed the player for £3,000, a fee that turned out to be a bargain. As Gillespie came in, Hunter left to join Forfar Athletic, Hay went to Arbroath and Martin was released. United then completed their League Cup group stage with a 4-0 win at Queen's Park to win the section and set up a play-off against Falkirk. In the first leg at Brockville on 31st August, United appeared to have established a good platform into the quarter finals with a creditable 1-1 draw. But at Tannadice in the second leg, Falkirk had the match sewn up by half time with a three goal lead for an aggregate 4-1 win.

Gillespie had been cup-tied for the Falkirk games. He made his debut along with trialist right back Tommy Graham of Shotts Bon Accord as the league programme resumed, with a 1-0 defeat at home to St Johnstone, a match in which poor finishing cost United the points. Graham was in the side again and then signed shortly after the next match, a 3-2 defeat at Dumbarton but at least the performance promised better things to come. Maurice Milne then returned to United in his old left wing position after his time in England but he was at Tannadice only three weeks before moving to Brechin City. After a slow start to the league campaign, United went to Hampden Park to face Queen's Park and, firing on all cylinders, recorded an 8-1 win which included a Gillespie hat-trick and four goals from Irvine. Davie Kidd was signed from Alloa Athletic in mid September along with Davie Crabb from Montrose Victoria whilst Goldie was released at his own request. McGrory appears to have been allowed to leave at around the same time, returning to Forfar Athletic.

United then won 2-1 at home to Stranraer on 19th September but with almost total domination throughout, it should have been a much bigger score line. Kidd made his debut as a run of wins continued, with a 2-1 result against Dumbarton, with all the action in the last half hour. An easy 3-0 victory was achieved at Stenhousemuir as United slowly climbed the league table and a week later, all the goals came in the first half when United beat Brechin City 3-1. In early October, United signed reserve goalkeeper Stewart Morrison from Whitburn Rovers.

The October Holiday Monday brought a visit from Newcastle United in a friendly arranged through Duncan Hutchison. The match drew a crowd of 8,500 and with United soundly beaten 9-2, it exposed the huge gulf between the teams. The English side were four goals ahead and although a revival looked possible when United scored either side of half time, it was only a brief respite. However, Newcastle were no doubt aided by fresh legs when they brought on three substitutes at half time. United fielded the same eleven, which included Crabb, making his first appearance. There then seemed to be a backlash from that result as United stuttered to a one goal defeat at East Stirlingshire and could only draw 1-1 at Morton. Kerr then made another significant move in the transfer market when he brought Tommy Neilson from East Fife. His first appearance was unspectacular as United drew 0-0 at home with Albion Rovers on 24th October. That was followed by a 2-0 defeat at Hamilton Academical, which left United in ninth position but it also marked the turning point of the campaign. At the same time, Dundee United Sportsmen's Club announced they had donated £11,800 to the football club in season 1958-59 and membership had risen to 62,000, a fantastic achievement in just three years.

A Newton double gave United the points in a 2-1 win at Cowdenbeath on 7th November but a week later Montrose deservedly won by the same score at Tannadice. Jim Bell from Dalkeith Thistle was the latest of Kerr's acquisitions and he made his debut in that match. The fans showed what they thought of it all and just 2,200 turned out to watch United recover from a goal down to win 2-1 against Alloa Athletic. Only 1,500 watched the midweek Forfarshire Cup tie against Arbroath at Tannadice, where United lined up with several reserve players. The crowd were treated to a 7-3 win, including an Irvine hat-trick. The good form was carried into the next league match as a powerful United display resulted in a 3-1 win at Forfar Athletic. November ended with Welsh and Collins accepting free transfers, whilst Reid moved to East Fife as Kerr made room for other players to come in.

The first match in December was at home to Queen of the South and an Irvine hat-trick helped United to a 4-3 win. Leading by four goals at half time, a three goal fight back by the visitors almost cost United a point. Kerr then added left winger Peter Prior from Aldershot, on a one month trial. He went straight into the side that just managed to beat Falkirk 1-0, with Gillespie scoring very late. Prior scored one of United's goals in the 2-1 win at Berwick Rangers where the defence had to work hard to ensure the points were won. Another addition to the playing staff was Dave Whytock from Brechin City. He scored a debut hat-trick in a 6-0 win over East Fife on Boxing Day. That result put United third in the league and for the first time in the campaign, the players collected the £2 bonus. They would receive the bonus every week over the remainder of the season as United never fell below third place. By then crowds were improving and a belief in promotion was growing.

A post-war record crowd of 15,700 was at Muirton Park, Perth on New Year's Day for the meeting with fellow challengers St Johnstone. In an entertaining match, Whytock scored a second half equaliser for a share of the points in a 1-1 draw. The same player was on the mark again in the 3-1 win over Queen's Park at Tannadice the next day. Prior scored in that match also but he was not retained after his trial period ended a few days later. Instead, new signing Eric Walker made his first appearance on the left wing as United won 3-0 at Stranraer on 9th January after a slow start. Walker was another player brought by Kerr from Alloa Athletic and as part of the deal, Newton went in the opposite direction.

United went to extreme lengths to clear snow from the pitch to ensure that the match against Stenhousemuir was played a week later, but after the 2-1 defeat inflicted by the visitors, they may have wished it had not gone ahead. The promotion challenge then seemed to falter with a 1-1 draw at Brechin City on 23rd January. On a bitter cold sleety day at Tannadice the following week, Cowdenbeath pulled off a shock 3-2 win with their keeper in top form and Gillespie missing a penalty. The race for promotion was back on as United, with Crabb in for his league debut on 6th February, hammered East Stirlingshire 6-1, after a goalless first half. The Board then announced that the financial year ended July 1959 had resulted in a loss of £5,696 but with the donation from the Sportsmen's Club, Dundee United were £6,594 in credit at the bank and well placed for the future. Jimmy Littlejohn returned to the Board, replacing Bill Robertson who had retired. More ground improvements had been carried out and if promotion was achieved, there would certainly be a new stand built. Outline planning permission for a new stand in Sandeman Street was obtained in March 1960.

The Scottish Cup then took priority and the eagerly awaited visit of Partick Thistle was seen as a test of United's top flight ambitions. A 14,000 crowd witnessed a thrilling match in which Thistle twice hit woodwork before taking the lead but a solo Norris goal restored parity. United fell behind again with just six minutes left, but within a minute a Gillespie thunderbolt made it 2-2 and a replay was required. On the following Wednesday, United travelled to Firhill and lost 4-1. Kerr gambled on Yeats who was not fully fit but it cost the game as the centre half struggled to cope with the Partick attack. The only consolation for United was a share in total gate receipts of £2,300 over the two games. In any event, the cup exit may have been a blessing in disguise as it left United with only one objective – promotion! The win against East Stirlingshire two weeks earlier had moved the Black and Whites up to second place and, with nine games to go, all that was required was to stay there!

Mid table Morton were the first obstacle of the run in and at Tannadice on 20th February, both sides had chances but in the end, 3-3 was a fair outcome. After an unsuccessful attempt to bring Doug Moran from Falkirk, Gibby Ormond was acquired from Airdrieonians after some difficult negotiations and he made a scoring debut in United's 4-1 win at Albion Rovers. Kerr said there would be no more signings and then promptly bought Tommy Campbell from Albion Rovers for £2,000! The new man made his first appearance on 5th March and became the second player that season to score a debut hat-trick as United thumped Hamilton Academical 5-1. With a free Saturday the following week, United arranged a Tannadice friendly with English Second Division side Derby County. The 3-2 win for the Black and Whites perhaps gave an indication that United were heading in the right direction.

United's fans were by now caught up in the excitement of the promotion race and their exuberance overflowed at the next match, a visit to Montrose. The official attendance of 6,500 was a league record for Links Park, but that number excluded several hundred who broke in through the main gate! The Angus side later received several donations from both United and Montrose fans to help pay for the damage. The result was 3-1 to United with the home side offering little against a strong attack. Shortly after that match the Manager penned a five year contract with the Club.

Yeats was badly missed a week later while he was playing for his army side in Germany. United lost 3-2 at Alloa Athletic and looked very vulnerable without the big centre half. On 2nd April, when Forfar Athletic were the visitors at Tannadice and Yeats was back in the side, a Campbell hat-trick was the highlight of a 4-0 win. Keeper Morrison made his debut and had to pull off two good saves to keep a clean sheet. Morrison was in goal again on 16th April when United went to meet Queen of the South, one of the main challengers for promotion. A real end to end match finished 4-4, with the home side grabbing a last gasp fourth. It was a little unusual but, prior to the match, United had announced that ten players were to be released including Morrison. The others were Robertson, Napier, Bell, Dickie, Kidd, Peter Smith, Sturrock, Stalker and provisional signing Jack Scott, who had made just one appearance in a Forfarshire Cup tie. Andy Young was leaving for Canada and was released at his own request. MacFadyen was initially on the retained list but left before the new season began. The others retained were Brown, Briggs, Graham, Douglas, Neilson, Doug Smith, Norris, Ormond, Walker, Campbell, Gillespie, Irvine, Whytock and McDonald, along with recently signed Wattie Carlyle from Shettleston and provisional signing Jack Jackson from Carnoustie Panmure. Yeats, Craig and Fraser were on national service and retained.

30th April 1960 – The line up to face Berwick Rangers
Standing: Coats (Trainer), Graham, MacFadyen, Brown, Neilson, Yeats, Fraser, Briggs,
*   Kerr (Manager)*
Kneeling: Norris, Irvine, Campbell, Gillespie, Ormond

Promotion was just in sight prior to the penultimate encounter of the season, at Falkirk on 23rd April. United faced a tough match and emerged with a 2-1 win after falling behind just before half time. It was a crucial win, with Briggs holding his nerve to level from the penalty spot with five minutes left. Then right on full-time, Irvine got the winner. To ensure promotion, all United had to do after that, was beat Berwick Rangers at Tannadice in the last game of the league campaign.

16,000 spectators crammed into Tannadice for the most important match United had played in decades and they were in ecstasy when Campbell scored with a shot on the turn, in just eight minutes. For the remaining eighty-two minutes, it was United on the attack although the visitors produced some nervous interludes for the home support. The final whistle sounded at 4.40 pm on 30th April 1960. A tidal wave of thousands spilled on to the pitch and engulfed the players, some of whom were carried shoulder high. United's return to the big time after

The promotion-winning goal

almost three decades was celebrated by players and fans for a long time after the final whistle. Up in the stand, former players John Coyle and Jock Bain applauded, whilst Jimmy Brownlie in his inimitable calm manner, rose from his seat, lit his pipe and said, "That's fine. I'm happy now."

Four days later, there was an anti-climax at Forfar Athletic where the home side won a Forfarshire Cup tie 2-0. The Black and Whites lacked hunger and a poor display was capped by a penalty miss near the end. Making his first appearance for United, Carlyle was one of the few to receive a pass mark.

30th April 1960 – Promotion celebrations

It is perhaps surprising that 36 players were used during the league campaign and over the season the line up was frequently altered but none the less, promotion was achieved in a highly competitive Second Division. The front men had played their part as the team scored 90 league goals, with Irvine netting 22 plus two in the cups for a total of 24. Gillespie was not far behind with 18 in the league and one in the League Cup. These two missed just a couple of league games each and were ably supported by the other forwards. Brown in goal and centre half Yeats were outstanding throughout the campaign.

Just as the season ended, there were two significant developments. The first was the arrival of former Dunfermline Athletic manager Andy Dickson as the new trainer. Then Kerr announced that he intended travelling to the continent to look at training methods adopted by foreign clubs. Following the European Cup final at Hampden Park, he was particularly keen to visit Eintracht Frankfurt or Real Madrid and had already spoken with the managers of both clubs. During June, private trial matches were held. From these, Kerr signed Tommy McLeod from Ardeer Thistle and former Swansea City, Celtic and Middlesbrough goalkeeper Rolando Ugolini from Wrexham.

1960-61

Back in the Big Time

There is no doubt that gaining promotion was a tremendous achievement for the Club, but throughout the summer speculation on the future at Tannadice was rife. Could Dundee United stay in the top league and compete with teams such as Celtic and Rangers? Would they suffer the same fate as Arbroath who had gone up in 1958-59 only to crash straight back down? How did Jerry Kerr feel about the prospect of First Division football? He summed it up in an interview with the *Peoples Journal* of 16th July when he said, "My outlook is the same as last season. I have a definite standard, which I look for in every player. If that standard is not maintained then I must act. This is the only way we can make headway." A few days later, there was an injection of cash into the Club when Directors George Fox, J Johnstone Grant, Duncan Hutchison and Ernest Robertson collectively purchased almost 5,000 new shares.

Following the Manager's trip to Germany to see for himself the training methods at Eintracht Frankfurt, changes were implemented. It had been open house at Tannadice with players from other clubs allowed to join in the training sessions but there was to be no more of that. Training was to be more focused with the emphasis on fitness and ball skills. Of course, the most important change at Tannadice was the decision that United should be completely full-time and for the first time in the history of the Club, the season would begin with a full-time team under a full-time trainer, Andy Dickson. There were no pre-season matches except the trial match that ended with a 5-0 win for the first team against the reserves and a few trialists. To complete the pre-season activity, Jackson signed professional forms and former Colchester United defender John Roe was added to the squad. With just four new players, Kerr was relying heavily on a reduced squad of existing players to retain First Division status.

Carlyle played his first game in major competition for United and Ugolini made his debut as the season got under way with a 2-1 away win on 13th August at newly relegated Stirling Albion, in a League Cup section that also contained Brechin City and Stenhousemuir. At home to Brechin City in the next match, United won again but only after Fraser snatched a last minute goal for a 2-1 victory. Despite a hat-trick from debut man Tommy McLeod, United had to settle for a 3-3 draw at home to Stenhousemuir three days later. The first league match interrupted the League Cup section on 24th August. United deservedly recorded an emphatic 3-1 home win over Hibs with Gillespie, Walker and McLeod getting the goals. Unfortunately, a promising start came off the rails with a 3-0 League Cup defeat at home to Stirling Albion and a 2-1 reversal in the same competition at Brechin City, where Roe made his debut. By the time United went to Stenhousemuir in the last game in the section, interest in the League Cup was all but over. Kerr made sweeping changes to the line up and the match ended in a 1-1 draw. On the same day, Willie Rumbles was added to United's reserve strength after he signed from Hibs. Shortly after that, Alec Smith from Frances Colliery and Harry Smith from St Joseph's also joined the reserves. Neither of this trio made it into the first team.

1960-61

Back Row: Briggs, A Smith, Brown, Ugolini, Neilson, Jackson, Fraser

Middle: Kerr (Manager), Norris, D Smith, Crabb, Campbell, Rumbles, Carlyle, Whytock, Douglas, Dickson (Trainer)

Front: Graham, McDonald, Irvine, Walker, Gillespie, McLeod, Ormond, Craig

After playing well in a Second XI Cup tie against Cowdenbeath 'A', unattached Kevin Cairns made his first team debut as the league campaign continued with United in top gear to win 2-0 at St Johnstone on 10th September. Two days later a side containing many of the first team and a few reserves took on a Combined Services XI, including Jim Baxter of Rangers. With the help of four goals from

McLeod, United won 5-0. Then it was back to league business with a Dundee derby in prospect at Tannadice, with a very low key build up. A controversial hand ball decision against Ure allowed Briggs to open the scoring from the spot but Penman levelled for the Dark Blues. Campbell restored United's advantage before the interval and, to cap a fine team performance, he added another, ten minutes from the end for a 3-1 win. That was the beginning of an astonishing turnaround in derby successes that would last for decades.

Norwich City enquired about Yeats but Kerr issued a statement declaring that United would not be selling any of their top players under any circumstances. Indeed, he was keen to add to the squad and at the end of September he made an audacious bid for Wilson Wood, then with Newcastle United. The clubs agreed terms but Wood declined the move although he would join up with United several years later. At around the same time, Douglas was released.

After winning the derby, form slipped and United took just five points from the next nine games, beginning with a 1-0 defeat at Partick Thistle. With the news that Manchester United were reputedly willing to pay £30,000 for Yeats, United took to the pitch at Tynecastle and managed a 1-1 draw with Hearts on 1st October. Then on the Holiday Monday, United gained a creditable 1-1 result with Sheffield United in a friendly at Tannadice. In the second half of that match, Ormond was injured and replaced by Jackson, who had been watching the match from the stand. The following day, the Sportsmen's Club held their AGM and announced that in the year to July 1960, they had donated in excess of £6,000 to the football club for ground improvements and almost £14,000 to assist with running costs and transfer fees. Membership of Taypools by then had reached 73,000. Shortly afterwards it was announced that United planned to rebuild the South Stand (now the Jerry Kerr Stand) at a cost of £40,000. After a lengthy debate at one of their meetings, the Sportsmen's Club agreed to help with the initial cost of £10,000. Plans to construct a stand costing £70,000 behind the North Terracing on Sandeman Street were then abandoned.

United lost, rather unfortunately, 2-1 to Airdrieonians on 8th October and then George McKinney from Brechin United became the latest player to join United reserves. Dave Reid, a former junior international, who had been with Dunfermline Athletic, was added to the first team squad and scored on his debut in a 2-0 win at Raith Rovers. At this point, United were in second place in the league but it appeared that several players were struggling to cope with the demands of the top flight. So, as good as his word, Kerr acted quickly, acquiring seventeen year old Bert Howieson from Leeds United at the end of October. Just before that signing, United lost by a single goal to Motherwell on 22nd October and a week later, a late goal from Campbell secured a 2-1 win over Clyde. That was followed by heavy defeats in Glasgow, where Third Lanark won 6-1 and then United lost 4-0 at Rangers. Still just seventeen years old, Jackson made his league debut in that match.

Kerr then dipped into the transfer market again to bring in Jimmy McMichael from Bathgate Thistle and Alec Gordon from Armadale Thistle. However, the most significant move of the whole season was perhaps the signing of the very experienced former Scotland international Neil Mochan from Celtic. Mochan and Howieson both debuted against Kilmarnock on 19th November. Mochan scored twice to put United 2-1 up early in the second half, but Killie netted three in six minutes for a 4-2 win to stun United and inflict yet another defeat. The return of Gillespie from injury the following week inspired a 3-1 win at Aberdeen and that was followed by a 2-0 home win over St Mirren. Next came United's first visit to Celtic Park in 29 years and with an injury-hit squad they left with a deserved point from a 1-1 draw.

On 17th December, a late thaw allowed the match against Ayr United to proceed, and the Black and Whites recorded a good 2-1 win. The remainder of the festive season programme saw a slump in form and the next four games ended in defeat. Dunfermline Athletic won 3-2 on Christmas Eve with a freak opener and a late winner. Then McMichael made his debut in a 2-0 defeat at Hibs a week later. United provisionally signed Bobby Dougan from Armadale Thistle just before the match against St Johnstone on 2nd January 1961. With a 2-0 win for the Perth side, 'Tannadice has no terrors for the Saints' was the by-line in the *Evening Telegraph*. Around this time it appears that the nickname of the 'TERRORS' first came into common use. The second derby of the season with Dundee saw their new boy Wishart grabbing all the headlines on his debut. The game was goalless at half time but after the interval, two-goal Wishart was man of the match as he inspired the Dens Park side to a 3-0 win. United needed a tonic and it came against Partick Thistle in a comprehensive 3-0 win, followed by arguably the best performance of the season as United won in style, 3-0 against Hearts. Interestingly, the *Sporting Post* that evening referred to United as the 'Tannadice Trojans' as the local press tried to find a fitting nickname. A few months later even the 'Tannadice Terriers' was tried but it was the 'TERRORS' that won the day and has remained.

In the third derby of the season, United met Dundee in a Forfarshire Cup tie at the end of January and United won 2-1 at Tannadice. On 1st February, George Sievewright from Broughty Athletic gave up his job as a baker to join a growing band of teenage talent at Tannadice, as United got back to the task of accumulating league points. At Airdrieonians, United came from behind four times to snatch a deserved point in a 4-4 draw. The Scottish Cup then paired United with St Mirren on 11th February. The prospect of a good cup run diminished when Gillespie was forced to retire injured after only fifteen minutes. Just two minutes later St Mirren scored the only goal of the game. The Terrors tested the Buddies' defence for the rest of the game and were denied two good penalty claims but could not find a goal to earn the replay they deserved.

Norris, Crabb, Whytock and Rumbles were all offered free transfers and soon left. Alec Gordon made his debut as a new look United beat Raith Rovers 4-1 on 18th February. United then lost 3-1 at Clyde, 4-3 at Motherwell and 2-1 at home to Third Lanark but each time, the breaks went against the Terrors. The season concluded with some creditable results, beginning with a 1-1 draw on 18th March against league leaders Rangers. Davie Boner, a nineteen year old signed from Everton in January, scored on his debut that day to put United in front but Rangers were level before the break. A week later United ran eventual league runners-up Kilmarnock ragged at Rugby Park but had just a point to show for their efforts in another 1-1 draw. A third draw in succession came on 1st April, with United three times in front. Each time, Aberdeen levelled in a match played like a cup tie, although there was nothing at stake for either side. Next, St Mirren were beaten 3-0 away, with all the goals coming in the last twenty minutes and United earned a good point in a 1-1 draw when Celtic came to Tannadice.

With the season all but over, a trip south to play two friendly matches was arranged, one at Cambridge City and the other at Millwall. Included in the trip was a visit to Wembley for the traditional Scotland v England match, although the players probably wished that, like all the Scots at that match, they had never gone. It was Scotland's worst ever defeat, losing 9-3 to the Auld Enemy. On the bright side, United won both friendly matches 2-0. There were just two league matches left and United had also agreed to provide the opposition to Forfar Athletic in a testimonial for former United defender, Doug Berrie. After losing 3-0 at Ayr United and winning 5-1 in the testimonial, United entertained Dunfermline Athletic in the final league match. The Pars brought with them the Scottish Cup they had won three days earlier and it was paraded around Tannadice to warm applause from both Pars and United fans. United then demolished the visitors who seemed to be suffering a Scottish Cup hangover. The 5-0 result could so easily have been more if United had built on Gillespie's early opener but it remained 1-0 at half time. After the interval, Gillespie completed a hat-trick and Mochan got the other two. The final league position of ninth, was United's best ever and was achieved thanks to the shrewd management of Kerr. Following the establishment of Dundee United Sportsmen's Club in 1956, Jerry Kerr was the second key element in the turnaround in the fortunes of Dundee United. His unfailing eye for talent produced an exceptional blend of youth and experience and a consistency in team selection, which would continue in the years ahead.

To round off a successful season, the Forfarshire Cup final was won comfortably 6-3 by United against Montrose. Howieson was the star with four of the six goals. There was some very good news for the fans after that match. After initially refusing to re-sign, Yeats and Briggs had agreed terms along with all the other players retained. Sidney Dick had joined United from Arbroath Lads Club, initially as an amateur as he was still at school. The team then went on a short highland tour, fielding strong line ups to beat an Inverness Select 5-1 and Elgin City 3-1. Only Jackson, McLeod, Walker, Reid and Alec Smith were freed, whilst Campbell, who had refused a free transfer, was put on the transfer list. One of seven players racking up over thirty appearances, the top scorer was Gillespie with 15 goals. Just behind him was Mochan, scoring one fewer.

With First Division status assured, the Board turned their attention to ground improvements. Demolition work on the old stand and pavilion began at the end of May. Jerry Kerr, a master joiner to trade, was appointed Clerk of Works for the new 3,000 seater stand, which would be the first cantilever stand in Scotland. In addition, the North Terracing was to be extended with a dozen extra flights of concrete steps and a new wall was to be built along Sandeman Street, with new turnstiles and exit gates. The next project the Directors were considering was floodlighting. The Sportsmen's Club would again be providing financial assistance from Taypools, which by then had 87,000 members and had donated a total of over £60,000 to the football club.

1961-62

Gaining a Vital Foothold

In June, centre half Eric Brodie was signed from Milton Rovers and was immediately farmed out to Armadale Thistle. He would later join the second eleven but failed to break into the first team. Hugh Cochrane from Dennistoun Waverley and Jimmy Hughes from East Stirlingshire were also added but they too featured only as reserves. United then signed another Tommy Campbell. This one came from Clackmannan Juniors but unlike his namesake, did not make any impact other than in the reserve side. Former Airdrieonians player Alex Stewart was also signed on a short-term trial. Following the success of the previous season, Kerr had his sights set firmly on establishing United as a First Division side and the aim for 1961-62 was to gain that vital foothold. His philosophy remained unchanged and he was again relying largely on the players who had done so well in the two previous campaigns.

Yeats though, was still unhappy with his terms and there were rumours in early June that Napoli were preparing a bid of £65,000 for the player. That never transpired of course and in mid June, Liverpool came in with an offer, but it was well short of the valuation placed on the player by United. Negotiations continued for almost a month and the Merseyside club increased their offer twice before Yeats was eventually allowed to sign for them, for a record fee of £30,000 on 21st July. The fans reckoned he was irreplaceable but waiting in the wings was another stalwart who would give many years of resolute service at centre half. It was of course Doug Smith. Another signing for the future was made in the run up to the new season when Sandy Davie joined United on a provisional form from Butterburn Youth Club, after showing exceptional ability in the trial match at Tannadice on 5th August. Davie had also been on trial with Dundee and West Ham United. Just as the season began, Carlisle United began to show an interest in promotion winning goal scorer Tommy Campbell but shortly afterwards he joined Tranmere Rovers for a fee of around £1,000.

The League Cup section threw up a tough trio of opponents in Motherwell, Aberdeen and Dunfermline Athletic and the campaign got off to a losing start at Motherwell on 12th August. Without Ian St John, who had joined Yeats at Liverpool, the Lanarkshire side emerged 5-3 winners. With Arsenal watching Gillespie against Dunfermline Athletic in the next match, United played well but could not break down a stuffy Pars defence and it ended goalless. Work was still under way on the new South Stand and initially season ticket holders were to be allowed in for that match. However, city officials would not allow this as

The South Stand – 19th August 1961

there was no handrail installed. Instead, the season ticket holders sat on benches along the track! For the next game, against Aberdeen on 19th August, season ticket holders were seated in the stand, although it was far from the finished article. The match was a phenomenal spectacle and one to remember as United controlled the play to win 5-3.

After beating Dunfermline Athletic 3-2 at Tannadice in a midweek league match, United then faced Motherwell in the League Cup, with cash-paying fans permitted to take their seats in the South Stand for the first time. Unfortunately, they were not treated to the same spectacle as they had when Aberdeen were the visitors, and two quick goals early in the second half sealed a 2-0 win for the Lanarkshire club. Facing a third meeting with Dunfermline Athletic in two weeks, United met a side intent on extracting some revenge and the Pars deservedly won 3-0 at East End Park. Stewart made his only first team appearance in that match and he was released soon after, along with Hughes. There was nothing at stake for either side in the final match of the League Cup section when United played Aberdeen at Pittodrie. A 2-2 draw was a fair outcome in an entertaining game.

The serious business of the league campaign then got under way but it was a bad result for United, with a derby defeat at Dens Park. The 'Tannadice Terriers', as the press referred to United in a local report, were 3-0 down within half an hour and the eventual 4-1 score line did not flatter the Dark Blues. United then strolled to a 3-0 victory against St Johnstone. But the press reported 'a black day for the Tannadice Terrors' after the next match at Celtic Park, where the home side won 3-1 comfortably. Next, Carlyle turned on the style to completely bamboozle Hibs in a 4-0 win, in which he scored twice. Davie made his first appearance in the United goal as a second half substitute, and Jim Baxter made a return to Tannadice in the British Army side that lost 3-1 to United on Holiday

Monday, 2nd October. On the same day, a bricklayers' strike halted all work at Tannadice. It would be two months before the dispute was settled to allow work on the new stand to resume.

26th August 1961 v Motherwell
Standing: Gordon, Neilson, Brown, Smith, Briggs, Fraser
Kneeling: Boner, Gillespie, Mochan, Howieson, Ormond

In the previous season, Harley and Hilley of Third Lanark had given United a torrid time in a 6-1 win at Cathkin Park. That same pair did it again as United lost heavily for the second time. This time it was 7-2. An inconsistent run of form continued with a well earned 3-1 win over St Mirren at Tannadice, with Sievewright making his league debut. Kilmarnock's failure to improve on two goals in their 2-1 win on 21st October was attributed largely to the goalkeeping of Brown. A drab goalless draw at Raith Rovers was followed by a visit to Airdrieonians, where a last gasp Gordon equaliser gave United a deserved point in a 3-3 draw. Just prior to that match, United signed another Eric Brodie, a centre forward who cost around £1,000 from Forfar Athletic. The help of Dundee United Sportsmen's Club was again acknowledged by the Directors of the football club. By this time, Taypools had 650 agents collecting a shilling (5p) each week from 89,000 members. In season 1960-61 Dundee United had benefited from donations totalling £33,000.

Against Stirling Albion, United dominated and won 2-0 but it took until ten minutes from the end for Neilson to get the vital opener and then Carlyle got the second. In the next match, at Motherwell on 18th November, centre forward Brodie made his debut as United took the lead, but eventually lost a hard fought encounter 2-1. The visit of Rangers was eagerly anticipated and a full house witnessed a valiant effort from United, who took the lead, but Rangers came back to go 3-1 up. Mochan pulled one back with a thunderbolt ten minutes from the end and Rangers ended the match 3-2 winners, hanging on grimly to their lead. That was followed by a good 2-1 win at Falkirk prior to a Scottish Cup tie at Motherwell on 13th December. At Fir Park, United dominated the first half of the cup tie but went in a goal down. They continued to play good football after the interval but Motherwell had more than their fair share of good fortune and scored three more for a truly flattering 4-0 win.

United then scored a comfortable 3-1 win at Aberdeen. Against Partick Thistle two days before Christmas, United were in control and leading 3-2 when they threw the match away, losing 5-3 after Ewing netted a hat-trick for the Jags in ten second-half minutes. After that the Dundee derby was postponed because Tannadice was snowbound.

United collapsed in the second half on 6th January at Dunfermline Athletic where they lost 4-1 but the visit of Celtic a week later almost witnessed the fight back of the season. With the Glasgow side 5-1 up just minutes into the second half, United regrouped and Irvine scored twice to add to the one he netted in the first half. Carlyle then reduced the deficit further as United came forward in waves. At 5-4, Celtic were left clinging to their narrow lead in the last ten minutes, just as Rangers had a few weeks earlier. The local press hailed another great showing from the 'Tannadice Terriers'. A 2-1 win at muddy St Johnstone was followed by narrow defeats against each of the capital clubs in Edinburgh, where Hibs won 3-2 and Hearts were 2-1 winners.

For the visit of Third Lanark on 3rd February 1962, United officially opened the newly completed South Stand. Formerly with both clubs, Jimmy Brownlie was the guest of honour along with his two granddaughters and they saw United gain some revenge for the earlier thrashing at Cathkin Park, with a 3-0 win. It was one of United's best performances of the campaign, with Carlyle scoring twice and Mochan getting the other. After a deserved 1-1 draw at St Mirren, United had a free Saturday and 9,000 turned up for a friendly against Manchester City, complete with their international keeper Bert Trautmann and £45,000 signing Bobby Kennedy from Kilmarnock. It was another good test of United's progress and after falling behind to a controversial penalty in the first half, a much improved United won 2-1, with goals from Carlyle and Gillespie. At Kilmarnock four days later, United were rocked by four goals from Andy Kerr as Killie led 4-0 within an hour and finally won 5-3. A comfortable 4-2 win against Raith Rovers followed. Then, despite being in the lead twice, United had to settle for a point in a 3-3 draw with Airdrieonians on a snow covered Tannadice pitch.

Two more players were added to the United squad in early March. First was Tommy Millar, who had returned to Scotland after he was released by Colchester United following the tragic death of his infant son. George Pattie of Blairgowrie Juniors had just been demobbed and was signed after playing well in a closed doors trial match.

A solitary Irvine goal sealed the points at Stirling Albion and after the match, McDonald accepted a transfer to the visitors for a nominal fee. With Millar making his debut, the Terrors then drew 1-1 at home to Motherwell when they really should have won. The next match brought a trip to Ibrox with Rangers riding high in the league and on course for the championship. Without the injured Doug Smith, United were given little chance of returning with anything. However, Carlyle scored the only goal of the game with fifteen minutes played, as the team produced a sensational performance for a deserved 1-0 win. The result severely dented Rangers' championship aspirations and gave a helping hand to the prospects of eventual league winners Dundee.

Out with the old South Stand (1961)

In with the new South Stand (1962)

A comfortable 4-1 win against Falkirk followed, and some of the United players were beginning to draw attention from south of the border. Aston Villa manager, Joe Mercer and Newcastle United's Director, Stan Seymour were at the next match to see Gillespie and Carlyle, who both put on a dazzling performance against Aberdeen in a 2-2 draw. The rescheduled league derby meeting on 9th April at Tannadice was crucial to Dundee's league challenge. After Irvine put United ahead, the followers of the Dark Blues had a nervous time until Gilzean equalised before half time. He then scored the winner with a dipping effort that bounced over the head of Ugolini six minutes from the end for a 2-1 win.

On a rock hard and uneven surface, Davie made his league debut along with Pattie in the match at Partick Thistle on 23rd April. Despite a 4-2 defeat, both acquitted themselves well. The final league game, against Hearts, was a fairly ordinary encounter, which the Edinburgh side won 1-0. That gave United a tenth place finish in the league, one place lower and one point less than the previous season, but overall it was considered a highly successful campaign as United had retained top league status. With a team put together at a cost of around £6,000, Kerr had achieved what no other Dundee United manager had, a third term in the First Division, built on a consistency in team selection. Briggs was the only ever present but Doug Smith, Fraser, Neilson, Gillespie, Mochan and Gordon were not far behind. Mochan and Carlyle each scored 17 league and cup goals, and just behind them on 16 each were Gillespie and Irvine.

To round off the season, United put out a strong side to beat Arbroath 5-2 in a testimonial for Jim Fraser but suffered a shock 4-3 home defeat from Montrose in the Forfarshire Cup. End of season free transfers were handed to both goalkeepers, Brown and Ugolini, along with Craig, Graham, Ormond, Boner, Cairns, McMichael and reserves McKinney and Campbell. All the others were retained and quickly re-signed, as Kerr intimated that the full-time squad was being reduced to a pool of around 18 players. A closed doors match was arranged on 10th May to try out a potential new goalkeeper, twenty-three year old Donald Mackay, who then signed for United from Forfar Athletic.

With the season over, United began more improvement work at Tannadice. Over the summer months Briggs, Gillespie, Dougan, Sievewright and Smith all helped with the work. The North Terracing was completely demolished and then reconstructed several feet further back to accommodate a new playing surface. Once completed several weeks later, the new North Terracing would provide one of the best views in Scottish football.

Gillespie and Briggs assisting with the improvements at Tannadice

As far back as December 1961, the Directors had decided to put in floodlights and the cabling work was carried out during the close season. The cost of all the work being done was met largely from donations by the Sportsmen's Club but the fee received from the Yeats transfer had been a big boost to the bank balance. As a result, in the year to July 1961, United announced a loss of £13,500 but, with more than £32,000 donated by the Sportsmen's Club, carried forward a credit balance of £22,500. During the season, United also celebrated international recognition for two players, with Gillespie and Fraser both chosen to play for Scottish League sides. Gillespie was the first Dundee United player honoured at senior level, playing against the League of Ireland, whilst Fraser turned out against the English League side.

1962-63

The Origin of the Arabs

After retaining First Division status, Kerr's next priority was to consolidate and improve the Club's position in the top flight. It perhaps came as a surprise to many that he intended to undertake the task with a smaller squad but the Manager was confident in the ability of the players he had. There were only four signings before the season started. In June, Ronnie Simpson joined United from Greengairs United along with Hector McKinlay from Armadale Thistle. A few weeks later Kerr brought in another young star when he signed sixteen-year-old schoolboy international Ian Mitchell from Woodburn Athletic. His signature was gained ahead of competition from several clubs, including Spurs, Manchester United, Rangers, Hibs and Hearts. Mitchell felt that he would have more opportunities to develop his skills at Tannadice. The last pre-season signing was Ally Riddle from Montrose.

The final touches were put to the South Stand and with the improved North Terracing nearing completion, the Board turned its attention to the floodlighting, ordering the installation of lights to be ready for use before the winter nights arrived. The season approached without pre-season friendlies yet again, but the Manager arranged a series of practice matches at Craigie Park and at Tannadice as well as the usual public trial. The progressive Board at Tannadice came up with another innovation when they introduced the first junior supporters section ever established in Scotland and possibly the entire United Kingdom. At the beginning of the season, around 500 young fans registered free. Membership soon reached over 1,000 and offered a special section within the ground, located west of the new stand. There were also opportunities for young fans to win a place on the team bus for away games.

The season began as usual with the League Cup and United were drawn in a tough section containing Dundee, Celtic and Hearts. Mackay was the only player making a United debut in the opening fixture on 11th August in a Dundee derby at Tannadice, the first of five that season. Stand tickets were sold for 5/6 (27 ½p) and in front of a near full house of 25,000, with the new stand and terracing completed, United turned out in their new white strip with black trim. Gilzean had the Dark Blues ahead twice but each time United levelled through Carlyle. After the interval, United had the lion's share of play and Irvine netted near the end for a well deserved 3-2 win. United then lost 3-1 at Hearts and 4-0 at Celtic to dispel any thoughts of progress in the competition. These two reversals were followed by a comprehensive 4-0 defeat at home to Dunfermline Athletic in the opening league fixture. United also lost their groundsman when Frank McCusker took a job outside the city. He was quickly replaced by Albert Lorimer.

1962-63

Back Row: *Riddle, Neilson, McKinlay, Mackay, Davie, Brodie (centre half), Mochan, J Smith, Ernie Ewen*

Middle: *Jerry Kerr, Dougan, D Smith, R Smith, Briggs, Sievewright, Fraser, Roe, Gordon, Dick, Andy Dickson*

Front: *Carlyle, Millar, Brodie (forward), Gillespie, Howieson, Cochrane, Simpson, Irvine, Pattie, Mitchell*

Riddle made his debut in the return League Cup derby on 25th August but that too ended in defeat, with a Gordon Smith inspired 2-1 win for Dundee. However, United pulled off a couple of shocks after that, beating Hearts 2-0 with Bobby Smith appearing for the first time. He had joined United from Burnley at the end of January after he failed to settle with the English side. The Terrors then drew 0-0 with Celtic, to continue a run of results at Tannadice that would ensure United remained undefeated at home for the remainder of the season.

The league campaign continued on 8th September with a 1-0 defeat at Queen of the South. Then the third Dundee derby in a month produced great entertainment in a 1-1 home draw that brought United's first point of the new league campaign. After another 1-1 draw at Third Lanark, and despite swamping Hibs 5-0 with Mitchell playing exceptionally well on his debut, there were those who doubted the Board's wisdom with the question – "Floodlights or forwards?" The criticism was unfair as Kerr was constantly on the look out for new talent and soon added youngster Jackie Smith from Musselburgh Windsor and John Auchie from Burnley on a free transfer, although neither made it into the first team. The Terrors then lost 3-0 at Partick Thistle and followed that up with a 1-1 draw with St Mirren at Tannadice. It was the thirteenth match in which Kerr had changed the line up in his quest for a successful combination. A further change took place the following week when Davie came in to replace the injured Mackay for the match at Celtic Park. United lost by a single goal but the keeper was one of the stars of the match. He then retained the No. 1 jersey for the rest of the season as Mackay remained on the sidelines much longer than expected. The turning point in the league season came in the last game of October as luckless Raith Rovers were hammered 8-1 at Tannadice, with Gillespie netting a hat-trick. After a 0-0 draw at Motherwell, United took on undefeated league leaders Rangers at home. Floodlights were used for the first time at Tannadice in the second half of the match and United outshone the Gers with a late Irvine volley to win 2-1. The lights were partly paid for by donations from the Sportsmen's Club which, by that time, had 91,000 members and had paid out prizes of almost £80,000 in the previous season as well as giving United around £40,000. There can be little doubt that the creation of Dundee United Sportsmen's Club was the pivotal event in the history of Dundee United FC.

More reserve players were added with the signing of John Reddington from Lochore Welfare and Jimmy McManus from Edinburgh Norton. Later, former Hibs goalkeeper John 'Jacky' Wren joined United reserves as cover for the injured Mackay. On 17th November, United recorded a 3-1 win at Clyde and then, on a pitch that only just passed a late inspection, the Terrors drew 3-3 with Kilmarnock at Tannadice. Momentum was temporarily lost in a 4-1 defeat at Falkirk but United were soon picking up points again, coming from behind twice to draw 3-3 with Aberdeen. On 15th December at Tynecastle against Hearts, a 2-2 draw was achieved, with United again recovering after the home side had twice taken the lead. With winter weather closing in and football about to be frozen out for weeks at a time, United won 3-1 at home to Airdrieonians and 2-1 to Queen of the South.

January 1963 – ice bound Tannadice

The worst winter on record for years wiped out the derby on 2nd January and a frozen pitch knocked out the match against Third Lanark to begin three weeks of inactivity on the pitch. Even the help of snow-blowers was not enough, as the real problem was ice beneath the snow. Off the pitch however, things were still happening. Fraser had a transfer request refused and Mochan was being linked with a move to Airdrieonians, whilst Riddle was transferred back to Montrose. Keeper Bobby Reid was signed from Arbroath just after Wren was released. The team trained whenever and whereever they could and were frequent visitors to Broughty Ferry beach.

The winter freeze, which had even created large ice floes on the river Tay, caused the postponement of United's Scottish Cup tie against Albion Rovers four times before a squad of 25 workmen was employed to break up the ice with picks. That proved inadequate and Kerr then arranged for tar-burners to be brought in to melt two inch thick ice. That resulted in a waterlogged pitch and over a hundred tons of coarse sand was then used to make it playable for the match on 26th January. It cost United over £600 but it was money well spent.

The conditions were described by one reporter as 'Sahara-like' and by another as 'a beach after the tide had gone out'. In fact, the pitch was a sticky quagmire and sapped the strength of both sides. United's superior stamina prevailed and the Terrors advanced to the next round with goals from Irvine, Gillespie and Howieson, all in the final fifteen minutes. In news reports a few days later United were likened

A tar burner and workmen with picks get the pitch cleared of ice

to the 'Desert Rats', so well did they adapt to playing on the sand. This incident may also have given birth to (or perhaps reinforced) another new nickname for United – the 'Arabs' – a term which later attached to the fans rather than the team. However, in establishing the origin of the Arabs, consideration must be given to another possibility; a Scottish Cup tie against Third Lanark on 14th February 1959, which was played on a similarly sanded pitch with the conditions also described as 'Sahara-like'. On the Monday following that match a cartoon in the *Dundee Courier* depicted Manager Andy McCall seated on a camel. This would have provided the perfect opportunity for the nickname to begin.

A week after beating Albion Rovers, only one match in Scotland survived the winter conditions. In it, United met Ayr United in a tough Scottish Cup

How the pitch looked on 26th January 1963

tie, which the Terrors won 2-1 at Somerset Park, to move into the next round. It would be another month before they played again. In the meantime, efforts were made to remove all the sand from Tannadice, but the work was continually interrupted by snow storms. Kerr tried, but failed, to arrange a friendly against Celtic in Dublin to get some much needed match practice. As the grip of winter continued, Scottish clubs met to discuss summer football. In view of the conditions at the time, it is perhaps surprising that the proposal was soundly defeated, with two thirds of clubs voting to retain the status quo!

The season resumed on 2nd March with United at Raith Rovers in a league match. The Terrors recorded an emphatic 7-2 win that took the Kirkcaldy side's goals against tally to 79 in only 21 games. A week later, United revealed their all black strip in the next match, a 2-1 home win over Motherwell. After that, they made heavy weather of getting past Queen's Park in the next round of the Scottish Cup and only a last gasp Carlyle equaliser to make it 1-1 gave United a second chance. They then faced Rangers at Ibrox in a league match and were thrashed 5-0, with all the goals coming in the first half. The Scottish Cup replay followed on 20th March and United won 3-1 at Tannadice with a convincing performance.

First Division football was guaranteed for the next season by this time and United, with McKinlay making a scoring

Cartoon from Dundee Courier 16th February 1959

debut, hammered Clyde 4-1 on 23rd March to set the fans' sights on a coveted Fairs Cities Cup place. Dunfermline Athletic were beaten 2-1 as United remained on course for a top five finish. The Club then faced a strength sapping three match Scottish Cup marathon against Queen of the South. The first two matches ended 1-1 and before the second replay, United, playing in a harlequin style strip, had a tough time beating Falkirk 1-0 at Tannadice in a league match. The tie against Queen of the South was settled on 8th April at Ibrox, where United produced a stunning last thirty minutes in which they scored all four goals in their 4-0 win.

United signed Andrew Waddell for the reserves as the team prepared for their first ever Scottish Cup semi final, against Rangers at Hampden Park on 13th April. Jimmy Millar, who had netted four goals against United in the recent league match, had the Glasgow side 2-0 up before Gillespie and Mitchell levelled the tie. Brand scored as United faded out of the game and Millar completed his hat-trick before the interval. United put up a brave fight after the break but Rangers wrapped it up at 5-2 with a late McLean strike. United were later fined £10 by the SFA for not wearing the Club's registered colours of white with black hoops!

Four days later United got back to league business in a Dundee derby that provided United's first win in a major competition at Dens Park. On a rain-sodden pitch, Mitchell was the man of the match, with the winner in the second half to seal a deserved 2-1 victory. United continued to pick up points and Davie was outstanding in a goalless draw with Hearts on 20th April. He starred again as United drew 1-1 at Hibs four days later. In between these two games, Pattie asked for a transfer and Newcastle United were twice rebuffed when they made offers for Fraser. Indeed Kerr was in the market to recruit players, not to sell, and he added Jim Moore from Lochore Welfare and Doug Soutar from Butterburn Youth Club. The latter made his debut at Airdrieonians where United lost 4-2. That result put a severe dent in any Fairs Cities Cup aspirations harboured at Tannadice.

United continued their undefeated home run with a 1-0 win over Third Lanark and immediately afterwards, Kerr announced that Sievewright, Roe and Pattie along with reserves, Jackie Smith and Cochrane were being released. Also, perhaps surprisingly released was Mochan.

The final five matches provided a mixed bag of results and performances, beginning with the 2-2 draw at Kilmarnock. That match was a typical end of season affair, with nothing of note other than the goals. A 2-1 defeat at St Mirren was harsh on United who deserved to take at least a point. Two points were taken from the visit to Pittodrie with United winning 2-1 thanks to a bizarre own goal. Most notable amongst the end of season results was a 3-0 home win on 11th May against Celtic, in which the Terrors' spirit was very much in evidence as Gillespie, Brodie and Carlyle got the goals. The league season ended a week later with a 2-2 draw against Partick Thistle to leave United in a best ever seventh place, just two points away from gaining entry into Europe. The success of the season was again built on consistency, with Doug Smith, Fraser, Millar, Irvine, Gillespie and Carlyle making 40 or more appearances. Davie, Briggs and Neilson were not far behind, with Mitchell and Gordon also playing regularly. Carlyle was the top scorer with 22 goals followed by Supporters' Club Player of the Year, Gillespie on 18, along with Irvine. One major highlight during the season was the performance of Fraser, who netted an unforgettable hat-trick for the Scottish League against the League of Ireland.

There was still a lot of football to be played before the curtain came down on season 1962-63. After beating Dundee 2-0 in the semi final of the Forfarshire Cup on 22nd May, Carlyle's extra time goal brought the cup to Tannadice in a 2-1 win over Arbroath five days later. In between these matches the reserves, who had already won the Second XI League, added the Second XI Cup, beating Hearts 'A' 3-2 on aggregate. In early June, as United prepared for a month long tour of Southern Rhodesia and South Africa, centre forward Brodie left to join Shrewsbury Town. Included in the tour party was new free transfer signing Benny Rooney from Celtic and youngsters Dougan and Dick. These three all made their first appearances for United during the tour as United played nine games and tasted defeat only once. In the process, they scored 29 goals with Mitchell bagging 9 of those. The United travelling party returned to Dundee on 17th July after delays in Rhodesia and in London stretched the homeward journey to 30 hours.

1963-64

Experience and Youth

With little time to prepare for the new season, it was just as well that there were few additions to the playing staff. For the reserves, United had signed Ken Brown from Tynecastle Boys Club and James Baigan from Edinburgh Emmett in late June. The next pre-season signing was sixteen-year-old Francis Munro who joined United after an unhappy year at Chelsea. The public trial was held on 6th August and more than thirty players took part. Those on show convinced Kerr that he had sufficient strength in the team for the season ahead. The only addition afterwards was David Allan of Edinburgh Athletic for the reserves. He was joined in early September by Bobby Benzie from Drumchapel Amateurs. Also in September, John Watson signed from Edinburgh Athletic and he was farmed out to Whitburn Juniors. Although the Manager was still living in Armadale and travelling daily, he decided that unmarried players should all live in Dundee and accommodation was arranged. At Board level, it was agreed that the players would receive extra bonus payments based on league position each week.

After making a handful of appearances on the recent tour, Rooney made his league debut in the opening match of the season, against Aberdeen at Tannadice in the League Cup on 10th August. The Dons took a first half lead but Mitchell levelled after the interval and it finished 1-1. In the next match United made a visit to Hibs, where a thrilling encounter ended 3-2 to the home side who netted a quick fire double to win midway through the second half. St Mirren were the fourth team in the section and at Love Street on 17th August, it was 1-1 at half time. Then, despite having Neilson badly injured and ineffective, United shocked the Buddies with goals from Briggs and Carlyle early in the second half to win 3-2. United returned to the same venue in midweek for the opening match of the league campaign but lost 2-1 following a defensive error. Interest in the League Cup ended after a 2-0 defeat at Aberdeen in which McManus made his debut. A few days later, Moore made his first appearance in a 4-2 home reversal against Hibs. That match also ended an undefeated home record that stretched back twelve months. United won the last of the games in the section, 3-2 against St Mirren at Tannadice.

The league campaign continued at home on 7th September with a hard fought 3-1 win over St Johnstone. A week later, a 22,000 crowd witnessed a pulsating Dundee derby at Dens Park, where Mitchell scored to earn United a well deserved point in a 1-1 draw. A 2-0 home win against East Stirlingshire followed, but a week later United lost 4-2 away to a good performance from top of the table Dunfermline Athletic. Airdrieonians were the next visitors to Tannadice and on the day that Ronnie Simpson made his league debut, United players scored all ten goals in the 9-1 win. Millar, Irvine, Gillespie and Mitchell scored two each with Briggs netting the ninth for the Terrors with a 20 yard thunderbolt. The visitors' counter was lobbed over keeper Mackay by Fraser of United. After such a stunning display by United, it was a huge disappointment when they lost a week later by a single goal at Partick Thistle. The visitors to Tannadice the following week were Celtic and they won 3-0 with United rarely threatening.

1963-64
Back Row: R Smith, Rooney, Brodie, Neilson, Davie, Mackay, McKinlay, Briggs, Munro
Middle: Jerry Kerr, Ernie Ewen, Fraser, Brown, Carlyle, Dick, Irvine, Moore, Gordon, Dougan,
*   D Smith, Andy Dickson*
Front: Simpson, Gillespie, Baigan, Howieson, Reddington, Millar, McManus, Mitchell, Soutar

The Manager had little doubt that the players were good enough but there were concerns at the lack of goals from the centre forward position. Both Rooney and Gillespie had not quite filled the role adequately and Kerr tried to sign Willie Hamilton from Hearts, before the 3-0 win at Motherwell. He ran out of time and played Howieson but was able to conclude a deal to bring Norrie Davidson from Hearts three days later, for a fee of around £4,000. Davidson made his first appearance for United, along with right winger Jocky Clark from Nairn County, in a testimonial for long-serving Charlie McFadyen of St Johnstone in Perth, where it ended 2-2. The new centre scored one, had another disallowed and hit the post. Clark and Davidson were in the side again in United's 3-1 win over Falkirk the following weekend and the centre was on the mark with two goals. Championship challengers, Kilmarnock then scored a 2-0 win over United at Rugby Park.

At the beginning of November, Millwall offered £6,000 for Carlyle and it looked as if the player would sign for them after he went down for talks. However, on 7th November he became a Motherwell player for a similar fee. United kept the season on the boil with a 0-0 draw against Hearts, although on chances, the Terrors should have won by a decisive margin. It was then announced that Ernest Robertson, United's longest serving Chairman, was standing down, although he would remain as a Director. The new Chairman, with a connection to the Club stretching back more than thirty-five years, was Duncan Hutchison. In his first match as Chairman he saw the Terrors win easily, 4-1 at home to Third Lanark and a week later at Queen of the South, the two sides gave the fans an action packed game that ended 1-1. United then met Rangers at Tannadice and although 3-1 down with just a few minutes left, a Mitchell goal reduced the leeway. That set up a storming last five minutes by the Terrors but they still lost 3-2. A week later Aberdeen were the visitors and another good performance failed to bring a just reward as the Dons won 2-1. With Dick appearing for the first time in major competition on 21st December, United met Hibs at Easter Road and returned with a 3-2 win after playing well on a bone hard frozen pitch.

United had been drawn to meet St Mirren in the Scottish Cup at Tannadice in January and on 28th December the Buddies were at Tannadice for a cup rehearsal. If this game was an indicator of what to expect, a cup sizzler was in prospect. The match was level at one goal each and in the second half United took the lead. Howieson was sent off along with Allan of St Mirren but United took full control after that and won 6-2, with Mitchell scoring a hat-trick. On New Year's Day, United again showed their Terrors' spirit as they came back from a two goal deficit to draw 2-2 at St Johnstone. In the Dundee derby, the next day, Mitchell was again the hero with a double, including a last minute winner as United beat Dundee 2-1. Two days later, United had to play East Stirlingshire away. After the exertions of the previous two games, there was no surprise when they struggled to a 1-1 draw.

Howieson's 21 day ban for the sending off meant he missed the Scottish Cup tie against St Mirren and the match failed to live up to the pre-match hype generated by the league meeting. In a poor game, the 0-0 score line was about right. In the midweek replay, United took a second minute lead through Irvine but failed to make the best of their possession and lost 2-1. Against Dunfermline Athletic three days later, neither side adapted well on a heavily sanded Tannadice pitch, and although United took an early second half lead, they eventually lost 2-1. With no game the following week, United travelled to Northampton Town where they lost a friendly 2-1.

On 1st February at Airdrieonians, United introduced George Smith to the side following his transfer from Partick Thistle in a swap deal that saw Davidson heading in the opposite direction after a short stay at Tannadice. Fraser gave United the lead in the match but after half time, the home side took control and deservedly won 3-1. A few days later the Sportsmen's Club paid a record £1,630 to a Taypools winner in a week when a total of £2,200 was paid in prizes.

United then lost their fifth game in a row when Partick Thistle left Tannadice with full points against the run of play. Norrie Davidson scored the decisive second goal for his new club in their 2-1 win. Again, with no match on Scottish Cup weekend, United played a friendly, travelling to Bury where Millar netted the only goal late in the game. Bobby Samuel was added to the reserves in mid February when he signed from Aberdeen Sunnybank.

As the more attacking side in a midweek rearranged match at Celtic Park, United should really have done better but lost to a single Chalmers goal. The Terrors had only themselves to blame for the failure to convert several good opportunities to score. Next came a home game against Motherwell who fielded former United men Bert McCann and Wattie Carlyle. On a snow covered pitch, United mastered the conditions but McCann opened the scoring for the visitors. United mounted a second half recovery to win 4-1, including a rare Briggs double from inside right! On the last day of February, United visited Falkirk where the home side had not recorded a win all season. The Terrors were severely hampered by injury to four players and lost 2-1, with a hotly disputed spot kick at the end bringing the decisive goal.

In early March, the Board announced that the area in front of the South Stand would be improved to provide an additional standing area for fans and an additional covered area was under consideration. Around the same time, centre forward Bobby Young (ex-Celtic) was signed and made his debut against Kilmarnock on 11th March. United gave one of their best performances of the season to beat a strong Rugby Park outfit 2-1. A few days later, United revelled in muddy conditions at Tynecastle and totally outplayed Hearts to win 4-0. The arrival of Young prompted a transfer request from Rooney but he was still very much in Kerr's plans and was not allowed to leave.

There was little left at stake as the league season drew to a close with a rather fortunate 2-2 draw at Third Lanark, thanks to a very late Gillespie strike. Then visitors Queen of the South were beaten 2-1 but only because their keeper, Alan Ball fumbled a late Bobby Smith effort. United then went to Ibrox where Rangers, needing just one point to take the championship, won 2-0 with United offering little resistance. With the league campaign almost over, United went to Arbroath for a Forfarshire Cup tie and a late goal gave the home side a 2-2 draw and a second chance. At Tannadice a week later, United completely dominated the replay to win 4-0. The penultimate match in the league was typical end of season fare. With neither side showing much invention at Aberdeen, United took a point from a dull goalless draw. Against Hibs in the last match, a dramatic second half produced a 1-1 draw. United took the lead through Young and then Gillespie missed from the spot. Baxter of Hibs was sent off and the visitors had a goal disallowed before grabbing a late equaliser.

The annual clearout of players resulted in free transfers for Simpson, Clark, Dougan, McKinlay and Reddington. George Smith was transfer listed at £4,000 after just three months with United. All the others players were retained. Kerr made the decision to move through to Dundee after five years of daily commuting. It was also decided that all players should live in Dundee and not just the unmarried ones. It was not compulsory and the Club agreed to give financial assistance to those who moved, but for those who decided to continue travelling, there would be no help with their costs.

In the semi final of the Forfarshire Cup on 28th April, United overwhelmed Brechin City to win 4-0. Although the league season was over, the newly introduced Summer Cup was about to begin and based on a regional set up there was plenty to hold the fans interest. Although crowds did not match those of league matches, an attendance of 13,500 was recorded for the opening game on 1st May against Dundee at Tannadice. Jimmy Hill of Coventry City was in the stand to watch Davie. Hill may have left impressed by the young keeper but not by the game, which was a poor goalless draw. The next match was in Perth and United won 1-0 against a dour St Johnstone. On 9th May, United lined up new signing Lewis Thom to face his old club Aberdeen and the Terrors were much the better side in the 4-1 win. Then, in a complete contrast to the game at Tannadice, the Dundee derby at Dens Park produced a cracking 3-3 draw that kept United at the top of the group. They consolidated that position with a 1-0 win against St Johnstone and went into the final match against Aberdeen as favourites to go through to the knockout stages. Only a win for Aberdeen by three goals or more could stop United advancing. However, it all fell apart for the Terrors, as the Dons hammered in five without reply, to end United's interest in the Summer Cup.

Despite disappointment in all three cup competitions, it was a successful term for United with an eighth place finish in the league built on a blend of experience and youth. The points haul was down, but six players made over forty appearances, including Supporters' Club Player of the Year, Doug Smith. Another three players made over thirty appearances each, including top scorer Mitchell, who netted 16 league and cup goals. Briggs, Gillespie and Irvine each scored 13 times. The latter player was not long for Tannadice and on 25th May, he signed for Middlesbrough for £25,000. It was a huge fee and the Board pledged to use the money to bring in new players. The Club could also boast more international honours, with Davie capped at Under-23 level against France. In the reserves, United had some talented young players and they had won the Reserve League Cup, beating Kilmarnock over two legs.

1964-65

A Season of Two Halves

As good as their word, the Board lost little time in ploughing the money from the Irvine transfer back into players and right winger Johnny Graham was signed from Third Lanark in early June, for a fee of around £6,000. Despite competition from Dunfermline Athletic and Falkirk, former Hibs and Falkirk centre forward, Doug Moran was quickly added from Ipswich Town for a similar fee. Most of the players who had been retained were re-signed, except for Briggs, who had requested a transfer, although he did eventually put pen to paper. Gordon also refused terms but he too was soon back in the squad, but initially agreed to sign only on a month to month basis. The public trial match on 1st August proved little as far as the Manager was concerned. He felt that the end was in sight for this type of match, as it no longer served any useful purpose.

1964-65
Back Row: *Gillespie, Welsh, Mitchell, Davie, D Smith, Mackay, Brodie, Fraser, Moore*
Middle: *Young, Moran, R Smith, Graham, Dick, Gordon, Brown, Briggs, Benzie*
Front: *Munro, Millar, Samuel, Thom, Howieson, Neilson, McManus, Rooney, Allan*

The season opened with a League Cup tie against Dundee at Dens Park on 8th August and, with Moran and Graham making their debuts, United got off to a good start. There was a big build up to the game and it was fully justified, as both teams served up a thrilling match. United won 3-2, thanks to a late goal from teenage sensation Munro, also making his first appearance in major competition. Sixteen year old Munro was the star of the show again in the second game of the section against Falkirk, scoring the first goal early in the second half and he played his part in the other two as United won 3-0. In the next match, Spurs were represented at Fir Park to watch Gillespie and he did not disappoint, running the show against Motherwell and scoring the only goal of the game. The excellent form in the League Cup however, was not repeated in the opening league match against Partick Thistle at Tannadice, where the Jags won 2-1 with a Billy Hainey double.

The return derby at Tannadice was another pulsating match with all the goals coming in the first half. United came from behind to win 2-1, with Munro again getting the winner, stretching the Terrors' undefeated run of derby matches to nine. Although United lost 5-2 at Falkirk in the next League Cup match, they won the section, even before playing Motherwell and winning 2-1 in the last game. Just after the League Cup section concluded, United signed reserve player Frank McCormack who had returned to Scotland after a short stay at Charlton Athletic. Kerr also added Bobby Welsh of Whitburn Juniors to the reserve squad.

Despite the good form shown in the League Cup, the next league performance was poor as United struggled at Perth, losing 2-0 to St Johnstone. The League Cup quarter final on 9th September brought United up against Hamilton Academical but the Second Division side were no match for the Terrors, who were 7-0 up at half time. After the interval, United eased off and scored just one more. Mitchell, McManus, Munro and Thom netted two each. Before meeting in the second leg at Hamilton, United played Dundee at Tannadice in the third derby in a month. This time the Dark Blues emerged 4-1 winners after United took the lead. The second leg of the cup tie against Hamilton Academical followed and United, with nothing to prove, won 2-1 easily for a 10-1 aggregate to set up their first League Cup semi final, against Rangers. Before that match though, United had two league games to play and firstly took a surprise point at Celtic Park in a 1-1 draw. That was followed by a visit from Hibs who left with both points after a narrow 1-0 win.

United's second major tournament semi final, excluding the Emergency War Cup of 1940, took place at Hampden Park on 30th September 1964 in front of 39,584 spectators. A large contingent of United fans witnessed a fine display from their team, who deservedly took the lead through Moran. Gillespie twice came close to increasing the lead but with just four minutes left, Forrest scored to take the match into extra time. Unfortunately, Rangers scored the winner seven minutes from the end to deny United a place in the final.

League form continued to cause concern with a 2-1 defeat at St Mirren where United went ahead, then missed two penalties and numerous other chances to finish off the Paisley side. A search for players was on and the Manager, along with Directors Hutchison and Grant, flew over to Ireland. The target was Irish international Jack Mooney of Shamrock Rovers but no deal was done. The Club officials were stranded by fog in Dublin but were back in time to see United collect full points for the first time in the league campaign. The 4-1 win over Third Lanark was not achieved without cost when Davie was injured and replaced by Briggs in goal. Just afterwards, reserve player Benzie was released at his own request.

A Forfarshire Cup tie against Montrose was played on 14th October and although the visitors were reduced to ten men after former United man Riddle went off in the first half, it did not detract from a controlled 4-0 win for United. Just after that match, the first hint of Kerr's interest in Scandinavian players emerged. Following the lead of Morton's Hal Stewart, who had already brought in Scandinavian players, Kerr tried and failed to sign Agne Simonsson, a Swedish international who had played for Orgryte against Dunfermline Athletic in a Fairs Cities Cup tie at East End Park. Also in that Swedish side were Orjan Persson and Lennart Wing. After taking a fortunate point in a 0-0 draw at Falkirk on 17th October, the Manager arranged to fly to Sweden.

United came from behind three times, to earn a point at Airdrieonians in a 3-3 draw, but the home side were the better team and were justified in feeling hard done by. United should have done better in the next match a week later at Tannadice, as they dominated for long periods against Kilmarnock but lost 1-0. Meanwhile, news filtered through to the fans that Kerr was hot on the trail of two Danish players who had been recommended to him by a Scot living in that country. Kerr flew to Denmark to see them in action and then opened negotiations for Persson in Sweden. The Swede had seventeen international caps and was attracting interest from Dunfermline Athletic, but despite complicated contractual negotiations, Kerr was confident of getting the player for United. There was no problem as far as paying the fee was concerned, as the Sportsmen's Club was still providing big donations. Over eight years, Taypools membership had risen to more than 93,000, and their contributions had allowed donations totalling almost £200,000 to the football club during that period. The money received had not only assisted in bringing players to the Club but had also helped pay for the new stand, upgrading the standing areas and installing floodlights. The cost of all that work was estimated at over £100,000. Unfortunately, the cash received could not guarantee results and another two points were dropped in a 2-0 defeat at Clyde on 7th November.

In early November, United were approached by Partick Thistle for Howieson but an offer was not forthcoming, even after Kerr suggested a swap for Billy Hainey. Instead, United signed Kenny Dick from Forfar Athletic on 10th November and three days later, in a surprise move, Moran was transferred to

Falkirk. Dick made his debut against Dunfermline Athletic four days later, when a rare Fraser double ensured two points in a 2-0 win. United lost by the same score at Morton the following week and then the chase for Persson gathered pace when St Johnstone disclosed their interest. The Manager and George Fox hurriedly arranged a trip to Sweden and after a seven hour meeting, the deal was all but concluded. They were back in time to see United lose 3-0 at home to Aberdeen but the only signing that week was Terry Preston, from Tranent Juniors, for the reserves.

On 1st December, all entrances to Tannadice were firmly locked whilst a private trial match was under way. The only information on the match came from residents of the Sandeman Street flats overlooking the ground. They were able to disclose that a big unidentified centre forward was playing and he scored four times. The following day another trial match was played

Finn Dossing is welcomed to Tannadice by Andy Dickson and Jerry Kerr

and immediately afterwards Kerr announced the signing of Persson. He also surprised everyone by revealing that he had signed the unknown Finn Dossing from Viborg in Denmark. Dossing, like all Danish players, was an amateur and he wanted to play professionally to earn enough money to eventually set up a business in his home country. The pair cost an estimated £10,000 and both made their debuts on 5th December against Hearts in a 3-1 defeat at Tynecastle. Persson impressed but Dossing did not, even though he scored United's single goal.

Before the next match, at home to Rangers, Kerr added another Scandinavian import when he signed the towering Danish international, Mogens Berg from Boldklubben 1909 Odense. He was the second Dane who had been recommended. Berg made his debut as the United fans got their first sight of him, Dossing and Persson at Tannadice, against Rangers on 12th December. United lost 3-1 but the result was in the balance until the visitors scored the third with two minutes left. Young was released at his own request just before United went to Motherwell, where they played with ten men after Fraser was carried off with a broken ankle, just half an hour into the match. Dossing scored late to give United the lead but the home side levelled almost at the end for a 1-1 draw. The draw was a commendable result in the circumstances but United were nonetheless second bottom in the First Division table, with just eight points from seventeen games, exactly half way through the season. The transformation that followed in the second half of the campaign was nothing short of astonishing. Players were still being added to the squad and Ian Grassick arrived on a one month trial after he was released by Hearts. Jim Stewart of Chelsea was training at Tannadice but he then joined Arbroath, although he signed for United in February.

The weather interrupted the league programme until 1ˢᵗ January, when United met St Johnstone at Tannadice. Dossing cancelled out an early lead for the Perth side but it took three late goals to give United a deserved 4-1 win. That was Johnny Graham's last game and he left soon after to join Falkirk for an undisclosed fee. Eight days later a first half Dossing double helped United pull off a stunning 3-1 win over Celtic at Tannadice. On 16ᵗʰ January, thirty times capped Swede, Lennart Wing was a guest of the Club at Easter Road, where a Dossing hat-trick was the foundation of a 4-0 lead against Hibs at half time. The Edinburgh side were revitalised after the interval and United were a shade lucky to return home with two points after it finished 4-3 in their favour. Two days later, the Manager flew to Sweden to complete the formalities that brought Wing to United. He made his debut against St Mirren on 23ʳᵈ January and another Dossing double earned two points in a 2-0 win. The Scottish Cup intervened and United found the going tough at Forfar Athletic, where the 3-0 win could have been more if the Loons' defending had not been top class. United then released George Smith to become player/manager at Ballymena, collecting an undisclosed fee in the process.

United continued their steady climb up the league, winning 4-1 against Falkirk, even without Dossing who was out through injury. He was back in his usual place the following week and scored both goals in the 2-1 win at Third Lanark, but early in the second half the centre limped off, injured again. He missed the Scottish Cup tie on 20ᵗʰ February as United went out of the competition, beaten 2-0 by Rangers. A week later, Dossing marked his return with a first minute goal as United took a fortunate two points in a 3-2 win over Airdrieonians. United then had the opportunity to face continental opponents with the midweek visit of Orgryte. In sub-zero temperatures neither side were at their best as United won 2-0, with goals from Munro and Dossing. As the freezing weather continued, United travelled to Kilmarnock on 10ᵗʰ March and lost 4-2 in a close game.

The side got back on the winning trail with a vengeance in a 6-0 win against Clyde, with Dossing, Berg and Gillespie each scoring twice. Dossing was on the mark again as United beat Dunfermline Athletic 1-0 at East End Park. That was followed by a midweek derby at Dens Park against Dundee, played in intermittent blizzard conditions and United won a fairly even contest 4-2, with Persson scoring twice. On the following Saturday both United and Morton lined up with four Scandinavians. United won 3-2 with a late Munro goal securing the points. At Aberdeen in the next match, the Terrors lost by a single goal and then top of the table Hearts came to Tannadice and were fortunate to leave with a point from a 1-1 draw, as United were by far the better side. An Easter Holiday fixture in the Forfarshire Cup against Forfar Athletic resulted in a 5-3 win for United, but it was a much better win for the Terrors than the score line suggests.

United then faced a trip to meet Rangers at Ibrox where just 7,000 spectators turned up to see United well ahead of the Glasgow side on play, but with only a Mitchell goal to show for all their efforts in a 1-0 win. A drab goalless match at Partick Thistle followed on 19th April. Two days later United won the Forfarshire Cup with a Dossing goal in a 1-0 win over Dundee. The league season then concluded with United winning 3-1 at home to Motherwell for a ninth place finish that no one could have predicted four months earlier. A testimonial match for Alan Kennedy at Arbroath was notable only for the appearance of Jim Stewart in his one first team game for United. It was a dull 0-0 result in front of a crowd of just 900.

There were no surprises as the Manager announced free transfers for Howieson and Stewart, along with reserves Allan, Brown, McCormack, centre half Brodie and Welsh. The season was far from over though, with the Summer Cup next on the card. The sections were again sensibly arranged on a regional basis to ensure the best chance of big attendances. The first match for United handed them another derby at Dens Park on 1st May and United gave Dundee a lesson in taking chances, winning 4-1. That score line was repeated as United were always the better side against a stuffy St Johnstone. At Aberdeen in the third match, United had to hang on to win 2-1 against a late surge from the Dons. United then recorded their sixth derby win in seven meetings against Dundee that season. The Dark Blues took the lead twice but United recovered to draw level both times before Berg netted his second goal of the match to complete a well deserved 3-2 win. In the next match, United led by a single goal at half time but ran riot in the second half to trounce St Johnstone 5-1 in Perth and finally, to complete a 100% record in the section, United beat Aberdeen 3-0 with ease.

That set up a two-leg semi final with Partick Thistle and United went off the boil and had to defend in depth to achieve a goalless outcome at Firhill. The second leg however, brought out the real United and the final beckoned after a comfortable 3-0 win at Tannadice. Motherwell were the other finalists and when the sides met in the first leg at Fir Park on 29th May, United were the better team in the first half and took an early lead. The home side equalised quickly and after the break, United faded from the game and were beaten 3-1. There was tremendous optimism for the second leg four days later and when Berg scored in the fourteenth minute, it looked as if United would wipe out the deficit. In the end, a combination of bad luck and over eagerness denied the Terrors and Motherwell took the trophy. All through the tournament, United had been without Persson and Wing who were on international duty for Sweden, taking part in a World Cup qualifier and a series of friendlies. There were many who thought that having this pair back for the final would have resulted in a win. However, the Manager was unwilling to recall them and based on the results in the sectional stages he was correct.

When the time came to review United's season, the changes in fortune following the arrival of the Scandinavians stood out for all to see. Only eight points were gained in the first half of the campaign and in the second half only six points were dropped. What might have happened if Dossing, Persson, Wing and Berg had been brought in earlier, is anyone's guess. Certainly, Dossing was well out in front in the goal scoring department, with 21 goals in 19 league matches. He also scored one in the Scottish Cup and nine in the Summer Cup. Briggs, Millar and Doug Smith played in all league and cup games and Gillespie missed out just twice all season. The emerging Munro played a big part in the second half revival and was chosen to represent Scotland in a youth international tournament in West Germany. The reserves also had a good season, reaching the final of the Second XI Cup, only to lose to Kilmarnock.

1965-66

The Scandinavian Influence

In early June, Thom and Moore went to Shrewsbury Town for talks but both returned after failing to agree terms, although Thom did move there in September. Re-signing talks with the rest of the squad took place in June. Initially, only Gordon and Fraser held out but by the end of the month both were signed. However, Gordon left United to join Bradford Park Avenue before the season began. There was little other movement of playing staff, with only youngster Donald McDonald signed in June for the reserves from Portsmouth, and Bobby Carroll joined the squad in late July from St Mirren. The annual public trial match was not being held and instead, the Manager tried to arrange a friendly. However, he was hindered by SFA rules, which precluded such matches at home, and the only option was to play a match outside Scotland. Finding opposition was a different matter and the plan for a pre-season match was abandoned.

Further improvements were being made to Tannadice and work was well under way to complete the enclosure below the South Stand before the season started. Players' welfare was also a high priority with the Directors and arrangements were made to pay part of their wages in cash, and the rest to bank accounts. In addition, many of the players participated in a voluntary savings scheme. The Board had also approved the purchase of two properties in Seafield Road, Broughty Ferry for use as a players' hostel and upgrading work was being carried out. There had been a drop of £8,000 in gate monies in season 1963-64 and at the financial year end, a loss of £13,700 was reported. However, the Sportsmen's Club donated over £37,000, which kept the bank balance healthy.

The League Cup threw up a very tough section, with Celtic, Dundee and Motherwell in United's group. Carroll marked his debut with a goal against Celtic on 14th August at Tannadice in the opening match. Although the Glasgow side levelled, Gillespie netted late for a 2-1 win. A goalless but action-packed Dundee derby at Dens Park came next before United faced Motherwell at

Tannadice, taking two points from a 4-1 win, with all United's goals coming after the interval.

1965-66
Back Row: Briggs, S Dick, Davie, Mackay, Moore, Smith
Middle: Andy Dickson, McDonald, Persson, Rooney, Dossing, Neilson, Munro, K Dick,
          Jerry Kerr
Front: Wing, McManus, Millar, Fraser, Gillespie, Thom, Mitchell

Just after that game McManus was suspended by the Club for a breach of discipline and soon left to join Falkirk. The league campaign opened against Celtic on 25th August in the midst of the League Cup section. The Glasgow side extracted revenge for their opening day defeat with a 4-0 win at Tannadice. At Celtic Park three days later on League Cup business, United lost again, this time 3-0. The double defeat seemed to knock the fight from United and they lost the

Dossing celebrates his second goal in the 5-0 win over Dundee

remaining two matches in the section, 3-1 at home to Dundee and 3-2 at Motherwell. The Lanarkshire side then provided United's next signing, young centre forward Hugh McLeish. Shortly after McLeish arrived, Kenny Dick left to join Queen of the South.

The league campaign continued with a trip to Dens Park on 11th September 1965, a date now revered by the fans as the 'Dens Park Massacre of '65'. A song penned shortly afterwards recalls a hat-trick by Dossing, a Gillespie rocket and a Wing penalty for a 5-0 win. Dundee had no answer to a hard tackling, fast moving United and the only Dundee player to emerge with pass marks was debutant Jim McLean, later to manage United. The Terrors scored another five goals a week later, beating St Johnstone 5-1 at Tannadice.

In the second half of September, forward David Robertson (ex-Motherwell, Crewe Alexandra and Morton) and right back George Rollo (Carnoustie Panmure) joined United reserves, whilst Kerr paid an estimated £5,000 to bring Ian Stewart from Arbroath. Without Wing and Persson, who were on international duty with Sweden, United's winning run continued with a 2-1 victory at St Mirren, and another five star performance brought two points in a 5-2 win against Partick Thistle. The Terrors also returned from a visit to Dunfermline Athletic on 9th October with a 4-2 win, although the home side were hard done by. At that match, United had Finn Seemann over from Norway as a guest, accompanied by John Sveinsson, who had played for United during WW2 and was by then an official at Seemann's club, Lyn Oslo.

With former United men Moran, Graham and McManus in the line up, Falkirk were the next victims of the United goal machine in a Dewar Shield tie. The Terrors ran riot in the second half to win 6-1. Hamilton Academical were the visitors on 16th October in the league as United romped to a 7-0 win, their sixth league win in a row, to move into second place. However, a week later, United lost a Forfarshire Cup tie 1-0 to Dundee at Dens Park and in midweek, Rangers ran out 2-0 winners at Ibrox in a league match. Seemann had signed by then and made his debut that night. The addition of the fifth Scandinavian brought United's total estimated spending on the imports to around £30,000. The Manager's success had not gone unnoticed elsewhere and Wolverhampton Wanderers tried to lure him south with a tempting offer of a £7,000 annual salary, a very substantial amount at a time when a player's basic wage was around £25 weekly! He stayed at Tannadice though, knowing that he had put together a side capable of mounting a strong league challenge.

Success on the field was reflected in the activities of Taypools, which reached its peak in late February 1965 with membership of 95,000 and over 700 agents. In season 1964-65, 2,800 winners had benefited from prize money of £95,000. However, the success of the operation meant that betting tax of more than £45,000 had to be paid! In the nine years since it had begun, the Sportsmen's Club, through Taypools, had paid out almost £600,000 in prizes and donated £235,000 to the football club. Chairman George Fox was lavish in his praise, going as far as to suggest that without the cash from that source, Dundee United FC may very well have gone out of existence. Dundee United Sportsmen's Club was the envy of every other football club in Scotland.

When Morton came to Tannadice on 30th October, United got back into a winning way with a 4-2 victory. Three days later, Stewart made his debut as a substitute in a 3-2 friendly win at Carlisle United. He played again and scored as United returned to league action in a 2-2 draw against Hearts, a result achieved without Wing and Persson, who were again on international duty. The league challenge was maintained with a 4-1 win at Falkirk and a second half Dossing hat-trick secured a 3-0 win at Motherwell, but United lost 2-0 at home to Clyde the following week. On 11th December, a goalless draw at Aberdeen was poor reward as United missed a hatful of chances. It was a similar story in another 0-0 draw a week later at home to Kilmarnock, and United made short work of beating Stirling Albion 4-2 on Christmas Day. A few days later, Jeanfield Swifts' Ally Campbell joined United reserves.

In the return league derby at Tannadice against Dundee on 3rd January, Mackay was the star of the show, making sure the Dark Blues were kept out, as United held on to win 2-1. High flying Celtic then snatched a narrow 1-0 win on a sodden Celtic Park. Then, a comfortable 3-0 win over St Mirren kept United in touch with the leading pack at the top of the table. Realistically by then, the league challenge was over but a Fairs Cities Cup place was now the target. With the Scandinavians in the side, United had raised their profile and the offer of a tour of Iceland in the summer was already under consideration by the Board.

Fairs Cup aspirations were dented as United lost 4-1 at Partick Thistle on a heavily sanded pitch. A week later, championship challengers Dunfermline Athletic, still fresh after their midweek European exertions against FC Brno of Czechoslovakia, won 4-0 at Tannadice. Attention then switched to the Scottish Cup and after the home tie with Falkirk was postponed on Saturday, it took an enormous effort to have snow cleared from the pitch for the rearranged game on Monday 7th February. United had the best of the chances but the match ended goalless. A fairly easy 4-0 league win at Hamilton Academical preceded the replay with Falkirk and at Brockville, a titanic struggle ended with a 2-1 win for United. Falkirk went in front and it took a Briggs goal four minutes from the end of normal time to save the game before Dossing got the winner in extra time. That win set up a tie against Aberdeen in the next round only three days later but the match was postponed until Wednesday 23rd February. United still looked jaded as they lost 5-0 but their cause was not helped when they practically gifted the Dons a three goal lead with uncharacteristic defensive errors.

A Scottish Cup hangover was evident as Morton won 2-0 at Cappielow on the following Saturday. That was followed up by a good 3-0 away win over Ayr United in a friendly and then Falkirk exacted some revenge as they won 3-2 in a league match at Tannadice. Then Rooney, who had requested a transfer in January, was sold to St Johnstone for £3,500. United tried and failed to sign Jimmy Millar from Rangers and John Divers from Celtic but were successful in acquiring Billy Hainey from Partick Thistle for around £8,000. He went straight into the side on 16th March to face Hearts, who were on an unbeaten run of fourteen league games. United pulled off something of a shock result at Tynecastle and ended Hearts' run with a Mitchell goal in a 1-0 win. Dossing had failed to score in the previous nine league matches but got back in the groove with a hat-trick in the 5-1 win over Motherwell. United then beat Rangers 1-0 at Tannadice but had Mackay to thank for a top class save near the end to secure full points. At Clyde five days later, United lost 4-1 and followed that up with a narrow 2-1 win at St Johnstone on 30th March. The Manager then agreed to field a strong line up against a Scottish Youth XI side, which would include Munro. The young Scots, who were all playing for a place in the forthcoming international youth tournament in Yugoslavia, won 3-1 with a good performance. Ian Thompson from Valleyfield played as a trialist and McLeish made his first appearance for United in the match. Neither would play first team football for United again.

United went into the last five league matches not knowing if a Fairs Cup place would be achieved, as UEFA was considering allowing just one side from each country to participate in the tournament. Hibs were one of the teams still in the running and faced United on 9th April. A real thriller ensued with United emerging 5-4 winners. Aberdeen were the next visitors to Tannadice and United adapted to the muddy conditions to record a 3-0 win. United and Hibs produced another thriller in a 3-3 draw at Easter Road but at Kilmarnock, with the home side also challenging for a Fairs Cup place, United lost by a single goal in a poor match. United then turned out a full strength side in a testimonial for Bill Ogilvie, and were shocked by a lively Montrose who won 5-2. The final league match of the season ended in a 1-1 draw at home to Stirling Albion on 30th April and gave United a best ever fifth place finish but with still no decision on a Fairs Cup place. The success of the season was again built on consistent team selection, with Millar, Briggs, Neilson and Doug Smith solid at the back. Top scorer Dossing notched 27 league and cup goals, despite a slight lull in form midway through the season. Mitchell and Munro also netted regularly with both well into double figures. In the supporting roles, Persson and Gillespie were outstanding, with Mackay at his best.

In early May, United announced the appointment of Doug Cowie as coach with responsibility for youth development. United also planned to employ eight scouts to cover all of Scotland, and over two hundred applications were received. At the end of the month, reserve team coach Ernie Ewen left United. Only a handful of players were released at the end of the season. Reserves Preston, McDonald and Rollo left, along with fringe players Bobby Smith and Soutar. All the others re-signed except for Millar and Doug Smith. Both these players would not be allowed to join the party touring Iceland and Denmark in June unless they put pen to paper first. Possibly in anticipation of that, Ronnie McFall was signed from Portadown for around £4,000 and Ian Scott, who was with Musselburgh Athletic and already on a provisional form, was added to the reserves in mid May.

The summer tour was a great success with United winning all three games in Iceland, scoring 17 times. In Denmark, United won both matches scoring 9 goals. Mitchell netted 10 times and Dossing got 7 in the five games. Neither Millar nor Doug Smith went on the tour but McFall travelled, making his debut in the opening game. In the case of Millar, he decided to return to his job as a printer. Smith re-signed on a three year deal when the team returned. Shortly after that came the news that United would be one of three Scottish teams taking part in the Fairs Cities Cup. When the draw was made on 25th July 1966, both United and Kilmarnock received byes.

1966-67

Europe – The First Time

The Scottish League had considered a proposal to restructure on a three league 16-12-12 basis but a two thirds majority was required to make the change and the clubs rejected that idea by a vote of 20-17. One long overdue change was however in the pipeline. After many years of debate, the introduction of a substitute would be in place in Scotland for all national competitions from season 1966-67, but the replacement of a player was only to be allowed for injury.

July 1966 began with the announcement that United had made a loss of £37,500 for the year ended July 1965, even after an increase of £30,000 in gate receipts. However, the Sportsmen's Club donated £36,500 and that kept the bank balance in credit. Thompson joined the rest of the players for pre-season training, but there was no Millar, as he had still refused to sign. United had also turned down an offer of £10,000 from Liverpool for him. There were no other changes to the playing staff until the season was under way. In mid August, Ian Stewart left United in exchange for Jackie Graham of Morton on the recommendation of Doug Cowie. Millar finally re-signed on 20th August but on a part-time basis. The reserve strength was increased with the addition of Philip Prain who had been with Peterborough United. Davie Kennedy from Comrie Colliery was also added to the reserves later that month.

Meanwhile, the season got underway at Keith on 9th August, in a friendly which United won 2-0 but only after toiling for much of the game. The League Cup came next and United's section comprised Dundee, Aberdeen and St Johnstone, which meant that there could potentially be some big derby crowds. Attendances did not reach the levels anticipated but the section produced some good games, beginning with United's 2-0 win over Dundee at Tannadice on 13th August. With the rules changed to allow substitutes, that match also witnessed the first United substitute in a competitive match. Gillespie was replaced in the second half by Hainey who scored United's second goal. Four days later United and St Johnstone served up an ill-tempered 1-1 draw in Perth and on the following Saturday, the Terrors were always second best as they lost 4-1 to a strong Aberdeen side at Pittodrie. United's interest in the tournament was all but over as the next match ended 1-1 against Dundee at Dens Park, with Jackie Graham making his debut. The Terrors then gave a great performance to win 5-3 at home to St Johnstone but lost the last match in the section against Aberdeen, by the odd goal in seven.

The league fixture list then threw up two matches against teams from the League Cup section. United lost 2-0 at St Johnstone and 4-1 to Dundee at Tannadice. Huddersfield Town expressed an interest in signing Munro, but a price tag of £15,000 was too much for them and they dropped their interest in the player. Some Fairs Cup news emerged. Barcelona won the 1965-66 final 4-3 on aggregate, after beating Real Zaragoza 4-2 in the second leg on 21st September. The final had been held over from May.

1966-67
Back Row: Berg, Mitchell, Mackay, McAlpine, Davie, Munro, Thompson
Middle: Moore, Briggs, Carroll, Gillespie, McLeish, Smith, Wing
Front: Persson, Dick, McFall, Dossing, Stewart, Neilson, Hainey

After two poor results in the league, United were firing on all cylinders at Ayr United, where a second half own goal was followed by two each for Dossing, Persson and Mitchell in a resounding 7-0 success. That was followed by a narrow 3-2 defeat at home to Rangers and the news that United were prepared to listen to offers for Sidney Dick. Meanwhile, the Manager was showing keen interest in Ashfield players Jim Cameron, Walter Smith and Gerry Hernon. On 3rd October, the Fairs Cup draw handed United the toughest possible European baptism, against the holders Barcelona and the following day, Kerr was bombarded with offers of hotel accommodation from Spain. Over the next couple of weeks, protracted negotiations with the Catalan giants took place before fixture dates were finally agreed.

In the meantime, gathering league points was the priority and a 4-1 win at Stirling Albion was achieved after the home side had taken the lead. Munro left United to join Aberdeen for a substantial but undisclosed fee before the next match on 15th October, in which United took a four goal lead by half time against Clyde. The visitors fought back and United were left defending desperately for a 4-3 victory.

Barcelona bound

Cameron and Hernon were signed the following day. A week later, Hainey was sent off but the Terrors still managed to take a point in a closely fought 2-2 draw at Easter Road with Hibs. United then prepared to fly out to Spain with a pool of fourteen players for their historic first match in European football. They returned, of course, with a glorious 2-1 first leg victory courtesy of an excellent team performance and goals from Hainey and Seemann, the latter a twice taken spot kick. The Barcelona heroes lined up:-

Davie, Millar, Briggs; Neilson, D Smith, Wing; Seemann, Hainey, Mitchell, Gillespie, Persson.

Jaded after their European trip, United lost 4-2 at home to Dunfermline Athletic and a week later drew 2-2 at Airdrieonians. Walter Smith was signed before the next match, a 1-1 draw at home to Kilmarnock, as United geared up for the return leg against Barcelona. The Terrors lined up with the same eleven for the second leg on 16th November. Another superb team performance in front of a record crowd of 28,000, created history. United won 2-0 with Mitchell and Hainey scoring the goals to complete a famous double over the Spanish side.

Mitchell and Seemann celebrate after Hainey scores against Barcelona at Tannadice

Back on league business three days later, United tired as the game at Motherwell progressed and could only draw 1-1. A week later, they were unlucky to lose 3-1 at home to Aberdeen. On 30th November, the Manager was in Portugal to witness the defeat of Vitoria Setubal by Juventus, which meant that the famous Italian side would be United's next opponents in the Fairs Cup, but the first leg would not take place until February 1967. United then had an easy passage to win 3-0 at Falkirk with all the goals coming in the first half. Millar came back on the United full-time payroll after he lost his job as a printer, primarily because he took time off to travel for the Fairs Cup match in Spain.

United lost 2-1 at Hearts on 10th December and could then manage only a 2-2 draw at home to St Mirren, despite pounding their goal for much of the second half. On Hogmanay 1966, Celtic arrived at Tannadice on a 46 game unbeaten run, which United ended with a 3-2 win, thanks to a good second half performance, in which Mitchell got the eventual winner. His goal against St Johnstone two days later was enough to seal another win. A treble of festive victories was achieved with a Jackie Graham hat-trick in only his second game for United, as the Terrors beat Dundee 3-2 at Dens Park. The winning sequence continued with an easy 4-0 home success against Ayr United but at Ibrox against Rangers, the home side established a three goal lead in the second half. Although United never gave up, they had only a late Gillespie goal to show for a lot of effort in a 3-1 defeat. The next game brought a 2-0 win over Stirling Albion at Tannadice, where United dominated for most of the match. It was not considered a good result in view of the impending cup ties against strong opposition. Nevertheless, United rose to the occasion the following week and won 3-0 against Hearts at Tynecastle in the Scottish Cup. Perhaps with too many players thinking about the forthcoming trip to Italy, United then lost 2-0 at Clyde.

United travelled to play Juventus and on the day of the match, only 6,000 fans turned out on the freezing cold afternoon of 8th February 1967, to see the Italian side win 3-0. Fielding the same eleven that beat Barcelona twice, United took great credit for their performance and the score line was a little flattering to Juventus, but it has to be said that they had an impressive domestic record, both in defence and in attack, and deserved to win. The following day, Kerr was still in confident mood and warned that United should not be written off.

United appeared to suffer another European hangover as they lost 3-1 to Hibs three days after the Juventus match. But a week later, a tremendous thirty-five yard Persson goal gave United a deserved 1-0 win in the Scottish Cup against Falkirk. The league campaign continued with a highly controversial 3-3 draw at Dunfermline Athletic, where it was claimed that two of the Pars goals should have been disallowed for offside. With the second leg against Juventus imminent, United won comfortably, 3-1 at home to Airdrieonians.

There were reports in the press of discord in the Juventus camp and rumours of player injuries, but no-one at Tannadice was being taken in by these stories as the team lined up for the second leg on 8th March, with just one change, Dossing for the injured Mitchell. Another 28,000 crowd witnessed another United performance to remember, but for all their effort, United managed just one goal from Dossing with eight minutes remaining. United went out on a 3-1 aggregate but they had firmly established the name and reputation of the Club on the European stage. Indeed Juventus' Sandro Salvatore said after the match that he was just glad they did not have to play United every week. Bearing in mind the disappointment felt by the players, they then did exceptionally well to beat Dunfermline Athletic 1-0 three days later in the Scottish Cup, with Dossing netting the only goal five minutes from the end of a highly competitive encounter.

The emphasis was now on a Scottish Cup semi final against Aberdeen at Dens Park and an all ticket sell-out crowd of 41,500 was expected. In the meantime, the league matches continued, with a 1-1 draw at home to Motherwell followed by a 4-0 away defeat at Kilmarnock, where Walter Smith made his debut. A cup rehearsal at Aberdeen on 25th March resulted in a nervy encounter for both sides and United just edged it 1-0 with a Graham goal. The Scottish Cup semi final a week later was also settled by a single goal but it was an unfortunate Millar own goal after just four minutes, that knocked United out.

A midweek match against Falkirk resulted in an astonishing 4-4 draw, with United recovering from being 4-1 behind. Three days later, a poor home crowd witnessed a good performance in which United beat Hearts 2-0. Then, without ever getting into top gear, United took two points at St Mirren on 12th April in a 1-0 win, with Hernon scoring the only goal on his debut. Next, United travelled to London to face Crystal Palace in a friendly and drew 1-1. A few days after returning, the third of the trio of players from Ashfield, Jim Cameron, made his debut in a 2-2 draw at home to Partick Thistle. On 3rd May, United embarked on a daunting trip to Celtic Park, where the home side needed just one point to win the championship. The Terrors spoiled the party by winning 3-2. It was the second time United had won against Celtic that season, the only team to do so as the Glasgow side won everything, including the European Cup. Around that time, Wing returned home to Sweden after his contract expired. Then Scott made his debut as United lost 3-0 at Partick Thistle in the last league match of the season.

United finished the league campaign in ninth place. Along with a good Scottish Cup run and two memorable European ties, that made season 1966-67 one of the best the Club had ever had. More success for the Club had arrived with international recognition for Mitchell at Under-23 level. Doug Smith with 48 appearances was the only ever present in a settled side, whilst Briggs, Millar, Neilson, Wing, Persson and Mitchell played over 40 games each. Mitchell was top scorer with 22 goals, followed closely by Dossing on 16. Perhaps surprisingly, Fraser was one of eight players released and the others allowed to leave were Dick, McFall, McLeish and Carroll along with reserves, Samuel, Campbell and Kennedy. Most of the others were re-signed, along with a new reserve inside forward Peter Stuart, who had recently joined the Club from Aberdeen Sunnybank, but Mitchell and Briggs had still to re-sign. Neither of the latter pair would travel to America, where United were to take part in the North American Soccer League, although Briggs re-signed in time to play in the latter stages. Persson was also unsigned and would not travel either. In any event he joined the Swedish national side taking part in European Championship qualifying matches.

The trip to America was arranged mainly because of United's raised profile after their European exploits. The Club were invited to participate in the North American Soccer League, which was being organised in an attempt to get the American public interested in the game. With the permission of the SFA, United took part as Dallas Tornado, playing twelve matches during a seven week period between 29th May and 8th July 1967. The tour however, was a strength sapping exercise involving travel over huge distances. Some of the matches were played

in intense heat, and although the Club benefited from an estimated £15,000, overall it was not a successful venture on the field, with just three wins, three draws and six defeats. The players had little time to rest before the new season was due to begin again.

Whilst the team and the Club officials were in the USA, groundsman Chick Boath was busy supervising improvement work at Tannadice. New drainage was being installed and the pitch was then re-turfed for the new season. In the South Stand, there was still fixed seating in some sections and these were replaced with more practical tip-up seats.

1967-68

Below Expectation

Throughout the early summer months of 1967, there was an ongoing saga concerning Orjan Persson. He had returned to Sweden claiming that his contract had expired but according to officials at Tannadice, there was a one year option still remaining. Although the Scottish League confirmed that the player was still under contract to United, in mid July, Persson stated that he would not play for United again. When he returned to Scotland to resolve the issue, it appeared that Rangers, who had been watching the situation closely, were poised to sign him. It then transpired that Persson would need a new work permit, and the deal looked unlikely to go ahead, but he did eventually join Rangers on 3rd August and United acquired winger Davie Wilson and half back Wilson Wood in exchange.

These new arrivals increased the number of new players formerly with Rangers to three, following the capture of free transfer Jimmy Millar (brother of United's Tommy), two weeks earlier. During all this activity, Mitchell re-signed and pre-season signings continued with the addition of Pat Purcell, who had been released by Chelsea. Doug Clark was provisionally signed from Broughty Athletic for the reserves. Almost unnoticed, United added provisional signings Jim Henry from Carnoustie Panmure and Iain Brown from Lochee Renton. Already in the ranks of the reserves, provisional signing Hamish McAlpine from local junior side North End was just about to sign professionally.

Season tickets for the stand were on sale at £6.5/- (£6.25) with a ground season ticket at £4. United kicked off the season with the first ever home pre-season friendly against an English side. Sheffield United were the visitors and with Millar, Wood and Wilson making debuts in the starting eleven and Purcell coming on for the second half, an entertaining match ended in a 1-0 defeat. The three former Rangers players then made their debuts in major competition for United at Celtic on 12th August, as the League Cup got under way. Despite a fighting performance, United lost by a single goal scored in the final minute. In a tough League Cup section, United faced Aberdeen next and after a goalless

137

first half, a Wilson-inspired performance left the Dons bemused and beaten 5-0. United then added Walter Borthwick from Morton to the reserve side on a one month trial. A few days later the Directors announced a loss of £23,000 for the year to July 1966 but the Sportsmen's Club had donated £37,000, to more than offset the deficit.

A League Cup visit to play Rangers at Ibrox was next, and United were unfortunate to lose 1-0 to a second half penalty. In the midst of an important League Cup section, United agreed to meet Brechin City in a Forfarshire Cup tie and in the 7-3 win, seven different players scored for United. A full house was packed into Tannadice for the visit of Celtic on 26th August and although Mackay saved a first half penalty, Celtic won with the only goal of the game after the break. The League Cup section wound down with a 2-2 draw at Aberdeen where United twice came from behind. In the last match of the section, Rangers came to Tannadice and won 3-0, after gradually taking control in the second half.

As the League Cup campaign ended, the league began with three draws in the first three matches, all 2-2. With Purcell making his first and only appearance in major competition, United were fortunate to take a point against St Johnstone in the first match but fully deserved a share against Dundee. The Terrors should have won against Hibs after coming back from a two goal deficit to take control of the match. United had already added reserves Tommy McKeith and Eric Bayolsen to the squad, and two further additions were made with the signing of Billy Bremner from Forrit Brae, and Andy Rolland from Cowdenbeath. The latter went straight into the first team at Airdrieonians on 30th September, but it was a poor United display and the home side scored two early goals for a 2-0 win. The first win of the season was achieved after a first minute Dossing goal and one each from Mitchell and Jimmy Millar gave United a three goal lead against Morton. After Davie was injured, Briggs took the keeper's jersey and he conceded two late goals, but the 3-2 win was well deserved.

On 14th October, United travelled north to Aberdeen to find the Dons in top form and the home side scored six without reply. A week later, a nervous United performance resulted in the loss of a point in a 2-2 draw at home to Partick Thistle. At this time Hainey was unsettled, having spent much of the season in the reserves and he asked for a transfer. United agreed to listen to offers but none were received. Kerr made changes to the side for the visit to Falkirk and for the first time in three years, there were no Scandinavians in the line up. The result should have been put beyond doubt but after leading 2-0, United allowed the home side back into the game and the 2-1 win was much closer than it should have been. Motherwell were the next visitors to Tannadice and an early goal by them and an outstanding performance by keeper McCloy almost won the day but Wilson scored a deserved equaliser for United and it ended 1-1. The next match resulted in a 1-0 defeat by Hearts at Tynecastle and United left with nothing, after Wilson missed the chance to level the match from the spot.

United won 1-0 on a visit to Raith Rovers on 18th November and followed that up with a midweek 5-1 Dewar Shield win over St Johnstone at Tannadice. Hainey was by then restored to the attack and he netted the winner in a 3-2 victory over Kilmarnock. The contrast in fortunes during the season was never better illustrated than during December. Firstly, United emerged with a well deserved point from a 1-1 draw at Celtic but two weeks later the fans witnessed a total collapse as United were hammered 5-0 at Clyde. Shortly after that, Dossing returned home to Denmark as his contract had expired and Neilson requested a transfer. A 2-2 draw resulted at Dunfermline Athletic, where United were by far the better side but had to wait for Scott's second goal of the game in the last minute to get a point. In the final match of the month, Scott and Mitchell each scored a hat-trick as United thrashed Stirling Albion 9-0, to end an erratic month of form.

A pulsating derby with Dundee at Tannadice on 2nd January produced plenty of entertainment for both sets of fans, but no goals. Then at Easter Road, Hibs won 3-0 although United were the better side in the opening stages. The Club was faced with another transfer request when Davie asked away just before the team travelled to Morton where they lost 5-2. Cameron and Berg were both injured in that match and a week later Briggs suffered a broken leg just three minutes into the 3-1 win over St Mirren in the Scottish Cup. A 3-2 home defeat by Aberdeen and 1-0 reversal at Partick Thistle followed, as United continued an inconsistent season. No-one could have predicted the drama that would follow in the remarkable Scottish Cup match on 17th February against Hearts at Tannadice. The visitors took a two goal lead but Wilson and Rolland levelled the tie, all in the first eighteen minutes! A Mitchell brace put United ahead but Hearts pulled one back and it was 4-3 to United at the interval. Soon after Seemann had his penalty saved by the Hearts keeper early in the second half, it was all square. Hainey put United in front again before the visitors levelled the tie from a penalty. With five minutes left, former United player Jim Irvine scored, for a 6-5 win to Hearts.

Bad weather meant it was two weeks before United were back in action in the league and a controlled display brought a 3-1 win at Motherwell. United beat Falkirk 3-2 in a rearranged midweek game, but with numerous chances coming their way, it should have resulted in a bigger winning margin for the Tannadice side. It was the Terriers versus the Terrors in a 2-2 friendly draw at Huddersfield Town, after which United met Raith Rovers at Tannadice. The visitors were the better side in a 3-3 draw, with Gillespie scoring the third, to earn a fortunate point for United from the spot, after a soft penalty was awarded. A measure of revenge was gained against Hearts four days later. After the visitors took the lead almost from kick off, United won 2-1 with second half goals from Mitchell and Wilson. In the third of a series of five home matches, United struggled to beat Airdrieonians 1-0 but on 30th March, they were outplayed as Celtic romped to a 5-0 win at Tannadice. Four days later a better organised United held Rangers to a goalless draw in a rearranged midweek game. On 6th April at Ibrox, United gave as good as they got, but lost 4-1 after being reduced to ten men as a result of injuries. Leading by two goals at half time, United almost threw away the points in the next match at home to Clyde as they eased off, allowing the visitors to pull one back, but it ended 2-1. A midweek match at Kilmarnock on 17th April gave Brown his debut as a substitute but it was an unhappy event for all concerned, as United lost 4-0. The Tannadice side then lost 4-1 at home to high flying cup finalists Dunfermline Athletic and lost again a few days later, 2-1 to St Johnstone in Perth.

With the season nearing completion, United signed Tommy Dunne from Albion Rovers for £5,000 and announced that fringe players Moore, Purcell, Thompson and Hernon were being released, along with the experienced Hainey and reserves Bayolsen, Stuart, and Clark, whilst Henry and Brown joined the full-time staff. Prain had already left and joined the junior ranks with Lochee United. Neilson was also released and shortly afterwards he went to Cowdenbeath. Dunne made his debut in the last league match of the season, away to bottom club Stirling Albion. The home side established a two goal lead, before late goals from Gillespie and Rolland earned a 2-2 draw. United then lost the first of a series of Forfarshire Cup ties, 4-3 to Dundee in the 1965-66 final at Dens Park on 4th May. At around the same time, Berg returned to Denmark.

In view of United's achievements in previous seasons, 1967-68 was below expectation, with an eleventh place finish. There had been several changes in personnel over the campaign, which saw the end of the Scandinavian influence. Doug Smith was again an ever present in the side but only Gillespie, Wood and Wilson came close to his 42 appearances. Mitchell was top scorer again on 16 goals, with Wilson closest to him on 10. The fans would surely be looking for improvement next season. Kerr found just the player to provide the spark that was needed, moving quickly to secure the signature of Kenny Cameron for a fee of £7,500 after the player put in a transfer request at Kilmarnock. A highly regarded striker, Cameron made a phenomenal early impact. In his first outing with United, a Forfarshire Cup match at Forfar Athletic on 8th May, he scored a hat-trick in the 3-3 draw. The replay went on at Gayfield, Arbroath, as the Tannadice pitch was being replaced. Cameron recorded another hat-trick in United's comfortable 5-0 win. In the next round, United were away to Arbroath and the home side earned a well deserved second chance with a 1-1 draw. There was no time to arrange the replay as United were preparing for a brief tour of Norway.

Davie Hogg was signed on a free transfer from Hibs and joined the travelling party to Norway, whilst Norman Robertson of Clackmannan Juniors was added to the reserves. Hogg made his first appearance on 19th June for United against Viking Stavanger in a 4-1 win, in which Cameron netted his third hat-trick since joining the Club. In a three team tournament, United met Brann Bergen FC the following day and lost 3-1 but won the tournament on goal difference. The final match of the tour was a 2-0 defeat by Lyn Oslo in a friendly, which was Seemann's last game before completing a £25,000 move to DWS Amsterdam. Shortly after returning home, United signed Alec Reid on a free transfer from Rangers ahead of stiff competition from several other clubs. Douglas Johnstone of United Crossgates was then signed for the reserve side in mid July.

1968-69

Last of the Black and Whites

Most of the signing activity had taken place in the early summer and the Manager arranged three pre-season friendlies against English opposition to put the players to the test. Kenny Cameron scored in the first match, at home to Preston North End on 2nd August and Reid scored a debut goal in that 2-1 win. In the return match at Preston, Cameron scored again as the home side reversed the score line. Cameron continued an amazing sequence of goal scoring, notching his fourth hat-trick since joining United, when the Terrors drew 4-4 at Hartlepools United. In that match, McAlpine and Henry made their first appearances for United. Just before the League Cup sectional stages kicked off the season, Kerr signed Stuart Markland on a free transfer from Berwick Rangers. The player initially came to United on a one month trial but was soon signed for the season. Patrick Murray and Eric Rooney joined the reserves after working on the ground staff and Tommy Flannigan of West Calder United was added to the second string in mid September.

Kenny Cameron, Reid and Hogg made their first appearance in major competition for United in the opening League Cup match on 10th August at Dunfermline Athletic. Gillespie and Cameron established a two goal lead but United threw the match away, conceding three times. The same 3-2 score line saw United lose at home to Clyde. Then at Aberdeen, United had only a late Mitchell penalty as consolation in a 4-1 defeat. Interest in the League Cup was already over when United faced Arbroath in a Forfarshire Cup replay on 21st August. Kenny Cameron again showed his scoring prowess, hitting all four goals as United won 4-0. Having lost the first three League Cup games, United then won the return matches, first coming from behind to beat Dunfermline Athletic 2-1. Markland made his debut on 28th August at Clyde where the Terrors were always in command to win 4-0 and when Aberdeen came to Tannadice, United won 1-0 with more than a little good fortune from a Jimmy Smith own goal.

1968-69
Back Row: *Rolland, Davie, W Smith, D Smith, Wood, Briggs, McAlpine, J Cameron*
Front: *Hogg, Reid, K Cameron, Gillespie, Mitchell, Wilson*

The good run of results continued as the league campaign got under way with a fairly easy 4-1 win at St Johnstone on 7th September, followed by a controlled 3-1 derby victory over Dundee at Tannadice. United then faced a tough trip to Aberdeen but emerged 1-0 winners after Kenny Cameron gave them an early lead. A week later, at home to Arbroath, United made it four league wins in a row but only after scoring two late goals to win 4-2. The next two matches ended in defeat. In the first, at Celtic Park, United were never completely out of contention until near the end, when the score went to 2-0, but at Kilmarnock it was all over by half time as the home side stormed forward to win 3-0. That result was preceded by the news that, for the first time in several years, United had made a trading profit for the year ended July 1967, even if it was just £1,275. Gate receipts showed a huge jump of £23,000 to £63,750, due largely to the Fairs Cities Cup matches. Transfer dealings showed a net gain of £5,000 and the trip to Dallas had brought in payments of around £15,000. In addition to the trading profit, United had also benefited by a further £36,000 from the Sportsmen's Club.

United returned to winning form with a 2-1 win over Airdrieonians on 19th October and with Mackay firmly established as first choice keeper, Davie left a few days later to join Luton Town, for a fee of £8,000. Hibs and United shared the points in a 1-1 draw at Easter Road and the Terrors stayed close to the leading teams with a 1-0 win at home to Clyde, thanks to a very late goal from Rolland. A close 2-1 result at Raith Rovers earned a hard fought two points and in an action packed game at Tannadice, another Kenny Cameron hat-trick was the highlight of a 4-2 win over Hearts. United, by then firmly established in second place, had another good day with a 2-0 win over Morton before a visit to third placed St Mirren resulted in a top class match, with both sides adopting a policy of all out attack in a 1-1 draw. The Paisley side took a 1-0 first half lead but Kenny Cameron headed a deserved United equaliser.

On 7th December, Falkirk were at Tannadice and after a goalless first half, a shaky United went 2-0 in front through Mitchell and Kenny Cameron, before the visitors scored late, to give United fans a nervous last few minutes. Then, after eight games unbeaten, a visit to Ibrox to meet Rangers ended in a 2-1 defeat for United but the result was anything but certain until the final whistle. The Terrors were back on track again a week later, winning 2-1 win over Partick Thistle but it took a goal from Rolland with five minutes left, to preserve the season's 100% home league record. At Dunfermline Athletic on 28th December, United were 2-0 down at half time but Mitchell scored a quick brace to take a point that was barely deserved. The festive season programme continued on New Year's Day, with a 4-2 home win over St Johnstone in a thrilling match. However, on the following afternoon, United were fortunate to return from Dens Park with both points in a close fought 2-1 win over Dundee. Two days later United's home record lay in tatters after Aberdeen won 4-1 with a commanding performance. A week later at Arbroath, a lacklustre United seemed to be caught on the rebound from the Aberdeen result as the determined home side won 3-1. In mid January, Kerr considered adding to the squad and whilst German centre half Dirk Stucklen trained with the reserves, he was gone after a week.

The visit of Celtic on 18th January brought in the biggest crowd of the season. United fought back from a Lennox first half goal to level through Mitchell with ten minutes left. A draw looked to be on the cards but Celtic stormed forward to score twice and win 3-1. The following week in the Scottish Cup third round tie, United were fortunate to go in front against Queen's Park after a soft penalty was converted, and the fighting amateurs never gave up and only just lost 2-1. Kilmarnock were the league visitors on 1st February and led by two goals before United rallied for a 2-2 draw, thanks to goals from Rolland and Kenny Cameron. Former Falkirk and Berwick Rangers winger, George Blues returned to Scotland after a spell in South Africa and joined United reserves on a one month trial along with Alex McCall who had been with Motherwell. Both were released in early March. United then lost Jimmy Millar when he moved to become player/manager at Raith Rovers. In between these two moves, United played Ayr United in the next round of the Scottish Cup at Tannadice. The gulf between the sides was evident in the first half hour with the visitors five goals down and early in the second half, Kenny Cameron scored United's sixth to complete a hat-trick.

The final score of 6-2 to United could have been greater had the Terrors not eased off toward the end.

Three weeks of bad weather meant that the next game was not until 1st March in the Scottish Cup. The lack of matches seemed to affect United as they lost a two goal advantage at home to Morton, who won 3-2. Relegation-threatened Raith Rovers came to Tannadice, and despite losing Mackay to injury, United deepened the Starks Park gloom with a 3-1 win. The absence of Mackay for the next match, against Hearts at Tynecastle on 8th March, gave McAlpine his league debut. The young keeper performed admirably as United lost narrowly to a single goal from Traynor near the end. United were fortunate still to have McAlpine as he had been on loan at Montrose and might have signed for them. However, his undoubted talent had already been recognised and he had been persuaded to give up his job in the accountancy offices of George Fox to sign for United on a full-time contract. After a 2-2 draw at Clyde, United's next match was at Morton, where they gained some revenge for the cup defeat, with a 2-1 win. On the same day, Jerry Kerr and Johnston Grant were involved in an motor accident in Glasgow that left the Director in hospital with several fractures. The Manager was out of action for two weeks also, and Andy Dickson was therefore in charge for the visit of St Mirren on 22nd March. United recovered from a two goal deficit to earn a point in a 2-2 draw with Hogg scoring the second very late in the game.

Another 2-2 draw was achieved at Falkirk, where the Terrors were again two goals behind and had to fight back for the point. A Fairs Cities Cup place was firmly in sight two days later as United entertained Hibs. New £8,000 signing Alan Gordon from Hearts made his debut in a comfortable 3-0 win for the Terrors. Shortly after that match, Kerr signed a new five year contract, which reputedly made him one of the highest paid managers in Scotland. The team celebrated Kerr's new deal with a 2-1 home win over Rangers. It was something of a shock result but no less than United deserved for a confident display. United followed that up with a dull 0-0 draw against Partick Thistle at Firhill.

A first round Forfarshire Cup tie against Dundee at Tannadice on 14th April produced a match worthy of a Scottish Cup final. With both sides all out to win, it was settled with a goal by Kenny Cameron for United from the penalty spot. The last two matches of the league campaign followed. A 2-2 draw with Dunfermline Athletic and a 1-0 defeat at Airdrieonians made no difference to United's final position of fifth, equalling their best ever placing and points total, which guaranteed a Fairs Cities Cup spot.

It had been a relatively successful season, achieved with a solid backbone in the team, from Mackay in goal through Rolland, Jim Cameron, Gillespie, Doug Smith and Wood, to front men Reid, Mitchell, Hogg and goal scorer extraordinaire Kenny Cameron, who had netted 36 league and cup goals. The bulk of the squad was retained although Wood refused terms to re-sign. Tommy Millar and Jackie

Graham were the only experienced players released and they were joined by reserves, Flannigan, McKeith, Robertson and Murray. United then prepared to leave for America to take part in the International League.

Football had never taken off in the USA and the International League was the latest of many attempts to get the attention of the American public. Unfortunately, it was another failure as crowds were poor throughout. United began with a match against Wolverhampton Wanderers on 4th May which ended in a 4-2 defeat. What was interesting about that match was the fact that FIFA had authorised an experiment in which there was no offside rule during the game. It seemed to open the game up but the experiment was not extended. The tournament in America was not a success for United, who had a poor run of results and only won the final two matches, 1-0 over Kilmarnock and 3-2 over Wolves. Amongst the other results, United were hammered 6-1 by West Ham United and the London club also beat United 8-2 in a friendly. Before returning home to Scotland, United showed something of their true form with a 2-0 friendly win over Dallas Tornado and in Jersey City, Gillespie scored the only goal in a memorable win over Juventus. The most positive outcome from the trip to America was the change of colours. The Directors were keen to discard black and white in favour of a more individual colour for United. It was Mrs Kerr who suggested the change to the tangerine strip favoured by the Dallas Tornado.

*Doug Smith and
Bobby Moore (West Ham)*

1969-70

New Colours

The summer of 1969 brought a rush of fresh teenage talent, in line with the Club's youth development policy. After being on the ground staff, David Munro and Eric Rooney were called up for the reserves. Former Butterburn player Bryn Williams was also signed for the second string along with Norrie Porter, a sixteen-year-old Dundonian released by Liverpool. Donald Yeaman from Kinnoull was also added, along with Ian Letford from Cambuslang Rangers and Allan Liddle of Easthouses Boys Club. A promising local schoolboy, Tommy Kierans, was also added. Later in the season Walter Bojczuk of Northfield signed on an 'S' form along with Gordon Menzies of Royston Boys Club and Alan Balfour and Alan Devlin both of Tynecastle Boys Club. Unfortunately, of these teenagers, only Devlin made any sort of mark at Tannadice, whilst Liddle and Letford made just a few first team appearances between them. The others remained at reserve level. The only experienced player added to the squad over the summer was Alec Stuart, a free transfer from Dundee. Unhappy at Tannadice, Wood had refused new terms and requested a transfer.

The Club was looking forward to the new season with the mouth-watering prospect of a Fairs Cities Cup tie against holders, Newcastle United. Financially the Club were by this time on a very solid base, which allowed the Directors to maintain season ticket prices at the same level as the previous year. Players' wages were then at £30 weekly, with a generous bonus scheme which would add an extra payment of £16 per week if United were in one of the top two places. Below that the bonus was £8 for third/fourth and £4 for fifth/sixth.

For the pre-season warm-up, Kerr had arranged a stiff test for United with three matches against English opposition, all away from home. The first match was at Everton on 2nd August where, wearing the new tangerine strip for the first time, United took the lead through Scott but Everton won comfortably, 4-1. Against Millwall two days afterwards, a late goal gave the hosts a 2-1 win.

On the next evening, the exertions of such a hectic schedule became evident as Ipswich Town won 3-0. It might have been more if Mackay had not been in such good form.

1969-70
Back Row: Briggs, Williams, Gordon, McAlpine, Mackay, Bremner, Stuart, W Smith
Middle: Jerry Kerr, Johnstone, Rolland, Henry, Gillespie, Munro, Reid, Brown, D Smith, Yeaman, Markland
Front: J Cameron, Dunne, Hogg, Keirans, K Cameron, Porter, Mitchell, Rooney, Scott

Stuart, who had played for the first time against Everton, made a scoring debut in major competition against Hearts on 9th August in the first of the League Cup matches. The pre-season woes appeared to have been left behind as he netted the second and United cruised to a 2-0 lead at Tannadice, but after half time, it all went wrong for United and the visitors netted three, to win 3-2. Worse was to follow at Morton, where the home side left United reeling after a 4-1 defeat. Letford then made his debut along with Bremner at St Mirren in a fighting performance, from which United returned with a 1-0 win, thanks to a Kenny Cameron goal. Morton made the trip to Tannadice and won 2-0, and at Hearts it was a single goal defeat for United. The final match of the League Cup section against St Mirren at Tannadice was witnessed by Keith Birkenshaw of Newcastle United, there to learn about his future opposition. He left none the wiser as United ended the match with a 2-1 win after recovering from a poor first half. The visitor from Newcastle would also have heard the news that United's reserve keeper, McAlpine, had undergone an operation for ligament damage and had been replaced by sixteen year old Ged Reilly from Montrose.

The league campaign started on 30th August with a good performance from keeper Mackay as United drew 0-0 with Rangers at Tannadice. The Terrors then struggled at Clyde and were fortunate to get a 2-2 draw, capitalising on two defensive errors. A visit to Morton saw the Greenock side totally overwhelm United to win 6-0, although at half time there appeared to be little between the teams, with the home side just one goal ahead. With the first leg of the Fairs Cities Cup tie against Newcastle United just days away, United then produced a stunning performance to beat Airdrieonians 5-2.

It was a memorable night for the 15,000 fans (including 5,000 supporting the visitors) when Newcastle United came to Tannadice on 15th September 1969. Their star striker, Wyn 'The Leap' Davies, scored with two headers in the first twelve minutes for a deserved lead. United played well in a match that swung from end to end, but came up against a side in top form. A head wound to Mackay meant he had to leave the action. That gave Reilly his debut with eighteen minutes left and five minutes later, Scott headed United's only goal. The next match was a local derby against Dundee at Dens Park. With Mackay restored to the goal, wearing a protective scrum cap, the Terrors emerged 2-1 winners with Gillespie netting the second from the spot, to secure the points.

A visit from high flying St Johnstone a week later gave United a stern test, but they emerged 1-0 winners against a Perth side that had scored 47 times in thirteen previous matches. That set the players up for the second leg in Newcastle on 1st October. The Tangerines were the better team on the night, but the home side scored the only goal of the match during injury time for a 3-1 aggregate win. Three days later United continued their good run of league form with a deserved 2-0 win at Motherwell, followed by a midweek visit from Dallas Tornado in a friendly that United won 3-2. Another two points were then collected as the Tangerines beat Ayr United 3-1 with some ease at Tannadice. A week later a Hogg hat-trick was the highlight as United blitzed an Inverness Select 10-2 in a friendly in the Highland capital. United then added former Hearts player Billy Higgins to the reserve strength, although it took several weeks to obtain clearance from the football authorities in South Africa where he had been playing.

The match on 25th October against St Mirren marked a debut in major competition for Henry, who had been sidelined since the start of the season with a broken foot. A defensive approach by the Buddies almost won them the points with a breakaway goal in the second half, but United wore them down and won 3-1, with all three goals coming in the last twenty minutes. Against Partick Thistle a week later, United had all the possession but won by just a single goal, scored late in the match by Mitchell. At Pittodrie, the Tangerines survived a relentless Aberdeen attack to leave with a point from a goalless draw. United's luck ran out at Tannadice against Hibs who won with a single goal, as both sides put on a great display of football. A few days earlier, Wood finally re-signed for United. He had been for trials with other clubs including Nottingham Forest but had decided that he would be better playing for United, even if it was in the reserves. United then lost Stuart to Montrose as their new player/manager and shortly after he left, he took youngster Porter to Links Park on loan.

United were still amongst the leading pack with a European place again the target. The challenge was maintained with a 1-0 away win over Raith Rovers and that lifted the Club into second place in the table. That position would have been consolidated if Kenny Cameron had not missed twice from the spot, as United drew 2-2 at home with Kilmarnock. Dunfermline Athletic then saw their unbeaten home run come to an end as United came from behind to win 3-2 at East End Park but United's challenge was about to become derailed. Two visits to Glasgow to play each half of the Old Firm ended in defeat. At Ibrox, Rangers were a little fortunate in their 2-1 win but against Celtic, United were thrashed 7-2, although they were not quite as bad as the score line suggests. The Terrors then slipped further behind after picking up just a point in a 2-2 draw at Hearts and at St Johnstone on New Year's Day, the home side won by a single goal. Two days later another derby win was recorded. United scored three goals before half time to control the match and beat Dundee 4-1. That was followed by a hard tussle at Tannadice against Hearts, with the visitors winning 3-2. A week later a Mitchell hat-trick in the first half had United 3-2 up at Airdrieonians but the home side took full control after the break to win 6-3. On 24th January, United just eased Ayr United out of the Scottish Cup with a 1-0 win, thanks to a Mitchell penalty.

In January there was some transfer activity as Wood had talks with Crystal Palace and then Falkirk. A swap deal for Craig Watson was agreed with the Brockville club but Wood could not agree terms and it fell through. Earlier, a similar arrangement involving Traynor from Hearts had also failed to materialise. United did sign a new player though, bringing in Morris Stevenson from Luton Town on a free transfer. An incredible match ended the month as United entertained Morton. Both sides adopted an all out attack, leading to a score line of 4-4 with just a few minutes remaining. Then a pass back beat the Morton keeper to give United a fifth goal and full points. United then travelled to Celtic Park for the next round of the Scottish Cup, only to suffer a comprehensive 4-0 defeat.

Stevenson made his debut on 11th February as United went into the final third of the league campaign against Kilmarnock at Rugby Park and lost 3-1. United then faced Newcastle United for the third time that season, in a friendly at St James' Park and a close game ended 3-2 for the home side. On 25th February, United played out an entertaining goalless draw with Motherwell, before the last game of the month was won 3-2 at Ayr United, with the Terrors scoring a deserved winner late in the game. Kenny Cameron then continued his astonishing record in the Forfarshire Cup, with five of United's goals in a 10-1 win over Brechin City.

Celtic came to Tannadice on 7th March and left with both points in a hard fought 2-0 win. United were in determined mood and matched the Glasgow side in every department but came up against a resolute defence. In a midweek match at home to Clyde a few days later, United won 3-1 comfortably but then lost by the same score line at St Mirren, where defensive slackness cost the points.

Eric Rooney made his only first team appearance in the Forfarshire Cup final against Arbroath on 18th March at Tannadice. United won 2-0 thanks to goals from Wilson and Gordon but it was a close run match with the Red Lichties giving United a difficult time. Three days later, United notched their first league win ever at Firhill against Partick Thistle, coming from behind to win 2-1. A fine 2-0 win over an uncharacteristically defensive Aberdeen kept United on track for the Fairs Cities Cup place. The Tangerines then suffered a 3-1 defeat to Hibs at Easter Road but a 4-2 win over Raith Rovers, which included a Mitchell hat-trick, brought European football again, despite a last game of the season 3-1 defeat at home to Dunfermline Athletic.

In late April, Wood finally left Tannadice to join Hearts, with Tommy Traynor moving to United in exchange. The Club had already indicated that they would listen to offers for Mitchell and Hogg before the list of players to be released was announced. Hogg was then included along with reserves, Reilly, Bremner, Brown, Johnstone, Porter, Rooney and Munro. A veteran of fifteen years at Tannadice, Jimmy Briggs was also allowed to go. Although he considered taking a coaching position, he joined Montrose a few months later. Recently added 'S' signings were brothers Ian and Gordon McDonald who had been signed as reserves along with Ian Clyde from Melbourne Thistle, and George Hill, who had been released by Dundee.

Ten years after gaining promotion, United were now a firmly established First Division side. For the second season in succession they finished fifth in the table, with a team built on a solid defence of Mackay, Rolland, Jim Cameron, Gillespie and Doug Smith, all of whom turned in over forty league and cup appearances. Mitchell was the top scorer with 20 goals from 40 games. A measure of how far the Club had progressed was evident when the Directors indicated their intention to include a social club at Tannadice, with the addition of a bar and rooms below the South Stand.

United turned down a tour of Portugal but invitations to play two games in Mexico and a match in Greece were accepted. During the trip to Mexico, United played sides containing a number of internationals who would soon take part in the World Cup. The Tangerines lost the first match 6-0, struggling in a high altitude venue. The second game was also a defeat but the 2-0 score line at least restored some respectability. After their return home, United were in trouble with the SFA over the first of these games, accused of breaking the rules by playing, what was in effect, an international side. However, the Club argued that they could not have known who the players in the sides were and after deliberations lasting six months the SFA accepted that and cleared United of any wrongdoing.

That United lost 3-1 to Panathinaikos in Greece only three days after leaving Mexico is no surprise, bearing in mind the arduous travel schedule that had to be undertaken. It is also no wonder that the Directors turned down two offers to take part in tournaments in Spain in June.

1970-71

Continued Progress

There was little rest for the Manager during July. He added Steve Petrie and Rangers free transfer Tommy Matchett to the reserves and brought seventeen-year-old former Queen of the South forward Ian Reid to Tannadice from Nottingham Forest on a free transfer. Better known in later years as a coach and manager at several clubs, 'S' signing Dick Campbell was also called up for the reserves. Later in the month the last remaining unsigned player, Alec Reid, put pen to paper, perhaps encouraged by the Directors' announcement that all first team and reserve players had been granted an increase in their basic wage and the same bonus structure was agreed for the forthcoming season. Mitchell was still on the transfer list and on 25th July he went to Newcastle United for a fee reported at £50,000. Even without that money, the Club were not short of ready cash and with approval from the council for the £20,000 project, the plan to add a social club progressed. Also approved was the addition of a souvenir shop in the South Stand. At the end of August, Club Treasurer George Fox confirmed that the financial situation was the best it had ever been and there was cash in hand which was not earmarked for any specific purpose.

Following his move to England, Mitchell made his first appearance for his new club in a friendly at Tannadice on 1st August and for United, both Ian Reid and Clyde made their debuts, the latter as a substitute. United were two goals behind before Ian Reid pulled one back and although the Terrors lost 2-1, a draw would not have been unjustified. However, in the return friendly at St James' Park a few days later, with Traynor making his first appearance, the home side were far superior and should have won by much more than the single second half goal they scored. On the same day, United found out that they would be meeting Grasshoppers of Zurich in the Fairs Cities Cup.

Traynor and Ian Reid made their debuts in major competition as the season got under way with a 1-1 draw in a League Cup visit to Clyde on 8th August. It was an uninspiring performance from the Terrors and it took a late Wilson goal to secure the point. A few days later, United beat Hearts 2-1, thanks to an early Ian Reid goal and a Wilson effort. Hearts scored after the break but also missed the chance to level from the spot. A trip to Celtic Park in the next game produced a 2-2 draw, with Gordon scoring in the final minute but United deserved the point, matching the home side in every area. The League Cup section continued with a goalless draw in an attacking performance at Hearts. Then at home to Clyde, a Henry equaliser in the second half brought another deserved point in a 1-1 draw. By the time Celtic came to Tannadice, the Glasgow side had already won the section but United completed the six games undefeated with a 2-2 draw.

1970-71

Back Row: J Cameron, Rolland, Williams, Gordon, W Smith, McAlpine, Mackay, Letford, Gillespie, Devlin, K Cameron

Middle: I Reid, Hill, A Reid, Matchett, Markland, Liddle, Henry, Petrie, Wilson

Front: Campbell, Dunne, Clyde, Scott, Jerry Kerr, D Smith, Balfour, Stevenson, Bojczuk

The league campaign began on 29th August. United took the lead through a Doug Smith penalty at home to Hibs but the visitors levelled and 1-1 was a fair outcome. It was the same score line a week later at St Johnstone, where United took the lead from an own goal. The visit of Dundee to Tannadice on 12th September was eagerly awaited and in an entertaining match won 3-2 by United, the fans were not disappointed. The Tangerines held the upper hand and led twice, but Dundee equalised both times before Gillespie got the winner. It was the perfect warm-up before the first leg of the Fairs Cities Cup tie at home to Grasshoppers of Zurich on 15th September. Ground and enclosure prices for the European match had been maintained at the usual level and only a small increase had been made for stand tickets. The 8,500 fans at the match were stunned when the visitors scored either side of the interval to lead by two goals in a game dominated by the Terrors.

However, Ian Reid pulled one back, before United earned a 3-2 win, with goals from Markland and Alec Reid.

On the following Saturday, United appeared to be suffering a European hangover, and after losing the first goal in just ten minutes, they went down 3-0 at Morton. A week later, Rangers came to Tannadice and won 2-0. United played well in the first half before losing two quick second half goals, but they never gave up. The same attitude was evident as United went to Switzerland for the second leg against Grasshoppers on 30th September. Gordon had two great opportunities to put the match beyond doubt but then the Swiss side came at United in strength and Mackay kept United in the competition with three outstanding saves. United were under the cosh but played a controlled game and a goalless draw ensured progress to the next round. The draw, made the following day, paired United with the formidable Sparta Prague.

It was back to gathering league points on 3rd October at Clyde, where a 2-1 win was achieved with a good first half showing and a winner from Gordon against the run of play after the interval. Gordon was on target again, with a goal in each half against Airdrieonians at Tannadice, but whilst retaining possession for much of the game, United allowed the visitors to come back twice and it ended 2-2. The visit to Kilmarnock a week later resulted in a 2-1 defeat as United again failed to make the best of their play after Gordon had opened the scoring. The team then left for the Fairs Cities Cup tie in Czechoslovakia on 21st October. The match in Prague brought another splendid United performance but Sparta took an early lead before United took the initiative and Traynor equalised midway through the first half. United then maintained control until they lost Mackay to injury late in the game. McAlpine took over in goal for just his second major appearance and with just ten minutes left the home side scored their second. Worse was to follow when Rolland was sent off for kicking the ball away at a Sparta free kick. Then the home side scored again in the final minute, to win 3-1. The team suffered another European backlash at home to Dunfermline Athletic in the next game and after leading by two goals, United tired and it ended 2-2.

Twin brothers Joe and Sandy White from Glenrothes provisionally signed in October and there was a further addition to the playing staff with Harry Mollison of St Francis joining on an 'S' form. Alec Rice from Club Romano signed a provisional form and joined the ground staff. Following a 4-0 defeat at Aberdeen on 31st October, with just McAlpine available in goal, George Whisker was signed from Lochore Welfare. He received the swiftest promotion of any United keeper when he was named as the substitute goalkeeper for the visit of Sparta Prague on 4th November. Kerr also tried, unsuccessfully, to sign an experienced full back to cover for the suspended Rolland and the job was given to Markland instead. On the night, 8,500 fans braved heavy rain and Gordon reduced the deficit with half an hour played. United came close to scoring several times but chances were missed, in particular a Traynor effort in the last minute, and United went out on a 3-2 aggregate.

The league campaign continued on 7th November with a 4-2 win over Ayr United with a reduced attendance after the BBC had erroneously announced the match was off! At Hearts a week later, United were holding their own and were denied a good penalty claim with ten minutes of the game played. They then lost Rolland to injury, which gave Liddle his debut as a substitute. United then conceded the only goal of the game. More players were signed, including teenager Martin Reid, who arrived on a one month trial in the reserves after an unsuccessful spell at Charlton Athletic. George Wood signed on a provisional form from West Calder United. Henry, who had gained international recognition playing for the Scottish League against League of Ireland, put in a transfer request around this time, stating he wanted away because he was the victim of verbal abuse from the fans. His request was turned down. November continued with a 2-2 draw at home to Motherwell, who came from behind twice for a point, in a game neither side deserved to lose. A week later United returned with a 2-0 win from a dull game against Cowdenbeath and on 5th December, the Terrors were unfortunate to lose 2-1 at home to Celtic. At Falkirk a week later, United had Traynor to thank for an equaliser and Mackay saved a penalty in a 1-1 draw.

Before the next match on 19th December, the Directors announced a profit of almost £11,000 on trading income of £74,000 for the year to July 1969. In addition a further £37,000 was received in donations from the Sportsmen's Club. United then signed centre forward Jackie Copland from Stranraer for £10,000. Letford was offered in part exchange but the Stair Park side insisted on a cash only transaction. However, Letford did go to Stranraer three weeks later on loan. Copland made his debut that weekend against St Mirren as United won 2-1 with both goals coming from Stevenson. On Boxing Day, United met Hibs at Easter Road and Copland scored a very late goal as United notched a 1-0 win against the run of play. In a reversal of that situation on New Year's Day, St Johnstone stole both points, beating United 2-0 at Tannadice.

Devlin made his debut as a substitute and scored one of the goals on 9th January against Morton but United lost 3-2 when the visitors scored the winner with the last kick of the ball. United's next match was away to Rangers on 16th January, the first match there since the tragic Ibrox Disaster two weeks earlier. Many lives had been lost when barriers on Stairway 13 collapsed and caused a horrific accident. A minute's silence was observed for the victims. The match was played in a subdued atmosphere and United left with a deserved 1-1 draw thanks to an Alec Reid equaliser in the second half. Following that match, United faced Clydebank away in the Scottish Cup but a goalless draw meant a midweek replay at Tannadice. It was a different story at home and United completely overwhelmed the Bankies with four second half goals to win 5-1.

In early February, United gave a trial to centre half Joe Cruickshank of Chelsea but he was not offered terms. Williams, who had never played beyond reserve level, went to Forfar Athletic on a free transfer. The league programme continued on 6th February with a 2-1 win at Airdrieonians, where United came from behind to win with a quick double from Gordon just after half time. The Scottish Cup was next. At home to Aberdeen, United should have done better than a 1-1 draw, with just a Doug Smith penalty to show for the lion's share of play. In the replay at Pittodrie, McAlpine kept the Dons at bay in the first half but just when United looked to be gaining the upper hand, a long range effort gave the home side the lead. A late second goal sealed a 2-0 win for the Dons, and United were left with just the league to concentrate on.

They were good value in their 3-2 win at home to Kilmarnock on 20th February. But relegation-threatened Dunfermline Athletic took the initiative and won 3-1 when United went to East End Park the following week. Three days later, the White twins, Hill and Gordon McDonald all made debuts, as a young United side played Raith Rovers in a friendly that ended 1-1. Another friendly was arranged on 5th March and a strong United line up went down 2-0 at Partick Thistle. A 2-0 league defeat at home to Aberdeen was followed by a 1-0 reversal at Ayr United but on 20th March, United produced a stunning 4-1 win over Hearts at Tannadice. Shortly before that game the unsettled Dunne was handed a free transfer and he was replaced a week later by Joe Watson, signed from Nottingham Forest after a successful trial in the reserves.

United went to Motherwell next and were leading 2-1 at half time but had to endure sustained pressure from the home side to take both points. On 3rd April, a Kenny Cameron hat-trick did most of the damage in a 4-2 win over Cowdenbeath. Doug Smith scored the third goal in that game, from the spot, to record United's 3,000[th] Scottish League goal. A Monday evening visit to Dens Park was next in the fixture list and debut winger Watson stole the show. He hit the bar twice and provided much of the ammunition as United beat Dundee with more ease than the 3-2 score line suggests. The win at Dens Park was followed by a 1-1 draw at Celtic where Rolland gave United the lead. The Tangerines lost concentration only briefly in a match they controlled and Celtic equalised. Clyde were the midweek visitors at Tannadice next and a nine man defence by the Bully Wee was only breached by a late Doug Smith penalty as United won 1-0. With United still on the fringes of a Fairs Cities Cup place, a 3-1 win over Falkirk was welcome. However, after losing the last league match of the season, 2-1 to a St Mirren side battling for First Division survival, the chance of European football for 1971-72 evaporated. The last match of the season was a 5-0 win for United over Forres Mechanics, in a testimonial for Bob Porter.

Scott had been released in early April and signed for Dundee. At the end of the season Letford went to Stranraer permanently. The other players released were Balfour, Clyde, Hill, Matchett, Yeaman and Liddle. The remainder were re-signed, except for Alec Reid and Markland who initially refused the terms offered. St Columba's players Steve Mellon and Graeme Payne were signed on

'S' forms and the White twins were called up and signed on professional forms. In late May, Frank Esposito joined the ground staff.

The sixth place league finish was considered satisfactory, although everyone at Tannadice was disappointed that the Club lost out on a Fairs Cities Cup place

The first Souvenir Shop – located in the South Stand

to neighbours Dundee. Gordon was the top scorer with 20 league and cup goals from his 44 appearances. A settled line up also saw the emergence of McAlpine in goal with 30 appearances and Rolland, Jim Cameron, Doug Smith, Henry, Wilson and Alec Reid racked up over forty appearances each. Financially, United were one of the healthiest football clubs in the country and the future was secure. Applications for membership of the new Dundee United Social Club were pouring in to Tannadice. It opened for the first time on 20th August 1971, around a month after the Souvenir Shop.

1971-72

Jim McLean – The Third Key to Success

It had been intended that a three match tour in East Africa would take place in late May, but negotiations were not concluded to the satisfaction of the Club and that trip was cancelled just days before United were due to fly out. Instead, a pre-season tour of South Korea was organised at short notice, with a guarantee that the hosts would contribute around £16,000 to the cost of the trip. United also arranged pre-season friendlies at Blackpool, MSV Duisburg in West Germany and Antwerp in Holland but the Club declined an invitation to play against Dutch sides DWS Amsterdam and Telstar. Before leaving for the Korean tour, Kerr called Mollison up for the reserves and then signed Billy Gray from Morton for an undisclosed fee. Gray was the only experienced player added to the squad for 1971-72.

On tour in South Korea

United returned from South Korea undefeated, with two wins and a draw. However, once again they faced an SFA inquiry, just as they had after the trip to Mexico, after an alleged breach of the rules, which precluded a Scottish club side playing any national team. Prior to the tour, Kerr had pointedly informed the

Koreans that United would not play the national side. He repeated his argument of the previous season to the SFA, that if this had happened, United were blameless, as they could not possibly have known. In the end the SFA accepted the reasoning and no further action was taken. The match against Antwerp was cancelled, just as Gray joined the pre-season preparations for the match at Blackpool, where United were the better side, but lost 3-1. The trip to Duisburg turned into a nightmare as United turned in a jittery performance. They were hammered 6-0 and had Alec Reid sent off after twenty minutes. The Manager made few excuses but there was a greater than usual injured list after the match. On his return, Kerr added Frank Campbell from St Francis to the reserves. He was joined shortly after by Douglas Findlater from West Bromwich Albion on a month's trial, along with George Butler from Broughty Athletic, on a provisional form. Stand season tickets went on sale at £7.25 with a ground ticket costing £5.

The season opened on 14th August with a League Cup tie at Tannadice, where United won a hard fought game against Kilmarnock 1-0, with Gray making his debut in major competition. At Easter Road in the next match, United lost 2-0 after Hibs scored two quick goals in the second half, and then defended until the end. Back at Tannadice, United were twice in front but it ended 2-2 with Motherwell, in a match United really should have won. When Hibs came to Tannadice on 25th August, United were confident of a result and with just ten minutes left, the match was finely poised at 1-1. Jim Cameron was then sent off and Hibs took full advantage, netting three times for a flattering 4-1 win. That effectively ended any interest United had in the League Cup and they lost the next match 4-2 at Kilmarnock. In the final match of the section at Motherwell, a Rolland double and one from Alec Reid gave United a 3-1 win to ensure they did not finish in bottom spot.

The league campaign did not get off to a good start at home to St Johnstone on 4th September. United had a commanding 3-1 lead at half time but the Perth side recovered to level the match at 3-3. The game that followed was one of the highest scoring competitive derby matches between United and Dundee. At Dens Park, where United were unbeaten in league meetings since 9th September 1961, a pulsating match finished 6-4 to the Dark Blues. A previously solid United defence conceded another six goals when they were soundly beaten 6-2 at

Dundee United Social Club at Tannadice
– opened 20th August 1971

Derby County in the Texaco Cup. They then lost 4-1 to Hibs at Tannadice for the second time in less than a month. Surprisingly, the Manager did little more than tinker with the line up and he became the target for the frustration felt by some fans. The Club's financial statements for the year ended July 1970 were made public around this time. On trading income of almost £115,000, including the Mitchell transfer fee, United recorded a profit of over £23,000. In addition, the Sportsmen's Club had donated a further £34,000. There was therefore no shortage of money.

In late September, United indicated that they were negotiating the return of Ian Mitchell in exchange for Alec Reid, who had let it be known that he wanted away from United. An offer from Carlisle United, involving a swap with Tommy Murray, had already been rejected, and the Mitchell/Reid swap went through a month later with no cash changing hands.

The league campaign continued with a 2-0 defeat at Kilmarnock on 25th September. A brief return to form brought a win over Derby County in the second leg of the Texaco Cup, although it looked grim for United as they conceded twice in the opening stages. Sandy White made his first appearance in major competition in that match but it was Copland who caught the eye, with a goal either side of half time. Devlin scored in between these, for a respectable 3-2 result on the night. Copland was on target again, with a hat-trick in the first half of a 5-0 home win over Airdrieonians and he netted again in a 2-1 win at Morton.

1971-72
Back Row: J Cameron, Traynor, Whisker, Mackay, McAlpine, W Smith, J White, Stevenson
Middle: Jerry Kerr, Watson, Esposito, Gillespie, A White, Gordon, Campbell, A Reid, Rice,
*   Gray, Andy Dickson, Doug Cowie.*
Front: Rolland, Wood, K Cameron, I Reid, D Smith, Devlin, Wilson, Markland, Henry

With Doug Smith already out injured, Watson was hospitalised just before the visit of Rangers on 16th October. United were 4-0 down to the Glasgow side at half time and the final score of 5-1 to the visitors could have been worse. Smith was back the next week and Mitchell made his comeback as United recovered to record a good 3-0 win at Clyde. However, the Terrors were then beaten 5-3 at home by Falkirk, a result made worse by a Smith penalty miss, Rolland's sending off and a serious injury to Gray who was carried off and taken to hospital. At around this time a leading bookmaker offered to install an electric scoreboard at Tannadice and the SFA gave permission, but the project was not advanced.

Stevenson had been out with a long-term injury and he returned to face Partick Thistle at Firhill, where they paraded the League Cup they had won two weeks earlier after famously beating Celtic 4-1 at Hampden Park. A McQuade hat-trick of headers for the home side gave the Jags a 3-1 win against a tired United. Just a few days later on 11th November, United called their first ever press conference, to announce the resignation of Jerry Kerr. The longest serving manager in Scotland, Kerr was stepping up to become General Manager, to leave team matters to a new, younger man. The Directors fully supported the Manager who had been under enormous pressure. His position was made all the more untenable by the barracking from a section of the support. Kerr remained in charge and in his final few weeks he added provisional signings, George Steel from Linlithgow Rose, John Ogilvie (East Craigie) and Brian Rankin (a nephew of Dennis Gillespie) from Vale of Clyde. The day after United announced the Kerr news, coach Doug Cowie decided that he was leaving Tannadice.

The next match brought a visit from Celtic and against the odds United held a one goal half time lead, but the Glasgow side then took control to win 5-1 with ease. Dunfermline Athletic made a bid for Kenny Cameron, offering cash plus Pat Gardner but they were rebuffed. At East Fife in very wintry conditions, Traynor got the goal that mattered in a 1-0 win. Then, despite the prevailing uncertainty and speculation over the new Manager, United beat Motherwell 2-0 at Tannadice, with Mollison making his debut.

Although the names of George Farm, Davie White and Alec Stuart were all touted for the United Manager's job, Neil Mochan emerged as the likeliest candidate. It therefore came as a surprise to many when, on 3rd December, Jim McLean was appointed. A coach at Dundee (who had just lost their manager John Prentice, replaced by Davie White), McLean had not even applied for the job at Tannadice. He had been approached by the Directors of Dundee United and accepted their offer with little hesitation. Although not due to take charge of the team until Monday, the new Manager was in the dugout the next day as United faced Hearts at Tynecastle and lost 3-2. It was perhaps unfortunate for Mollison in particular, who gave Hearts the lead with an own goal, in his second and last game for United.

McLean made his mark as soon as he took charge on 6th December. He started the players on double training stints for a minimum of three weeks, in order to assess the squad. He also attended all the evening sessions with the part-timers and 'S' signings. He was quickly into the transfer market, but an enquiry concerning Preben Arntoft of Blackburn Rovers, brought a request for a fee in excess of the £13,000 they had paid Newcastle United only months before. Needless to say, United did not make a formal offer.

McLean's first game in charge officially was at home to Ayr United on 11th December. The 2-2 draw was a point dropped as United led twice, only for the visitors to level each time. Injuries became a real problem in the week before the next game at Aberdeen, where Joe White came in for his debut in major competition. It was only thanks to McAlpine that the Dons won just 3-0, when their dominance could have resulted in a much bigger defeat. The new boss chalked up his first win a week later on Christmas Day, against Dunfermline Athletic. Jim Cameron scored his first and only goal, as United won 3-2 with a good team performance. The New Year's Day match at St Johnstone ended in a 2-0 defeat on the same day that Frank Kopel joined United on a free transfer from Blackburn Rovers. He had been recommended to the Manager by Ian Mitchell. Initially Kopel arrived on a one month trial but was quickly signed up on a longer contract. Two days later, two evenly matched sides served up a 1-1 draw in the Dundee derby at Tannadice. That was followed by a record bid by United for Dundee half back Doug Houston. The offer was rejected, as was McLean's initial offer to St Mirren for Archie Knox but he signed soon after for a fee estimated to be in excess of £5,000. Almost unnoticed, the new Manager also completed the 'S' form signing of St Johns schoolboy Dave Narey, and just over a month later, tucked away in the pages of the *Evening Telegraph,* was the name of another 'S' signing, Stobswell Secondary schoolboy, John Holt.

Knox went straight into the side to face Hibs at Easter Road on 8th January in a game that was much closer that the 3-0 result in favour of Hibs suggests. United were on the fringes of the relegation battle and lost 2-1 at home to Kilmarnock a week later. However, a sequence of transfers was about to turn the season around. On 21st January, United signed Pat Gardner from Dunfermline Athletic for £6,000, concluding negotiations that had been ongoing for six weeks. On the same day, Alan Gordon who worked in Edinburgh and could not get time off to attend training in Dundee, as required under the new regime, left United to join Hibs for a fee of £12,000. To complete a trio of moves involving United, George Fleming was signed from Hearts for £7,000. Kopel and Gardner made their debuts in the next match, which United won 2-1 at home to Morton on 29th January. United then went out of the Scottish Cup, beaten 4-0 by Aberdeen at Tannadice and there could be little cause for complaint at the score line. Wilson was the next player to leave Tannadice, turning down a move to Dunfermline Athletic to join Dumbarton. Then, on 12th February, with Fleming making his debut, United had the better of the chances but lost 1-0 at Rangers. A week later, United faced Clyde and were two goals behind but laid siege to the visitors' goal and eventually secured a point in a 3-3 draw.

With no league match scheduled the following week, United entertained Peterhead in a Dewar Shield tie and won 3-0 easily. On 4th March, the Tangerines were fortunate to return from Falkirk with a point from a 1-1 draw. It also emerged that the out of favour Henry, was going to Fulham for £50,000 and he left for London two days later. However, within days he was back at Tannadice after Fulham refused to complete the deal, because they said the player was carrying an injury, a fact they had been made well aware of. United referred the matter to the Scottish League but no action was taken. Henry therefore remained a United player for the time being. More new players arrived with the addition of Brian Eddie from Whitburn Juniors and teenager Allan Forsyth from Larkhall Thistle. United also had Jim Robertson in the second eleven.

With Copland playing at right half, United recorded a good 1-0 win on 11th March, at home to a stubborn Partick Thistle. After the 1970-71 Forfarshire Cup final 2-0 defeat by Dundee a week later, Copland's move to the half back line became permanent. United then dropped a point at home to East Fife, who scored a late equaliser for a 2-2 draw and that was followed by a 1-1 draw at Airdrieonians. Relegation worries began to disappear with a Knox goal in a 1-0 win at Motherwell. A few days later at Gayfield, a resilient Arbroath eventually succumbed to a 6-2 Forfarshire Cup defeat by United, with Gardner and Kopel each scoring a hat-trick. United then collected another two valuable league points against Hearts, coming from behind to win 3-2, with two goals in the last ten minutes. In a testimonial for Charlie Dunn at Brechin City, Ian Reid scored twice to level the match, but the best goal in the 3-2 win came from a neat Kenny Cameron back-heeler.

United travelled to meet an in-form Ayr United on 15th April as the season drew to a conclusion and lost 4-2, with George McLean scoring all four home goals. A week later a 2-0 win over Aberdeen was well deserved, and just as deserved was the 3-0 defeat at Celtic Park that followed. The final league match was at Dunfermline Athletic, where United's 1-0 win relegated the Fife side. A 2-0 Forfarshire Cup win at Forfar Athletic on 3rd May brought a first appearance for Eddie, and the last at United for the long-serving Dennis Gillespie, who came on as a substitute. He had been offered a part-time coaching position but declined, preferring to keep playing. He was therefore released along with Mackay and Stevenson. Those three were the most experienced players allowed to go and they were joined by Watson plus reserves, Mollison, Whisker, Menzies, Gordon McDonald, Ian McDonald, Petrie, Rice, Wood, Steel, Campbell and Esposito. Markland was transfer listed, whilst the majority of the first team players and the rest of the reserves were retained.

After such a poor start to the season, the final position of ninth in the league was perhaps better than expected. With a mid season change of Manager, it was not surprising that there were more alterations to the side over the campaign than there had been in recent seasons. The most consistent of the players were McAlpine, and defenders Rolland and Cameron. Another indication of the lack of a settled line up was that top scorer Copland had only just managed to get into double figures with 11 goals. His closest challenger was Gordon with 10, and he had left in January. There would be no European football for United fans in 1972-73 but top level English opposition was assured with qualification for the Texaco Cup once more.

It had been intended to undertake a tour of Iran but an earthquake in that region in April caused that trip to be cancelled. United immediately arranged an alternative trip to Nigeria at the end of May. The Tangerines played five games in strength-sapping heat, winning just once and recording two draws. The players suffered badly, with only Doug Smith completing the full ninety minutes in all the games. The tour party included Sandy Davie who had returned to United in mid May from Southampton, for a fee of around £5,000. Even after the team returned home on 12th June, they were still in demand and a three match tour of Holland was declined.

1972-73

Quiet Dissatisfaction

Outwardly, there appeared to be little happening at Tannadice, but the new Manager was quietly preparing for his first full season in charge. The seeds of success that had been planted back in 1956 with the formation of Dundee United Sportsmen's Club, followed by the appointment of Jerry Kerr in 1959, were about to bear fruit. McLean would become the third and final key, which unlocked the door to success for Dundee United.

Like his predecessor, McLean had an eye for spotting talent and soon brought in many more provisionally signed young players and 'S' forms, including Graeme Payne and Jim Coates (St Columba's), Jim Spink (Fintry CC), Graeme Rogers and Jim Lorimer (Broughty Athletic), Allan Boath (Celtic), Cammie Fraser (Invergowrie Boys Club and later to play for Dundee, Rangers and Hearts) and Robert McKell (Sandyhills). In mid July, Bobby Gray was signed on a one month trial after he was released by Nottingham Forest and soon after, teenager Ian Steen from Blackpool was added. To conclude the pre-season signings, McLean brought in Joe Fascione who had been with Chelsea before moving to South Africa in 1969. With the high priority given to the development of youth players, additional coaching assistance was added when former Forfar Athletic manager Ian Campbell joined United.

Three pre-season matches were arranged in England, beginning at Crystal Palace on 29th July. It was not a good opening as United were outplayed with just a Knox consolation in a 3-1 defeat. Two days later, non league Guildford Town gave United a tough workout in a 1-1 draw. Then on 2nd August, the same result was recorded at Bournemouth where a fair outcome was achieved with Fleming's very late goal. Fascione was the only new player to see action in these matches but he was released soon after. The last of the pre-season matches was at home and McLean expected it to be the toughest test. MSV Duisburg were the opposition and United were looking for revenge for the 6-0 hammering twelve

166

months earlier. Knox scored early in the match but the visitors equalised against the run of play. United went on to dominate but could not find another goal and it ended in a disappointing 1-1 draw.

The Scottish season began as usual with League Cup action and in the opening match at Tannadice on 12th August, United won 2-0 against Dunfermline Athletic, but only secured the victory with a late Doug Smith penalty. He scored from the spot again for the first of three late United goals in the next match against Kilmarnock, to help United to a flattering 3-2 win after they had struggled at Rugby Park for much of the game. There was no struggle three days later however, as United thrashed Stenhousemuir 5-0 at Tannadice with the captain opening the scoring in just two minutes, again from the penalty spot. Continuing a 100% record in the section, United played at the peak of their form to beat Kilmarnock 2-1 and then won 1-0 at Dunfermline Athletic, where the home keeper defied the Terrors for much of the game. In the final match of the section, from which two teams would qualify under the amended rules of the competition, United travelled to Stenhousemuir aiming to finish with full points from all six games. However, the home side had to win to qualify for the next round and they were the hungrier side, beating United 2-0.

1972-73
Back Row: Rolland, Kopel, Davie, McAlpine, McKell, Narey, Devlin, Fleming
Middle: Jim McLean, Steen, J Cameron, Copland, Eddie, W Smith, Knox, Gardner, Traynor,
*   Gray, Andy Dickson*
Front: Henry, Fascione, Reid, A White, D Smith, K Cameron, Mitchell, Markland

The league campaign got under way against Airdrieonians on 2nd September with a comfortable 3-1 win at Tannadice. United recorded the same result at St Johnstone a week later but only after enduring some intense pressure from the home side in the first half. Shortly after that match, Devlin was offered and accepted a free transfer and United added Alex Brown (Broughty Athletic) to the reserves. A visit to Leicester City in the first round first leg of the Texaco Cup brought a 1-1 draw thanks to some safe handling by McAlpine and a late goal from Sandy White. That was followed on 16th September by a derby win against Dundee at Tannadice. Although the Dark Blues took the lead, Gardner levelled the match before half time and Sandy White made it 2-1 with another late goal. Four days later, United suffered an unbelievable 5-2 defeat in the League Cup against Hibs. Leading 2-0 just after half time, United conceded two quick goals and then collapsed in the latter stages. The next game was also against Hibs, at Easter Road in a league match, and although United put up a good fight they lost two late goals to go down 3-1.

Next came the second leg of the Texaco Cup against Leicester City on 27th September and although United were much the better side, they came across an in-form Peter Shilton in goal. At full-time, the sides were level at 1-1. The visitors took the lead before a Doug Smith penalty conversion three minutes from the end of extra time took the match to United's first ever penalty shoot-out. Smith went first for United and missed. Shilton then saved from Cameron and Fleming, whilst the visitors scored three to put United out of the competition.

The league campaign continued with a 1-0 win against Morton, thanks to yet another Smith spot kick and then in the second leg of the League Cup tie against Hibs, it ended goalless, with neither side able to break down the other. On the following Saturday, United went to the top of the Scottish League with a stunning 4-1 win at Motherwell, where the match soon ended as a contest, with United four goals in front at half time. Top spot was maintained a week later after Smith scored United's third goal from the spot to secure a 3-2 win at home to Hearts. Unfortunately, United were knocked off the top a week later after a shock 1-0 defeat at Falkirk. In mid October, United announced that the players' hostel in Broughty Ferry was to close, as it was no longer financially viable to operate such a facility. Many of the players coming through were local so there was little need for a hostel.

The final of the 1971-72 Forfarshire Cup had been held over from the previous season and on 23rd October, United faced Dundee at Tannadice to decide the winner. In a fast paced match, United handed the Dens Park side a lesson in taking chances to win 4-0, for what McLean described as the Club's best performance of the season. At home to Ayr United in the league a few days later, the visitors scored in just two minutes but the Terrors hit back to win 2-1, with Smith yet again sealing the points from the spot. Shortly after that match, United announced that they would listen to offers for transfer listed Jim Cameron, Markland and Billy Gray. The latter of this trio left to join Raith Rovers in late November.

A visit to Celtic Park on 4th November held no fears for United as they matched the Glasgow side all the way. It was 1-1 after Gardner levelled just before half time. United played well in the second half and should have gone in front but it was the home side who took the initiative to win 3-1. The 3-0 defeat a week later at home to Partick Thistle left United fans stunned. The Terrors attacked incessantly but could do nothing right in the final third of the pitch. That was followed by another shock defeat as United lost 1-0 at East Fife. Those three defeats in a row saw United slip out of the top six in the league for the first time that season. But after a well deserved 3-2 win against Aberdeen and a 4-2 victory at Arbroath, United climbed back up again. However, when Rangers came to Tannadice on 9th December, they adapted better than United to a slippery pitch which had been heavily sanded. As a result the Glasgow side left with both points from a 4-1 win.

With the emphasis at the Club firmly on youth, McLean indicated that Joe White, Rankin and Steen might soon get their chance in the first eleven. Brian Goodall was signed on a provisional form from Lochee Harp, whilst Traynor was added to the list of players available for transfer. Joe White was in the side a few days later as Mitchell scored the only goal in the last minute, for two points at Kilmarnock on 16th December. Shortly after that match, Brian Cooper was signed from Brechin City. In the next match, against Dumbarton, United won 3-2 and in the course of the game, scored all five goals! Dumbarton held a 2-1 half time lead after two unfortunate own goals by Markland and McAlpine but United fought back. Doug Smith was again the match winner, scoring the third from the spot with five minutes left. On 30th December, United threw away a two goal lead to draw 2-2 at Airdrieonians. Two days later in the New Year's Day fixture, United were a goal down to St Johnstone at Tannadice but an incredible match ended 5-1 in favour of the Terrors, stunning the visitors, who had been the more attacking side. Following that, Dundee won a rare two points against United in a 3-0 derby win at Dens Park.

Despite reasonable performances from the team, attendances were poor and McLean made no secret of the fact that players might have to be sold if the situation did not improve. The Club tried everything to bring in paying customers including some novel ideas, but it soon became obvious that gimmicks would not induce the supporters to turn up. United organised a posse of Santas to hand out free chocolate just before Christmas and a pie eating contest was arranged on New Year's Day. There were also penalty kick competitions, including one where all the participants were called Jim Brown. A more serious attempt was made on 13th January 1973, when United staged an exhibition boxing match between Dick McTaggart and Sandy Mathewson at half time. That match against Hibs also marked the passing of Duncan Hutchison, with a minute's silence. The match ended 1-0 for United, with Rolland scoring the only goal.

Next, Motherwell recorded their first victory at Tannadice in twelve years, with a deserved 2-1 win after United had failed to convert their first half superiority into goals. On 3rd February, a Scottish Cup tie against Rangers at Ibrox went the way of the Glasgow side with a Quinton Young goal. But again United could not convert good play into goals. Recently signed Cooper got his first chance in United colours as a substitute against Hearts in a surprise 2-0 win at Tynecastle. Eleven days later, Morton netted one in each half for a 2-0 win against a poor United. A friendly at Southampton to fill a blank Saturday on 24th February ended 1-1 and a week later, United lost 2-1 at Ayr United after a defensive error gave the visitors the advantage. Rolland had to be substituted early in the game and although United equalised, Ayr regained the lead and held on to win. A midweek match against Falkirk was littered with errors by both sides and United were lucky to get a 1-0 win, with the help of a Kennedy own goal.

Eddie made the first of his three appearances in major competition for United as they put a slight dent in Celtic's title bid, earning a 2-2 draw in an even contest. The Tangerines then took both points at Partick Thistle, where a midweek rescheduled match ended 3-0 for United, in a game they controlled from start to finish. A lacklustre first half against East Fife on 24th March, resulted in United going in a goal down at half time but a revitalised side eventually earned a deserved point in a 1-1 draw from a last gasp Traynor effort. At Aberdeen a week later, United lived dangerously at times but were still worth their point in a goalless draw. A third draw in succession resulted when Arbroath were the visitors at Tannadice. Their keeper kept United's attack at bay and it took a Winchester own goal to give United the 1-1 score line. There were two end of season additions to the playing staff, starting with Duncan MacLeod on 10th April after he was released by Dundee, and Barclay Gunn was signed from Bankfoot Juniors on a provisional form.

With the season winding down, any lingering thoughts of achieving a European place disappeared, after losing 2-1 at Rangers on 14th April. United defended well in that match but produced very little in the way of goal threat. A week later, Walter Smith scored his first goal for United in a 2-1 win over Kilmarnock. A Forfarshire Cup tie against Dundee at Tannadice followed two days after that and once again United fans had bragging rights over their neighbours, as the Terrors came from 2-1 down at half time to win 4-2. MacLeod and Steen made their first United appearances in the match and Steen was on for his league debut in the final game of the campaign at Dumbarton. It was not the usual end of season fare and produced a match filled with drama. The Sons had to win to ensure First Division safety but United took the lead through Fleming within ten minutes. The match then turned on an incident that saw Dumbarton given a hotly disputed penalty, from which they scored, but Copland was sent off for protesting. By half time the home side were in front and it ended 4-1 in their favour as they took full advantage of the extra man. Only two more matches took place after that. The first was a Forfarshire Cup tie against Forfar Athletic at Tannadice. United won 3-1 on a rain-sodden pitch, in front of just a few hundred hardy fans. To end the season, 10,500 turned out to honour Dennis Gillespie in his testimonial match against a Dundee Select. United, complete with several guest players, won 2-1.

Markland was released and joined Montrose before the end of the season. Free transfers saw fringe players Brian Eddie and Joe White allowed to leave. They were joined by several who had only seen reserve football, including Robertson, Brown, Ogilvie, Butler, Rogers and several 'S' signings. Mitchell was placed on the transfer list and all the others were retained. The retained list included McKell, Payne, Narey, and Gunn, who were all added to the reserve squad for the following season. In addition, there were several new 'S' signings, including Ray Stewart. One piece of shock news from Tannadice was the announcement that Jerry Kerr was leaving United, having given notice as far back as November. Other news from the Boardroom was the appointment of new Director, George Grant.

The season had been relatively successful with United finishing in seventh place, improving on the 1971-72 position and the players were still benefiting from a bonus scheme based on league placing throughout the season. Gardner was top scorer with 15 league and cup goals, followed by Kenny Cameron who had just one fewer. Next was, surprisingly, Doug Smith with 9 goals, all from the penalty spot. The captain had made over forty appearances along with Kopel, Gardner and Copland. Not far behind came McAlpine, Rolland, Fleming and Kenny Cameron. On the face of it, a relatively settled side had done well but McLean expressed himself 'quietly dissatisfied'. Having been in the top six for most of the season, United dropped out of that group in the final match. McLean believed that the team should have done much better.

1973-74

A First Scottish Cup Final

Youth development at United now had the highest priority it had ever received, with more than a dozen 'S' signings training regularly at Tannadice, and in the reserves, a batch of teenage stars were learning their trade. Included in this number was Andy Gray, signed from Clydebank Strollers in May 1973. Gray had attracted attention from many other clubs but had chosen United because he was impressed by McLean and, like many of the other emerging players at Tannadice, he saw United as the best Club with which to progress. Next to join the growing band of teenage talent was Lochee United's Derek Addison, signed at the end of May ahead of competition from other Scottish sides. The cost of team building and the youth development programme became evident when the figures for the year ended July 1972 were disclosed. A loss of nearly £12,000 had been made, even after a donation of over £36,000 from the Sportsmen's Club, but Dundee United were still in a comfortable financial position with a substantial credit balance in the bank. Season tickets were on sale at £10 for the stand and £6.50 for the ground.

United were offered a pre-season tour of France but turned it down as they were not given enough information about the trip. Instead the Club agreed a three match trip to Holland. The tour produced a 1-1 draw against Dordrecht, a 1-0 win over Fortuna Sittard and a 2-1 defeat by Telstar Velsen but the Manager was happy with the outcome as he prepared for the new season. The last of the pre-season call ups to the reserves was John Holt from Invergowrie Boys Club.

For the League Cup and Dryburgh Cup competitions, the Scottish League put in place an experimental offside rule. Players would not be flagged offside between the eighteen yard lines in each half, in the hope that it would open up the game. Along with MacLeod, Payne made his debut in major competition on 11th August in a 2-1 win at East Fife in the first match of the season, a League Cup tie. Such was the young midfielder's desire to make the grade at Tannadice, he missed the wedding of his brother, Arbroath player Kenny Payne, on the same day. United then earned a point in a hard fought 0-0 draw at home to a strong Aberdeen side. A few days later, Gray made his first appearance when he came on as a substitute at Motherwell, on the wrong end of a 4-0 result. McLean tried to bolster the squad with the addition of Graham Fyfe, a reserve centre forward at Rangers but the fee requested was too much, and a bid to bring another attacking player to United was also rejected. United then went to Pittodrie and won comfortably 2-0, although McAlpine had to be at his best in the latter stages of the game. Even after a 3-0 defeat at home to Motherwell, United still had a chance of qualifying for the next round of the League Cup and they ended the section with a great display to win 5-2 over East Fife. However, the two goals conceded and a draw between the other two sides in the section, left United in third place and it was Motherwell and Aberdeen that went through with better goal differences.

First Team Squad - 1973-74
Standing: MacLeod, J Cameron, Kopel, W Smith, McAlpine, Copland. Knox, Gardner, Fleming
Seated: Henry, Rolland, White, D Smith, Mitchell, Traynor, K Cameron

The league season began on 1st September with a 2-1 win at Dumbarton but only after a half time pep talk from McLean transformed United, following a jaded first half. Against St Johnstone, teenagers Gray and Payne were outstanding in a 2-0 win a week later. As United prepared to meet Dundee in the first derby of the season at Dens Park, former Dundalk and Preston North End attacker Sean Sheehy was added to the squad. Mitchell was then released but was quickly signed by Falkirk.

United's dominance in the Dundee derby stretched to another win, with Walter Smith scoring the only goal in a match controlled by United's midfield. The result was an excellent tonic as United prepared to travel to Sheffield United in the first leg of a Texaco Cup tie. The match ended goalless with United the better side but defences were on top throughout. Meanwhile, Ian Reid, who initially refused a move to Queen of the South in August, joined the Dumfries side on 17th September. Around the same time, Jim Cameron joined Falkirk for a fee of £7,000 and Cooper was released, joining Arbroath soon afterwards.

On 29th September, Motherwell recorded their third win of the season against United, with a 4-0 victory, achieved without much opposition. That was followed by an excellent United team display with two goals from Henry, to beat Sheffield United 2-0, to advance to the next round of the Texaco Cup. Back on league business, United completely dominated at home to Clyde and two goals in each half brought a 4-0 win. McLean tried and failed to bring Czech international right winger Josef Jeliner to Tannadice. The Manager then signed South African, Rodney Bush, who was already training at Tannadice. He had been recommended by former Dundee player, Alec Hamilton. United made it known that any of the senior players who were not regularly in the first eleven were available for transfer, but rejected a bid by Montrose for Knox.

The team continued to play well and a 2-0 win at Morton on 13th October could have been more, as United dominated. At home to Rangers a week later, a fairly even match ended 3-1 to the Glasgow side when a draw might have been a more accurate reflection on play. United then travelled to Leicester City to find an in-form Peter Shilton for the second season in succession, and were thankful for a Kopel equaliser after the home side had gone ahead from a soft penalty award. The proverbial game of two halves saw Aberdeen win 3-1 at Pittodrie but the next match, against Falkirk at Tannadice, did not count, as the game was abandoned due to fog five minutes from the end, with United leading 2-0. On 7th November, Leicester City were at Tannadice for the second leg of the Texaco Cup tie and in a dour struggle, it took a Fleming goal in the second half to liven up both sides. United won by that single goal and went through to meet Newcastle United in the semi final.

At Hearts a few days later, both sides failed in the final third of the pitch and it ended 1-1 but only after Rolland netted with two minutes remaining. A lifeless 0-0 draw at home to East Fife was followed by the rearranged match with Falkirk. A Wednesday afternoon kick-off, due to power restrictions because of industrial action by miners, resulted in a crowd of just 1,250 witnessing a 2-1 victory for United. Narey made his first team debut and United fully deserved the win, although it took a last minute goal by Knox to settle it. Shortly after that match, keeper McKell went to East Fife on loan. United drew the next two matches, both away from home. Sandy White scored with a wind-assisted shot for a 1-1 draw at Ayr United, and then at Celtic Park, United produced a real Terrors display to fight back from a two goal half time deficit for a 3-3 draw, with Knox again scoring a late goal.

United entertained Newcastle United in a Texaco Cup semi final first leg at Tannadice on 12th December and early goals from Kopel and Knox secured a comfortable 2-0 win. In the second leg a week later, the Terrors were left to rue chances missed in the first leg. In an afternoon kick-off at St James' Park, the home side scored within a minute but United showed resilience with a Gray goal before half time. United had more chances before Newcastle United scored another in the second half and a third with nine minutes left. The Tyneside club netted the winner in extra time to go into the final on a 4-3 aggregate. Although despondent, United had the consolation of £5,000 from the sponsors and the receipts from three good home gates. They then banished memories of the defeat with a 3-2 win at Dunfermline Athletic after being two goals down. That was followed by a stunning 6-0 win over Dumbarton, with Gray getting four goals and missing a penalty. That match also gave Bush his only first team outing with United, in the last eleven minutes of the game.

Two days into the New Year, United were lucky to take a point at St Johnstone in a 1-1 draw and then lost 2-1 in an all action Dundee derby at Tannadice. The Dark Blues took an early two goal lead and Gardner scored in the second half but despite intense pressure, United could not engineer an equaliser, which would have been fully justified. Soon after, Henry moved to Aberdeen for around £20,000 and McLean called up provisional signing Steve Mellon from Dundee North End. The commitment to youth was demonstrated with a debut for Addison on 12th January against Hibs in a 3-1 defeat at Easter Road. Then Holt made his first appearance as United lost 1-0 at home to Motherwell.

Amidst unfounded rumours of a £50,000 bid from Newcastle United for Copland, United prepared for the Scottish Cup tie against Airdrieonians and produced their best form of the season to advance to the next round with a confident display in a 4-1 home win. Although he had been with United for over three years, it was the first appearance in the side for Rankin. After being unable to play for several weeks due to injury, Sheehy was the next player to make a debut, coming on as a substitute at Clyde in a 2-1 win on 2nd February.

A major new development in Scottish football took place before United played their next match. Dunfermline Athletic were the club that proposed the change in January and, after some fine tuning, at a meeting of the Scottish League in mid February, the new 10-14-14 league set up was formally intimated. A month later it was approved by a majority of the clubs, although United were one of several who voted against the new set up. The next season, 1974-75 would be the last of the two-division Scottish League. It would be replaced in 1975-76 with a ten club Premier League and two lower leagues of fourteen clubs each. One other change of immediate importance was the agreement that matches could go ahead on Sundays. Some fans were against this and vowed not to go to games. In the case of United season ticket holders, the Directors agreed to refund 25p for each Sunday match not attended. Nevertheless, Sunday football was here to stay as United proved, playing their next four matches on Sundays.

The first of these was a Scottish Cup tie against Morton on 17th February at Tannadice. It was a scrappy 1-0 win for United but the goal scored by Rankin was a 25-yard rocket, worthy of winning any game. A week later United lost 3-1 to Rangers at Ibrox in a league match. A poor first half United showing meant the home side were three up by half time, although an improved second half brought a goal for United. Aberdeen visited Tannadice next and took the lead against the run of play. United could not find any fluency and eventually lost 3-0. To encourage support in a season of low attendances, United arranged buses from the outlying housing estates but it was an unsuccessful service that was soon withdrawn.

The Scottish Cup brought a quarter final at Dunfermline Athletic on 10th March and with many United fans already on their way home, Traynor snatched a last gasp equaliser for a 1-1 draw and a replay that was less than deserved. At Tannadice two days later, a transformed United dominated proceedings to win 4-0. Fleming was the architect of the success with two well taken first half goals. That set up a semi final against Hearts and in a cup rehearsal on 16th March at Tannadice, the visitors came from two goals behind to earn a point in an enthralling 3-3 draw, on a pitch resembling a quagmire. Shortly after, Bush announced he was returning to South Africa and Davie gave notice that when the season was over he was leaving to begin a new life in New Zealand. That was bad news for United, as McAlpine was already out of the side for the rest of the season with knee trouble requiring surgery. It took some time to find another keeper to cover but eventually former Brechin City player, John Ritchie, was signed from Bradford City on a free transfer.

Smith scores from the spot in the Scottish Cup semi final replay

United won the next three league matches, beginning with a 2-0 win at East Fife thanks to late goals from Traynor and Gray. Then on 30th March, the Tangerines recorded a close 2-1 home win over Ayr United, with Doug Houston, recently signed from Rangers for £10,000, making his debut. United then won 1-0 at Falkirk on 2nd April. Four days later, United travelled to Hampden Park for the Scottish Cup semi final and were a goal down to a lively Hearts at half time. A revitalised United improved in the second half and earned a replay from a 1-1 draw, with Gardner netting a vital equaliser from a 30 yard free kick. The replay went ahead in midweek amidst rumours that Gray was attracting interest from Spurs. The team appeared unsettled in the opening exchanges of the game and played poorly in the first half, conceding a goal early in the match. However, after Doug Smith scored from the spot to level the tie with an hour played, it became a teenage rampage as Payne and Gray hit top form with a goal each. Knox scored the other for a well deserved 4-2 win to reach the Club's first ever Scottish Cup final.

Just as it had been with Hearts, United immediately faced a cup rehearsal. At Tannadice, Celtic took an early lead and then played a containing game to win 2-0. United then beat Arbroath 3-1 at Tannadice and 2-1 at Gayfield but could only draw 1-1 at home to Partick Thistle despite dominating possession. A week before the cup final, Dunfermline Athletic came to Tannadice needing a win to have any chance of avoiding relegation and achieved their aim with the only goal of the game in the second half. Two days later United faced Partick Thistle away and lost 2-1, after the Jags scored a late winner. It was not a good run up to the final but United received a boost when it was announced that Copland was in Scotland's initial forty for the World Cup in West Germany. It was yet another indication of United's progress under McLean.

On 4th May 1974, United walked out on to the Hampden pitch in front of a crowd of almost 76,000. 6/1 outsiders for the cup, the Terrors were the better side in the opening twenty minutes but fell behind to two goals in six minutes in the first half. United had two clear cut goal scoring opportunities just after the interval but the chances were not taken and Celtic gradually took control. There was no real surprise when Celtic netted a third. Beaten 3-0 but not disgraced, United fans made the long trek home. It would be 20 years before they made that same journey as winners. The line up for that first attempt was:-

Davie, Gardner, Kopel; Copland, D Smith (Traynor), W Smith; Payne (Rolland), Knox, Gray, Fleming, Houston.

By virtue of being losing finalists, United did at least have the consolation of a place in the Cup Winners' Cup for the next season. In terms of prestige this was good for the Club but in terms of hard cash it could be costly. United might have preferred the Texaco Cup which involved less travelling and better income prospects from sponsorship and gate money.

United still had two league fixtures to complete and lost 4-1 at home to Hibs, who then finished second in the league for a UEFA Cup slot. The last match of the season ended in a 4-2 win over Morton, with MacLeod netting a hat-trick. Most of the players were retained but as well as losing Davie and Bush at the end of the season, Sheehy left and United announced free transfers for McKell, Gunn and Mellon, along with the experienced Kenny Cameron. United had come a long way in just two full seasons with McLean in charge, and consistency of selection was a major factor. Rolland, Kopel, Doug Smith, Walter Smith, Copland,

Fleming, Gardner and Traynor had all made over forty appearances each and not far behind came McAlpine and Gray. The young striker was also top scorer with 19 goals. Another satisfying feature of the season was the inclusion of Narey, Payne, Gray and Holt in the Scotland professional youth squad. The production line of young talent was fully operational and Graham Mooney from Salvesen Boys Club had joined the reserves in February. The next player to come under the expert care of McLean was sixteen-year-old Paul Sturrock, signed from Bankfoot Juniors in June. Also called up for the reserves were 'S' signings Davie Dodds (Sporting Club) and Kenny Murphy (St Columba's).

1974-75

Aiming for the Top Ten

During the close season, the only addition to the squad was a promising pair of Rangers free transfers, Jimmy Murray and Iain McDonald. Both were signed in early July and joined the rest of the squad in pre-season training. All the retained players re-signed, although Copland had requested a transfer saying he would like to try his luck elsewhere if the opportunity arose. A proposed tour of Holland was cancelled in late June and instead United fixed up friendlies in the Highlands. McDonald made his first appearance for United, scoring on his debut and Brian Goodall got his only first team game, as United won 2-1 at Inverness Clachnacuddin on 29th July. In the second match, a Copland hat-trick was enough to ensure a 3-0 win at Elgin City. The last of the pre-season matches was a stiffer test against Sheffield Wednesday at Tannadice, where United did most of the attacking. However, it took a Kopel header late in the second half to make it 1-1 and cancel out the visitors' first half lead. Season tickets were on sale at £11.50 for the Stand and £7.50 for a ground ticket and the take-up was encouraging.

The experimental rule, in which players could not be flagged offside between the eighteen yard line in each half, was repeated in the League Cup and Dryburgh Cup competitions for a second season. But efforts to extend the experiment into league matches and the Scottish Cup were beaten. After the season ended the change was dropped as there was no appreciable improvement in the game.

United started the season in a tough League Cup section including Ayr United, Motherwell and Celtic. All the goals came in the first half in the first match on 10th August, as United comfortably won 3-1 at home against Ayr United, with McDonald making his first appearance in major competition as a late substitute. At Motherwell in the next game, United were under pressure and were grateful to leave with a point from a goalless draw. The Terrors then lost by a single first half goal at Celtic Park, after outplaying the Glasgow side for much of the match.

It was also a first half goal that gave United a home win over Motherwell on 21st August, but the points were only secured with a solid second half display by the home defence. The visit of Celtic a few days later resulted in another 1-0 defeat and again United could claim to have been the better side, missing chances to recover from an early setback. The last match of the section was at Ayr United where a two goal lead was squandered and it ended 2-2. It had not been a particularly good start but already United's teenage stars were attracting attention. Several English sides were showing interest in Gray, and Narey was also drawing his fair share of admirers. It was no surprise when a bid, believed to be £75,000, was received from Nottingham Forest for Gray. It was the third offer in as many months but like the others, it was rejected.

1974-75
Back Row: *Gardner, Rankin, Copland, McAlpine, W Smith, Narey, Knox, Houston*
Middle: *Jim McLean, Dodds, Brown, Sturrock, McDonald, Goodall, Forsyth, Mooney, White, Holt, Andy Dickson*
Front: *Payne, Rolland, MacLeod, D Smith, Gray, Kopel, Fleming, Traynor*

The value of Gray was confirmed in the opening match of the league season on 31st August as he netted the first and last, in a stunning 5-0 win over Motherwell. It was said that the rustle of English First Division clubs' cheque books could be clearly heard in the Tannadice stand! A week later United lost 2-0 at St Johnstone, who adapted better on a heavy pitch. That match was followed by a derby against Dundee, with a 6.30 pm kick-off to avoid a clash with the Leuchars Air Show. United won 3-0 with a commanding display that kept Dundee confined to their own half for most of the game. Alan Munro, signed from Partick Thistle on the morning of the match, made his debut and scored one of the goals. By now, it was not just the progression of teenage talent that drew envious eyes to Tannadice. The

Manager was also becoming a desired commodity and following the loss of their manager, Ian St John, Motherwell tried and failed to lure McLean to Fir Park.

The win over Dundee was an excellent warm-up for the forthcoming Cup Winners' Cup tie against Jiul Petrosani of Romania, considered one of the weaker sides in the tournament. The match on 18th September was a 3-0 win for United, with goals from Narey, Copland and Gardner and gave them a cushion for a tricky away leg. Sturrock made his debut when he came on as a second half substitute and left fans in little doubt that another talented player had been unearthed by McLean. United struggled in the away league match against leaders Hibs on the following Saturday and the 3-0 defeat reflects a bad day generally. A 1-0 win against Dunfermline Athletic a week later was achieved courtesy of a second half own goal but United passed up enough earlier chances to win the game. That was followed by the second leg against Jiul Petrosani and although United lost 2-0 in an intimidating atmosphere in Romania, they went through on a 3-2 aggregate. After such an arduous trip into Eastern Europe, the draw for the next round was not kind, handing United an even longer journey to face Bursapor of Turkey.

It was a jaded team that drew 1-1 at Airdrieonians on 5th October with Gray the hero, heading United into the lead before becoming the villain, by heading an own goal with only two minutes left. Hearts were the next visitors to Tannadice and the match was a personal triumph for their former player Traynor, who netted a hat-trick as United cruised to a 5-0 win. Just prior to the next match Gardner left United to join Motherwell for a fee of around £10,000. As United prepared for the visit of Bursapor, they drew 1-1 at Ayr United in a match that either side could have won had they taken their chances. The Cup Winners' Cup tie at Tannadice on 23rd October was played almost entirely in the Bursapor half but United could not find a route to goal and it ended goalless. The visit of Dumbarton three days later resulted in a 3-3 draw, with Gray scoring twice to give United a 2-1 lead before the Sons went ahead. Gray completed a hat-trick with a very late equaliser.

With a long journey to Turkey the following week, United tried unsuccessfully to rearrange the match scheduled at Arbroath on 2nd November to the day before. Gray scored the first goal and the last in the 3-1 win. The match at Bursapor was played on a fiery pitch and United had to endure some uncompromising tackling as they went out to a 30-yard shot scored after just nine minutes. The return journey left United little time to prepare for a match against Celtic. It ended 0-0 with McAlpine saving a penalty but United were arguably the better team against the Glasgow side.

In his search for a partner for Gray up front, McLean made an offer to Hamilton Academical for twenty-year-old Paul Hegarty. Initially it was cash plus two players, including Rankin but that offer was rejected. However, Hegarty was signed for £40,000 in a straight cash deal on 13th November. Rankin then had talks with Hamilton Academical, signing a week later. Shortly afterwards, Munro ended his brief career at Tannadice when he accepted a move to St Mirren. Hegarty made his United debut coming on as a substitute against Partick Thistle in a 5-0 win at Firhill. In a midweek match against Aberdeen at Tannadice, a Fleming double set up a comfortable 4-0 win, but at Ibrox, United could do little to prevent a 4-2 defeat against a powerful Rangers display. That was followed by a visit from lowly Clyde on 7th December. The Bully Wee played the better football in the early stages and had the lead until Copland and Hegarty scored in the last five minutes to snatch a 3-3 draw. Shortly after that it was announced that former player Kenny Dick was joining United as a scout. He would also be coaching the ever growing band of 'S' signings at Tannadice.

United carried on their league campaign with a 6-0 win at Morton, with the Greenock side held captive in their own half for almost the entire match. Murphy made his one and only first team appearance in the last nine minutes of that match. McLean then brought a trialist over from Iceland for a week and, after impressing the Manager, the player returned to his home country to make arrangements to join the Tannadice set up but that was the last United heard from him. A few months later the player, Johannes Edvaldsson signed for Celtic. On 21st December, United lost 4-3 at home to Kilmarnock after gifting the Ayrshire side a four goal lead. United mounted a late recovery but three goals in the last fifteen minutes were just not enough. A week later, United won 1-0 at Motherwell with a first half Gray goal against the run of play but should have scored more in the second half after the home side had two players sent off. St Johnstone then put on their best performance of the season to draw 1-1 at Tannadice after Narey had given United an early lead. The festive programme concluded on 4th January at Dens Park, where Dundee won 2-0 with a controlled display. McLean then signed Jason Walker as a reserve from St Mirren for a small fee.

After almost three years in United reserves, Forsyth made his debut in the first team on 11th January as third placed Hibs, beat fourth placed United, 3-1 at Tannadice. Over the next three weeks the weather caused several postponements until 1st February, when United struggled to beat a stubborn Airdrieonians 1-0. Included in the postponements had been the home Scottish Cup tie against Berwick Rangers, which was played three days later. Gray gave United the lead but a fighting performance by the visitors brought a late equaliser and a replay on the following evening. At Berwick, the home side matched United in the first half but tired in the second and incessant United attacking produced the winner from Gray in injury time. The next round was due to bring Aberdeen to Tannadice but that too was postponed and before the rescheduled cup tie, United lost 3-1 at Hearts and won 2-1 at Dunfermline Athletic. The cup tie against Aberdeen went ahead on 19th February and the Dons took an early lead and held on to win by that single goal. United should have equalised from any number of chances and missed the best opportunity when Kopel sent a spot kick past the post near the end. Already assured of a top ten place, that left the Terrors with a single objective – to achieve a best ever fourth place finish and with it, entry into the UEFA Cup.

The side went all out over the remaining weeks of the season and a McDonald double on 1st March resulted in a 2-1 win at Dumbarton. That was followed by a 3-1 win over Ayr United and then, crucially, United won 1-0 at Celtic Park with a goal scored by Gray. Not only was the win fully deserved to keep the momentum going but it also ended Celtic's slim hope of winning the league. All the goals came in the first half when United won 3-1 at home to Arbroath. On 22nd March, in a scrappy game against Partick Thistle, two Forsyth penalties, the second with just minutes remaining, gave United a 2-1 win at Tannadice. The good run of results ended at Pittodrie, where United were fortunate to lose just 2-0 against a lively Aberdeen, who were themselves aiming for the all important fourth place. United however still had the advantage, even after the defeat at Pittodrie.

United went on to complete the league campaign without losing another match. On 5th April they might have won against Rangers at Tannadice instead of drawing 2-2. Sturrock scored twice in the first half but the Glasgow side levelled it and although United were swarming around the visitors' goal in the final stages, they could not get a winner. A 2-1 win at Clyde followed, with the home side taking United all the way. A single Sturrock goal at home to Morton on a rain-soaked pitch was enough to win another two points in the penultimate league game. The final match of the league campaign was at Rugby Park on 26th April. A big home support left disappointed after United won 4-2, keeping Kilmarnock out of the top ten of the newly instigated Premier League. United had two Forfarshire Cup matches to end the season and only managed to beat Brechin City 2-1 in the first, with the help of two defensive errors. The 1973-74 final against Montrose had been held over from the previous season and the Angus side deservedly beat United 2-1 to win the cup.

United did finish in fourth place and although there had been disappointment in all of the cup competitions, McLean was satisfied with the progress that had been made and a place in the top ten of the Scottish League's Premier Division was assured. Gray was top scorer with 26 goals in his 46 appearances but no other player managed to get into double figures. McAlpine, Rolland, Narey, Kopel and Copland made over forty appearances each and Doug Smith, McDonald, Houston and Fleming all topped thirty. During the season, several of United's rising stars were involved with the national squads; Sturrock and Holt with the professional youth set up and Gray, Narey and McDonald at Under-23 level.

Sandy White went to Forfar Athletic at the end of the season and a free transfer was given to Steen, along with reserves Goodall, Ritchie, Mooney, Murray and Walker. There were still a large number of young players on 'S' forms and provisional signings, including recently signed Billy Kirkwood from Cornbank Boys Club in Penicuik. Although the figures would not be disclosed until the following summer, 1974-75 had been a poor year with a loss of £65,000 recorded, due largely to the payment of transfer fees and the considerable cost of the two trips to Eastern Europe. However, a donation of £36,000 from the Sportsmen's Club kept the bank balance in credit at around £25,000.

Immediately the season ended, United had season tickets on sale at £18 for the stand and £11.50 for the ground and to encourage early purchasers, a payment plan was available. An offer to participate in a tournament in late June in Salamanca, Spain, was accepted. The travelling party included sixteen-year-old Davie Dodds, together with Billy Steele, signed in May on a free transfer from Rangers. The matches in Spain were played just hours apart, with the first, a 2-1 defeat by Spartak Moscow on the evening of Saturday 21st June. On the following afternoon, Dodds played for United for the first time, against the hosts. In the heat of the midday sun, it was no surprise that a tired United lost 2-0. On returning from Spain, McLean signed Henry Hall from St Johnstone, with MacLeod and a small cash adjustment going in the opposite direction as part of the deal. Alex Rennie also joined United after he had been released by St Johnstone. Leaving United was Kenny Dick who returned to Forfar Athletic in a coaching capacity.

1975-76

A Narrow Escape

For the new season, the Directors announced a £20,000 improvement scheme for the floodlights, to bring them up to a standard suitable for colour television broadcasts. There were further additions to the playing staff with reserve keeper, David Cooper from Glenrothes, joining United in mid July and amongst a number of 'S' signings was Derek Stark from Glenrothes. From Tain Royal Academy, Jim Oliver was signed in early August as a striker for the reserve side and Kenny Brown was called up from St Columba's Boys Club, along with schoolboy international Allan Boath. Although Boath would never make it into the first team at Tannadice, he went on to play at international level for New Zealand and starred in their World Cup campaign in 1982. Graeme Buchanan of Cumbernauld Juniors and provisionally signed Alistair Coupar of Forfar West End, were also brought into United's second eleven.

The pre-season programme started on 28th July at Fraserburgh with debuts for Rennie and Steele, the latter as a substitute, in a benefit match for the home side's long-serving player Brian McCann. Gray scored a hat-trick of headers as United won 3-0 and he netted another hat-trick against Elgin City in a 4-0 win on the following day. To conclude the Highland tour, United won 5-0 at Golspie Sutherland with a commanding display a day later. Cooper played in goal in that match for what turned out to be his only first team outing. In a Forfarshire Cup tie at Brechin City on 2nd August, with Hall coming on as a substitute for his first appearance, the Angus side gave United a tough match and it took two Gray goals in extra time to secure a 2-1 win. The last of the pre-season matches was at Tannadice and United did all the attacking to win 2-0 against Preston North End.

In the opening match of the League Cup on 9th August against St Johnstone, Hall and Steele made their debuts in major competition for United. The Tangerines dominated against the Perth side for most of the match but it took a goal near the end, from substitute Steele, to secure the 2-1 win. A few days later, United did not play well and lost 3-1 at Partick Thistle. United bounced back against Kilmarnock and two goals from Gray brought a relatively easy 2-0 win. Partick Thistle were the visitors at Tannadice next and left with a 2-1 result after scoring a late winner but United had only themselves to blame for failing to capitalise on some excellent build up play. With Rennie making his first appearance in major competition at Kilmarnock in the next match, United had the better of the first half but faded after the break and lost to a single goal. That meant there was nothing at stake in the final match on 27th August at St Johnstone and United had to come from behind, with two second half goals, to win 2-1.

Coincidentally, United then opened the Premier League campaign on 30th August in Perth against St Johnstone. The first penalty awarded in the new league went to United after four minutes but Steele had his effort saved and United were left ruing that miss when the home side scored the only goal of the game four minutes from the end. Another penalty decided the outcome of the match against Hibs a week later, with Payne netting in the second minute for a 1-0 win. A full-blooded encounter at Aberdeen was next and United emerged 3-1 winners in an enthralling match. A few days later, Walter Smith left United to join Dumbarton for a fee of £8,000.

1975-76
Back Row: Rennie, Addison, Narey, Copland, Dodds, Kopel, Houston, Buchanan
Middle: Holt, Rolland, Hegarty, McAlpine, W Smith, Cooper, Gray, Forsyth, Stewart
Front: Steele, Sturrock, Hall, D Smith, Payne, Fleming, McDonald, Traynor

Penalties were fast becoming the highlight of United matches and during the visit of Motherwell each side had one awarded in the first half. United failed to convert and the visitors scored to lead at half time. However, Sturrock pulled it level and United took a deserved point from the 1-1 draw. United then travelled to Iceland to meet IBK Keflavik in a UEFA Cup first leg tie and won 2-0 with ease against the amateurs. Man of the match Narey scored two first half goals and almost made it a hat-trick as United cruised to the win.

United were scheduled to face Celtic away in the league on 27th September and the fans awoke to the news that they would do so without Gray. There had been several enquiries about him, with Leeds United and Schalke 04 the most recent. But it was Aston Villa who made the successful offer of £110,000, a record for a Dundee United player at the time. The match at Celtic resulted in a 2-1 defeat but with the Glasgow side leading by two goals, they had to hang on for the win after Payne scored from the spot with fifteen minutes left. The second leg of the tie against IBK Keflavik followed three days later and United trampled the Icelandic side under, in a comfortable 4-0 win. Over the two legs of the tie, United lost around £1,000, as the expense of travelling to Iceland outweighed the income from the home tie.

On 4th October, United faced Ayr United at Tannadice and established a three goal lead but a fight back by the visitors made the final score 3-2. United lost 1-0 at Hearts a week later after conceding a first half goal, and a second half fight back proved fruitless against a solid defence. The following week, United took control in the first derby of the season against Dundee at Tannadice and went in front through Houston. Dundee were level by half time and as United faded, the visitors scored again to win 2-1. It was not the best preparation for the impending UEFA Cup tie against FC Porto at Tannadice a few days later. United were hampered by injuries and appeared to be a little overawed by the Portuguese side. The situation was not helped when Payne missed a first half penalty and at half time United were a goal down. Rennie scored an equaliser but it ended 2-1 for the visitors, who scored the winner against the run of play in the latter stages of the match.

There was some more player news in October. After the visit to Iceland, striker Oskar Tomasson came to United but returned home after four weeks in the reserves. Doug Smith turned down a move to Raith Rovers and United signed Stuart Baxter from Preston North End, but he was released after a month playing in the reserves. McLean had not been idle in his search to find a replacement striker for Gray and an offer for Dom Sullivan was rejected. He then made a bid for Tom McAdam of Dumbarton and that too was initially turned down. An increased offer of around £37,000 was made on 31st October, at which time he became a United player. McAdam went straight into the side the next day, scoring twice on his debut as United won 3-1 with a polished display against St Johnstone. That set up the trip to Portugal for the second leg against FC Porto and United left in confident mood. In a torrid match, United had to face some dubious tactics but still took the lead midway through the second half. However, that advantage lasted just three minutes. It ended 1-1 on the night and United went out on a 3-2 aggregate. Worse still, Fleming was sent off near the end and subsequently received a three-match ban.

A match at Easter Road against Hibs on 8th November was next up and a McAdam goal gave United a deserved point from a 1-1 draw. That was followed by a midweek encounter at Ibrox where Rangers won 4-1 but only after scoring two late goals, whilst United were chasing an equaliser. Aberdeen then came to Tannadice and won 2-1 in a finely balanced match. At Motherwell a week later, McAdam gave the Terrors a first half lead and after United soaked up intense pressure, they succumbed to a brace of late goals, to lose 2-1. For the visit of Celtic to Tannadice on 29th November, the new concept of segregation of the fans was in place for the first time. Celtic took an early lead and United had chances to get back into the game but paid the price for not taking them as the visitors scored two more. It ended 3-1, with Hegarty scoring a late consolation. Shortly after that match, Rolland was suspended by the Club for breach of contract after he moved with his family back to Glenrothes. It took several days to resolve the problem but eventually a compromise was reached, with the player staying in Dundee on training days.

29th November 1975 – Segregation of fans at Tannadice for the first time

On 6th December at Ayr United, some silky football by the Terrors resulted in a two goal half time lead but the home side improved after the break and earned their point in a 2-2 draw. At Tannadice a week later, Hearts adapted better to a hard surface and won 1-0. McLean then failed in a bid to bring an experienced keeper in from a First Division side but was successful in getting ex-Brighton & Hove Albion and Preston North End defender, Alan Kershaw. By then with Morton, Alec Reid returned to Tannadice on 31st December in exchange for Traynor and £10,000. The year ended with goalless draws away to Dundee and at home to Rangers. On both occasions the game might have gone either way.

New Year's Day brought a 1-1 draw at St Johnstone with a goal from Rolland in a quite superb first half performance. But after the interval, United fell out of it and an improved Perth side levelled. United then lost 5-3 at Aberdeen, with all the damage done in the first half as the Dons established a three-goal lead. United's fight back was commendable but not enough. The visit of Motherwell on 17th January produced a poor United display and although it was level at half time, the Fir Park club outplayed United to win 4-1. On a snow covered pitch a week later, United found the way to goal as they faced Hamilton Academical in the Scottish Cup at Tannadice and won 4-0 with ease. United travelled to Celtic on the last day of January and were a goal up through Hall after just two minutes. A second goal was disallowed, before Celtic scored twice to make it 2-1. United had another one chalked off before the interval but took the game to Celtic, who were glad to hear the final whistle. The next round of the Scottish Cup beckoned and a pulsating match at Easter Road against Hibs ended 1-1 after the home side levelled the match with just ten minutes left. Prior to the replay with Hibs, United beat Hearts 1-0 at Tynecastle in a match they dominated and should have wrapped up long before Hall's goal midway through the second half. When Hibs came to Tannadice for the cup replay, a big crowd turned out anticipating a United win but the visitors scored twice with long range shots to win 2-0. Reid had a great chance to bring United back into the match but United's penalty woes continued, as he hit the post with a spot kick. After that, United offered little and more or less gave up in the final quarter of the game.

The league battle was then the priority, as by then St Johnstone appeared doomed in bottom spot but United were slightly adrift and flirting with the second relegation place. The derby against Dundee at Tannadice on 28th February therefore took on a huge significance. It was a fairly tame affair until McAdam scored the only goal of the game in the second half. As the better side, United deserved the points, but they were still five points behind Dundee. The next four matches were crucial and seven points out of a possible eight closed the gap. United hammered fellow strugglers Ayr United 5-0 at Tannadice, with McAdam netting a hat-trick. It was more than two weeks before the next match and in difficult conditions at Hibs, United had to withstand a late onslaught after Hall scored the only goal of the game in the first half. On 27th March, Aberdeen were the visitors and United did well to hold them at bay against a strong first half wind. The Terrors turned the tables after half time and won 1-0 with a Fleming header. Four days later, a freak goal gave St Johnstone the lead but with time running out, Hegarty made it 1-1.

United were unlucky to lose 3-2 at Motherwell on 3rd April, with the home side scoring the winner right at the end. A week later, United faced a make or break visit from second top Celtic. McAdam scored a late first half goal but Celtic levelled soon after the interval. The United players then rose to the occasion, with Fleming and McAdam scoring, before a very late Celtic goal made the final score 3-2 for a memorable win. On 14th April, the visit to Ayr United deepened the gloom again as the home side won 1-0 with a good second half performance. The emotional roller coaster for the fans sped on, with the visit of cup finalists

Hearts. United missed a penalty after five minutes but Hegarty scored before half time and as the Terrors dominated, McAdam wrapped up a 2-0 win with a second half strike.

A midweek visit to Dens Park to meet Dundee resulted in a tense encounter, with the home side scoring either side of half time. Hall pulled one back and then United stormed forward looking for another but the Dark Blues held out for a 2-1 win. That result left United level on points with Dundee and Ayr United. Rangers were United's next visitors and a win for the Glasgow side gave them the title. In just twenty-two seconds, Derek Johnstone scored the only goal to give them the flag. Incidentally, in the pre-match entertainment that day, United 'S' signings played a Celtic Boys Clubs team which included Ralph Milne, who was also by then a United 'S' signing. At that time, United also had Ray Farningham and Don McVicar on 'S' forms. The penultimate match of the season brought Hibs to Tannadice and with twelve minutes gone, United were awarded a penalty. After missing so many that season, the fans wondered who might take it, until keeper McAlpine ran the length of the pitch, placed the ball and scored with a powerful shot to put United in front. Hall made it 2-0 shortly after and that was how it ended. There was more drama yet to come as United, needing one point to ensure survival, travelled to Ibrox to face Rangers in the last match of the season. The Terrors outplayed the champions for most of the game and with five minutes left a penalty was awarded. McAlpine came forward again but his shot came back off the post and a frantic few seconds passed as he raced back to his goal. It ended 0-0 and United were safe, retaining top league status on goal difference, ahead of Dundee. It is interesting to note that in the ten team league, only three points separated Hearts in fifth place and relegated Dundee in ninth.

The league campaign had been a tough one for most clubs, with more than half of the sides fighting for survival. United had to consider themselves fortunate to be looking forward to another Premier League season, after just narrowly escaping relegation, in what must be considered one of the most important campaigns in the history of the Club. McAlpine was the only ever present in the side and he racked up 49 appearances. Also with forty or more were Narey, Houston, Fleming, Kopel, Hegarty and Supporters' Club Player of the Year, Rolland. McAdam and Hall shared the top scorer spot with 13 goals each.

After seventeen years with the Club, the list of free transfers brought to an end the playing career of Doug Smith. Knox was also released along with McDonald who had been plagued with injury and had been advised to give up the game. Reserves Cooper, Coupar, Murphy, Buchanan, Oliver and Kershaw were also allowed to go. One of the gaps left by the departures was already filled by Ray Stewart, who had been called up for the reserves in December from Errol Rovers. He was joined in May by Kirkwood and Derek Stark. McLean also signed Dave McKellar, a goalkeeper from Ipswich Town. To encourage supporters to buy season tickets costing £21 for the stand and £13.50 for the ground, an instalment plan was again being offered.

Further evidence of the progress being made at Tannadice was seen during the season, with the inclusion of Dodds and Stewart in the Scottish professional youth squad, whilst Narey was part of the Under-23 set up and Rolland had played for the Scottish League against their English counterparts. 1975-76 was also a good year financially, as disclosed at the AGM a year later. The Club recorded a profit of £29,000 and the Sportsmen's Club donated £27,500, to boost the bank balance to around £60,000.

1976-77

A Big Improvement

McLean made an unsuccessful bid for Aberdeen's Jocky Scott in July, whilst teenagers David O'Neil, Kenny Johnston, Ronald Boyle, David Rae and Norman Vannart, who had all signed on 'S' forms, were called up for training with the rest of the squad and joined United reserves. There was little further signing activity but Archie Knox was re-engaged for one of the shortest stays on record when he returned on 31st July. He played for the reserves against Brechin City and left United two days later to join Montrose.

There were no new faces in the line up in the first match of the season, a friendly at St Johnstone on 31st July, which United lost 2-1. Reserve goalkeeper McKellar made his first senior appearance in the 2-2 draw at St Mirren in the second warm-up match. United completed the pre-season programme, winning the 1974-75 Forfarshire Cup final with a 3-1 victory over Montrose but it came at a cost, with Houston breaking a collar bone, forcing him out of the side for several weeks. Following withdrawal by the sponsors of the Texaco Cup, it had been replaced by the Anglo-Scottish Cup in which United faced Aberdeen in the first round on 7th August. The Terrors won an all action first leg 1-0 at Tannadice and went into the second leg in confident mood but did not make the best of some early creative play. Aberdeen scored three times before a late McAdam goal set up a thrilling finale, but United lost on a 3-2 aggregate and went out of the competition.

The League Cup section had drawn United in a group containing Arbroath and Dumbarton, but the main obstacle to progress in the competition was Celtic. In the opening match on 14th August, the Glasgow side were fortunate to leave Tannadice with a single goal victory, after United failed to make the best of their first half superiority. Dodds made his debut in major competition in the next match at Arbroath. After a goalless first half he scored twice and Sturrock netted a late counter to give United a 3-1 win. After conceding the first goal to give Dumbarton a shock lead in the next match, the Terrors recovered to equalise in the second half but it took a late Hegarty goal to earn a deserved 2-1 win. The visit of Arbroath on 25th August then produced a 2-0 win, with both United goals coming in the first four minutes. There appeared to be an excellent chance to qualify but at home to Dumbarton, a missed penalty left United with just a point from a 1-1 draw. That meant that a win by four goals over Celtic was needed if United were to go any further. Just prior to the match, McLean signed former Dundee striker Gordon Wallace from Seattle Sounders and he went straight into the side for his debut, along with Stewart. United controlled the first half but could not find the net and when Celtic scored in the second half it was obvious that the Tangerines were not going to pull off the required miracle. Hegarty levelled the match and in the end it was a commendable 1-1 draw but there was no further involvement in the League Cup.

The league campaign began well with a 2-1 victory at Hibs on 4th September, with a McAlpine penalty and a last minute Wallace goal sealing the points. United then produced another controlled performance against Celtic at Tannadice for a 1-0 win, with Wallace scoring, whilst two other United efforts were disallowed. Ayr United were the next victims of a good opening run, as a stylish performance from the Terrors produced a 4-1 away win. Shortly after that, Steele left to join Dumbarton for around £5,000. A visit from Partick Thistle followed, and the Jags took a shock lead in just three minutes but McAdam scored twice, as United recovered to make the score 2-1. A fifth win in a row came with a deserved 2-0 victory against Motherwell on 2nd October to keep United at the top of the league. There was a break of almost three weeks before United played the next league match. Prior to that came a testimonial match for Iain McDonald, forced out of football due to serious injury, aged just twenty-four. Torrential rain almost had the match postponed but the 5,057 fans that turned up were glad it went ahead, as they witnessed a 7-7 draw with Dundee. Both sides fielded guest players, with Ronnie Glavin and John Greig in the United line up and Kirkwood got his first outing when he came on as a second half substitute. United led 6-3 at one point but a late surge from the visitors put them in front and only a last gasp goal from Payne levelled the match again.

The league campaign picked up again on 20th October as United travelled to Celtic where an early Wallace goal was disallowed and United lost Rennie to injury, with Hegarty taking his place in the centre of the defence. At half time, Celtic's one goal lead did not look insurmountable but midway through the second half, the home side netted four times in fifteen minutes and United could manage just a late Sturrock consolation. The 5-1 score line flattered Celtic but United stayed top and they consolidated that position with a 2-1 win at Hearts three days later. Top spot was maintained the following week, even after a closely contested match at Aberdeen ended in a 3-2 defeat. Surplus to requirements, Reid left United to join Ayr United for £7,000. Sadly, a subsequent injury restricted him to just two appearances for his new club before he was forced to quit the game.

On 3rd November, United played Kilmarnock and earned two valuable points from a 3-0 win. United then retained top spot at home to Hibs, but only after a late goal from McAdam brought a 2-1 win. Despite losing 3-0 away to Rangers, United held on to first place in the league. With no match on 13th November, McLean wanted to keep the players sharp and arranged a friendly at Everton, where an entertaining match resulted in a goalless draw. The most significant event of the day was a positional switch, which saw Hegarty move from an attacking role into defence, from the start. Before the next match, Copland left United to join St Mirren in the First Division, for a fee of £17,000. United had turned down a bid of that same figure by Premier League club Partick Thistle just two months earlier. United stayed at the top of the table with a 2-2 draw at home to Ayr United on 20th November, with Wallace scoring a late equaliser. By the following week however, Aberdeen had taken over at the top after playing their game in hand. United then thumped Partick Thistle 5-1 away to keep up a strong challenge.

Weather problems meant that the next match did not take place until 18th December on a snow covered Rugby Park, where Kilmarnock's direct approach won the points with a single goal. Half priced season tickets went on sale in early December and the first home match afterwards was played on 27th December against Hearts, on a pitch more like an ice rink. The visitors took the lead but Payne levelled it at 1-1 for a point. The festive season programme was disrupted by the weather and United's next match was against Hibs on 5th January at Easter Road, where a fortunate point was taken in a goalless draw. Three days later, United lost more ground in the league race with a 2-1 home defeat by Celtic and then more bad weather wiped out football for three weeks. During that lean spell on the pitch there was a lot happening off it. Hull City expressed some interest in signing Sturrock. United declined the offer of a summer tour in Bangladesh. Memories of difficult conditions during previous visits to exotic locations were the deciding factor. McLean then added 'S' signing John Reilly from Tayside Boys Club.

After the three week lay off, United faced St Mirren in a Scottish Cup tie in Paisley but never got going. In front of a crowd of over 15,000, the home side ran United ragged to win 4-1. United were left with just the league to concentrate on and were still in touch near the top. To reinforce the challenge, the Terrors went to Ayr United and won 4-1 with ease. On 12th February they produced their best display of the season to beat Rangers 3-2 at Ibrox, coming from two goals behind. Walter Smith had just returned to United for a fee of £4,000 and went straight into the side to play his part, as a solid team effort won the day. Sturrock was by now attracting admirers from elsewhere and Stoke City had him watched against Rangers. Narey had also drawn attention from Spurs but McLean warned there would be no bargain buys for any side interested in the young stars at Tannadice. Money was not a problem and the Manager had around £30,000 at his disposal to bring in players if he wanted. Some of that was used when Billy Williamson left Aberdeen to join United for £14,000 on 22nd February. Just prior to that move, United had taken a point in a 1-1 draw with Motherwell and followed that up with a resounding 4-0 win over Kilmarnock, after establishing a three goal lead in the first thirteen minutes.

Williamson made his debut as a substitute against Partick Thistle on 1st March at Tannadice, where a doggedly defensive visiting side frustrated United in a 0-0 draw. The challenge at the top was maintained with a nervy 1-1 draw at Hearts and a goalless game at home to Rangers. The next two matches were crucial as United faced Aberdeen at Pittodrie and then at Tannadice, within a few days. In the first encounter United won 1-0, with Sturrock getting the only goal but it took some solid defending near the end to make sure of the points. The match at Tannadice was a 3-2 triumph and was built on outstanding goals by Narey and then Hegarty, within the opening six minutes. Aberdeen got one back but McAdam made it 3-1 by half time and the visitors scored again, keeping the result in doubt until the very end.

United then played Hibs at Tannadice and an even contest ended 1-0 to the Terrors. That left United just three points behind leaders Celtic, the team they faced next. The visit to the league leaders was therefore the most significant match of the campaign and

A McAlpine spot kick – but this one was saved

proved to be the turning point. United started well and McAlpine had an early first half penalty saved before United faded, going a goal down by half time and eventually losing 2-0. From that point onward, United slipped out of contention in the league race.

At the end of March, sixteen-year-old Derek Murray from Oakley United signed on a provisional form. United lost by a single goal at home to Ayr United. Then at Firhill the second goalless draw of the season with Partick Thistle, was the outcome of a fairly even match. Aberdeen gained some revenge for the double header defeat, beating United 3-2 at Tannadice on 13th April. There was no sign of any fight from United as they succumbed 4-0 too easily at Motherwell. Next, already relegated Hearts pulled off a shock 2-1 win at Tannadice. One bright spot in that match was the league debut of Kirkwood, who scored United's goal. A disappointing match against Rangers was lost by a single goal after a defensive error and United finished the season with a scrappy 2-1 win at Kilmarnock and a dull 1-1 draw at Motherwell. The season ended with a fourth place finish, which at least brought a UEFA Cup place.

1976-77 witnessed a big improvement on the previous season but still, everyone connected with United had to be disappointed. After such a good start to the league campaign there was no apparent reason for the collapse in the latter stages. It had been a settled line up throughout, with McAlpine, Hegarty and Payne the ever presents in the side, with 45 appearances each. Narey, Kopel, Fleming, McAdam and Sturrock all topped forty outings. Payne, Narey and Sturrock had been involved with the national side at Under-21 level. Narey had in fact gone as far as making his first full international appearance, coming on as a substitute against Sweden in a friendly, making him the first United player to turn out for Scotland at that level. Sturrock was top scorer with 17 goals. His development was certainly aided by playing alongside the experienced Wallace, who was next in line, scoring 13. Further down the development chain, Stewart and Dodds were still part of the Scotland professional youth squad and several of the 'S' signings were showing promise. United's progress could also be measured off the field with a prestigious sponsorship agreement reached with sports manufacturers Adidas. For the year ended July 1977 the Club made a loss of almost £16,000 but received £51,000 from the Sportsmen's Club to leave the balance in the bank at £87,000, although this information was not disclosed until the AGM in November 1978.

When the list of free transfers was released at the end of April, Hall was the only first team player leaving. Reserves Rae, Brown, Johnston, Boyle and McKellar were also released. Other than a few 'S' signings, all the rest of the players were retained and United also called up the provisionally-signed goalkeeper Gordon Archibald of Brechin Victoria.

1977-78

Aiming Ever Higher

Tannadice was buzzing with activity in early July, beginning with the signing of Jim McIntosh on a free transfer from Hull City. The former Montrose player was a long-time target of the Manager but did not progress beyond reserve level except to take part in two friendlies. McLean also confirmed that Walter Smith was coaching around thirty 'S' signings, and called up teenager Raymond Lorimer from Celtic Boys Club for the reserves. Also called up were provisionally-signed goalkeeper Derek Neilson from Tartan Boys Club and Jackie Myles from Edina Hibs. Moving out of Tannadice, Houston went to St Johnstone for a fee of £4,000.

The draw for the UEFA Cup paired United with the little known KB Copenhagen of Denmark. The Terrors would have to face that tie without Rolland, suspended for one game, and Fleming who was suspended for three. An offer of a friendly with Sligo Rovers in Ireland had to be turned down as United already had a full programme of pre-season matches lined up. Season ticket prices were held at the same level as 1976-77 and were on sale at £21 for the stand and £13.50 for a ground brief.

On 30th July, the pre-season build up began at home against Montrose in a Forfarshire Cup tie, in which United were fortunate to achieve a 2-1 win after underestimating the visitors. Two days later, United made a similar mistake and lost 3-1 at Alloa Athletic in a friendly. Trialist keeper Sandy Thomson, from Alloa Athletic, made his debut along with McIntosh and Vannart, the latter coming on as a substitute. A fourth debutant in that match was future star, Ralph Milne. On 3rd August, United faced a visit to Kilmarnock in another friendly but this time they won comfortably 3-0. The pre-season was completed with a controlled performance to win 2-0 at Arbroath. Then, to open the new Waterstone Crook Park in Newport-On-Tay, United played out an entertaining 1-1 draw with East Fife. Murray and Stark made their first appearances in that match whilst keeper

Thomson made his last for the first team, before being released two months later. On 9th August, almost 5,000 fans turned up at Tannadice for Doug Smith's testimonial match against a select side containing, amongst others, former United favourites Yeats, Dossing and Berg and several stars from other Premier League sides. Gillespie and Briggs were introduced later in the game as substitutes. It was a treat for the fans and although United won 5-4, the score did not really matter.

Football began in earnest on 13th August with a tough opening league match at Celtic Park where McAlpine was the United hero in a goalless draw. A surprise move two days after that match saw Williamson leave United after just six months to be replaced by Bobby Robinson from Dundee, in a player swap with a modest cash adjustment to the Dark Blues. Robinson went straight into the side to face Albion Rovers in the League Cup in its new format. The opening sectional stages had been scrapped in favour of a two-leg knockout competition. The Terrors cruised to a 5-0 win over Albion Rovers in the first leg at Tannadice, with debut man Robinson netting the fifth. Newly promoted St Mirren then came to Tannadice for a league match and United were grateful to McAlpine for a penalty save, after the Tangerines came from behind to win 2-1. In the second leg of the League Cup tie at Albion Rovers, in front of just 800 spectators, United brushed the home team aside to advance to the next round on a 10-1 aggregate.

The next league match resulted in a hard fought 0-0 draw at Aberdeen. That score was then repeated when United met a defensive Partick Thistle in the first leg of their League Cup tie on 31st August at Firhill. At Tannadice a few days later the Jags faced a barrage of attacks from United in the second leg but only a single goal from Dodds separated the sides at the end. Then on 7th September, United made the shock announcement that McAdam, who had been unable to hold down a first team place, had gone to Celtic for almost £60,000. McLean promised that the money would not lie in the bank for long. As good as his word, he signed John Bourke from Dumbarton for a similar fee. The initial offer, on the day after the McAdam transfer, was declined but Bourke joined United a week later.

On 10th September a flawless performance resulted in a 2-0 win over Hibs as United prepared to meet KB Copenhagen in the UEFA Cup. Although they did not make the final selection, teenagers Neilson and Vannart were included in the squad as United prepared. On the night of the match, the Terrors dominated play throughout but found the visiting keeper in form and had just a one goal lead from a Sturrock effort in the second half. It would not be enough.

With Bourke making his debut and scoring one of the goals, United continued a good opening sequence in the league, with a 3-0 win at Clydebank, to gain second place in the league table. United's Under-21 trio of Sturrock, Payne and Narey were in action for Scotland in midweek and watched by Richard Dinnis, the manager of Newcastle United. His interest was focused on Narey and just after the match United rejected what McLean described as a "ridiculously low offer".

Bourke scored again in the 3-2 win over Motherwell at Tannadice on 24th September but after taking a three goal lead, United had to endure a nervous last few minutes as the visitors fought back. Perhaps the player's thoughts had drifted to the impending second leg against KB Copenhagen in Denmark, where United faced a tough test to advance in the competition. A fluent display in the first half hour seemed to have United on track but they found the keeper in form again and star striker Torsten Andersen, who had missed the first leg, scored just after half time. That goal gave the Danes fresh heart and Andersen went on to complete a hat-trick and knock out a deflated United. It was a disappointing exit but United recovered well to win 2-0 at Ayr United in the league match following their return. They followed that up with a very good 4-0 first leg League Cup win at Arbroath, with teenage striker Kirkwood netting a hat-trick. Arbroath then took Dodds on loan for a month.

United suffered their first defeat of the league campaign, losing by a single goal late in the game, at home to Rangers on 8th October. A week later they lost again at Partick Thistle where the home side cancelled out United's silky football and won 2-1. Rennie was the subject of transfer talk involving a player swap but nothing happened. United then made another surprise signing, bringing Gordon Wallace (the younger of the two players with the same name then at Tannadice) from Raith Rovers for £12,000 on 21st October. He made his debut, coming on as a substitute, in a 2-1 home defeat against Celtic a day later. United then met Arbroath, without Dodds, at Tannadice in the second leg of their League Cup tie and lost an early goal. Kirkwood levelled the match and Sturrock scored the winner against the resilient Red Lichties for a 6-1 aggregate victory. United recorded a somewhat fortunate 1-0 win at St Mirren in the next league match but lost by the same score line at home to Aberdeen a week later. McIntosh then left United and returned to Montrose, whilst Jimmy Page (Macalpine Thistle) signed on an 'S' form.

Hearts were the next League Cup hurdle and an attacking display by United at Tannadice, resulted in a well deserved 3-1 first leg win on 9th November. That was followed by a trip to Easter Road where a dull league match against Hibs ended goalless, with neither side producing anything for the fans to shout about. United were back in Edinburgh a few days later to meet Hearts in the second leg of the League Cup tie and in atrocious weather, the home side went for all out attack. They scored twice to level the tie at 3-3 on aggregate and even extra time failed to separate the sides. It went to a penalty shoot-out which United lost 4-2, to exit the competition. After that late knock out, United had to get back on their feet for the visit of Clydebank and reacted well to win 4-0. A week later defences were on top in a goalless draw at Motherwell. Then at Ibrox, the loss of Bourke to injury early in the match upset United after a good opening period and they were beaten 2-0 in an ill-tempered match against Rangers. A point was dropped in a 2-2 draw at home to Partick Thistle and United were unfortunate to leave Celtic Park with nothing, after losing 1-0 on Christmas Eve.

There was some transfer activity in December, all involving reserve players. Former Middlesbrough player Ally Link was signed and he was joined in the second string by Andy Graham from Johnstone Burgh. Shortly afterwards, Vannart left to go to Forfar Athletic, where he joined a band of ex-United men that include former reserves, Allan Boath and Ken Brown and the experienced Hall, Rankin and player/manager Knox.

United ended 1977 with a 2-1 win over St Mirren, thanks to a last minute Hegarty header but then lost the opening match of 1978, to a late Aberdeen goal. Another point was collected on 7th January in a 1-1 draw with Hibs but the weather wiped out United's league matches for the rest of the month. Another new player arrived when keeper Tommy Hughes signed on loan from Hereford United, but he had little opportunity to show his ability due to several postponements because of the bad weather. His only first team outing before returning to his own club, was in the second half of a 3-0 friendly win at Raith Rovers late in the month.

Training had been difficult to arrange, due to the winter weather over the three weeks leading up to the Scottish Cup tie against Hamilton Academical on 28th January. When the match kicked off it was on a Douglas Park pitch resembling a muddy field, but United did well to master the conditions and win 4-1. United then won comfortably at Ayr United by a single goal and a few days later, Gordon G Wallace (the senior of the two players with the same name) left United to join Raith Rovers for a small fee. There was also welcome news that Dodds had been called up for the national Under-21 side. Another weather-enforced three week break meant that the next match was on 25th February at Partick Thistle and with Payne running the game, United won 2-0. The Scottish Cup fourth round match against Queen of the South had been one of the victims of the bad weather and eventually went ahead at Tannadice two days later. A stubborn Dumfries side frustrated United but after half time Fleming scored the opener to set up a 3-0 win.

The league campaign continued with a narrow defeat by one goal from Celtic on the same day that Scotland manager, Ally McLeod, announced his World Cup 40 for Argentina, including Narey, Hegarty and Payne. None of the trio was in the final 22 for the trip but just being chosen was enough to confirm that United had progressed beyond all expectation. The Scottish Cup quarter final on 11th March brought Queen's Park to Tannadice, where United had no easy passage in the 2-0 win against the plucky amateurs. The next match was a personal triumph for Forsyth, who had been struggling with injury for more than a year. In his first team comeback game at St Mirren, the pitch was muddy and pooled with water in places but United won 2-1. There was little to choose between the sides in the next match as United drew 0-0 with Aberdeen on 18th March. A week later, defensive lapses cost United dearly as they lost 3-1 at Hibs.

In late March, Link ended his short Tannadice career. Rolland also ended his time with United when he was released and went to America. During this flurry of player movement, United drew 1-1 with Motherwell, thanks to a late Holt equaliser and then United faced Rangers in the Scottish Cup semi final on 5th April at Hampden Park. The Terrors were the better side until Rangers scored late in the game, against the run of play. The advantage was doubled soon after and United left the national stadium beaten but unbowed, after a good performance.

United were of course aiming for a good finish in the league but McLean admitted frankly that the prospect of European competition, whilst important for maintaining a high profile, was not good for the bank balance. He preferred the Anglo-Scottish Cup, with less travelling costs and the prospect of bigger gates. In the final stages of the campaign, there were eight league games to be played in four weeks and at Motherwell in the first of these, Fleming scored within five minutes. United then had to defend in depth to achieve a 1-0 win. The Tangerines had a tough time beating Clydebank by the same one goal margin a few days later, relying on a late Hegarty goal to secure the points. McLean then withdrew Payne and Hegarty from a Scotland practice match in the Highlands, as he needed the players for the important league matches coming up at home to Ayr United and Rangers. United beat the Ayrshire side by a single goal but lost by the same margin to Rangers. In a second match against Rangers a few days later at Ibrox, United went down to a 3-0 defeat.

United had had a problem finding the net all season but then netted eight goals in two games, beating Ayr United 3-1 on 26th April with three goals in the first half, then scoring a 5-2 victory over Partick Thistle. However, in the last league match of the season on 2nd May, with Graham and Stark making their debuts in major competition, United lost 2-0 at Clydebank, the relegated side. The final match of the season drew a crowd of 10,778 to Dens Park for the 1975-76 Forfarshire Cup final against Dundee, who were then still in the First Division. It was a full-blooded encounter, settled in extra time with two headers by Hegarty, for a 3-1 win.

United's third place finish in the league was their best ever and guaranteed UEFA Cup football for the next season. Success was measured in the lengthy runs in both domestic cups and a good league campaign, despite the lack of goals. Top scorer was Kirkwood with 11 goals, of which 7 were in the League Cup, and Fleming was close behind on a total of 10, with all bar one of those in the league. The only ever present was Hegarty, with 50 outings and McAlpine, Kopel, Narey, Fleming, Payne and Sturrock recorded more than 40 appearances. In addition to the players selected for the World Cup 40 and the Scotland Under-21 side, Lorimer was in the professional youth set up, along with Stewart, who captained the international youth side. Another honour collected by a United player came in the form of the first ever SPFA Young Player of the Year award, which went to Graeme Payne.

McLean sent a youth squad to France at the end of the season and they returned with the Under-19 Ville De Dunkerque Trophy. Kirkwood, Milne, Stark, Dodds and Murray were part of the winning squad. They had also played in the Reserve League Cup final which was lost to Rangers on penalties. The Manager was happy with his squad of players and as a result, there was just one free transfer at the end of the season, when Myles was released. Rennie was forced to retire because of injury. The Club's AGM for the year ended July 1978 was not held until a year later, when United again posted good results, with trading income showing a profit of £46,000 and added to that was a donation of £36,000 from the Sportsmen's Club.

An interesting postscript to the season came at the Scottish League AGM, where the subject of betting shops at football grounds was discussed. United had been refused permission by the SFA in October 1977 to have a betting shop at Tannadice because, in the words of Chairman Rankine Grimshaw, "gambling and football should not be seen to go hand in hand." Obviously there was an eventual change of mind by the Scottish football authorities! There is now betting available at many grounds, including Hampden Park, the home of the national side and its ruling body.

1978-79

Towards a Brighter Future

United had been advised that a reduced crowd capacity of 10,000 would be in force for the new season, pending safety enhancement at Tannadice. Only then would the new capacity of 18,465 be permitted. With these restrictions in mind, supporters were encouraged to get to Tannadice early for their season tickets, costing £26 for the stand and £17 for the ground. However, over the season the Club was involved in various appeals at both regional and national level and the new regulations were not implemented. A friendly with Eintracht Frankfurt was tentatively agreed until it was ascertained that the German side wanted to play United at Tannadice. The Directors then decided against the match, as a substantial guarantee was being requested by Frankfurt. Instead, all the pre-season matches were arranged against Scottish opposition, with the exception of a trip to play Port Vale.

Training started in early July with around fifty players taking part. Included with the full-time and part-time players were teenagers Neil Clark (Fraserburgh) Peter Dolan, Graham Marshall, John Milliken (Tobago Boys Club) and Dean Kay (Tartan Boys Club) who had just been called up to the squad. They were joined by 'S' signings Colin Craig, Steve Moran, David McCabe, Paul O'Brien, Gerry Lesslie and Paul Cavanagh (Tartan Boys Club). Most of this group would play in the reserves during the season but few progressed much beyond that level. The only player missing was Bourke, who had opted to stay away from Tannadice and had been suspended by the Club. He never played again and in October he left to join Kilmarnock for £40,000. Walter Smith was also in the news, linked with a move to Aberdeen in a coaching role but he decided to remain with United. There was a reported £½m bid from one of the big English clubs for an unnamed United player, thought to be either Hegarty or Narey but the offer was declined. It was also revealed that this had not been the first big offer for a player and partly in response, the Directors introduced a pension scheme for players who signed long-term contracts, to ensure a substantial lump sum payment when they finished their playing careers. It proved to be a very astute move by the Board and guaranteed that in the coming years, United would retain many extremely talented players. The only player who left United in the close season was Forsyth, who joined Raith Rovers for around £15,000.

The pre-season matches began on 29th July at Raith Rovers with a comfortable 3-0 win but two days later, United received a rude awakening in a one goal defeat at East Fife. It then took a last minute Kirkwood goal to achieve a 2-1 win at Queen of the South and a deflected Robinson shot settled an ordinary game at Port Vale. The only pre-season home match was on 7th August when visitors Montrose were beaten 1-0 in a Forfarshire Cup tie. Shortly after that United signed Second Division top scorer Derek Frye from Stranraer, for a fee of around £15,000. The new striker made his debut at Tannadice when he came on as substitute against Hibs during a 0-0 draw in the opening league match on 12th August. He scored the opening goal in his next game but opponents Partick Thistle levelled the match at Firhill, 1-1 after half time. United then played a midweek Forfarshire Cup semi final against Forfar Athletic and had Holt to thank for an early goal that won the match. The third league draw in succession was recorded when Aberdeen were the visitors to Tannadice on 26th August. Both sides adopted an attacking policy and it ended level at 1-1.

The first round of the League Cup intervened four days later and United entertained Celtic in the first leg of their tie on 30th August. It was a closely contested match with both sides having their share of dominance but it ended 3-2 to the visitors. With all to play for in the second leg three days later, United held their own at Celtic Park and came close to levelling the aggregate score. However, the loss of Fleming to a red card early in the second half was crucial and Celtic made the best of their advantage, scoring from a disputed late penalty to knock United out on a 4-2 aggregate. A week later, as the team prepared for a visit to Standard Liege of Belgium in the UEFA Cup, Frye missed a penalty as United lost 2-1 at home to Morton, who scored a late winner. The match in Belgium had been brought forward by a day to Tuesday 12th September and had been moved to Ghent following crowd trouble at Liege the previous year. United were hampered by the loss of Payne and Sturrock to first half injuries and that contributed to the 1-0 defeat.

On returning from Belgium, it emerged that there had been an alleged illegal approach to Narey by Derby County assistant manager, Frank Blunstone, whilst both teams were returning from their European matches. The English Club had already made their interest in Narey known. This latest action angered United and an official complaint was made through the SFA. After the investigation, five months later, Blunstone was severely censured and fined £500.

United recovered from their European disappointment with a determined performance to win 1-0 at Motherwell and a week later recovered from an early setback to win 3-1 at St Mirren. That set United up for the second leg of the UEFA Cup tie against Standard Liege at Tannadice on 27th September. With an enthusiastic support behind them, the Terrors were unfortunate in the first half, having a good penalty claim denied and a Kopel effort disallowed. The Tangerines were not at their best though, and the match ended goalless, putting United out 1-0 on aggregate. Again, the side recovered and comfortably disposed of Hearts in a 3-1 win at Tannadice. That was followed a week later by a hard fought 1-1 draw at Rangers, where United had to withstand some pressure to leave with a point. On the same day, it was announced that Sturrock had requested a transfer and the Club agreed to listen to offers. Within days a bid for an unnamed United player was rejected.

The next match, on 14th October, was settled when Kopel scored in the first minute against Celtic at Tannadice. United went on to play with style and confidence, but there were no more goals in a narrow, but deserved win. A point was gained in a 1-1 draw at Hibs a week later. Then on 28th October, buoyed by the recent inclusion of several players in the various Scotland international squads, United went to the top of the Premier League with a controlled 2-0 win at home to Partick Thistle. The Terrors would go on to retain top spot for the next fifteen weeks, even after losing 1-0 at Aberdeen and 3-1 at Morton in the next two games. Graham Honeyman, who had just returned after playing in Australia, was signed on a trial basis and made his debut as a substitute in the match against Morton on 11th November. Other additions to United's list at the time were 'S' signings, David Beaumont and Maurice Malpas, while John Reilly was added to the reserves.

Top spot was consolidated with a 2-1 win over Motherwell and a 1-1 draw with St Mirren and then Iain Phillip was signed from Dundee for £25,000. That was followed by the news that Narey had been selected to play for Scotland from the start against Portugal, coincidentally on the same day that his long overdue cap from his Sweden debut arrived by post at Tannadice. United were so thrilled that they hoisted the Lion Rampant in his honour but were apparently ordered to take it down, as it was the Royal Standard in Scotland, to be used only for a royal occasion!

December began with the news that Motherwell had tried for a second time to lure McLean to Fir Park but he was not interested. Nor was he interested three months later, when a lucrative offer was received from Canadian side Toronto Metros. After six years at Tannadice he was only part of the way towards his goal. As if to underline how the players felt, on

*Dave Narey
– The first Dundee United
player to turn out at full
international level for
Scotland*

9th December they faced Rangers at Tannadice and played at the peak of their form against the Glasgow side to win 3-0 with a classy performance. Shortly afterwards Honeyman was released at the end of his trial period. The win over Rangers was followed by a creditable 1-1 draw at Celtic, with Phillip making his debut as a late substitute.

United beat Hibs 2-1 at Tannadice on 23rd December to top the league at the halfway stage. From that point on however, severe winter weather caused serious disruption to the football card and in the next two months United were restricted to just three league matches and two friendlies. They struggled to find a suitable training surface and managed to arrange a friendly on 9th January at Raith Rovers where they won 3-1, whilst a second team lined up at Forfar Athletic and won 4-1. Jim Kerr from Stonehouse Violet was then added to the reserve strength.

In a Scottish Cup rehearsal, United lost 2-1 at St Mirren in the league on 20th January and did not play again until 3rd February at Arbroath, where they won 3-0 in another friendly. A week later United were knocked off the top spot in the league, after losing by a single goal at Rangers. The Scottish Cup tie with St Mirren at Tannadice was postponed and did not go ahead until 26th February. A crucial penalty failure left United ruing chances missed. They had the lion's share of play but lost 2-0, conceding both goals in the final stages.

United again paid the price for not converting outfield superiority into goals when they lost 1-0 at Hibs on 3rd March but after playing at their best to beat Motherwell 4-0 and Morton 4-1, the Terrors were back at the top again. Further good displays followed, with a 2-1 win at home to Partick Thistle and a 2-0 win at Aberdeen, and even after losing 3-1 at Morton, United stayed top. The run of good results continued with a deserved 2-1 win at Partick Thistle but at home to Motherwell it took a late surge and two goals from Addison in the last four minutes to secure a fortunate 2-1 result. At struggling Hearts, the title challenge took a severe knock as the home side defended in depth to steal the points in a 2-0 win. United won the next three games, beginning with a 2-0 win against St Mirren to partly avenge the Scottish Cup defeat. Against Celtic, United came from behind to win 2-1 on 11th April. They stretched the lead at the top with a 3-0 win at Hearts but then faced Rangers at Tannadice in a crucial encounter. United wilted under first half pressure and were two goals behind at the interval. They fought back with an early second half goal by Stewart from the spot but lost 2-1. With just three matches to go, United were six points clear of Rangers in second place, with Celtic a point further behind, but the Glasgow duo each had five games in hand.

United maintained the challenge with a 2-1 win over Hearts but then lost another important match 2-1 at Celtic, after playing the better football and leading at half time. A 2-2 draw at home to Aberdeen concluded United's programme. They were still in top spot but were eventually overtaken by Celtic and Rangers when the Glasgow clubs played out their games in hand. It was another disappointing end to a league campaign, added to the early cup exits in all three major competitions. Nevertheless, United had come a long way since McLean had arrived. Fans were now turning up more in expectation, rather than in the hope of winning, as had perhaps been the pre-1960 scenario. With another third place finish, the best season to date had been built on a solid defence, with ever presents McAlpine, Hegarty and Narey ably supported by the emerging Stark and Stewart. In attack, no-one set the heather alight, with top scorer Kirkwood netting 11 times and Dodds one fewer.

The number of United players involved at international level was unprecedented. Narey and Hegarty had been with the Scottish League squad to meet the Irish League in November 1978. In addition, McAlpine had been selected in the initial squad for that match. United's central defensive pairing had also been on full international duty, with Hegarty making his debut against Wales in the Home Internationals in May. Stewart was involved at Under-21 level and also in the international youth side along with Milne, Lorimer and keeper George Tulloch, who had been signed from Everton. In the team as a whole, what was more evident was a belief in their own ability and that would result in better things in 1979-80 and beyond. McLean had faith in the players, and released just reserves Kay, Marshall, Dolan and McCabe. United's reputation was enhanced further as Paul Hegarty collected the SPFA Player of the Year award and Ray Stewart was presented with the Young Player award.

The last match of the season brought Dundee to Tannadice for a Forfarshire Cup tie on 14th May. In front of a bumper crowd of 12,170, an exciting game ended 2-2 after extra time and the sides were finally separated in a penalty shoot-out which Dundee won 3-2. It had been tremendous entertainment and whet the appetite of the fans for the forthcoming derby matches in the next season, as Dundee had just won promotion. That was not quite the end of the season. United had been invited to tour several countries, including America, Canada and Norway but elected to take up an invitation to play in the Japan Cup. On the way to a semi final against Fiorentina, United drew 2-2 with Argentinian club side, San Lorenzo, and beat the Burmese national side 4-0 and a Japan B side 2-0. The semi final resulted in a 1-1 draw, which put United into the final against Spurs. United missed a penalty in the first half and the English club took the lead, leaving United chasing an equaliser. Spurs scored another goal late in the game to win 2-0. The tour party was made up of the first team players and included Ian Ballantyne. Recently signed from Queen's Park, he had made a scoring debut in the Forfarshire Cup tie against Dundee.

The results of the Club's financial year ended July 1979 were published in April 1980, and showed the best ever financial position for United, with the bank balance standing at £133,000, after the Club made a profit of almost £32,000. Dundee United Sportsmen's Club had donated almost £50,000. An additional source of income had come on stream, with a payment of £32,000 from Littlewoods Lotteries, following the introduction of an instant win ticket scheme at the beginning of the season.

The end of season 1978-79 marked a highly significant turning point in the history of Dundee United. After a period in the doldrums following the end of WW2, the Club had drifted along for over a decade. The first sign of real progress came with the creation of Dundee United Sportsmen's Club, which provided the much needed cash over the next crucial period, to turn the fortunes of the Club around. Jerry Kerr came in with his undoubted eye for talent and laid the foundations for success on the field of play, introducing many exciting players. Following Kerr's departure, Jim McLean then further developed the youth programme, and that combined with shrewd transfer dealing took the Club to the next level. The rise of the Terrors was now complete, as an even brighter future beckoned. There would soon be tangible evidence that Dundee United were now amongst the elite of Scottish football.

The Players

Listed in order of the season that they first played for the Club, the following pages contain career details of all the players known to have signed for Dundee United from August 1945 until May 1979.

To qualify for inclusion, the player must have played at least once in the first team either signed provisionally, professionally, on loan or as a temporary transfer. A player is also included from the point that he made his first appearance as trialist, junior, senior, A N Other or under an assumed name and later signed.

1945-46 Player Profiles

George Barron was a left back signed from Aberdeen Muggiemoss. He made his only first team appearance for United in a friendly against a Polish Army XI on 10th April 1946. George was re-signed for the following season but never played in the first eleven. He was however, frequently in the Dundee United 'A' side, which played in C Division. In December 1946, he went to Huntly on loan and was released by United in April 1947.

Martin Buchan was signed from Aberdeen. He went straight into the United side for his debut at inside right against East Fife on 19th January 1946, in the final game of Southern League B Division. He never missed a match over the rest of that season, playing in more than a dozen cup ties. Martin was re-signed for the return of Scottish League football in 1946-47. He started the season well with a scoring league debut against Dunfermline Athletic on 10th August 1946. Later in the campaign, he found it more difficult to keep his place and he was demoted to the reserves by December 1946. He was released in April 1947.

Bob Collins was a left winger signed from Dundee Arnot. He made his debut for United in the Southern League Cup play-off against Ayr United at Hampden Park on 3rd April 1946. Bob started season 1946-47 playing for Dundee United 'A' in Scottish League C Division but was released at his own request three months into the season.

John Cruickshanks was a left half who joined United on loan from Aberdeen in the latter stages of season 1945-46. He made his debut in the last Southern League B Division match of the campaign, against East Fife on 19th January 1946. John played in most of the remaining matches in various cup competitions that season and then returned to his own club.

Charlie Ferguson was an inside forward who had been with Middlesbrough, Notts County and Luton Town before WW2. During the war he had played with Arbroath and Aberdeen. He made his United debut on 1ˢᵗ September 1945 against Ayr United in a Southern League B Division match but was not with United for long. His work took him to North Shields in November 1945 and he was released to join the local side there as player/manager.

Bill Harrow

Bill Harrow was a right half with Elmwood. He signed for United and made his debut against Cowdenbeath in a Southern League B Division match on 29ᵗʰ December 1945 and was frequently in the line up over the remainder of the season. He was retained as a reserve for the next two seasons, playing regularly for Dundee United 'A' in Scottish League C Division. He made just two more first team appearances in friendlies before he was released in April 1948.

Lloyd Hull was a half back signed from Lesmahagow Juniors. He made his debut on 23ʳᵈ March 1946 against Ayr United in a Southern League Cup tie. Lloyd played just a few more times before the end of that season. He was re-signed for 1946-47 and played briefly for Dundee United 'A' in Scottish League C Division but he was released early in the season.

John 'Jacky' Hunter joined United from Morton on loan, making his debut at centre forward on 25ᵗʰ August 1945 against Albion Rovers, in a Southern League B Division match. He made just four more appearances for United before returning to his own club.

Alex Jardine was signed from Wishaw Juniors as a direct replacement at left back for Frank Shufflebottom, who was about to leave the area after he was demobbed. Alex made his debut on 9ᵗʰ March 1946 against Dumbarton in a Southern League Cup tie. When the Scottish Leagues were restarted the following season he was in the line up that faced Dunfermline Athletic on 10ᵗʰ August. Over the next three years Alex was a regular in the side, usually at left back but he also played on the right side and occasionally in the half back line. In the latter stages of season 1949-50 several new players arrived at United

Alex Jardine

and Alex found it harder to get into the side. He then played out his time at Tannadice for Dundee United 'A' in Scottish League C Division. After refusing to re-sign the following season, Alex was transfer listed and was very quickly signed by Millwall for an undisclosed fee, later reported at £700. He remained with the London side for eight years but his career ended prematurely in 1958 through injury.

Willie Kelly was a centre half signed from St Mirren. He made his debut on 18th August 1945 against St Johnstone in a Southern League B Division match. Willie missed very few games until the return of John Ross kept him out of the side and he requested a transfer in late January 1946. Within a few weeks he moved to Morton where he was later suspended *sine die*.

Alec MacFarlane was a right half with Crosshill Hearts and then Arbroath. He played his first game for United as a trialist on 1st September 1945 in a Southern League B Division match against Ayr United and signed the following day. Alec was a frequent starter in the side until he was called up for national service in February 1946. Over the next two years he played once in a Forfarshire Cup tie and also turned out in a couple of Scottish League C Division matches for Dundee United 'A', when his military duties allowed. After he was demobbed in the Spring of 1948, he returned to United for season 1948-49 but he was restricted to just a handful of first team games, playing mostly in C Division matches until he was released in April 1949. He then signed for Cowdenbeath.

John McGowan was a left back signed from Thornliewood United. He made his debut in a Southern League B Division match against Dunfermline Athletic on 11th August 1945. Signed on a short-term deal, he turned out just a few more times and appears to have been released in December 1945.

Ed McInally was an inside right signed from Lanark United. He made his Dundee United debut in a Southern League B Division match against Cowdenbeath on 29th December 1945. The arrival of other players to fill the forward positions left Ed making just a handful of appearances and he was released in April 1946.

Neil McKinnon made a scoring debut as a right winger against Albion Rovers on 24th November 1945 in a Southern League B Division match. He joined United from Rangers and was a regular in the side for the rest of season 1945-46. He re-signed for the next season in the Scottish League but midway through the campaign he was transferred to Albion Rovers. Neil later played for Queen of the South.

Willie Martin had been an inside right with Huddersfield Town and Bradford Park Avenue before WW2 and he joined United from junior side St Rochs. He made a scoring debut against Dunfermline Athletic in a Southern League B Division match on 17th November 1945. He made just three more appearances for the Club before being released.

George Mudie was a right half signed from Brechin City. He made his debut on 24th November 1945 against Albion Rovers in a Southern League B Division match, his only appearance for United at any level.

Emilio Pacione was a Lochee Harp centre forward who made his first appearance for United as a trialist on 20th October 1945 against Stenhousemuir in a Southern league B Division match. He scored two of the goals in a 7-0 win and scored another brace a week later in his second trial. That was enough to convince new Manager, Willie MacFadyen to sign the player and he became a regular in the side from January. In 17 league appearances that season he was top scorer with 13 goals, and then re-signed for 1946-47. Half way through that campaign he moved out to the right wing where he performed regularly over the next two seasons. In the latter part of 1948-49 he was more often in the Dundee United 'A' side in Scottish League C Division. Emilio played regularly for the second string in the next term, making just three more first team appearances before he was released in May 1950. After he left United, he spent a short time with Coleraine in Northern Ireland before returning to Scotland to join Brechin City.

Emilio Pacione   *Len Rae*   *Frank Shufflebottom*   *John Tivendale*

Len Rae was an inside forward signed from Inverurie Locos. He made his debut in a Southern League Cup tie against Ayr United on 23rd March 1946 and showed enough potential in the final stages of the season to remain with United for the next campaign. Len started that season playing for Dundee United 'A' in Scottish League C Division, only breaking into the first eleven in December 1946, at which point he became a regular in the side. He found a new lease of life in the half back line until January 1948 when he lost his place following the arrival of new players. Len ended his career at United back in the reserve side and after he was released in April 1948, he joined Brechin City.

Devon Reid was a young goalkeeper who joined United from Brechin Victoria. He made his debut as a trialist on 2nd January 1946 against Dumbarton in a Southern League B Division match. He then signed a short-term deal, playing just twice more before he was released.

Frank Shufflebottom was a full back with Ipswich Town before WW2. During the war he played with Nottingham Forest, Raith Rovers and Kilmarnock before he signed for United, making his debut against Dundee in a Southern League B Division match on 8th September 1945. He was stationed in the Dundee area and was a regular in the United line up until he was demobbed in April 1946. Shortly after that he returned to Nottingham Forest and later played for Bradford City.

Harry Smith was an inside left who began his career at Stobswell. He then spent five years with Dundee. In 1934, he joined Clapton Orient where he remained until the outbreak of WW2. After the war he signed for United, making his debut on 22nd December 1945 against Airdrieonians in a Southern League B Division match. He was in and out of the side over the next few months and was released in April 1946.

William Smith was signed from St Monance Swifts after he showed up well in the 1945 pre-season trial match. He made his debut at right half in a Southern League B Division match on 11th August 1945 against Dunfermline Athletic. William made only three appearances throughout the season and he was released in April 1946.

Percy Steele was an full back with Tranmere Rovers. He joined United on a temporary transfer, making his debut against Dundee on 1st January 1946 in a Southern League B Division match. Percy played inside left at United for a month but in that short time, he scored five times in five appearances. He returned to Tranmere Rovers where he spent the next ten years.

Alec Stewart was a surprise signing from St Johnstone. He made his debut at inside left against his former club on 10th November 1945 in a Southern League B Division match, but after just one more outing with United, he was released.

John Tivendale was a Watford reserve player who made his United debut on the right wing against East Fife on 27th October 1945 in a Southern League B

Division match. John made just four more appearances in early 1946. Although he re-signed for the next campaign, he played just twice in the first eleven but turned out frequently for Dundee United 'A' in Scottish League C Division. He was released in April 1947 and joined Leith Athletic.

Jack Wilson was a former United Juniors player who made just one appearance at outside right for Dundee United, playing in a Forfarshire Cup tie against Arbroath on 16th February 1946. He may also have previously turned out for United several times during WW2.

Benny Yorston had started his senior career at Montrose and then spent five years at Aberdeen where he also collected his only Scottish international cap. He then played for Sunderland and Middlesbrough during an eight year spell in England before WW2. Benny played just once for United at inside left against Albion Rovers on 24th November 1945 in a Southern League B Division match.

Hugh Young played in the 1945 trial match and then signed from local junior side YMCA Anchorage. He was a right winger and made his debut in a Southern League B Division match against Dunfermline Athletic on 11th August 1945. Hugh was restricted to just a few appearances in season 1945-46 and was released at the end of the campaign.

Leslie Young was registered with Manchester United and he was stationed locally in the RAF. He signed for Dundee United as an amateur, making a scoring debut as a right winger against Stenhousemuir on 20th October 1945 in a Southern League B Division match. Leslie made several more appearances but seems to have left United at the end of December 1945.

Trialist, Junior, Senior, Newman, A N Other

The following players, listed as one of the above, are those known to have played during the season.

Aitken of Croy Celtic at inside left against Stenhousemuir on 20th October 1945 in a Southern League B Division match, scoring a hat-trick.

Bob Carrie of Dundee Violet in goal against Cowdenbeath on 6th October 1945 for the first of three appearances in Southern League B Division matches.

Davis of Renfrew in goal against Airdrieonians on 29th September 1945 in a Southern League B Division match.

Wood (ex-Dunfermline Athletic) at centre forward on 4th May 1946 against Arbroath in a Forfarshire Cup tie.

Roy Young of Kirkintilloch Rob Roy at left half on 22nd December 1945 against Airdrieonians for the first of two appearances in Southern League B Division matches.

1946-47 Player Profiles

Doug Berrie

Doug Berrie was a versatile full back signed from local junior side Stobswell. He began his career in August 1946 in United reserves playing in Scottish League C Division matches. His first team debut came on 14th December 1946 against Cowdenbeath in a Scottish League B Division match. Doug was frequently in the first team line up over the rest of the campaign. He re-signed for the following season and became a regular in the side in either full back position over the next six years until he was released in May 1953. He then signed for Forfar Athletic. In April 1961, after eight years at Station Park, he was granted a testimonial for which United provided the opposition. Doug was released by Forfar Athletic in April 1964. His son, also Doug, was a United 'S' signing in May 1970 but never emulated his father as a first team player at Tannadice.

John Brannan was a seventeen-year-old inside forward signed from Maryhill Hibs. He played most of his three years at Tannadice in Dundee United 'A' in Scottish League C Division, making over 40 appearances at that level. John made his first team debut in a Forfarshire Cup tie against Brechin City on 30th April 1947 and his first appearance in major competition three days later against Albion Rovers in a Scottish League B Division match. He had just two more first team games before he was released in May 1949.

Willie Crothers was severely wounded on active service in Burma during WW2 but recovered after six months in hospital. He was with Dunipace Juniors when he first played as a trialist for United against Alloa Athletic in a Scottish League B Division match on 11th January 1947, scoring twice. He was signed immediately after. A centre forward, Willie was an ever present in the side for the rest of that season and was re-signed for the next. The arrival of Peter McKay meant that he found it harder to get into the side in 1947-48 and had to be content with playing from time to time in the first team or in the reserves. In March 1948, he spent a short period on loan at Stirling Albion. At the start of season 1948-49 he was playing well and scoring regularly for Dundee United 'A' in C Division. Willie was promoted to the first eleven again, demonstrating his ability with eight goals in an eight game spell including a hat-trick against Kilmarnock. However, he was soon back in the reserves where he spent the majority of that campaign and the next, with a brief spell on loan at Alloa Athletic in March 1949. After January 1950 Willie was not in the first eleven and played for Dundee United 'A' where, in total, he racked up an average of almost a goal a game in over 60 matches. He also had a good strike rate in his first team outings. He left United in late November 1950 to join Forfar Athletic and later played for Stenhousemuir.

Jake Davidson was an inside left signed from local junior side, Dundee Violet after showing up well in the 1946 public trial match. He made his debut on 10th August 1946 against Dunfermline Athletic in a Scottish League B Division match. In his second game for United, he scored a hat-trick against Stenhousemuir in a Supplementary Cup tie and was a regular in the side during the first half of the season. The arrival of Alex Lister created fewer opportunities for Jake in the first eleven and he played the remainder of the campaign for Dundee United 'A' in Scottish League C Division. He refused terms to re-sign in the summer of 1947 and was transfer listed, later joining East Fife, where his brother Doug was already playing, joining Kilmarnock in 1950.

Jake Davidson

Lou France was a right back signed from St Johnstone YMCA, primarily as a reserve. He began playing for Dundee United 'A' in Scottish League C Division in January 1947, making his first team debut on 14th April 1947 against Raith Rovers in a Scottish League B Division match. Lou played again the following day in a Forfarshire Cup tie against Brechin City but that was his last first team match. He re-signed for 1947-48 and spent the entire season as a regular in the reserves until he was released in April 1948.

George D Grant was an inside right signed from New Stevenston United, displacing former team mate George Stewart to make the position his own. He made his debut on 7th December 1946 in a Scottish League B Division match against Arbroath. George attracted the attention of Burnley after just a handful of games for United but stayed at Tannadice, missing only a few games that

George Grant

season. He was re-signed for the next seven seasons and during his career, he featured regularly in the line up, forming part of United's 'Famous Five' of Quinn, Grant, McKay, Dunsmore and Cruickshank in the early 1950s. George was regularly on the score sheet in his time with United, recording a remarkable hat-trick in three minutes against Hamilton Academical in October 1949. Burnley were watching the player again in early 1950 and he also attracted interest from Huddersfield Town, Hearts and Portsmouth but still he remained at Tannadice. His loyal service at United was marked with a joint testimonial with Jimmy Toner of Dundee in April 1954. In November 1954, he went to Falkirk in a swap deal that brought Willie Dunlop to United. George joined Hamilton Academical in 1956.

George Jeffrey was an inside right signed from Hamilton Academical. He made his debut in a Supplementary Cup tie on 28th August 1946 against Dunfermline Athletic and three days later made his Scottish League debut against St Johnstone. George was on a short-term contract and was released in late September 1946. He signed for Stirling Albion in December 1946 and then for East Fife four months later.

Tommy Kinloch was a right half who had been with Benburb and Glasgow Secondary Juveniles. In three seasons at Tannadice, he played mainly for Dundee United 'A' in Scottish League C Division, making 60 reserve appearances. He made his debut for the first team in a Scottish League B Division match against Albion Rovers on 3rd May 1947 but had only occasional first team appearances thereafter. Tommy was released in May 1949, going to Falkirk for a season before joining Carlisle United for 1950-51. After five years with the Cumbrian side, he moved to Workington and later played with Southport, Wigan Rovers and Colwyn Bay.

Alex Lister had been with Third Lanark and began his United career with trials in the reserves before signing. He made a scoring first team debut on 19th October 1946 against Dumbarton in a League Cup tie. Although usually an inside left he could play in most forward positions and was a regular in the first eleven. In his first season, Alex scored 18 goals in 22 league and cup games to become top scorer. He signed for the next campaign but made just a few first team appearances, playing mainly for Dundee United 'A' in Scottish League C Division. He then spent all of the next campaign in the reserves before he was released in May 1949. Alex then moved to Northern Ireland to join Glentoran and later played for Alloa Athletic, Rochdale, Montrose and Stenhousemuir.

Peter MacKay was a goalkeeper who began season 1946-47 playing for Dundee United 'A' in Scottish League C Division. He played just once for the first team, on 4th September 1946 against East Fife in a Supplementary Cup tie and appears to have left the Club soon after.

Alec Miller was a left half who had been with Celtic and Preston North End prior to WW2. He was with Motherwell and available for transfer at £400 when he signed for United, making his debut in a Scottish League B Division match on 10th August 1946 against Dunfermline Athletic. Alec was a regular in the line up that season, usually at left half but sometimes as centre half. He even played once at centre forward. He lived in the west and owing to travel difficulties, he requested a transfer in March 1947. His request was turned down and he re-signed for season 1947-48 but two months into the campaign he was transferred to Morton. He later played for Inverness Caledonian and Stranraer.

Tommy Muir was a goalkeeper with Bridgeton Waverley. He was signed as a reserve in August 1946 and was a regular in the Dundee United 'A' line up in Scottish League C Division in his first season. Tommy made his first team debut on 1st March 1947 against Rangers in a League Cup quarter-final first-leg tie. He shared the keeper's jersey with Dave Clark for a short spell but was soon back in the reserves where he played almost exclusively in 1947-48. Tommy racked up around 45 appearances at reserve level in his two years at Tannadice. He requested a transfer in November 1947 but did not leave United until April 1948 when he was released. He then joined Derry City in Northern Ireland.

Sammy Ross was a former Kilmarnock, Rangers and Falkirk right half who had also been on loan at Dumbarton and East Fife. He signed from Motherwell for £350, despite stiff competition from several English sides. He made his debut for United on 10th August 1946 against Dunfermline Athletic in a Scottish League B Division match and went on to miss just one game over the entire season. He re-signed for the next campaign but after just a handful of games, he was transferred to Morton.

Jimmy Salmond joined United from Jeanfield Swifts. He made a scoring debut at left half on 17th August 1946 against Ayr United in a Scottish League B Division match. It was his only first team game for the Club and after a short run for Dundee United 'A' in Scottish League C Division, Jimmy left to join Brechin City.

Robert Simpson was a right back signed from Lochgelly Albert after playing in a trial match in July 1946. He made his debut for United on 10th August 1946 against Dunfermline Athletic in a Scottish League B Division match. Robert was the first choice right back for the season, missing only a handful of games near the end of the campaign. He featured regularly again in 1947-48 and then signed for a third term but could not command a first team place in season 1948-49. Instead he played for Dundee United 'A' in the Scottish League C Division. Originally released in May 1949, he appears to have returned to play for the reserves in the early months of 1949-50.

George Stewart was an inside forward signed from New Stevenston United. After playing a few matches for Dundee United 'A' in Scottish League C Division, he was promoted to the first eleven and made a scoring debut at right half on 9th November 1946 against Alloa Athletic in a Scottish League B Division match. George Grant was signed from the same junior club, making his debut a month later and he then took over the inside right berth. As a result George Stewart was relegated to the reserves again and was released in April 1947. Just weeks later he died in a tragic accident.

Sammy Ross   *Robert Simpson*   *Tom Wyllie*

Tom Wyllie was a centre half signed from Arbroath Victoria in October 1946 as a reserve. He made his first team debut on 2nd January 1947 against St Johnstone in a Scottish League B Division match. In the next season, he continued to play regularly in the reserves, making just a few more first team appearances. In February 1948, his work took him to the Highlands and he went on loan to Elgin City. Tom did not play for United again but was still a registered player and went on loan to Arbroath for a short time in the early part of 1949-50 but he was then released by United.

Trialist, Junior, Senior, Newman, A N Other

The following player listed as one of the above, is known to have played during the season.

Peter Carroll from Banks O' Dee at centre forward on 14th December 1946 against Cowdenbeath in a Scottish League B Division match, scoring a goal.

1947-48 Player Profiles

John Barr was a former Queen's Park Rangers and Third Lanark centre half. He was briefly with Dunfermline Athletic before he joined United for a short stay, making his debut on 13th December 1947 against Ayr United in a Scottish League B Division match. John played just once more before leaving.

John Boyd was a goalkeeper with Dunipace Juniors. He made his United debut on 16th August 1947 against Leith Athletic in a League Cup tie, becoming the first choice keeper for the rest of the season. John was re-signed for 1948-49 but was temporarily displaced to the reserves by Fred Watson just after the new season began. He won his place back in October but then lost out to Alec Edmiston in January and was released in Aril 1949. However, after a season with Albion Rovers he returned to United and was briefly first choice again until he was ousted by another new keeper, Bob Wylie in November 1950. John was released again in May 1951.

John Boyd   *Jimmy Craig*   *Jack Dewar*   *Jimmy Dickson*

Jimmy Craig was an inside left with Rosslyn Juniors. He made a scoring debut for United against Cowdenbeath on 14th February 1948 in a Scottish League B Division match. Jimmy spent the remainder of the season with United but played mainly in the reserves in Scottish League C Division, making just a handful of first team appearances. He re-signed for 1948-49 and spent the entire season in the reserves. Jimmy was with United at the start of the next campaign but appears to have left in September 1949.

(William) Joe Dalling was signed from Tulliallan Juveniles in the summer of 1947. He was a right winger and made his debut on 16th August 1947 against Leith Athletic in a League Cup tie. He made just two more first team appearances over the season but played around 20 times for Dundee United 'A' in Scottish League C Division matches before he was released in April 1948.

Jack Dewar was one of three loan signings made in March 1948 to help the Club successfully avoid relegation. He was a left winger and made his debut against Raith Rovers on 20th March 1948 in a Scottish League B Division match. He went back to his own club, Hearts, at the end of the season but returned to United as a signed player for the 1948-49 campaign. Over the next two years, he was a regular in the line up on the left side of attack or the half back line. Jack began season 1950-51 in the first eleven but in the latter part of the campaign he featured only rarely and was released in May 1951. He then joined Forfar Athletic.

Jimmy Dickson joined United as part of the deal that took George 'Piper' MacKay to Dundee. Jimmy was a left half but made his debut at centre half on 27th December 1947 against Albion Rovers in a Scottish League B Division match. As the first choice at left half, he re-signed for season 1948-49 and featured regularly in the side. Although retained initially for the next campaign, Jimmy left to join Queen of the South in the summer of 1949.

George Henderson was a former Third Lanark player who was with Stirling Albion and in season 1947-48 he was Scotland's top scorer. A centre forward, he was one of three players signed on loan at the transfer deadline to help United in a successful bid to avoid relegation. George made a scoring debut against Raith Rovers on 20th March 1948 in a Scottish League B Division match. He also scored two crucial goals against Ayr United in the match that secured safety. After playing in all the remaining games, George returned to his own club at the end of the season. He later played for Dunfermline Athletic, St Mirren, Albion Rovers, Alloa Athletic and Stranraer.

Jimmy 'Soldier' Jones was a former Dundee right winger. He had a trial in United reserves before making his first team debut on 13th September 1947 against Cowdenbeath in a League Cup tie. His only other outing in the first eleven was in a friendly at Elgin City in October 1947 and he appears to have left United soon after.

Johnny Kerr was a lifelong United supporter signed from Dundee North End. He made a scoring debut at inside left on 13th August 1947 in a Scottish League B Division match against Alloa Athletic and became a regular in the side for the next few weeks. He fell out of favour and played most of the remainder of the season in Dundee United 'A' in Scottish League C Division, making around 20 appearances there. At the end of the campaign, he was released and went to Northern Ireland where he signed for Glentoran.

John McCormack was signed from Stenhousemuir and made his debut at inside left on 6th March 1948 against Leith Athletic in a Scottish League B Division match. He played in most of the remaining games that season and was retained for 1948-49 but played just twice at the start of the campaign. John was a regular in the reserve line up for most of his second season and was released in May 1949.

Johnny Kerr *Peter McKay*

Peter McKay was the first Dundee United post-war legend. An instant hero with the United fans, the centre forward was signed from Newburgh after he had netted sixteen times for the junior side in just five matches. He made his United debut on 13th September 1947 against Cowdenbeath in a League Cup tie and soon hit the goal trail. In just 20 appearances, he scored 13 times to end the season as top scorer. Peter repeated that feat the next year with 38 goals in 37 appearances including hat-tricks against St Johnstone, Hamilton Academical and Dumbarton. He also scored four goals in one game against Queen's Park. In the same season, he netted eight goals in just three Forfarshire Cup ties, including another two hat-tricks. In the summer of 1949, he became assistant groundsman at Tannadice. Peter just could not stop scoring and in 1949-50, he netted 35 goals in 36 games including another four hat-tricks. Part of United's 'Famous Five' of Quinn, Grant, McKay, Dunsmore and Cruickshank in the early 1950s, Peter became the object of attention for scouts from other clubs including Portsmouth, Hull City and Hearts. The next season brought 38 goals in 40 appearances, including four in one game against Alloa Athletic and another hat-trick. The following season he was top scorer again with 36 scored in 40 matches, including another five hat-tricks. Burnley and Portsmouth were showing interest but United issued a hands off warning. Another two hat-tricks and four in one game against Kilmarnock in 1952-53 helped him to 17 goals but for the only time in his seven seasons at United, he was not top scorer. He regained that honour in his final season, 1953-54, adding another 26 goals from 37 appearances, including three hat-tricks, to his tally for a total of 203 goals in 241 games in major competitions and another 27 goals in 20 Forfarshire Cup ties. In April 1954, Hibs wanted to take Peter on trial but that request was declined. However, with interest being shown by Dundee and Falkirk, Burnley made an offer of £3,000 and Peter decided to put his ability to the test south of the border. Just as he had been with United, the little centre was a big hit with the Burnley fans and in 60 appearances, he netted 36 times. He later moved to St Mirren before returning south to end his career at Corby Town. Peter was inducted into the Dundee United Hall of Fame in January 2009. The award was made posthumously and accepted on his behalf by his family.

Frank McKee was a versatile inside forward signed from Lochgelly Albert. He made his debut for United on 30th August 1947 in a League Cup tie against Albion Rovers. His talent was quickly spotted by other clubs and after just a short time at United, he was transferred to Birmingham City in February 1948. After three years at Birmingham he moved to Gillingham and then to Gloucester City.

Gibby McKenzie did not want to join United when they first tried to acquire him from Airdrieonians in December 1947 but a month later, he was persuaded to sign. A right half, he made his debut on 31st January 1948 against Dumbarton in a Scottish League B Division match, becoming a regular in the side for the rest of the season. He re-signed for 1948-49 but had just four first team outings at the start of the campaign, thereafter playing mainly for Dundee United 'A' in Scottish League C Division. Gibby left to join Dundee as a coach and then took up an SFA coaching position in Shetland

Gibby McKenzie

in March 1949 before moving to Kilmarnock in the same role. He went into management in 1954 with Northern Irish side Linfield. Gibby then became manager of Morton but returned to Northern Ireland to take over at Portadown. When United played Portadown in a friendly in October 1958, Gibby was linked with the vacant job of Manager at United.

Ralph McKenzie

Ralph McKenzie was one of three players who joined United on loan for the latter stages of season 1947-48 in a successful battle to avoid relegation. He was a centre half with Aberdeen and made his United debut on 20th March 1948 against Raith Rovers in a Scottish League B Division match. After playing his part in saving United from the drop, he then returned to his own club.

Alec Malcolm was with Jeanfield Swifts before he joined United. He was a left winger and made his debut on 27th August 1947 against Albion Rovers in a Scottish League B Division match. Alec played just a few times for the first team and around a dozen games for Dundee United 'A' in Scottish League C Division. Towards the end of 1947-48, he left to join Stirling Albion, initially on loan.

Malcolm Sinclair was a former Third Lanark player, signed by United on a free transfer from Falkirk. He made his debut at left half in a Scottish League B Division match against Dumbarton on 18th October 1947 and was a regular in the side until shortly after the arrival of Jimmy Dickson. Malcolm was unable to hold down a first team place after that and was released at the end of the season.

Trialist, Junior, Senior, Newman, A N Other

The following players, listed as one of the above, are those known to have played during the season.

Alex Collins of Carnoustie Panmure at right wing on 15th November 1947 against Leith Athletic in a Scottish League B Division match.

Bert Finlay of Dundee Violet at right back on 13th March 1948 against Hamilton Academical in a Scottish League B Division match.

1948-49 Player Profiles

James F Cameron was a right half with Blairhall Juniors. He had trials with Dundee, but joined United and made his debut against Stirling Albion on 26th February 1949 in a Scottish League B Division match. James became a regular in the side for the rest of the campaign and was re-signed for 1949-50. After playing in the early months of that season, he was dropped and finished his career at United playing Scottish League C Division football in the reserves. He was released in May 1950.

George Cruickshank

George Cruickshank was a junior international left winger signed from Banks O' Dee. He made his United debut as a trialist on 4th September 1948 against Kilmarnock in a Scottish League B Division match. George spent the next six years at Tannadice. Other than for a short period in early 1950, he was normally the first choice for the left wing, becoming one of United's 'Famous Five' of Quinn, Grant, McKay, Dunsmore and Cruickshank. At the end of season 1953-54 he was surprisingly released by the Club and then signed for Arbroath. It was several months before a satisfactory replacement was found.

Andy Dunsmore was an inside left signed from Blairhall Juniors against stiff competition from Blackburn Rovers and Southend United. He made his debut against Hamilton Academical in a Scottish League B Division match on 12th March 1949. Andy was re-signed for the following season but played just a few times whilst turning out regularly in the reserves. In 1950-51 he established himself in the first team forming United's 'Famous Five' front line of Quinn, Grant, McKay, Dunsmore and Cruickshank and was then a regular in the side for three years. Although normally a forward, Andy also filled in at half back on numerous occasions during his Tannadice career. In his final season, 1953-54, he featured less often and he was released in May 1954 and then signed for Arbroath. Andy also played for Albion Rovers.

Andy Dunsmore   *Alec Edmiston*

Alec Edmiston was a goalkeeper signed from St Andrews United. He made his debut against Dumbarton on 8th January 1949 in a Scottish League B Division match and then became the first choice keeper for the remainder of that season. Alec re-signed for season 1949-50 and played in goal for the major part of that campaign. He then fell out of favour and was demoted to the reserves, making just a few first team appearances at the end of 1950-51. Alec was called up for national service in August 1951 and four months later, he was posted to Germany but featured in the line up for United a few times whilst home on leave. He later served in Korea and after he was demobbed in the summer of 1953, he became a regular in the side again. Over the next four years, several keepers came and went but Alec was the usual first choice until the arrival of Bill Lucas at the end of 1956-57. By the time he left United, Alec was considered a legend at the Club. He was released in May 1957 and then joined Brechin City where he played for the next six years.

Willie Hume was an inside forward who had been with Hearts before he joined Aberdeen. From there he signed for United, making his debut on 14th August 1948 against Dumbarton in the first Scottish League B Division match of the new season. He featured occasionally in the first half of the season but was in the reserves thereafter playing in Scottish League C Division matches. Although retained for 1949-50, he did not play again at any level for United.

George Mitchell was a junior inside left with Aberdeen Sunnybank. He made his United debut as a trialist on 1st January 1949 against St Johnstone in a Scottish League B Division match and became a regular in the side for the rest of that campaign. In the following season, he took on a new role in the half back line where he played successfully. In 1950-51 George was more often in the Dundee United 'A' line up in Scottish League C Division but was restored to the first eleven for the next campaign. He was released in May 1952 and then moved to Forfar Athletic.

| *George Mitchell* | *Duncan Ogilvie* | *Frank Quinn* |

Duncan Ogilvie signed for Motherwell in 1932 and gained his only international cap a year later against Austria. In 1936, he joined Huddersfield Town but a few months later returned to Motherwell in a deal that took Willie MacFadyen to the Yorkshire side. After WW2, he joined Hamilton Academical. He played in a closed doors trial for United in early August 1948 and he was then signed. Duncan was an experienced defender and made his debut for United in a Scottish League B Division match on 14th August 1948 against Dumbarton. He featured regularly in the side until February 1949. Although he re-signed for season 1949-50 he was not used again and retired from the game when that season ended. He later became a director at Falkirk.

Frank Quinn was a right winger, signed on a free transfer from Celtic where he had been for two years without establishing himself in the side. He burst on to the stage at Tannadice with a hat-trick in a reserve match and then made his first team debut on 1st September 1948 against Alloa Athletic in a Scottish League B Division match. He was soon the first choice on the right, scoring nine league goals in his first season. In a Tannadice career spanning six years, Frank was a regular in the side and was one of the stars of the early post-war era, becoming one of United's 'Famous Five' of Quinn, Grant, McKay, Dunsmore and Cruickshank. Considering he was a winger, Frank had a fantastic scoring rate and netted 20 goals or more in each season bar his first and last at Tannadice. He also notched hat-tricks against Kilmarnock, Forfar Athletic and Dumbarton during that period. In 1952-53, he was the Club's top scorer, netting 24 goals in 37 games.

In his final season, he featured in just over half of the league and cup games and he was perhaps surprisingly released in May 1954. Considered a United legend, Frank then joined Hamilton Academical and later played with Cowdenbeath and Stranraer. He still had much to offer and proved that on several occasions with match-winning play against United.

Alfred 'Fred' Watson was a goalkeeper with Renfrew Juniors. He played his first match for United as a trialist against Dunfermline Athletic in a Scottish League B Division match on 18th August 1948. Fred was then signed and retained the keeper's jersey for the next nine games in preference to John Boyd, but thereafter played more often in the reserve side than in the first team. The arrival of Alec Edmiston left Fred surplus to requirements and he was released in May 1949.

1949-50 Player Profiles

Jimmy Colgan was an inside forward who had been with Partick Thistle, Airdrieonians and Bournemouth & Boscome Athletic before he arrived at United on a short-term deal. He made a scoring debut against Dumbarton on 17th August 1949 in a League Cup tie but after just one more game in the first eleven and three in the reserves, he was released.

Andy Donaldson was formerly with Aldershot and signed for United from Dunfermline Athletic. Although he was normally a full back, he made his first appearance for United at centre half on 6th September 1949 in a friendly against Newburgh Juniors. Six days later, he was in the side that played Kilmarnock in a Supplementary Cup tie and made his league debut against the Rugby Park side on 1st October 1949. Andy continued to play in the side at full back until November 1949 but then dropped out of the line up completely. He played in the reserves in the latter stages of the season but he was released in May 1950.

Earle Downie was a right half with local junior side Dundee Violet. He made an impressive start in United reserves and then made his first team debut on 15th October 1949 against Dunfermline Athletic in a Scottish League B Division match. Earle became a regular in the line up and was rarely out of the side over the next three seasons until he was released in May 1952. He then signed for Dunfermline Athletic.

Earle Downie

Jim Elliot was an inside left signed from Ayr United. After making a good early impression in the reserves, he made his first team debut on 27th August 1949 against Airdrieonians in a League Cup tie and featured regularly in the side for the next three months. He then lost his place and played out the season in the reserves until he was released in May 1950.

Willie Guthrie

Willie Guthrie was provisionally signed from Newburgh Juniors and made his first United appearance against his own club on 6th September 1949 in a friendly. He was called up for United reserves and scored a hat-trick in his first game, which meant he was quickly promoted to the first eleven. An inside right, Willie made a scoring debut in major competition against Albion Rovers in a Scottish League B Division match on 26th November 1949. He then had a short run in the side, but never made the breakthrough into the first team. Willie turned out for the reserves in Scottish League C Division until the end of the season at which time he was released.

Albert 'Bert' Hood joined United on a one month deal from Brechin City. The goalkeeper made his debut in major competition on 13th August 1949 against Airdrieonians in a League Cup tie but after just one more appearance, in a friendly at Newburgh Juniors, he returned to his own club. Ten years earlier, Bert had played for United as a trialist.

Ted Leven was signed from Brechin Renton. He made just one first team appearance for United, at inside right on 6th September 1949 in a friendly against Newburgh Juniors. He spent the next three months in the reserves before going on loan to Brechin City and at the end of the season, he was released.

George Morrison

George Morrison made a scoring debut for United with two goals against Stenhousemuir in a Scottish League B Division match on 25th March 1950, after successful trials in the reserves. He was signed from Thornton Hibs and initially played in the forward line but was soon converted to a half back. George stayed with United for three seasons but spent most of his time playing with Dundee United 'A' in Scottish League C Division, where he totalled more than 50 appearances. He had an extended run in the first team in the early part of 1952-53 but was released in May 1953.

Alec Shaw was a left winger, formerly with Strathclyde Juniors and Crewe Alexandra. He signed from Lovell's Athletic and made his debut on 18th February 1950 against Forfar Athletic in a Scottish League B Division match. Alec retained the left wing berth until the end of the season and was re-signed for 1950-51 but spent most of that campaign in the reserves playing in Scottish League C Division. He made just four more first team appearances before being released in May 1951.

Bob Sherry had played with Queen's Park as an amateur and then joined Kilmarnock. A centre half, he made his debut on 17th August 1949 against Dumbarton in a League Cup tie. Over the rest of the season he played mainly in the reserves, making just a few first team appearances. In the next campaign, he was again in the reserves where he racked up a total of over 40 appearances in two seasons. He was unfortunate to be in direct competition for a first team place with the dependable Bobby Ross, but remained with United until he was released in May 1951.

Bob Wyllie was a goalkeeper with Monifieth Tayside and signed provisionally for United in September 1949. After playing well in the reserves for three months he was promoted to the first team, making his debut on 19th November 1949 against Morton in a Scottish League B Division match. He then shared first team duties with Alec Edmiston for the remainder of the season. Bob began the next season as first choice and after a two month spell out of the side he reclaimed his place in November 1950. He was rarely out of the line up for the next two years other than through injury. In May 1953, he left United to join Blackpool and later played for West Ham United, Plymouth Argyle and Mansfield Town, before ending his career at non-league Ilkeston Town.

Bob Wyllie

Trialist, Junior, Senior, Newman, A N Other

The following player listed as one of the above, is known to have played during the season.

George Skinner of Comrie Colliery at left wing on 7th January 1950 against Dumbarton in a Scottish League B Division match.

1950-51 Player Profiles

Charlie Campbell was a left half signed from Dundee North End in December 1949 after successful trials in the reserves. He made his first team debut on 23rd September 1950 against St Johnstone in a Scottish League B Division match but after just three outings, he was back in the reserves. In total, he made around 50 appearances for Dundee United 'A' but just one more at first team level. He was called up for national service in October 1951 but remained a registered player until he was released in May 1953.

John Coyle

John Coyle was a centre forward with St Joseph's. He signed for United on a provisional form in September 1950 and made an early impact in the reserves, when he joined the squad in February 1951. His first team debut came on 30th April 1951 against Arbroath in a Forfarshire Cup tie. He made his first appearance in major competition against Cowdenbeath in a League Cup tie on 11th August 1951. Later that month, the fans were taking notice of the young centre as he scored all four goals in a 4-2 win against Stenhousemuir. Unfortunately for John, he was in direct competition with an in-form Peter McKay and although he turned out occasionally for the first team, the youngster was left to hone his goal scoring skills mainly in the reserves. To gain further experience he spent the latter part of 1952-53 at Brechin City on loan as United no longer operated a reserve eleven in Scottish League C Division by that time. On his return, John's appearances were infrequent, largely because he was on national service from the summer of 1953. However, after he was demobbed in June 1955, he became a Tannadice legend, scoring at a remarkable rate. In season 1955-56, he was top scorer with a Club record that still stands, 43 goals. That was an average of exactly one goal per game in major competition including four goals in games against East Stirlingshire and Berwick Rangers. He repeated that feat against Albion Rovers in the next season and also netted hat-tricks against Ayr United and Third Lanark. His total for that term was 38 goals in 49 games and he was top of the scoring charts at Tannadice again. His form continued in the same vein in 1957-58 and he netted hat-tricks against Stranraer and Morton. John was frequently the subject of transfer speculation and in late 1955, there were rumours linking him with Leeds United. Several other clubs were keeping close tabs on John and in January 1957, Falkirk made an approach but surprisingly dropped their interest. Two months later, Dundee tabled an unsuccessful offer of £1,750. United were determined to hold on to John and there was a benefit match being planned against top class English opposition. However, the player put in a transfer request in late 1957 and left to join Clyde in December 1957 for a fee of £5,000. At Clyde, John won a Scottish Cup winner's medal, scoring the only goal of the 1958 final, in a 1-0 win over Hibs. He was in the 1958 Scotland World Cup Squad in Sweden but did not play. Two years later, John went south to join Cambridge City and then played for Boston United. In January 2009, he was inducted into the Dundee United Hall of Fame.

Richard 'Dicky' Grieve had started his career at Montrose and had played for Rochdale. An inside forward, he signed for United from Wrexham on a free transfer in January 1951. He spent most of his time at United in the reserves but even there he played just a handful of games. He made only one first team appearance on 3rd February 1951 against Cowdenbeath in a Scottish League B Division match and he was released at the end of that season.

Dicky Grieve

Davie Johnstone was signed from St Johnstone on a one month trial. He made his debut at left back against Kilmarnock on 30th September 1950 in a Scottish League B Division match. After playing four times during his trial period, he was signed. However, Davie was unable to get back into the first team and spent the rest of his time at Tannadice in the reserves. He appears to have been released in February 1951.

David Kinnell was an inside forward signed from St Andrews United in the face of strong competition from Ipswich Town and Rangers. He made a scoring debut for United on 14th October 1950 in a Scottish League B Division match against Dunfermline Athletic. After just

David Kinnell

four games, he dropped out of the side and played the remainder of the season in the reserves, making just a Forfarshire Cup appearance at first team level at the end of 1950-51. He re-signed for the next season and turned out in three League Cup matches but was soon back in the reserves where he totalled over 30 appearances in his two years at Tannadice. David was released in May 1952.

Matt McIlwain was a former Ayr United inside forward who had been on trial at Reading before he joined United on a one month deal. He made his debut on 7th October 1950 in a Scottish League B Division match against Stenhousemuir. After playing in the next three matches he was released when his contract expired. Matt joined Bolton Wanderers in August 1951.

Archie McIndewar was an inside right, formerly with Rangers and Dumbarton. He took part in the public trial match in August 1950 and was then signed on a short-term deal. Archie made his United debut on 12th August 1950 against Stenhousemuir in a League Cup tie. After just one more game at first team level and three in the reserves, he was released. He then joined Stirling Albion and later played for Workington.

Hugh Ormond was signed from St Mirren on a free transfer in October 1950, primarily as reserve cover at left half. He made his United first team debut on 9th December 1950 in a Scottish League B Division match against Queen's Park. Hugh played just once more that season, in a friendly, spending most of his time in the reserves. He was re-signed for 1951-52 and turned out in League Cup ties early in the season but was again demoted to the reserves where he racked up almost 40 appearances in his two years at United. After just a few more first team outings, Hugh was released in May 1952.

Dave Stratton was a university student who played for United for four seasons, signing on for each campaign as an amateur according to the rules. He was signed from Elmwood on a provisional form in September 1949 and was a regular in the reserves playing at full back in Scottish League C Division matches throughout his first season. Dave began the next campaign in the reserves again, before making his first team debut on 2nd October 1950 against Hamilton Academical in a Scottish League B Division match. Soon after that, he broke into the first eleven as a left half and was frequently in the line up over the next two years. In his four seasons with United, he played just as often in the first team as he did in the reserves. He was recognised at amateur international level and played for Scotland against Wales, England and Northern Ireland in 1951. In his last season, 1952-53, he was less frequently in the first team and when the season ended, he did not re-sign for the next campaign.

Bob Swan was a right back signed from Alloa Athletic on a free transfer in December 1950. After a successful run in the reserves, he made his first team debut on 24th March 1951 against his former club in a Scottish League B Division match. Bob then kept his place for the few remaining games of the season. He re-signed for 1951-52 but was back in the reserves and did not reclaim a first team slot until November, becoming first choice until the end of that campaign. In his last season, 1952-53, he played for the first team several times in the early part of the campaign but dropped out of the line ups in January. He was released in May 1953.

1951-52 Player Profiles

Tommy Dunlop was a centre half signed for season 1951-52 as a reserve from local junior side Osborne. He had played well in the second string and got his chance in the first team with a debut on 10th November 1951 against Kilmarnock in a Scottish League B Division match. However, he had just one more league outing and one in a friendly before he was back in the reserves where he totalled more than 25 appearances. He was released in May 1952.

Neil Fleck was formerly with Alloa Athletic and Falkirk and played against United in a friendly at Llanelli. An inside left, he signed in the summer of 1951 and after just one game in the reserves, made his debut on 22nd September 1951 against St Johnstone in a Scottish League B Division match. Neil retained his place for the next six games but was then relegated to the reserves again for most of the rest of the season. He had just one other short run in the first eleven in January 1952 and was released in May 1952.

Jimmy Guy was a half back who had played for Third Lanark and Stirling Albion. He joined United from Falkirk on a free transfer, making his first appearance in a friendly against Crystal Palace on 12th May 1952. His debut in major competition followed on 9th August 1952 against Dumbarton in a League Cup tie but he made just a few appearances before he was released in May 1953.

Jimmy Irving was formerly with Motherwell, St Johnstone and Kilmarnock and signed for United at the end of season 1951-52. He was an inside left and made his first appearance in a friendly against Cowdenbeath on 19th April 1952, scoring one of the goals. Jimmy made his debut in major competition against Dumbarton in a League Cup tie on 9th August 1952 but featured in the side again only occasionally and was released in May 1953.

Jimmy Irving

Jimmy Knight was a right winger signed from Dundee Violet for United reserves, where he made more than two dozen appearances in total. He made his first team debut for United on 15th September 1951 against Queen's Park in a Scottish League B Division match. Jimmy played just twice more in the first eleven and he was released in May 1952.

Johnny McIvor was a left winger with Maryhill Harp and made his first appearance for United as a trialist on 10th November 1951 against Kilmarnock in a Scottish League B Division match. He signed soon after, but had just one more outing that season, spending most of his time in the reserves. He was called up for national service in 1952, and over the next two seasons he was in the line up only occasionally and was released in May 1955.

Johnny McIvor

George 'Lachie' McMillan was signed from Kirkmuirhill Juveniles and was considered one of the brightest prospects in the juvenile ranks. He was a left half and made his first team debut on 25th August 1951 against Cowdenbeath in a League Cup tie following some impressive displays in the reserves. After an initial run in the first team, he fell out of favour and finished the season back in the second string. George made just a few appearances in his second season and he was released in May 1953.

Jimmy McMillan signed from Whitburn Juniors on a provisional form in December 1950, joining United as a reserve in August 1951. He spent his first season at Tannadice in the second eleven, making more than 30 appearances in Scottish League C Division league and cup matches. Jimmy made his first team debut at left back on 19th April 1952 in a friendly against Cowdenbeath. His first outing in a major competition was against Dumbarton on 9th August 1952 in a League Cup tie. He was in the first team line up in the early part of the season but could not command a regular place and was released in May 1953.

Jimmy Melville was United's reserve goalkeeper signed from Dundee Arnot in September 1951 and played regularly for Dundee United 'A' throughout the season. He managed one outing for the first team but it was not in goal. Jimmy was on the right wing in a friendly against Coupar Angus on 23rd April 1952. He was released soon afterwards.

John Scott was a former Third Lanark centre forward who signed for United from Cowdenbeath. He made his debut on 29th March 1952 against Dumbarton in a Supplementary Cup tie but after one more outing, in a Dewar Shield match, he was released.

Richard 'Dickie' Sneddon joined United from Lochore Welfare in the latter stages of season 1950-51, primarily as a reserve right half but he also played inside right occasionally. He re-signed for the next campaign but made just two first team appearances, including his debut on 22nd September 1951 against St Johnstone in a Scottish League B Division match. He spent most of his time in the reserve side where he made over 30 appearances in total. Dickie was released in May 1952.

Trialist, Junior, Senior, Newman, A N Other

The following players, listed as one of the above, are those known to have played during the season.

Buchan (ex-Hearts) at left wing on 12th May 1952 against Crystal Palace in a friendly.

Cash (ex-Airdrieonians) at right back on 12th May 1952 against Crystal Palace in a friendly.

Pollock of St Johnstone at left half on 12th May 1952 against Crystal Palace in a friendly.

1952-53 Player Profiles

Alex Arnold was signed from junior side Dundonald Bluebell after a pre-season trial match. He was a centre half and made his debut on 16th August 1952 against Ayr United in a League Cup tie. Alex (also referred to as Sandy) became an important part of the United defence for the next five years and, apart from a spell on the sidelines in the latter half of both seasons 1953-54 and 1956-57, he was rarely out of the side until he was released in April 1957. He then joined Stirling Albion and later played for Berwick Rangers.

Alex Arnold   *Sam English*   *Johnny Laird*   *Jimmy Lovie*

Sam English signed for United from Albion Rovers where he had been unsettled. Formerly with Arbroath, he was a right back but made his debut at centre half on 15th November 1952 against Ayr United in a Scottish League match. He became a regular in the side until January 1954 at which time he lost his place and requested a transfer. Sam was however quickly back in the side again and was re-signed for the 1954-55 campaign but he was released in October 1954, shortly after Reggie Smith was appointed Manager.

Johnny Laird joined United from Rosyth Recreation. He made his debut as a trialist at left half on 29th November 1952 against Alloa Athletic in a Scottish League match and was signed immediately afterwards. Despite playing regularly in the side for the rest of the season, he was released before the new season began and signed for Montrose.

Jimmy Lovie was a versatile inside forward signed from Highland League side, Peterhead. He made his debut as a trialist on 28th February 1953 against Albion Rovers in a Scottish League match and signed shortly after. Jimmy played in every match for the rest of the season and was initially retained for 1953-54 but was transferred back to Peterhead before the new season got under way. He later played in England for Bury, Bournemouth & Boscombe Athletic and Chesterfield.

Charlie McMullen was a former Arbroath inside right signed from Hamilton Academical. He made a scoring debut against Stirling Albion on 13th August 1952 in a League Cup tie. Charlie failed to establish himself in the side, making just two more appearances before he was released.

George Munro had been with Irish side Shelbourne before he joined St Johnstone and then signed for United. A versatile full back, he made his debut on 13th August 1952 against Stirling Albion in a League Cup tie. He featured regularly in the defence until he was released in May 1953.

George Munro   *Jimmy Murphy*   *Jim Temple*

Jimmy Murphy was with Blantyre Celtic when he made his first appearance for United as a trialist on 14th March 1953 against Morton in a Scottish League match. He then appears to have joined Celtic but signed for United on a free transfer in August 1954. Jimmy was a regular in the side in season 1954-55, featuring on either wing. Re-signed for the following season, he played just twice more before he was released in October 1955, signing for Brechin City.

Jim Temple was the second signing of the season from Fife junior side, Dundonald Bluebell. He was an inside right and made his debut on 6th December 1952 against Dunfermline Athletic in a Scottish League match. Jim featured regularly in the side over the remainder of the season and was re-signed for the next campaign. As the new season progressed, Jim was often in the line up but he was released in May 1954. In December 1955 he joined Montrose but left them four months later.

Jimmy Timmins was a university student who was playing for Hamilton Academical. In September 1952, United urgently required players to fulfil a Second XI Cup fixture and Jimmy was one of the men signed. He could not be persuaded to remain with United but did make one first team appearance, against Stirling Albion in a Scottish League match on 11th October 1952.

Trialist, Junior, Senior, Newman, A N Other

The following players, listed as one of the above, are those known to have played during the season.

Barclay of Tranent at inside right on 21st February 1953 against Queen's Park in a Scottish League match.

Clark of Dennistoun Waverley at left back on 13th December 1952 against Forfar Athletic in the first of two Scottish League matches.

David Condie (ex-Raith Rovers) at left back on 9th May 1953 against Montrose in the first of two Forfarshire Cup ties.

Kenny Dick of Alyth United in goal on 10th January 1953 against Stenhousemuir in a Scottish League match. He also played in a friendly against Blackpool on 5th October 1953.

Jimmy Easson of Dennistoun Waverley at centre forward on 28th February 1953 against Albion Rovers in a Scottish League match.

George Gray of Glencraig Colliery at centre forward on 6th December 1952 against Dunfermline Athletic in a Scottish League match.

Alec Hood of Rosewell Rosedale at left wing on 7th March 1953 against Ayr United in a Scottish League match.

Dennis Logue of Blantyre Celtic at centre forward on 14th March 1953 against Morton in a Scottish League match, scoring a goal.

McLaren of Bridgeton Waverley at inside left on 6th December 1952 against Dunfermline Athletic in a Scottish League match.

Ian Muir (ex-Motherwell) at centre half on 9th May 1953 against Montrose in the first of two Forfarshire Cup ties.

John O'Hanlon of Easthouses Lily at right wing on 7th March 1953 against Ayr United in a Scottish League match, scoring a goal.

Johnny Raeburn of Lochgelly Albert at centre forward on 14th February 1953 against Hamilton Academical in a Scottish League match, scoring a goal.

Jerry Tracey of Ardeer Recreation at centre forward on 13th December 1952 against Forfar Athletic in a Scottish League match, scoring a goal.

1953-54 Player Profiles

Frank Callaghan joined United from junior side Paisley St Mary's. He was a versatile half back and made his debut as a trialist against Alloa Athletic on 21st November 1953 in a Scottish League match. Three weeks later, after a second trial, he was signed. At the time, Frank was nearing the end of his national service in the RAF. Based locally, he was able to turn out regularly over the remainder of the season. By the time season 1954-55 started, he had been demobbed and re-signed, again becoming a regular in the side until a knee injury kept him out in the early months of 1956. He was back playing regularly in 1956-57 but at the end of that campaign, he

Frank Callaghan

was released and then signed for Third Lanark. Frank later played for Morton, Forfar Athletic and Inverness Clachnacuddin.

Ernie Doig was a right half, formerly with Kilmarnock and Falkirk. He made just one appearance for United, at right half in a Scottish League match on 31st October 1953 against Forfar Athletic.

Jimmy Forbes spent some time at Rangers, and in his last season there, he was on loan at Dumbarton. He joined United, making a scoring debut against Morton on 8th August 1953 in a League Cup tie. A versatile player, he was able to fill either half back position or an attacking role. Jimmy was a regular in the side until January 1954, when he joined the RAF on national service. He did not play again until August 1954, making a few appearances in the early months of that season. He was back with United after he was demobbed in January 1956 and was again a regular in the side until he was released in May 1957. He then joined Stenhousemuir.

Jimmy Forbes

Phil Gormley was an inside right who had been with Celtic before joining Aldershot in 1950. He came to United on a two month deal and made his debut at left half on 8th August 1953 against Morton in a League Cup tie. Phil took part in four League Cup matches but left when his contract expired.

Jimmy Hamilton

Jimmy Hamilton was a former Alloa Athletic and Cowdenbeath left back. He made his debut for United on 17th October 1953 against Motherwell in a Scottish League match. Jimmy then became the regular left back and never missed a game during the remainder of the season. He attracted interest from Chelsea in April 1954 but stayed at United for season 1954-55. However, he managed only two appearances and requested a transfer in January 1955. No offers came in and he was released three months later.

Joe Locherty had been with Sheffield Wednesday, Colchester United and Scarborough before he signed for United on a free transfer. He had the misfortune to make his debut at left half in the side that suffered a record 12-1 defeat on 23rd January 1954 against Motherwell in a Scottish League match. It was his only outing for United.

Robert 'Bert' McCann signed for United as an amateur from Dundee North End. He made his debut on the right wing on 5th September 1953 against Dumbarton in a Scottish League match. Over the season, he also played at inside left and in both half back positions. As an amateur, his contract was for one year only and at the end of the season, he did not re-sign. Instead, he went to Queen's Park, still as an amateur and he won five international caps at that level whilst with the Hampden Park side. He signed for Motherwell in 1956 and was with them for eleven years, including five years as club captain. He spent his last season playing with Hamilton

Bert McCann

Academical. Bert gained full international recognition, playing for Scotland five times between 1959 and 1961.

James McKee joined United from Doncaster Rovers. He made just one appearance, at left back against St Johnstone on 19th September 1953 in a Scottish League match.

Des McLean was an experienced goalkeeper who had been with Queen's Park, Celtic and Arsenal. He joined United from Airdrieonians on a two month deal and started the season in goal against Morton on 8th August 1953 in a League Cup tie. After three games, all of which were lost, he was replaced by Alec Edmiston. Des was released when his contract expired.

Henry Morris signed for United in May 1953 from East Fife where he had won two League Cup winner's medals. An experienced centre forward, he had gained an international cap against Northern Ireland in October 1949, scoring a hat-trick in an 8-2 World Cup qualifier win. His opening goal in that match was the first goal ever scored by a British player in World Cup competition. He made his United debut against Morton on 8th August 1953 in a League Cup tie but after just one more game, he lost his place in the side. He requested and was granted a free transfer in November 1953.

Henry Morris

Johnny Samuel was an ex-Morton player signed from Third Lanark. He made his debut at centre half on 8th August 1953 against Morton in a League Cup tie. Johnny made some impact initially but lost his place in the side and was released in May 1954. He then signed for Portadown in Northern Ireland.

Alf Scrimgeour was a centre forward who joined United from Stobswell. He played his first game for United on 4th January 1954 as a trialist centre forward against Third Lanark and scored a goal. He was signed for the next season but made just three appearances.

John Shearer was signed from Airdrieonians. He made his debut for United immediately after signing on 12th December 1953, playing at centre half against Albion Rovers in a Scottish League match. He was in the line up for every game over the rest of the season but was released in May 1954.

Archie Smith joined United from East Fife and made his debut in a League Cup tie on 22nd August 1953 against Morton. A versatile full back, he made a good initial impact but after a two month run in the side, he was dropped and had only three more first team outings before he was released in May 1954.

Alec Stenhouse was a right sided attacking player, signed from junior club Auchterarder Primrose. He made his debut for United on 16th January 1954 against Kilmarnock in a Scottish League match and was in the line up a few more times before the end of the season. In April 1954, during a joint testimonial,

Alec Stenhouse

against Dundee, for George Grant and Jimmy Toner, Alec was the first United player to come on as a substitute and score a goal. A regular in the side during the following season, Alec left the area in the summer of 1955 to carry out his national service. He was retained by United for the next two years but made only two appearances whilst home on leave. In February 1957, he went to Portsmouth for a fee reported at £1,000. Alec later played for Southend United, Bedford Town and Corby Town.

Andy Tait was a left half signed from Dumbarton. He made his debut on 19th September 1953 against St Johnstone in a Scottish League match and was a regular in the line up until the end of the season. Andy was initially on the retained list for 1954-55 but never featured again and signed for Albion Rovers during that season.

Jimmy Ward was a former Rosyth Recreation junior signed by United from Blackburn Rovers on a free transfer. He made his debut at inside left on 22nd August 1953 against Morton in a League Cup tie. Jimmy was signed only for a short-term trial period and was released in December 1953.

Trialist, Junior, Senior, Newman, A N Other

The following players, listed as one of the above, are those known to have played during the season.

Roy Jenkins of Stobswell in goal on 10th October 1953 against Kilmarnock in a Scottish League match. He later moved to Kirrie Thistle and played again on 23rd March 1957 against Montrose in a Scottish League match.

Donald McIntyre of Duntocher Hibs at right back on 9th January 1954 against Arbroath in a Scottish League match.

Kenny McLaughlin of Carnoustie Panmure at right back on 4th January 1954 against Third Lanark in a Scottish League match.

Peter Turnbull of Glasgow St Anthony's at right half on 28th November 1953 against Ayr United in a Scottish League match.

1954-55 Player Profiles

Archie Aikman was a centre forward who had been with St Mirren, Falkirk, Manchester City and Stenhousemuir. He was signed from Falkirk after his second spell there, just in time to make his United debut against Brechin City on 5th February 1955 in a Scottish League match, scoring twice. Archie went on to complete the season, scoring seven times in just eleven games, including a hat-trick against Arbroath. He was re-signed for the next campaign and was a regular in the line up, mainly in the inside forward positions, supporting centre forward John Coyle. Archie continued in that role in season 1956-57 but made fewer appearances as the season progressed and he was eventually released in April 1957. He later became a football commentator on television.

Archie Aikman

Alex Anderson was an experienced full back who had been with St Johnstone, East Fife, Forfar Athletic, Southampton and Exeter City. He made his debut for United against Dunfermline Athletic in a League Cup tie on 18th August 1954 but played just a few more times before being released early in the season.

Danny Bell signed for United from Dumbarton on a free transfer after a private trial match in June 1954. A right back, he made his debut on 14th August 1954 against Ayr United in a League Cup tie. Danny was a regular in the side at the beginning of the season but by December that year he was no longer holding down a first team place. He was released at the end of the season and then joined Montrose.

Davie Cross signed for United from Airdrieonians in June 1954 after taking part in a private trial match. He was a left-sided defender, comfortable at full back or half back and also at centre half. Davie made his debut on 14th August

Davie Cross

1954 against Ayr United in a League Cup tie and was an ever present in the side that season. He missed very few games over the next two years but in his final season, 1957-58, he was only in the line up for around half of the matches and was released in April 1958.

Willie Dunlop joined United from Falkirk in a swap deal that took George Grant in the opposite direction. An inside right, Willie made his debut on 13th November 1954 in a Scottish League match against Dunfermline Athletic and retained the inside right position for much of the remainder of that season. He was reluctant to re-sign for the next campaign but eventually did. However, he had just two more outings before he was offered a free transfer and he appears to have left the Club in January 1956.

Vince Halpin was a very tall centre half signed from Hibs after taking part in a private trial match in June 1954. Due to injury, his debut was delayed until 16th October 1954 when he played against Ayr United in a Scottish League match. It was his only game for United and he was unfortunate to have a debut disaster, scoring two own goals as United lost 5-1. Vince was released in April 1955.

Lawrie Higgins was a left winger signed from Aberdeen on a free transfer. He made his United debut on 11th September 1954 against Stenhousemuir in a Scottish League match but after just two months with the Club, he was released.

Ian Irvine joined United from Huddersfield Town after taking part in a private trial match in June 1954. He made just one appearance for United, at left back against Ayr United in a League Cup tie on 14th August 1954. He was released in October 1954.

Ronnie Johnston was a centre forward, formerly with Rochdale, Exeter City and Brighton & Hove Albion. He made a scoring debut for United as a trialist on 18th December 1954 against Forfar Athletic in a Scottish League match. After another trial, he was signed and played a few more times but by the end of January 1955, he was out of the side. At his own request, he was released in April 1955.

John McBain was a former Elmwood player who was capable in most defensive positions and in attack. He signed for United from Arbroath on a free transfer and made his debut on 8th

John McBain

January 1955 against Airdrieonians in a Scottish League match. For the next eighteen months, he was a regular in the line up. In April 1956, he went to India to work but United retained his registration and when he returned in February 1957, he reported back to Tannadice. Unfortunately, injury forced him to retire from the game two months later.

Tom McGairy was an inside left who had played with Dunfermline Athletic, Hamilton Academical, Alloa Athletic and Dumbarton before moving to Walsall at the beginning of season 1954-55. It appears he did not settle there and signed for United, making his debut on 4th December 1954 against Hamilton Academical in a Scottish League match. Tom made a favourable early impact, including a hat-trick on Christmas Day 1954 against Stenhousemuir. He was an ever present in the line up for the rest of the season, and with just 11 goals to his credit he was top scorer. In the following season, he found it more difficult to get a starting berth in the side and he was offered a free transfer in January 1956. There were no offers for the player and he was released three months later.

Tom McGairy

Sandy McLaren was a goalkeeper with Perth Celtic. He made his debut for United as a trialist on 20th November 1954 in a Scottish League match against Queen's Park and after one more outing, he was signed for the rest of the season. Initially he displaced Alec Edmiston but by January 1955, the positions were reversed. Sandy re-signed for 1955-56 and started that campaign in the first team but very quickly fell out of favour and became the understudy. He was released in April 1956.

Tommy McLeod had been with Liverpool and Chesterfield and signed for United from Wisbech Town after playing in a trial match in August 1954. A left-sided attacker, he made a scoring debut against Ayr United in a League Cup tie on 14th August 1954. Tommy played just once more for United before being released in September 1954.

Duncan McMillan was a former Celtic player who had been at Grimsby Town for seven years before he signed for United in late 1954. He made just one appearance, in a Scottish League match on 27th November 1954 against Alloa Athletic and he was released just a few weeks later.

Alan Massie, who had been with Aberdeen, was signed from the ranks of Dundee reserves. He was a full back who could play on either flank and made his debut on 20th November 1954 in a Scottish League match against Queen's Park. He was a regular in the line up for the rest of the season and re-signed for the next campaign. Alan had a good run in the side again but in January 1956, he was offered a free transfer. There was no interest from other clubs and he was released in April 1956.

Maurice Milne

Maurice Milne was a left winger with St Joseph's when he made his first appearance for United as a trialist on 16th April 1955 against Arbroath in a Scottish League match and he was signed soon after. Maurice became a regular in the line up in the following season, by the end of which he was attracting attention from many other clubs, mainly in England, and Luton Town made an unsuccessful bid. He continued in his regular berth in the side and during 1956-57, Cardiff City and Leeds United monitored his progress but it was Norwich City who eventually came in with an offer and he joined them in May 1957. He made just a few appearances for the English side before moving to Gloucester City and then returned to Tannadice in September 1959. In his second stint at Tannadice, Maurice made two more appearances for United before moving to Brechin City and then to Forfar Athletic.

Jimmy Reid was an inside forward with St Joseph's and made his first appearance for United as a trialist on 26th March 1955 against Hamilton Academical in a Scottish League match. He was signed immediately after the game and featured regularly in the line up throughout the next season. Jimmy re-signed for 1956-57, becoming the first choice at inside left and he soon came to the attention of other clubs. Bury made an offer and he joined them in January 1957, still just twenty years old. He remained with the English side for two years and then had a short spell at Stockport County before returning to United in August 1959. After three months back at Tannadice he left to join East Fife and later played with Arbroath and Brechin City.

Jimmy Reid

Jimmy Robertson was an attacking player signed from Plymouth Argyle. He made his debut on 18th August 1954 against Dunfermline Athletic in a League Cup tie. After just a handful of appearances, he was released.

Tommy Robertson had been with St Johnstone and Cheltenham Town before signing for United on a one month trial. He made the first of three appearances for United at inside left against Dunfermline Athletic in a Scottish League match on 13th November 1954. Tommy was released when his trial period ended.

Tom Simpson signed on a short-term deal from Crusaders of Belfast after a good performance in a reserve match. Formerly with Hamilton Academical, he was a half back and made his debut on 11th December 1954 against Morton in a Scottish League match. Tom left a month later, after just five outings with United. He later played for Darlington and then Weymouth.

Sandy Stephen was signed from local junior side Elmwood and made his debut as a trialist on 6th November 1954 against Albion Rovers in a Scottish League match. A versatile attacking player, Sandy was frequently in the line up until he was called up for national service in January 1956. He made a few appearances in April whilst on leave and although he remained on United's retained list, he did not play again until he was demobbed in January 1958. Over the rest of that season, he had just a few first team outings and he was released in April 1958.

Eddie Stewart

Eddie Stewart was a versatile half back, signed for United from local junior side Osborne. He made his debut as a trialist against Stenhousemuir in a Scottish League match on 11th September 1954 and became a regular in the side until he was called up for national service in December 1955. During his time in the forces, he made several appearances whilst home on leave and also spent some time on loan at Norwich City. When he was demobbed in November 1957, the English side offered £1,500 for his transfer but United turned it down. Eddie lost his place in the side and requested a transfer in February 1958 but was refused. He started playing regularly again in 1958-59 but was still unsettled and was allowed to join Arbroath in February 1959 on a free transfer. He later played for St Johnstone.

Trialist, Junior, Senior, Newman, A N Other

The following players, listed as one of the above, are those known to have played during the season.

Billy Boyle of Osborne at centre forward on 18th September 1954 against St Johnstone in the first of two Scottish League matches. In the second match, he netted four goals against Alloa Athletic.

Frank Crossan of St Mary's Boys Club at centre forward on 2nd May 1955 against Albion Rovers in a Scottish League match.

Dickie Cruickshank of Aberdeen Sunnybank at centre forward on 25th September 1954 against Third Lanark in a Scottish League match, scoring two goals.

Billy Dawson of Irvine Meadow at centre forward on 6th November 1954 against Albion Rovers in a Scottish League match, scoring a goal.

Bobby Hope of Lochgelly Albert at left wing on 23rd April 1955 against Cowdenbeath in a Scottish League match.

Ian Hunter of Dundee North End at centre forward on 9th October 1954 against Brechin City in a Scottish League match.

Willie McMaster of St Mirren at right wing on 7th May 1955 against Montrose in a Forfarshire Cup tie.

Stan Neave of Dundee North End at right wing on 4th October 1954 against Burnley in a friendly. He also played in another friendly in 1956-57.

Billy Ritchie of Osborne at centre forward on 11th September 1954 against Stenhousemuir in a Scottish League match, scoring a goal.

1955-56 Player Profiles

Frank Barclay was a half back who had originally been with local junior side Dundee North End. He joined United following a free transfer from Nottingham Forest. Frank made his debut for United on 20th August 1955 against Forfar Athletic in a League Cup tie but played just twice more in the first team. He made several reserve appearances and was still with United at the beginning of the next season but appears to have left in October 1956.

Frank Barclay

Jimmy Briggs

Jimmy Briggs was one of a group of teenage players signed from St Mary's Youth Club in June 1955. He made an early debut for United, against Brechin City on 24th August 1955 in a Scottish League match. It did not take Jimmy long to become a regular in the side and after just two years at United there was interest being shown in the player by Manchester City. In March 1958, he was called up for national service. As a result he made just a few appearances over the next two years. After he was demobbed he was immediately back in the side, and for the next eight years hardly a week went by without the name Jimmy Briggs being on the team sheet. At the end of season 1959-60, Jimmy scored a crucial late penalty in the penultimate match of the promotion-winning season. A stalwart of the United defence in the sixties, his proudest moment was perhaps when he captained United in their debut European match against Barcelona in October 1966. He continued to command a regular place in the side until he was sidelined after breaking a leg in January 1968. Later that year he suffered another break to the same leg and rarely turned out for the first eleven after he recovered. Instead, he played frequently in the reserves where he was able to pass on the benefit of his years of experience to the younger players. Jimmy was offered a coaching role at Tannadice which he declined and was released in May 1970, later joining Montrose. With 401 appearances in major competitions for the Club in fifteen years, Jimmy ranks thirteenth in the all time appearances table and is considered a legend at Dundee United. His total appearances would no doubt have been much higher but for two years of national service and another two years lost to injury. It is perhaps surprising that his loyalty to United was not rewarded with a testimonial match. However in January 2008, Jimmy became the first player inducted into the Dundee United Hall of Fame.

Jimmy Coyle

Jimmy Coyle (brother of John Coyle) was one of five players signed from St Mary's Youth Club in the summer of 1955. A right winger, he made his first team debut on 24th August 1955 against Brechin City in a Scottish League match. Still just a teenager, he was very quickly established as a first team regular and was re-signed for the next season. However, he was out of the side by the end of October 1956 and played reserve team football until he was released in April 1957.

Ernie Fenton was a fourteen-year-old pupil at Harris Academy when he joined United reserves in late 1955. He was a left winger and made just one first team appearance, in a friendly against Arbroath on 12th October 1955. Ernie spent around a year at United playing reserve football and then appears to have been released.

George Grant was a former Lochee Harp left half who signed for United on a free transfer from Arbroath. He had a trial in the reserves for United before making his debut on 21st January 1956 against his former club in a Scottish League match. George played just a few times over the remainder of the season, including two games on the left wing, before he was released in April 1956 at his own request, for business reasons.

George Grant

Fred Grubb was one of five young players signed from St Mary's Youth Club in the summer of 1955. Whilst all the others had some success in the first team, Fred made just one appearance, at right back on 18th April 1956 against Morton in a Scottish League match.

Ian Hamilton was a pupil at Harris Academy when he joined United in April 1955. He was a half back but could also play at inside forward and spent two seasons in the reserves where he made over 25 appearances. Ian made his first team debut on 12th October 1955 in a friendly against Arbroath. Despite a good record in the reserves, he had just one more first team outing in a friendly, before he was released in May 1957.

Ian Lornie was signed as a reserve goalkeeper in September 1955. He had just left Harris Academy and was attending St Andrews University when he joined United reserves as an amateur. His first team debut was on 10th September 1955 against Queen's Park in a Scottish League match. He made just one more appearance in the league and one in a friendly before he was released at the end of the season.

Neil McKinven was a centre half released by Dundee in May 1955. He initially turned down an offer to play for United, signing for Arbroath instead. At the end of November 1955, he requested a free transfer from Arbroath and then joined United. Neil made his first appearance on Christmas Eve 1955 against a Combined Services XI in a friendly. A week later he made his debut in major competition against Dumbarton in a Scottish League match but was then out of the side until April 1956. At that time, he made a brief return to the team but he was released a month later.

Bob Penman was a right back signed from Jeanfield Swifts in March 1955. He made his debut against Motherwell on 17th August 1955 in a League Cup tie but had only occasional games in the first eleven and was released in April 1956.

Willie Penman was a former Raith Rovers left winger who signed for United from Montrose. He made his debut on 17th December 1955 against Berwick Rangers in a Scottish League match but made just a handful of appearances before he was released in May 1956.

Dave Sturrock was one of five young players signed from St Mary's Youth Club in the summer of 1955. Still just sixteen years old, he made his first appearance for United on 12th October 1955 against Arbroath in a friendly. After a good run in the reserve side, he made his debut in major competition against Queen's Park on 14th January 1956 in a Scottish League match. A versatile attacking player, Dave became established over the next few months and was a regular in the side for three seasons. In October 1958 he requested a transfer, which prompted an enquiry from Portsmouth, but he stayed at Tannadice. Dave was called up for national service in August 1959 and as a result missed out on most of the season that United won promotion, and he was released in April 1960. He was quickly signed up by Accrington Stanley and later played for Bedford Town, Corby Town and Stamford Town.

Willie Penman   *Dave Sturrock*   *Alex Will*   *Duncan Young*

Alex Will was one of five teenagers signed in the summer of 1955 from St Mary's Youth Club. He was a right half and made his debut on 24th August 1955 against Brechin City in a Scottish League match. He then played mainly in the reserves with only a few appearances in the first team that season. Just after Alex became established in the side, he was called up for national service in January 1956. He still managed to turn out quite frequently for United over the next twelve months but he was released in April 1958.

Duncan Young joined United from Butterburn Youth Club. He was a right back and made his first appearance as a trialist on 12th October 1955 in a friendly against Arbroath. Duncan signed soon afterwards and made his debut in major competition against Alloa Athletic in a Scottish League match on 25th February 1956. For the remainder of that season he was a regular in the side. Over the next season, he was still frequently in the line up and although retained for two more years he suffered an injury and was rarely included again. Duncan was released in May 1959.

Trialist, Junior, Senior, Newman, A N Other

The following players, listed as one of the above, are those known to have played during the season.

Mike Gilchrist of St Joseph's at centre half on 12th October 1955 against Arbroath in a friendly.

J Russell of Blairgowrie at inside right on 27th December 1955 against Brechin City in a Scottish League match, scoring a goal.

1956-57 Player Profiles

Alex Berry was a right winger signed on a short-term trial basis from Preston Athletic. He made his first appearance for United on 13th April 1957 against Cowdenbeath in a Scottish League match. Alex scored twice in his next game two days later and had one more outing before the season ended but he was not offered a deal for the following season.

Jimmy Brown

Jimmy Brown was a versatile player who joined United from Glencraig Colliery. He made his first appearance at right half as a trialist on 22nd April 1957 in a Scottish League match against Brechin City and was signed immediately after the game. Jimmy was with United for just one full season, spending the first few months of 1957-58 in the half back line and the latter part of his stay as an inside forward. He was released in May 1958 and then signed for Thornton Hibs, later spending some time with East Fife.

Archie Coats was the son of United's trainer of the same name. He was a goalkeeper with local junior side, Elmwood before he joined United. After three games in the reserves, he made his only first team appearance against Forfar Athletic on 16th March 1957 in a Scottish League match.

Sandy Evans was a former Dundee centre forward who was signed by United after playing in the trial match in August 1956. He made just one appearance for United. On 22nd August 1956 he was on the right wing against Alloa Athletic in a Scottish League match. Sandy then played over 20 times in the reserves, scoring regularly, before he was released in May 1957.

Davie Gray was a former Rangers, Preston North End and Blackburn Rovers full back who joined Dundee in 1952. He was released by the Dens Park club in 1956 and then signed for United, making his debut on 15th September 1956 against Dundee in a League Cup tie. Davie was a regular in the line up in the first few months of the season but dropped out of the side until the end of the campaign when he made another few appearances. He followed a similar pattern in season 1957-58, at the end of which he retired from playing and began coaching at Forfar Athletic.

Davie Gray

Andy Hamilton joined United towards the end of season 1956-57 from Dunfermline Athletic, making his debut on 13th April 1957 against Cowdenbeath in a Scottish League match. He played three more times before the season ended and was re-signed for the next campaign. However, Andy was unable to command a regular place and he was offered a free transfer in December 1957. He appears to have moved north to join Lossiemouth two months later.

Bobby Henderson was an experienced goalkeeper who had spent 13 years at Partick Thistle and then 5 years with Dundee. He was released in May 1956 and joined United at the start of the next season after playing well in a trial match. Bobby made his United debut on 11th August 1956 against Ayr United in a League Cup tie. Following an injury received in a Second XI Cup tie at Aberdeen in September 1956, he was replaced in goal by Alec Edmiston. Bobby made just one more first team appearance before being released in May 1957.

Bobby Henderson

Charlie Hutton was a goalkeeper signed from East Fife. He was one of a number of keepers used primarily in the reserves after Bobby Henderson was injured. Charlie made his first team debut for United on 27th October 1956 against Third Lanark in a Scottish League match but played just twice more before being released in December 1956. He planned on retiring from football but later played briefly for Brechin City.

Ian Inglis was formerly with Dundee and Carnoustie Panmure and signed from local junior side Elmwood. He was a versatile defender who joined United primarily for the reserves, where he made around 20 appearances over the season. Ian made a first team appearance on 29th December 1956 against a Dundee Junior Select in a friendly. His debut and only game in major competition was on 16th March 1957 against Forfar Athletic in a Scottish League match and he was released in May 1957.

Bill Lucas

Bill Lucas was a goalkeeper signed from junior side Broxburn Athletic. He made his debut for United as a trialist on 8th April 1957 against Arbroath in a Scottish League match. Bill quickly became the first choice keeper and in season 1957-58, he never missed a game in any competition. At the beginning of season 1958-59 he remained first choice until the arrival of Alec Brown created competition for the No. 1 jersey and Bill was demoted to the reserves. He was transfer listed in October 1958 after he requested a move but within two months, he was back in the side until the end of the season at which time he was released.

Willie McDonald was an inside forward with local side St Joseph's and made his debut for United as a trialist on 9th February 1957 against Stirling Albion in a Scottish League match. He signed shortly afterwards and played often in the side over the remainder of 1956-57. Willie was retained for the next season, becoming a regular in the forward line. Brechin City tried, unsuccessfully, to sign him from United in exchange for Norman Christie in November 1957. In the following season, Willie had another successful campaign and was top scorer with 15 league and cup goals, including a hat-trick against Stirling Albion. He remained with United for three more years but was less often seen in the first eleven, playing mainly in the reserves, where he notched over 70 games, with a very good scoring record. Willie was transferred to Stirling Albion in March 1962 for a nominal fee. He later played for Montrose.

Willie McDonald

John McGuinness was in the army serving as a regular in the RAOC and was a registered player with Dundee. He was released by them and signed for United, after making his first appearance as a trialist on 26th January 1957 against Hamilton Academical in a Scottish League match. John was an inside forward and turned out for United regularly over the next two months. At the end of the season, he was not re-signed.

John Markie was still a schoolboy of fifteen years old when he began playing for United in the reserves. After signing from Breadalbane, he made over 20 second eleven appearances during 1956-57 but had just one first team outing, on the right wing on 29th December 1956 against a Dundee Junior Select. He appears to have then gone into the junior ranks with Dundee North End and later played for Forfar Athletic, East Fife and Brechin City.

Clive Wallace made his first appearance for United on the left wing as a trialist against Berwick Rangers on 2nd October 1956 in a Scottish League match. At the time, he was with Kirrie Thistle and still at school and keen to take his exams. He signed a provisional form and played twice more, scoring three times but eventually, he decided to sign for Dundee. Clive was released by the Dens Park club in May 1958 and then signed for United. After just a few first team appearances in the early part of the season and a handful of

Clive Wallace

reserve outings, he was released in January 1959 and soon afterwards signed for Montrose. Clive later played in England with Bury and Stockport County.

Noel Wannan was a centre half, formerly with local junior side Downfield. He joined United from Montrose on a free transfer and made his debut on 22nd August 1956 against Alloa Athletic in a Scottish League match, followed by a short run in the side in the following month. In December 1956, he left United after deciding to retire from football.

Don Watt was at Aberdeen University when he signed for United as an amateur. He was a right winger but could also play through the centre. Don made his debut on 24th November 1956 against Montrose in a Scottish League match and became a regular in the line up over the rest of the season. He did not re-sign for the next campaign, choosing instead to join Dundee. Later in season 1957-58, he spent a short time at Brechin City.

Trialist, Junior, Senior, Newman, A N Other

The following players, listed as one of the above, are those known to have played during the season.

Leslie Hooley of Lochore Welfare at centre half on 8th April 1957 against Arbroath in a Scottish League match.

Jimmy Kemp of Jeanfield Swifts at right half on 30th March 1957 against Albion Rovers in a Scottish League match.

1957-58 Player Profiles

Alex Cameron was a right winger who joined United from Perthshire junior side, Luncarty. He made his debut on 23rd November 1957 against Stirling Albion in a Scottish League match and he was signed soon after. Alex played in almost half of the remaining matches that season and was re-signed for the next campaign. He made just one more appearance, in December 1958 and shortly after that, he was given a free transfer.

Alex Cameron

Jim Duncan

Jim Duncan was a former Celtic player signed by United from St Mirren. He was a versatile attacker and made his debut on 10th August 1957 against Clyde in a League Cup tie. Jim made an early mark in the side but fell out of contention and refused a free transfer in November 1957. He stayed on until the season ended at which point he was released. He then signed for Albion Rovers.

George Forrester requested, and was granted, a free transfer from Dundee. He had previously been with Raith Rovers and Sunderland. George was a full back who made his United debut on 22nd February 1958 against Dunfermline Athletic in a Scottish League match. He made several appearances before the end of the season and was re-signed for 1958-59. Just two months into the season, he left to join Brechin City. He later played for Accrington Stanley and several English non league sides.

George Fox (not related to the Director of the same name) was a half back signed from East Fife in May 1957. He made just one appearance for United, in a Scottish League match against St Johnstone on 21st September 1957.

Stewart Fraser was a half back who signed for United from junior side, Banks O' Dee. He made his debut as a trialist on 18th September 1957 against Arbroath in a Scottish League match. Initially he was to remain with his junior side but after they were knocked out of the Scottish Junior Cup, Stewart was allowed to sign for United earlier than expected, joining the Club in October 1957. He was quickly established as the first choice right half over the rest of that season. Re-signed for 1958-59, he was only in the side on a few occasions over the next two years whilst he completed obligatory national service. In the run in to the end of season

Stewart Fraser

1959-60 however, he was back in the line up and was a vital part of the team that gained promotion to the First Division. Over the next four years, Stewart was rarely omitted from the side and gained international recognition playing twice for the Scottish League. His international debut was against an English League side and in his second game for Scotland, he recorded a hat-trick against the League of Ireland in November 1962. He attracted interest from Newcastle United but two offers by the English side were turned down. In season 1964-65, a broken leg kept Stewart sidelined for the second half of the season and after that, he was unable to regain a regular place in the side. He stayed with United for another two years, playing mainly in the reserves with just a few first team outings before he was released in May 1967. He became player/coach at Brora Rangers and then spent a year in the USA with Philadelphia Flyers.

Allan Garvie joined United from junior side Perth Celtic. He was a left winger and made his debut as a trialist on 14th December 1957 against Albion Rovers in a Scottish League match. He was unable to fully establish himself in the side as a regular and was released in April 1958.

Alistair 'Alec' Gibson had been with Workington and Worcester Town and joined United from Queen of the South, making his debut in a League Cup tie against Clyde on 10th August 1957. He could play in any half back position and was a regular in the line up over the next two years until he was released in May 1959.

Wilson Humphries was a centre forward signed from St Mirren. He had previously been with Motherwell where he had scored six of the goals during United's record 12-1 defeat. He had also collected a Scottish Cup winner's medal in a 4-0 win over Dundee in 1952. Wilson, who had one international cap to his credit, was United's first £1,000 player and made a scoring debut on 10th August 1957 against Clyde in a League Cup tie. He went on to become top scorer for the season, with 27 goals in his 37 league and cup appearances, including hat-tricks against Stenhousemuir and Stranraer. He had only five fewer outings in his second season but did not repeat the same scoring rate, netting just 11 and he was released in May 1959. He then signed for Hamilton Academical for a short time and was a coach at Motherwell before becoming a teacher.

Jimmy King joined United from Cowdenbeath and made his debut on the left wing in a League Cup tie against Dumbarton on 28th August 1957. He appeared just briefly in the first team again, late in the season and he was released in May 1958.

Bobby McKillop was an inside forward signed from Dundee Violet. He made just one appearance for United on 4th September 1957 in a Scottish league match against Arbroath.

Allan Garvie   *Alistair Gibson*   *Wilson Humphries*   *Ally Rae*

Ally Rae was a full back with St Johnstone and signed for United after he was released by the Perth side. He made his debut on 22nd March 1958 against Hamilton Academical in a Scottish League match and was a regular in the line up for the rest of the season. Ally re-signed for season 1958-59 but played in just five more first team games and several friendly matches in the reserves before he was released in April 1959. He then joined Brechin City.

Joe Roy was an experienced inside forward who had been with Dundee and Third Lanark. He was signed in May 1957 but his debut was delayed by injury. He eventually turned out against Dumbarton on 28th September 1957 in a Scottish League match. Joe then became a regular in the line up and he was just beginning to have a positive effect on the side when his season was ended abruptly by another injury in January 1958. He was retained for the following season but was soon advised to give up the game entirely, although he stayed with United in a scouting role, covering the west coast for a time.

Joe Roy

Jimmy Wilson was a former Alloa Athletic, Leicester City and Mansfield Town winger who left the senior ranks and joined junior side Duntocher Hibs. He was tempted back into the senior game as a player/coach at Tannadice and made his debut on 4th September 1957 in a Scottish League match against Arbroath. Jimmy played just once more and he was released in October 1957.

Ron Yeats

Ron Yeats was a centre half with Aberdeen Lads Club. He was signed by United in December 1957 after the Manager had seen him play just twice. Ron went straight into the side on 2nd January 1958 against East Stirlingshire in a Scottish League match. He had an immediate positive impact and was an ever present in the line up for the rest of that season. Ron was re-signed for 1958-59 but a broken wrist sidelined him after just four games. His recovery took four months and he was restored as first choice centre half in December 1958. By January 1959 he was attracting interest from big English clubs, including Manchester City but the Directors were determined to hold on to him. At the beginning of season 1959-60, Ron was called up for national service. Manager Jerry Kerr worked hard to ensure that United would not lose such an important player, taking the unusual step of visiting Ron's commanding officer, Major Sharp, in Aldershot. A football fan himself, Major Sharp agreed to Kerr's request to have the player released to play for United as often as possible. As a result, Ron missed just four matches over the season and was a highly influential player in the side that won promotion at the end of the campaign. Season 1960-61 was Ron's last with United and he was still travelling regularly to take his place in the side. He helped United retain First Division status whilst the Club held off interest from clubs such as Norwich City and Manchester United. After the season ended there was more rumoured interest with Italian side, Napoli, said to be ready with a huge offer. Ron had re-signed for United but it was obvious they could not hold on to him for much longer and the player wanted to move. Liverpool made a bid of £20,000 in mid June but the offer was increased twice before Ron left to join the Merseyside club for a fee of £30,000 on 24th July. He was a big hit with the fans at Anfield. In ten years with Liverpool, he played over 450 times and then played for Tranmere Rovers, a side he later managed. Ron returned to Liverpool in 1986 for a lengthy term as chief scout. He gained international recognition whilst with the Merseyside club, playing for Scotland twice. Ron was a legend at Liverpool and achieved the same status with United in his three years at Tannadice.

Trialist, Junior, Senior, Newman, A N Other

The following players, listed as one of the above, are those known to have played during the season.

Boswell of Broxburn United at inside left on 5th April 1958 against Albion Rovers in the first of two Scottish League matches.

Herbert Cadenhead of Lewis United at inside left on 16th April 1958 against Alloa Athletic in a Scottish League match.

Charlie Chalmers of Dundee Osborne at right wing on 19th October 1957 against Alloa Athletic in a Scottish League match.

Frank Craig of Broxburn Athletic at left wing on 18th September 1957 against Arbroath in a Scottish League match.

Reg Dewar of Dundee Violet at left wing on 26th October 1957 against Dunfermline Athletic 'A' in a friendly, scoring a goal.

Jimmy Dick of St Joseph's at left wing on 16th November 1957 against Berwick Rangers in the first of two Scottish League matches.

Jim Galley of Vale of Leven Juniors at left half on 28th September 1957 against Dumbarton in a Scottish League match.

John Gwynne of Larkhall Thistle at centre half on 19th October 1957 against Alloa Athletic in the first of two Scottish League matches.

Charlie Henaughen of Rutherglen Glencairn at inside left on 26th April 1958 against Stranraer in a Scottish League match.

Jock Keddie (ex-East Fife) at centre forward on 3rd May 1958 against Berwick Rangers in a Scottish League match, scoring twice.

Dave Logie of Dundee North End at right wing on 15th March 1958 against Stirling Albion in the first of two Scottish League matches.

Jim Mann of Rutherglen Glencairn at inside right on 11th January 1958 against Dumbarton in the first of two Scottish League matches.

Jimmy Miller of Dunfermline Athletic at inside right on 26th October 1957 against Dunfermline Athletic 'A' in a friendly.

Charlie Milne of Brechin Matrix at centre forward on 28th December 1957 against Stranraer in a Scottish League match.

Andrew Murphy of Kirkintilloch Rob Roy at left wing on 21st September 1957 against St Johnstone in the first of two Scottish League matches.

Steve Reilly, a junior from Lanarkshire at left wing on 21st August 1957 against Cowdenbeath in a Scottish League match.

Alan Ross of Perth Kinnoull at inside right on 16th April 1958 against Alloa Athletic in the first of two Scottish League matches, scoring once.

Sime of Bathgate at left wing on 9th November 1957 against Forfar Athletic in the first of two Scottish League matches.

1958-59 Player Profiles

Jock Adie was a former East Fife and Hearts left back. He signed for United on a short-term contract and made his debut on 23rd August 1958 in a League Cup tie against St Johnstone. Jock was a regular in the first team until he lost his place to Charlie Robertson in October 1958. He appears to have been released soon after.

Alec Brown

Alec Brown was a goalkeeper who joined United from Lochgelly Albert. He made his first appearance as a trialist on 10th September 1958 against Brechin City in a Scottish League match and remained in the side as first choice keeper until December. He was replaced in goal by Bill Lucas for the next three months but by March, he was back in the line up again. Alec was first choice in the following season, playing in all but two matches. With some excellent displays between the posts, he helped United win promotion to the First Division. He was the understudy to Lando Ugolini for most of 1960-61 in Division One, playing in the reserves until he regained the No. 1 jersey again near the end of that campaign. Alec and Lando shared the goalkeeping duty in the next season and both were released in May 1962. Alec then joined Morton.

Bobby Craig was a half back signed from Rutherglen Glencairn. He made his first appearance as a trialist on 18th April 1959 against Morton in a Scottish League match. Signed shortly after, he was then retained for the next season. Bobby featured often in the United line up, until he was called up for national service in early 1960. He remained a registered player with United for the next two years, turning out occasionally in the second eleven. When Bobby was demobbed in March 1962, he returned to play in the reserves until he was released two months later and he then joined Morton.

Willie Dickie

Willie Dickie joined United from Dalry Thistle and made his first appearance as a trialist against Morton on 18th April 1959 in a Scottish League match at left half. He signed just a few days later and was retained for season 1959-60. Willie was regarded as a utility player and started the new season in the first team but was dropped in October 1959, spending most of the campaign in the reserves. He was released in April 1960 and joined Forfar Athletic briefly before moving to East Stirlingshire and then to South Shields.

Ian Douglas was a left half signed from Aberdeenshire junior side Banks O' Dee. He made his debut for United on 20th August 1958 against East Stirlingshire in a Scottish League match. Ian played quite frequently during season 1958-59 and was on the retained list for the next two seasons without ever making another first team start. He played in the reserves until he was released in September 1960.

Ian Douglas

Hugh Hay was transfer listed by Aberdeen at £1,000 when he signed for United. He was an inside forward and made a scoring debut against St Johnstone in a League Cup tie on 9th August 1958. Hugh was injured early in the season but within two months, he recovered and became a regular in the line up. He was with United for just one season, leaving to join Arbroath in August 1959 for a fee of £350.

Jackie Hunter signed for United from Motherwell for a fee of around £1,250. He made his debut at centre forward on 9th August 1958 in a League Cup tie against St Johnstone but for most of his United career he played on the right wing. Jackie was a regular in the line up over the season and was second top scorer with 12 goals, including a hat-trick against Stenhousemuir. At the end of the campaign, he was on the transfer list and joined Forfar Athletic in August 1959.

Andy Irvine

Andy Irvine was an experienced centre half who joined United from Falkirk where he had been since they signed him from Dundee in January 1957. Andy had won a Scottish Cup winners medal shortly after joining Falkirk. The initial bid by United was rejected but when it was ascertained that Ron Yeats would be out for longer than expected, the need for a replacement became urgent and the offer was increased to secure the player. He made his debut on 1st November 1958 against Alloa Athletic in a Scottish League match and was in the side until the return of Yeats in December. Andy made two appearances at full back towards the end of the season but he was released in May 1959.

Tommy Martin was a left winger signed from Forfar Athletic. He made his debut against St Johnstone on 6th September 1958 in a Scottish League match but he was gradually displaced from the side after the arrival of Ian Scott. Tommy was transfer listed in the latter stages of the season and left United in August 1959.

Andy Napier

Andy Napier was a six foot tall centre forward with Newburgh Juniors. After just four games with them, he played for United as a trialist against Hamilton Academical on 3rd January 1959 in a Scottish League match. Two weeks later, he had another trial and he was then signed. Andy was frequently in the line up in the remaining games that season but only found the net twice. Re-signed for 1959-60, he played just a handful of reserve matches and was released at the end of the season.

Watt Newton joined United from Forfar Celtic after making his first appearance as a trialist against Brechin City in a Scottish League match on 25th April 1959. A centre forward, Watt was signed for the next season and was a regular scorer in the opening stages of the campaign. He was moved out to the right wing following the arrival of Dennis Gillespie in September 1959. Two months later, Watt was relegated to the reserves. In January 1960, he went to Alloa Athletic in a swap deal that brought left winger Eric Walker to Tannadice.

Bobby Norris was a right winger who joined United from Rutherglen Glencairn for a fee of around £200 after two matches as a trialist. He made his first appearance on 4th April 1959 in a Scottish League match against Stranraer and he was signed after his second outing, a week later. Bobby was then retained for 1959-60 but in the early part of the new campaign, he was used infrequently. In the latter part of the season, he became established in the side again and played a major role in the team that gained promotion to the First Division. Re-signed for the following season, Bobby played just once and accepted a free transfer in February 1961. He then joined English non league side South Shields and later spent a short time at Brechin City and Stenhousemuir.

Charlie Robertson was a left back with local junior side, Osborne. He made his first appearance for United as a trialist in a Scottish League match against Stenhousemuir on 27th September 1958, remaining at left back for all but three matches over the rest of the season. Charlie was re-signed for 1959-60 but played just three times before being demoted to the reserves. He stayed with United for the season but he was released in April 1960.

(Alexander) Ian Scott was a left winger who signed on a free transfer from Brechin City, initially on a one month trial. He made his debut at inside left against Dumbarton in a Scottish League match on 20th September 1958. He was soon signed for the rest of the campaign, playing in every forward position during the season. Ian was released in April 1959 and then joined Montrose before returning to Brechin City.

Ian Scott

Doug Smith is a Dundee United legend. He made his first appearance on 22nd April 1959 against Alloa Athletic in a Scottish League match as a trialist at right half, playing alongside his former Aberdeen Lads Club team mate, Ron Yeats. Doug was signed in June 1959 and played just a handful of first team games over the next two years as understudy to Yeats. When Yeats left to join Liverpool in July 1961, Doug was his natural successor. Over the next ten seasons, Doug was a mainstay in the side and incredibly, missed just four games in major competitions, including matches

Doug Smith

in Europe. In 1964, he was named the Supporters' Club Player of the Year. In 1966, Doug was in the United line up that humbled Barcelona both home and away and in the late 1960s, he became Club captain. Into his second decade with United, he was still a regular in the side and was by then the usual penalty taker, rarely missing from the spot. Recognised as one of the country's best uncapped players, one of his proudest moments came on 4th May 1974 when he led United out at Hampden Park for the Club's first Scottish Cup final. Over the next two seasons, he completed his United career, declining a move to Raith Rovers in October 1975. Doug was released in May 1976, one of a rare breed of one-club players, having spent fully seventeen years at United. Although he left without winning a major honour, Doug had one major distinction – he was never booked in a career spanning 628 games in major competition. He ranks fifth in United's all time appearances chart. In August 1977 he was granted a testimonial, in which several former players and current stars from other Scottish Premier League sides took part. In 1983, he returned to United as a Director and remained on the Board until 2002, spending the last two years as Chairman. Well respected in Scottish football, after serving on various national committees, he became President of the Scottish League in 1997. Doug was included in the first group of players inducted into the Dundee United Hall of Fame in January 2008.

Jim Stalker

Jim Stalker was an inside forward with Dalry Thistle when he made the first of three appearances as a trialist for United on 7th March 1959 against Ayr United in a Scottish League match. He then signed and played regularly until the end of the season. Jim was retained for 1959-60 but played mainly in the reserves. He was used in the first team only sparingly as the Club won promotion to the First Division and was released in April 1960. Jim then joined Stranraer and was later with Stenhousemuir.

Gordon Tosh signed for United for a month on trial from Forfar Athletic. A centre half, he made his first appearance in a friendly against Portadown on 6th October 1958 and his only other outing was against Queen's Park five days later in a Scottish League match. Gordon then had a short stay at Dumbarton.

Jimmy Wallace was an inside forward who joined United from Aberdeen. He made his debut in a League Cup tie against St Johnstone on 9th August 1958. Jimmy was a regular in the side in either the half back line or the attack. He did not complete even a full season and in March 1959, he was released.

Jimmy Wallace

Jimmy Welsh was a left winger with Aberdeen Lads Club. He made his United debut in a Scottish League match on 28th March 1959 against Arbroath and was then re-signed for the next season. However, he played mainly in the reserve side and after just two further first team appearances, he accepted a free transfer, leaving United in November 1959.

Andy Young

Andy Young was a right back with Kirkintilloch Rob Roy when he made his first appearance for United as a trialist against Forfar Athletic in a Scottish League match on 3rd September 1958. He was signed immediately after the match and he then became almost a permanent feature of the United line up, missing just one game over the rest of the season. Andy was re-signed for 1959-60 but featured in just the opening few games. He stayed with United, playing in the reserves until April 1960 when he requested a free transfer and emigrated to Canada.

Trialist, Junior, Senior, Newman, A N Other

The following players, listed as one of the above, are those known to have played during the season.

Eric Anderson of Luncarty at centre forward on 13th September 1958 against Hamilton Academical in the first of two Scottish League matches, scoring in his first game.

Willie Denholm of Crossgates Primrose at inside left on 10th September 1958 against Brechin City in a Scottish League match.

Ray Ewen of Hall Russell at right wing on 11th April 1959 against Albion Rovers in a Scottish League match.

Jacky Gallacher of Benburb in goal on 3rd September 1958 against Forfar Athletic in a Scottish League match.

Jim Gordon of Dalry Thistle at right wing on 14th March 1959 against Cowdenbeath in a Scottish League match.

David Jeffrey of Broughty Athletic at centre forward on 10th January 1959 against Dumbarton in a Scottish League match.

Bobby Smith of Kirkintilloch Rob Roy at centre forward on 8th November 1958 against Ayr United in the first of three Scottish League matches, scoring in each of his first two games.

Dave Souter of Carnoustie Panmure at right wing on 17th January 1959 against Stenhousemuir in a Scottish League match.

1959-60 Player Profiles

Jim Bell was a left winger with Dalkeith Thistle when he made his first appearance for United as a trialist on 14th November 1959 against Montrose in a Scottish League match. He was then signed and played in the next four games but was quickly demoted to the reserves, where he spent the remainder of the season. He was released in April 1960.

Tommy Campbell

Tommy Campbell was a former Kilmarnock centre forward signed from Albion Rovers for £2,000. His first appearance for United was on 5th March 1960 against Hamilton Academical in a Scottish League match. He became the second player that season to record a hat-trick on his debut. Four weeks later, he hit another hat-trick against Forfar Athletic and ended the season with 9 goals in just 7 appearances. Crucially though, he scored the only goal of the game against Berwick Rangers on 30th April 1960. That secured the win that United needed to gain promotion to the First Division, thus repaying his transfer fee many times over. Tommy was re-signed for the First Division campaign of 1960-61 and started the season in good form. However, he dropped out of the side in November and spent most of the remaining months of the campaign in the reserves. Carlisle United showed some interest in signing him but he went to Tranmere Rovers in June 1961 for around £1,000. He did not settle there and was soon back in Scotland with Dumbarton and later played with Stenhousemuir before he returned to Albion Rovers.

Walter 'Wattie' Carlyle signed from Shettleston Juniors. He had also been with Rangers as a provisional signing. Both Motherwell and Liverpool were monitoring his progress but he signed for United, making his debut in a Forfarshire Cup tie against Forfar Athletic on 4th May 1960. He was then re-signed for the forthcoming First Division campaign. A right winger who played at centre forward occasionally, Wattie made his debut in major competition on 13th August 1960 against Stirling Albion in a League Cup tie and went on to play regularly that season. The following year, he became joint top scorer with 17 goals, helping United to consolidate top flight status. He also topped the Tannadice scoring chart in the next season with 22 goals. 1963-64 was just a few weeks old when Millwall made an offer of £6,000 and the player went down south for talks at the end of October 1963. Just as it looked like he would complete the move, Motherwell came

Wattie Carlyle

in with a similar bid and he elected to sign for them instead. He later played for St Johnstone, Queen of the South, East Stirlingshire, and Alloa Athletic.

Peter Collins was a full back signed from Partick Thistle in May 1959. He made his debut on 12th August 1959 against Montrose in a League Cup tie but had just one more first team outing for United. He played in several reserve matches before accepting a free transfer in November 1959.

Davie Crabb was a left half signed from Montrose Victoria, making his first appearance for United on 5th October 1959 in a friendly against Newcastle United. His debut in major competition was against East Stirlingshire in a Scottish League match on 6th February 1960. Davie spent most of his time with United in the reserve side, where he notched up around 20 appearances. In February 1961, he accepted a free transfer and left United to join East Fife.

Dennis Gillespie

Dennis Gillespie was signed from Alloa Athletic for £3,000 just after the start of season 1959-60. He turned out to be one of Jerry Kerr's most inspired acquisitions, making his debut on 5th September 1959 against St Johnstone in a Scottish League match. A forceful attacking player, Dennis was a vital part of the side that won promotion to the First Division that season, finishing as second top scorer with 19 goals, including a hat-trick against Queen's Park. He was top scorer with 15 goals in the next season, including a hat-trick against Dunfermline Athletic. Dennis was a regular in the side for the next four seasons and kept up his scoring rate, recording yet another hat-trick against Raith Rovers in October 1962. He became the first Dundee United player to turn out at senior international level for Scotland when he played for the Scottish League against the League of Ireland in 1961. A big favourite with the fans, he collected the Supporters' Club Player of the Year award for 1962-63 and a year later he was drawing attention from Spurs. In the mid 1960s, he took more of a supporting role, often playing in the half back line but was still a regular in the side and was in the line up as United faced and defeated Barcelona in the Club's first venture into European football. By season 1968-69 Dennis was the regular right half and he revelled in his new role for two seasons. He spent his last two years at the Club playing mainly in the reserves, passing on the benefit of his experience to the younger players. Offered a coaching role in April 1972, he elected not to accept as he wanted to continue playing and he went to Brechin City where he remained for four years. In May 1973, Dennis was awarded a testimonial in which several well known guest players joined his United colleagues in front of a crowd of more than 10,000 to pay tribute to a Club legend. He is ranked seventh in the all time appearances chart with 455 games in which he scored 115 goals. In January 2008, Dennis was one of the first players inducted into the Dundee United Hall of Fame. Sadly it was a posthumous award, collected on his behalf by his two sons.

Jim Goldie joined Aston Villa in 1957 and was with Raith Rovers and Falkirk before he signed for United on a free transfer. He was a left winger and made his debut on 12th August 1959 against Montrose in a League Cup tie. After just one more outing he was dropped and was given a free transfer at his own request in September. He later played with Kilsyth Rangers and moved south again, where he spent some time with Luton Town, York City and then non league Poole Town.

Tommy Graham

Tommy Graham was a right back with Shotts Bon Accord when he made his first appearance for United as a trialist on 5th September 1959 against St Johnstone in a Scottish League match. He was then signed and hardly missed a match over the rest of the promotion winning season, 1959-60. Tommy was re-signed for the next season but featured less often. In season 1961-62, he started out in the first team but he was quickly demoted to the reserves, where he racked up over 40 appearances in two seasons. He was released in May 1962 and joined English non league side Poole Town.

Jim Irvine was an inside right signed from Whitburn Juniors. He had attracted interest from a few English teams but decided to sign for United and made his debut on 19th August 1959 in a Scottish League match against East Fife. Jim went on to become an important player in the 1959-60 campaign, helping to take United into the First Division. On route to becoming top scorer that season with 24 goals, he netted a hat-trick against Queen of the South and scored four in one game against Queen's Park. Jim remained with United for the next four years, playing regularly and filling all of the forward positions during his Tannadice career. He continued scoring regularly and amongst his tally, he had a hat-trick against Celtic in January 1962. In May 1964, he left United to join Middlesbrough for a fee of around £25,000. His scoring rate with the English side was also impressive and after three years with them, he joined Hearts. Whilst with the Edinburgh side he played in a memorable Scottish Cup tie against United at Tannadice, scoring the winner for Hearts in a game they won 6-5. He later returned south and played with Barrow.

Jim Irvine

Davie Kidd was signed from Alloa Athletic and featured a few times in the absence of Ron Yeats at centre half. It was in that position that he made his debut on 23rd September 1959 in a Scottish League match against Dumbarton. He was normally in the left back slot where he frequently lined up during 1959-60. Davie played his part in the squad that gained promotion to the First Division but was released at the end of the season.

Ian MacFadyen

Ian 'Buddy' MacFadyen was the son of former United Manager Willie MacFadyen. Ian first signed for United as an amateur from Ashdale Amateurs in August 1950 and was with United for the next four years, making around 40 reserve appearances without breaking into the first team. He joined the RAF on national service in November 1951 but remained with United until August 1954 when he signed for Motherwell. Almost five years later, he returned to United and made his first team debut at left back on 8th August 1959 against East Stirlingshire in a League Cup tie. Ian was in the left back position frequently that season and played on 30th April 1960 as United beat Berwick Rangers at Tannadice to gain promotion to Division One, but he was released a few days later.

Frank McGrory was a left winger who had been with Arbroath, Dundee and Forfar Athletic. He made his debut for United on 8th August 1959 against East Stirlingshire in a League cup tie but after a few reserve outings and just one more first team appearance, he was released. He then returned to Forfar Athletic.

(David) Stewart Morrison was a goalkeeper who joined United in October 1959 from Whitburn Rovers. He spent most of that season in the reserves where he played more that 20 times, making just two first team appearances, including his debut against Forfar Athletic in a Scottish League match on 2nd April 1960. His next game was two weeks later, after which he was released.

Tommy Neilson began his senior career at Hearts and then moved to East Fife. From there he joined United for a reported fee of £300. Tommy made his debut on 24th October 1959 at inside left against Albion Rovers in a Scottish League match but quickly reverted to right half, where he remained for the rest of the season. He was an important part of the team that won promotion to the First Division at the end of that campaign. Tommy was an ever present in Division One in the Club's next season, and for the next six years, he was rarely out of the side. In late 1966 he was in the United team that was victorious against Barcelona home and away, as United entered the European football arena for the first time. In his final season with United, 1967-68, he was unable to retain a first team berth and asked for a transfer in October 1967. Three months later, he had a short run in the side but was released in April 1968. He was then with Cowdenbeath for a season before he emigrated to South Africa. Tommy achieved the status of legend at United and he is ranked nineteenth in the all time appearances chart with 316 games played.

Tommy Neilson   *Gibby Ormond*

Gibby Ormond was an experienced left winger signed from Airdrieonians. He went straight into the side, making a scoring debut on 27th February 1960 against Albion Rovers in a Scottish League match. Gibby became an ever present in the side for the remainder of the season and was in the line up as United clinched promotion to the First Division on 30th April 1960. He was re-signed for the next campaign and missed just four games in season 1960-61 in the top flight. During the following season, the arrival of Neil Mochan restricted Gibby's first team appearances and he was more often in the reserves until he was released in May 1962. He then joined Cowdenbeath and later played for Alloa Athletic.

Peter Prior was a left winger who joined United after spending a month on trial at Raith Rovers. Before that, he had been with Aldershot. Peter made his debut for United on 12th December 1959 against Falkirk in a Scottish League match. After his trial period ended, he was released and later joined Hamilton Academical briefly, before joining junior side Fauldhouse United.

Peter Prior

John 'Jack' Scott was a full back signed from local side St Joseph's. He played in the reserves for most of season 1959-60, making just one first team appearance in a Forfarshire Cup tie against Arbroath on 25th November 1959. He was released in May 1960.

Peter Smith was a former Hearts half back who signed for United in the summer of 1959. He made his debut on 8th August 1959 against East Stirlingshire in a League Cup tie and went on to play quite regularly in the side until February 1960. Shortly afterwards, the arrival of new players saw him dropped to the reserves. Peter was released in April 1960 and then he joined Alloa Athletic where he spent around nine years, before joining junior side Broxburn Athletic.

Peter Smith

Eric Walker was a left winger acquired from Alloa Athletic in exchange for Watt Newton. Eric made his debut on 9th January 1960 against Stranraer in a Scottish League match. However, after just eight appearances, he was out of the side, replaced by Gibby Ormond. He re-signed in 1960-61 but played mainly in the reserves. Limited to just five first team outings in his second season, he was released in May 1960, joining Brechin City.

Eric Walker

Dave Whytock was with Brechin City but trained at Tannadice. He was an inside forward who made his debut against East Fife on 26th December 1959 and scored a hat-trick. He kept his place in the side for the next two months but after that, he played most of his time with United in the reserves, making just two first team appearances in friendlies in 1960-61. He accepted a free transfer in February 1961 and then rejoined Brechin City. Dave later played for Forfar Athletic.

1960-61 Player Profiles

Davie Boner

Davie Boner was a right winger who joined Everton in 1958 but he did not break into the first team there. He arrived at United in the middle of season 1960-61 and played initially in the reserves. Davie made a scoring first team debut on 18th March 1961 against Rangers in a Scottish League match and kept his place in the side until the end of the season. He played most of the next season in the first team but was gradually replaced by Wattie Carlyle. Davie was given a free transfer at his own request following his marriage to a girl from Liverpool. He moved there but did not settle and returned north to join Raith Rovers. In July 1963, he joined Mansfield Town.

Kevin Cairns was from the Preston area and had spent a short time at Blackburn Rovers before playing for English amateur sides Weymouth and Carshalton Athletic. He was recommended to United by Ron Yeats who played alongside him in an army team. A right back, Kevin signed for United and then made his debut on 10th September 1960 against St Johnstone in a Scottish League match. He featured regularly in 1960-61 and was retained for the next campaign. However, the arrival of new players forced Kevin into the reserves for most of season 1961-62 and he had just one more first team outing. He was released in May 1962 and then signed for Southport, where he remained for six years. Kevin then moved to non league Wigan Athletic.

Henry Alexander 'Alec' Gordon was a versatile defender signed from Armadale Thistle in late 1960. He made a few reserve appearances before making his first team debut on 18th February 1961 against Raith Rovers in a Scottish League match. Over the next eighteen months, Alec was a regular in the line up but fell out of favour in October 1962. During his spell out of the first team he had a transfer request declined but by March 1963, he had returned to the first eleven to become a regular in the line up again. At the start of season 1964-65, Alec signed again after initially agreeing a month to month contract. He was rarely in the first team and featured more often in the reserve side for much of that season. Initially retained for the next campaign, Alec left to join Bradford Park Avenue in August 1965. He remained with them for two years before returning north in 1967 to join St Johnstone, where he spent around five years. Alec then joined Highland League Ross County.

Alec Gordon

Bert Howieson

Robert 'Bert' Howieson was signed from Leeds United when he was still just seventeen years old. He had not played in their first eleven. Bert made his Dundee United debut on 19th November 1960 against Kilmarnock in a Scottish League match. He was utilised at centre forward or inside forward during five years with United. Initially considered a reserve, he made just 20 first team appearances in his first two seasons. More frequently used in the first team during 1962-63 and 1963-64, he played mainly in the reserve side in the next campaign. Although never a prolific scorer in the first eleven, he scored four times in a Forfarshire Cup tie against Montrose in May 1961. He also hit more than 40 goals for the second string in almost 90 appearances. In November 1964, he almost joined Partick Thistle in exchange for Billy Hainey, but that deal did not work out. Bert was released in May 1965 and soon after, he joined Motherwell. He spent a year with the Fir Park club and then moved to South Africa to join Durban City.

Jack Jackson signed provisionally from local side Butterburn Youth Club in October 1959 and then made a few reserve appearances. He joined Carnoustie Panmure before becoming a signed United player in July 1960. Jack made his first team debut as a substitute against Sheffield United in a friendly on 3rd October 1960. He was primarily a reserve forward and turned out around 20 times for Dundee United 'A'. He made just one Scottish League appearance at first team level on 12th November 1960 against Rangers and he was released in May 1961.

Tommy McLeod was an inside forward with Ardeer Thistle and was signed in June 1960 after making a good impression in a private trial match. He made a spectacular debut, scoring a hat-trick against Stenhousemuir in a League Cup tie on 20th August 1960. Tommy was in the side at the beginning of the season

and was regularly scoring goals, including four in one match against a Combined Services side in a friendly. However, in November he was demoted to the reserves and made just one more first team appearance before he was released in May 1961. He spent a short time in Canada before joining Morton and later played for Cheltenham Town and Highland League side Inverness Caledonian.

Jimmy McMichael was an inside right signed from junior side Bathgate Thistle. He spent most of his two seasons with United in the reserves where he turned out around 40 times in all. He made his first team debut on 31st December 1960 in a Scottish League match against Hibs but played less than a dozen times in major competition before being released in May 1962.

Tommy McLeod

Neil Mochan was a very experienced centre forward who had started his senior career at Morton before moving south to join Middlesbrough for two years. He went to Celtic in 1953 and during a successful career with the Parkhead club, he gained international recognition, winning three caps for Scotland during 1954. Neil arrived at United for a fee of around £1,500 and made a scoring debut with two goals against Kilmarnock on 19th November 1960 in a Scottish League match. In his first season at Tannadice, he was second top scorer with 14 goals in 24 matches. In his second season, most of which

Neil Mochan

he spent playing on the left wing, he was joint top scorer with 17 goals, hardly missing a game. In his final season, 1962-63, he played frequently in the side but by then he was competing with Wattie Carlyle and Jim Irvine in the attacking roles. He was linked with a move to Airdrieonians in January 1963 but stayed until the end of the season when he was released. He then joined Raith Rovers. His last game for United brought the Second XI Cup to Tannadice when Neil scored the decisive winning goal against Hearts 'A' with a typical thunderbolt. In February 1964, he rejoined Celtic on the coaching staff and he remained there for many years. Following the resignation of Jerry Kerr in 1971, Neil was one of a number of candidates mentioned in connection with the Manager's role before Jim McLean was appointed.

Dave Reid was a centre forward, formerly with Dunfermline Athletic. He had also played alongside Ron Yeats in an army side. Dave made a scoring debut for United on 15th October 1960 against Raith Rovers in a Scottish League match. He played just once more in the first eleven before being demoted to the reserves. Even there he made just a few appearances and he was released in May 1961. He then appears to have gone to Australia to play.

John Roe was a defender, signed from West Calder after he played well in a public trial match. He had also spent a brief time with Colchester United at the start of 1958-59. John made his Dundee United debut on 31st August 1960 against Brechin City in a League Cup tie. John stayed with United for three seasons in the reserves, where he was a regular in the line up, making around 100 appearances. He made only infrequent first team appearances and he was released in April 1963, later playing for St Johnstone.

George Sievewright was a right half with Broughty Athletic and joined United reserves as a part-timer in February 1961. Six months later, he became a full-time player. He made his first team debut for United in a testimonial match for Doug Berrie at Forfar Athletic on 26th April 1961. His first appearance in major competition came on 14th October 1961 against St Mirren in a Scottish League match. George was at Tannadice for two years, playing just a few first team games, whilst he totalled around 80 appearances in the reserves. He was released in April 1963 and joined Oldham Athletic. George also played south of the border with Tranmere Rovers, Rochdale, Macclesfield Town and Mossley.

Lando Ugolini

Rolando 'Lando' Ugolini was signed from Wrexham after playing well in a private trial in June 1960. An experienced goalkeeper he had also been with Hearts, Celtic and Middlesbrough. He made his debut for United on 13th August 1960 against Stirling Albion in a League Cup tie. United had just earned promotion to the top flight and the keeper became the first choice for the No. 1 jersey. Lando was retained for the following season but as a result of injury, he only played in around half of the games. During that time, he coached some of the younger players in the reserves. In May 1962, he was released and later played briefly with Berwick Rangers and Cowdenbeath before announcing his retirement in September 1962.

1961-62 Player Profiles

Eric Brodie had played at international level as a junior. He was an inside forward, joining United from Forfar Athletic for a fee of around £1,000. Eric made his debut on 18th November 1961 against Motherwell in a Scottish League match but after a brief run in the first team, he was relegated to the second eleven. During season 1962-63, he was playing mainly in the reserves but had several games at first team level. Initially retained for the next campaign, Eric left United in June 1963 to join Shrewsbury Town. Five years later, he was with Chester and later spent time with Tranmere Rovers and Bangor City.

Eric Brodie

Sandy Davie

Tommy Millar

Sandy Davie had trials with both West Ham United and Dundee before he signed for Dundee United from Butterburn Youth Club in August 1961. He made his first appearance in a friendly against a British Army side on 2nd October 1961, when he came on as a substitute. He was the third choice keeper that season but on 23rd April 1962 he made his debut in major competition against Partick Thistle in a Scottish League match. Keepers Ugolini and Brown were then released but United signed Donald Mackay who began season 1962-63 as first choice. Following injury to Mackay early in the season, Sandy took over in goal and retained the No. 1 jersey for the next two years. His part-time position with the Club became a full-time post after he lost his job as a gardener in July 1963, when he chose to travel with United on the tour of Southern Africa. In May 1964, he was named in the Scotland Under-23 side to face France. United were fortunate to have two good goalkeepers throughout the early sixties and after Sandy was injured, he took the deputising role again in August 1964. By season 1966-67 he was again first choice and was in the line up that recorded famous home and away wins over Barcelona as United stepped on to the European stage for the first time. Another keeper role reversal occurred in the following season when Mackay was again established in the first eleven. Sandy requested a transfer in January 1968, accepting a move to Luton Town in October, with United receiving a fee of around £8,000. After two years with them he went to Southampton but was not first choice there. In a surprise move, Sandy re-signed for United in May 1972 for a fee reported at £5,000, replacing Mackay who had been released. Sandy was then seen as the deputy for the established Hamish McAlpine and spent the next two seasons at Tannadice, reaching the pinnacle of his United career in the side that faced Celtic in the Club's first appearance in the Scottish Cup final of 1974. Shortly afterwards, he emigrated to New Zealand where he signed for North Shore United. Sandy also played at international level for New Zealand, winning eight caps and he was later appointed Director of Coaching for the New Zealand FA.

Tommy Millar joined Colchester United in 1959 from the Scottish junior ranks and had become a first team regular there. However, he was released by his club following the tragic death of his young son and he returned to Scotland in January 1962. Initially, United offered Tommy training facilities but he signed soon after to become a regular in the United rearguard for several years. Although he was a defender, Tommy made his United debut at inside right against Motherwell on 17th March 1962 in a Scottish League match and remained in that position for the rest of the season. Early in the next campaign, he was firmly established at right back, although he still filled in as an auxiliary forward occasionally. This was the pattern throughout his Tannadice career over the next five years. In the summer of 1966, the player was reluctant to sign for United and a bid of £10,000 from Liverpool was rejected. He then decided to stay with United but went part-time. The fans were glad that he did, as Tommy was one of the United team that made their first venture into European football in late 1966 to famously record home and away wins over Spanish giants, Barcelona. Unfortunately for Tommy he lost his job as a result, because he took time off to play in the away leg but United then agreed to take him back full-time. In season 1967-68 Tommy was joined at United by his brother Jimmy and they played together for United several times thereafter. A broken leg in the midst of season 1967-68 marked the beginning of the end of Tommy's time at United and he was out for nine months. He returned to the side for a while in October 1968 but he was released in May 1969. He then joined Cowdenbeath and later played with Berwick Rangers and Hamilton Academical.

George Pattie joined United on a provisional form from Blairgowrie Juniors after playing well in a closed doors trial match. He had just been demobbed after completing his national service. A versatile attacking player, George made his debut in a Scottish League match against Partick Thistle on 23rd April 1962. He featured in the early part of season 1962-63 but he was soon relegated to the reserves. In April 1963, he lodged a transfer request and was released a few weeks later. He appears to have spent some time with English non league side Weymouth before returning north to join Montrose in 1963. George then joined Brechin City late in season 1964-65.

Alex Stewart joined United on a short-term basis from Airdrieonians. He made just one first team appearance, on the left wing against Dunfermline Athletic in a League Cup tie on 30th August 1961. Alex played in several reserve matches but he was released in October when his trial period ended. He then joined Albion Rovers and later played for Brechin City.

1962-63 Player Profiles

(James) **Sidney Dick** was a sixteen-year-old schoolboy when he joined United reserves as an amateur, signing from Arbroath Lads Club in April 1961. He could play at centre half or full back. After two full seasons in the second eleven, he made his first team debut on 26th June 1963 against a Northern Rhodesia XI during the Club's tour of Southern Africa. He made his first appearance in major competition at left back against Hibs in a Scottish League match on 21st December 1963. Sid spent the next four years with United but competing against other well established defenders, he was never able to earn himself a regular first team slot. He made just 20 first team appearances, whilst playing close to

Sidney Dick

200 games for Dundee United 'A', before he was released in April 1967. Shortly afterwards, Sid joined Forfar Athletic. During 1969, he went to South Africa where he played for the Jewish Guild.

Bobby Dougan was a seventeen-year-old left half, signed as a reserve in December 1960 on a provisional form from Armadale Thistle. After more than two years in the reserves, he made his first team debut for United during the tour of Southern Africa, coming on as a substitute against a Western Province XI on 2nd July 1963. He made one more appearance on the tour but never again featured in the first team. Bobby played exclusively in the reserves for the next season, finishing his United career with around 90 second eleven appearances in total. He was released in April 1964 and then spent a season with Montrose before moving to South Africa where he joined Addington.

Donald Mackay joined United from Forfar Athletic in May 1962 after keepers Ugolini and Brown had been released. Donald made his debut for United on 11th August 1962 against Dundee in a League Cup tie and as first choice keeper, looked

Donald Mackay

set to have a good season. Unfortunately, he sustained an injury in October, which kept him out of the side for the rest of the campaign. As his understudy, Sandy Davie did an excellent job to retain the No. 1 jersey for much of the following season. Unsettled, Donald was refused a transfer in September 1964. Soon after, Sandy Davie was injured and that allowed Donald to re-establish himself as first choice for the next two years. His good form led to an international squad call up and he was the travelling reserve keeper for the Scottish League against their English counterparts in March 1966. Following a role reversal for the keepers in 1966-67, Donald was again the deputy for a while but he was the first choice for much of the next three years. His new deputy was Hamish McAlpine and by 1970-71, Donald found himself back in the supporting role and he was released in April 1972. His football involvement was far from over and he went south to play for Southend United before taking up a coaching role at Bristol City in 1974 for four years. After a brief spell managing Norresundby in Denmark, he took the job of manager at Dundee between 1980 and 1983. After parting company with the Dens Park club, he returned to Denmark. He was back in the UK in September 1984 as assistant manager at Coventry City and was promoted to manager within three months. He then moved to Rangers as reserve and youth team coach in May 1986 and went to Blackburn Rovers as manager nine months later. Donald was in that post for four years before taking over as manager at Fulham until 1994. He also managed Airdrieonians for a short time in 2000-01 and after scouting for Middlesbrough, he joined Leicester City's coaching staff briefly in 2007.

Hector McKinlay was an inside right with Armadale Thistle and had his first trial with United in the reserves in November 1959. He did not sign at that time but joined the second eleven as a part-timer in June 1962. Over the next two years, he made over 60 appearances for Dundee United 'A'. Hector made a scoring first team debut on 23rd March 1963 against Clyde in a Scottish League match but played just once more in the first eleven before being released in April 1964. He then joined Dumbarton.

Hector McKinlay

Ian Mitchell was widely regarded as one of the best prospects in Scottish football when United signed him as a sixteen-year-old in July 1962, ahead of competition from Spurs, Manchester United, Rangers, Hearts and Hibs. A former schoolboy international, Ian joined United, initially on an amateur form from Woodburn Athletic. He became the youngest player to turn out for United when he made his debut on 29th September 1962 against Hibs in a Scottish League match. By the end of his first season, he was firmly established as the first choice left winger, finding the net frequently. He signed professional forms in May 1963. For the next seven years the name of Ian Mitchell was rarely missing from the line up and he continued in good scoring form. In 1963-64, still playing mainly on the left wing, he was top scorer with 16 goals including a hat-trick against St Mirren. Over the next two years United were aided by

Ian Mitchell

the prowess of Finn Dossing and his Scandinavian colleagues. They were ably augmented by Ian, by then taking an inside left position, and still reaching double figures in the United goal scoring charts. During a period when Dossing was out of the side, Ian took over at centre forward for a while in 1966-67. Whilst in this role he scored the crucial first goal at Tannadice against Barcelona as United made their home debut in European competition. In the same season, Ian was capped at Under-23 level against Wales and England. That season also saw him as top scorer again with 22 goals. Including a hat-trick against Stirling Albion, Ian scored 16 goals in the next campaign but that was enough for him to top the scoring list again. For the fourth time in his United career he was top scorer on 20 goals in season 1969-70 with hat-tricks against Airdrieonians and Raith Rovers. During his first spell at Tannadice, Ian had lodged transfer requests three times. He finally got his wish in July 1970 when he moved to Newcastle United for a fee reported at £50,000. However, just fourteen months later a possible return to Tannadice was being muted and in October 1971, he was back in a swap deal that took Alec Reid to Newcastle United. Ian spent the next two seasons with United in a supporting forward role but in May 1973, he was listed as available for transfer. There were no takers however, and he was released in September 1973. After training briefly with Dundee, he joined Falkirk and later Brechin City before retiring from the game. Regarded as a Dundee United legend, Ian is the fourth top all time goal scorer with 133 league and cup goals in his total of 314 games, which ranks him at twentieth in the all time appearances table.

Ally Riddle was an attacking player signed from Montrose. He made his debut for United on 25th August 1962 against Dundee in a League Cup tie but after just a few more first team matches, he was demoted to the reserves. He was transfer listed in January 1963 and was re-signed by his former club Montrose, moving to Brechin City four years later.

Benny Rooney was a promising twenty-year-old signed on a free transfer from Celtic, initially as a part-timer. Several other clubs including Liverpool, Leyton Orient and Crewe Alexandra were tracking the player at the time. A versatile forward, he immediately joined the United travelling party on a tour of Southern Africa and scored twice on his first appearance against a Nyasaland Select on 19th June 1963. Benny made his debut in major competition against Aberdeen on 10th August 1963 in a League Cup tie and was a regular in the side in the early stages of the season. However, he was relegated to the reserves in October 1963 and requested, but was declined a transfer in March 1964, after making just a few first team appearances. Over the next two years, he played mainly in the reserves where he scored more than 40 goals in around 60 appearances. He only had occasional first team outings, and in January 1966, he lodged another transfer request. This time it was granted and two months later, he left United to join St Johnstone for a fee of around £3,500. Benny was with the Perth side for a decade and then moved to Partick Thistle where he remained until he became manager at Morton in 1976.

Benny Rooney   *Bobby Smith*   *Doug Soutar*

Bobby Smith joined Burnley as a teenager but he had not settled in England. His registration was cancelled in January 1962 so that he could sign for United and he spent the rest of that season in the Tannadice reserves. He made his debut at first team level on the left wing against Hearts in a League Cup tie on 29th August 1962 and seemed to have made the breakthrough into a regular first team berth in early 1964. However, he was soon back in the reserves, where he played mainly on the left side of defence in a total of around 100 games. He made just fleeting first team appearances and in January 1966, he requested a transfer. He was released three months later and then joined St Johnstone for a season before moving to Montrose where he spent five years.

Doug Soutar was a centre forward who played trials in United reserves at the end of 1962 but stayed with Butterburn Youth Club until the end of season 1962-

63. He then signed for United and made his debut on 27th April 1963 against Airdrieonians in a Scottish League match. Doug spent three seasons at United but rarely made it out of the reserve side, where he played over 80 times and had a good scoring record, with around 40 goals. He spent a short time on loan at Forfar Athletic in early 1965. Doug was released in May 1966, joining East Fife and after five years at Methil, he moved to Elgin City in the Highland League.

1963-64 Player Profiles

Jocky Clark had attracted the attention of both Dundee senior sides before he signed for United from Nairn County. He was a winger and made his first appearance in a testimonial match for Charlie McFadyen at St Johnstone on 30th October 1963. Three days later, he made his debut in major competition against Falkirk in a Scottish League match. After one more outing, he was dropped to the reserves and was released in April 1964.

Norrie Davidson was a former Aberdeen centre forward who joined United from Hearts for a fee estimated at £4,000. He made his first appearance and scored against St Johnstone in a testimonial for Charlie McFadyen on 30th October 1963. Three days later, he netted twice on his debut in major competition, against Falkirk in a Scottish League match. The player was with United for just a few months, leaving to join Partick Thistle in January 1964 in a swap deal for George Smith. Norrie later played for St Mirren and English non league side Margate.

Jimmy McManus

Jimmy McManus was a versatile winger who signed as a reserve for United from Edinburgh Norton in November 1962. He made his first team debut on 24th August 1963 in a League Cup tie against Aberdeen, but over the next two years, he was in the side only occasionally. In three years with United he racked up around 80 appearances in the reserves. Jimmy requested a transfer in August 1965 and shortly afterwards joined Falkirk. In 1969, he moved to South Africa and joined Durban United.

Jim Moore was a centre half with Lochore Welfare when he signed for United at the end of season 1962-63. He made his first team debut on 28th August 1963 against Hibs in a Scottish League match, but competing with the well established Doug Smith, Jim had few first team opportunities. He almost joined Shrewsbury

Town in June 1965 but was unable to agree terms. His longest run in the United first team came in the last two matches of 1966-67 and during the subsequent trip to America, when he filled in at left half for Lenny Wing. Jim continued to play in the reserves, where he made a total of around 170 appearances before he was released in April 1968. He then spent five successful years at Cowdenbeath and finished his career in 1975 at Forfar Athletic.

Jim Moore

Ronnie Simpson was a right-sided attacking player signed from Greengairs United as a sixteen-year-old in June 1962. After playing well in United reserves, he made his first team debut on 5th October 1963 against Airdrieonians in a Scottish League match. He kept his place for just two more games before he went back to reserve football, where in total, he racked up almost 60 appearances in two years. Ronnie was released in April 1964 and then joined Stranraer.

Ronnie Simpson

George Smith had been with Partick Thistle for ten years before he joined United in a swap deal that took Norrie Davidson in the opposite direction. An attacking player with a good scoring record, George made his debut on the right wing against Airdrieonians in a Scottish League match on 1st February 1964. In a brief Tannadice career, he also played at centre forward and on the left wing. George was re-signed for the next season but was out of football due to injury or illness until February 1965. He then accepted the post of player/manager at Irish club Ballymena, with United collecting a nominal fee for the transfer.

Lewis Thom was twenty years old when he signed for United from Aberdeen at the end of season 1963-64. He was a left winger and made his debut in a Summer Cup tie on 9th May 1964 against his previous club. He went on to play regularly in that position until the arrival of Orjan Persson in December 1964. After that, Lewis found it harder to get into the side, spending much of his time in the reserves. Although he played throughout the Summer Cup of 1965, he was intent on leaving United. He had talks with Shrewsbury Town in June 1965 but was unable to agree terms. However, he joined them three months later. Lewis moved to Lincoln City in 1967 and then to

Lewis Thom

Bradford Park Avenue in 1969. The player then had a short spell at Altrincham before returning north to play for Highland League sides Elgin City, Inverness Clachnacuddin and Huntly.

Bobby Young was a former Motherwell, St Johnstone and Celtic centre forward who had been without a club for a short time before joining United at the end of 1963-64. He made his debut on 11th March 1964 against Kilmarnock in a Scottish League match and held on to the No. 9 jersey for several weeks. He re-signed for the next season but could not get back into the first eleven and after four months in the reserves, he was released in December 1964 at his own request. He then joined Airdrieonians and later played for Berwick Rangers, Dumbarton and Alloa Athletic.

1964-65 Player Profiles

Mogens Berg

Mogens Berg (Pedersen) came to United from Boldklubben 1909 Odense in Denmark and was the third Scandinavian player to join United at the end of 1964. Along with Finn Dossing, Mogens had been recommended to then Manager Jerry Kerr. The three-times capped Danish international was a versatile forward and made his debut at inside left on 12th December 1964 against Rangers in a Scottish League match. His bustling style soon made him a fans' favourite. Although not renowned as a goal scorer, he managed to score eight times in the Summer Cup of 1965, including a hat-trick against St Johnstone. A serious back injury shortly after that sidelined the player for all of the next season and he did not make a comeback into the side until late 1966. From that point on he was unable to fully re-establish himself in the team. Still restricted by injury, he played twenty first team matches in 1967-68 and was released in April 1968. Mogens then returned to Boldklubben 1909 Odense. He later gained more international recognition, collecting five more caps.

Kenny Dick signed for United from Forfar Athletic as a centre forward at a time when United were struggling to find a player who could score goals regularly. He made his debut on 14th November 1964 against Dunfermline Athletic in a Scottish League match. However, he had little time to prove himself before the arrival of Finn Dossing effectively ensured that Kenny would play in the reserves. Kenny was transferred to Queen of the South in the early part of season 1965-66, remaining with the Dumfries side for three seasons. He then returned to Forfar Athletic and in 1971 joined Brechin City, where he went into management a year later. Kenny became youth coach and a scout at United in 1974 but returned to Forfar Athletic again in June 1975. He later coached at Montrose and Dundee.

Kenny Dick

Finn Dossing

Finn Dossing (Jensen) arrived under a cloak of secrecy from Viborg in Denmark for trials on 1st December 1964. He netted four goals in a closed doors game and starred in a second trial match before he was signed along with Orjan Persson for a total of around £10,000. Finn made a scoring debut against Hearts on 5th December 1964 in a Scottish League match but did not impress some of the watching reporters. However, they quickly changed their opinions, as the tall Danish centre forward became a Tannadice scoring sensation. He was largely responsible for turning a mundane season that threatened relegation, into a memorable one that pushed United into a respectable mid table finish. In just 29 appearances, Finn was top scorer with 31 goals including a hat-trick against Hibs. In his second season at United, he topped the scoring charts again, with 27 goals from 41 appearances including one of the most famous hat-tricks in United history when he netted three against Dundee in a 5-0 win. He also netted hat-tricks against Motherwell, at home and away. Finn also holds the record for the fastest goal scored by a United player, netting after just 14 seconds against Hamilton Academical on 16th October 1965. His scoring rate dropped in 1966-67 and injury kept him out of the team as they went into European competition for the first time, but he had the satisfaction of scoring the only goal of the game at Tannadice against Juventus in his only European match. With his contract nearing the end, in 1967-68, he made only eight appearances before returning to his home in Denmark in December 1967. Despite his scoring exploits at United, as a professional player, Finn was unable to represent his country due to their strictly amateur policy at the time. His record at United is remarkable, with a total of 76 goals in 115 league and cup matches, ranking him amongst the Club legends. In January 2008, Finn was one of the first players inducted into the Dundee United Hall of Fame.

Johnny Graham joined United from Third Lanark in June 1964 for a fee of around £6,000. He was a right winger and made his debut against Dundee in a League Cup tie on 8th August 1964. Although he appeared to have slotted in well to the United set up, the arrival of the Scandinavian players at Tannadice forced Johnny out of the side by January 1965, and he left to sign for Falkirk. In 1969, he joined Hibs and later played with Ayr United. He returned to Falkirk in 1977 and a year later began coaching at Ayr United.

Johnny Graham

Doug Moran was an attacking player who began his senior career at Hibs. He then joined Falkirk, and whilst with them he was the subject of an unsuccessful offer by United in February 1960. Doug moved to Ipswich Town in July 1961 and after three years there was signed by United for £6,000 ahead of competition from Dunfermline Athletic and Falkirk. He made his debut at centre forward on 8th August 1964 against Dundee in a League Cup tie. Doug was in the side for the next two months but was not finding the net as often as had been hoped. In a surprise move he returned to

Doug Moran

Falkirk in mid November 1964 for an undisclosed fee and remained there for four years before moving to Cowdenbeath.

Frannie Munro

Francis 'Frannie' Munro began his senior career with Chelsea but did not settle there and returned north to join United in August 1963, still just sixteen years old. He spent his first year at Tannadice as a regular in the reserves before making a dramatic first team debut against Dundee on 8th August 1964 in a League Cup tie, scoring a late winning goal. Frannie was an inside right but was just as capable at right half and occasionally he filled the right wing berth. He even played at centre half a couple of times. He quickly became established as a first team regular and his undoubted talent saw him recognised at international youth level. After two seasons at United, the player was unsettled and was reluctant to agree terms for 1966-67. Although he did eventually re-sign, he was transfer listed. Huddersfield Town showed interest in September but were not prepared to meet the £15,000 price tag, but Frannie left United a month later to join Aberdeen. His career advanced with a move to Wolverhampton Wanderers two years later and whilst with them he won a League Cup winner's medal in 1974. He also gained the first of nine full Scottish caps in May 1971. In 1977, he joined Celtic for three years before moving to Australia where he spent the 1980s in coaching and management.

(Per) Orjan Persson joined United from Orgryte in Sweden on 3rd December 1964 after protracted negotiations over almost six weeks. He signed along with Finn Dossing for a total fee of £10,000. Orjan made his debut two days later against Hearts in a Scottish League match and he was quickly recognised as an exceptional talent. He became a regular in the side over the next three seasons, playing mainly on the left

Orjan Persson

wing but also filling in when required on the right. When United made their first appearance in European competition, Orjan was in the line up for the famous home and away wins over Barcelona. He had already been capped 17 times for his country and whilst with United, he added another 9 to his tally. Along with Lenny Wing, he was the first United player to be capped at full international level. A player of his calibre was always going to be the target for one of the bigger clubs and by the latter stages of 1966-67, he was being closely monitored by Rangers. At the end of that campaign the player severed his ties with United and there followed a complicated contractual dispute, which was never fully resolved. In the end, Orjan joined Rangers on 3rd August 1967 in exchange for Davie Wilson and Wilson Wood. Whilst with Rangers, he played in the 1970 World Cup finals for Sweden. After returning to Orgryte he continued his international career, turning out in the World Cup finals in 1974.

Jim Stewart had joined Chelsea as a teenager but following an injury, he was sidelined. Still just eighteen years old, he joined United in January 1965. He played around a dozen times in the reserves but made just one first team appearance, on the right wing in a testimonial for Alan Kennedy at Arbroath on 28th April 1965 and was released shortly after.

Lenny Wing

(Lars) Lennart 'Lenny' Wing joined United from Orgryte. He first came to the notice of Jerry Kerr, playing alongside Orjan Persson when the Swedish side met Dunfermline Athletic in a European match in October 1964. Lenny was a fire-fighter in his home town and had to obtain a leave of absence to play for United. A strong left half with 29 caps for his country, he made his debut on 23rd January 1965 against St Mirren in a Scottish League match. He went on to retain that position over the rest of the season and for much of the two seasons that followed. Whilst with United he collected another seven international caps. Along with Orjan Persson, he was the first United player to be capped at full international level. When his contract expired at the end of season 1966-67 the popular Swede asked for another extension to his already long leave of absence from the fire service. His request was denied and he returned home but continued to play part-time football, signing for Orgryte and then Kungsbacka.

1965-66 Player Profiles

Bobby Carroll was a former Celtic player signed by United from St Mirren. A right-sided attacking player, Bobby made a scoring debut against Celtic in a League Cup tie on 14th August 1965. After just a few games, he was relegated to the reserves where he played more than 50 times in his two years at Tannadice. He had just occasional first team appearances and was linked with a move to Raith Rovers in December 1966 but stayed with United until he was released in April 1967. Bobby later played with Coleraine in Northern Ireland. He was back in Scotland for season 1967-68 and

Bobby Carroll

finished his professional career at Queen of the South before joining junior side Irvine Meadow, where he had played before turning professional.

Billy Hainey

Billy Hainey was first mentioned in connection with a move to United in November 1964 but a transfer, which may have seen Bert Howieson move to Partick Thistle in exchange, did not work out. Billy was however, signed eighteen months later for a fee of around £8,000. He was a right-sided attacker and made his debut for United on 16th March 1966 against Hearts in a Scottish League match. At the beginning of season 1966-67, he became the first player to come on for United as a substitute in major competition and the first United substitute to score a competitive goal when he replaced Dennis Gillespie against Dundee in a League Cup tie on 13th August 1966. Billy was a regular in the line up that season and scored some vital goals but none more important than the opener against Barcelona in Spain as United made their first entry into European football. He then scored a stunning second goal against the Spaniards in the return leg at Tannadice. Out of the side early in the next campaign by October 1967, he handed in a transfer request.

There were no offers and he was released in April 1968. He then joined St Mirren and later played for Portadown in Northern Ireland.

Ronnie McFall

Ronnie McFall was signed from Northern Ireland side, Portadown for a fee of around £4,000. He was primarily taken on as a reserve right back and his first game for United was against Fram Reykjavik of Iceland on 1st June 1966 whilst United were on tour. Ronnie played in four of the tour matches that summer but never made the breakthrough into the first eleven, becoming a regular in the reserve side before he was released in April 1967.

Hugh McLeish was a teenage centre forward who had been with Motherwell and he signed for United in September 1965. He had around 40 reserve outings but just one first team appearance for United, against a Scottish Youth XI on 4th April 1966 in a friendly. The player had little chance of getting any first team experience at Tannadice as he was in competition with experienced players such as Dossing, Gillespie and Mitchell. Hugh was released in April 1967 and then joined Sunderland. He later played for Luton Town, non league Stevenage Town and Berwick Rangers.

Finn Seemann joined United from Norwegian side Lyn Oslo. He was a Norwegian international and had played in the 1966 World Cup qualifying stage matches but lost any chance of more international honours when he signed professional forms with United. Norway had a strict amateur rule that allowed only their home based players in the side. Finn was a right winger but played a few times on the left side during his time with United. He made his debut on 27th October 1965 against Rangers in a Scottish League match and went on to become a regular in the line up over the next two seasons. He was in the

Finn Seemann

side that faced Barcelona in Spain as United made their debut in the European arena and he scored the second goal, a penalty that ensured victory. After three successful years with United, he left in June 1968, playing his last game against his former club Lyn Oslo in a friendly in Norway. Finn then signed for DWS Amsterdam for a fee estimated at £25,000. When Norway scrapped their strict amateur rule in 1969, Finn was again able to play for his country and by 1970, he had accumulated 15 caps and scored 4 goals. Tragically, Finn died in a motor accident in September 1985.

Ian Stewart was a left winger who joined United from Arbroath for a fee of around £5,000 in September 1965. He made his first appearance as a substitute in the second half of a friendly against Carlisle United on 2nd November 1965. Four days later, Ian made a scoring debut in major competition in a Scottish League match against Hearts. He had just two more outings with United and after spending the remainder of his time at Tannadice playing reserve football, he joined Morton in August 1966 in a swap deal that brought Jackie Graham to Tannadice. He returned to Arbroath a short time later before moving to Forfar Athletic in 1967. Ian spent around seven years at Station Park and the next five with Montrose before he took the post of player/manager at Brechin City, from where he moved to become manager at Arbroath for three years.

Ian Thompson joined United from Valleyfield Juniors in the summer of 1966. In three years at United the tall left half, nicknamed 'Lofty', made more than 70 reserve appearances but played just once in the first eleven, in a friendly against a Scottish Youth XI on 4th April 1966. In competition with players such as Wing, Fraser and Neilson, he had little hope of a regular first team berth and he was released in April 1968. Ian then spent six years at Montrose.

1966-67 Player Profiles

Jim Cameron

Jim Cameron was a left back and one of three players who signed from junior side Ashfield, in late 1966. He turned down both Leicester City and Stirling Albion to join United. Jim made his debut against Partick Thistle in a Scottish League match on 22nd April 1967 after playing exceptionally well in the reserves. He then played in most of United's games as Dallas Tornado in the North American Soccer League in the summer of 1967. Following a serious injury to Jimmy Briggs, the new left back got his chance in the first team in February 1968. From that point on, Jim rarely missed a game over the next five years. The arrival of Frank Kopel into the side at the start of 1972-73 increased competition for the left back slot and with the new man soon recognised as first choice, Jim was transfer listed in October 1972. He played mainly in the reserves over that season and accepted a move to Falkirk in September 1973 for a fee reported at £7,000. In 1977, he moved to Montrose and a year later was at Forfar Athletic before moving to Australia, where he played with various clubs until he retired.

Jackie Graham was a versatile attacking player who joined United in a swap deal that took Ian Stewart to Morton. He made his debut for United in a League Cup tie against Dundee on 27th August 1966. On 3rd January 1967, in his first Scottish League match for the Club, against neighbours Dundee again, he scored a hat-trick which won the game for United. Although he spent three seasons at Tannadice, he was unable to stake a regular place in the first team, playing more often in the reserves. Jackie was released in April 1969 and he then joined Guildford City. In July 1970, he moved to Brentford where he spent ten successful years and later played for non league Addlestone & Weybridge, Hounslow and Burnham.

Jackie Graham

Gerry Hernon was one of the trio of Ashfield juniors signed by United in late 1966. He was a left-sided attacker, but could play in any forward position. Gerry made a scoring debut against St Mirren on 12th April 1967 in a Scottish League match. It was his only outing in the first team, except for an extended run of matches during United's time in America as Dallas Tornado in 1967. He made around 30 reserve appearances before he was released in April 1968 and he then joined Stranraer.

Ian Scott joined United from Musselburgh Athletic initially on a provisional form. He was a versatile forward and after playing well in the reserves, he made his first team debut on 6th May 1967 against Partick Thistle in the last Scottish League match of that season. Ian made the breakthrough into the first team by October 1967 and in December, he netted a hat-trick against Stirling Albion. Although he was a frequent starter in the line up over the next three years, the competition for places was intense and he played as often in the reserves as he did in the first eleven. Ian was released at

Ian Scott

the end of season 1970-71 and then joined neighbours Dundee, where he spent the next four seasons before retiring from the game.

Walter Smith

Walter Smith was one of three new signings in late 1966 from junior side Ashfield. He was a versatile player who made his mark in the second eleven before making his first team debut against Kilmarnock on 20th March 1967 in a Scottish League match. His first four years at United were spent mainly in the reserves with just a handful of first team appearances until he broke into the side in the latter half of 1970-71. Walter played initially at right half or inside right but was just as capable on the left side or at centre half. He was a regular in the line up over the next three seasons and in 1973-74, he hardly missed a match, including United's first Scottish Cup final against Celtic. It was also in that campaign that he famously scored the only goal in a derby at Dens Park against Dundee and then kissed his boot, an action he later described as his most embarrassing moment. He was not in the side as often in 1974-75 and just weeks into the next campaign, he left to join Dumbarton for a fee of £8,000. Eighteen months later in February 1977, he returned to Tannadice for half of that fee. He played regularly over the rest of that season but then, aged just 29, he suffered an injury which limited his first team appearances. Instead, he concentrated on a coaching role and played in the reserves. By the time he finished his playing career with United, he had made a record number of appearances in the second string, turning out approximately 360 times. He was linked with a move to Aberdeen as coach in the summer of 1978 but remained at Tannadice. By 1979 he was assisting with coaching the Scotland youth squad. Walter remained involved at national level, first with the Under-21 side and then as assistant to Alex Ferguson with the full national side in the lead up to the World Cup of 1986. He was elevated to the Tannadice Board in February 1986 but two months later, he left to become assistant manager at Rangers. In 1991, Walter took over as manager at Ibrox, following the departure of Graeme Souness. He went on to become one of Rangers' most successful managers and left them at the top of his profession. In 1998, he took over the manager's chair at Everton but enjoyed little success there before he parted company with them in March 2002. He was out of football for a short period but returned as assistant to Alex Ferguson at Manchester United until December 2004, when he was appointed manager of Scotland. Following a relatively successful time as the national team boss, he was firmly on track for a World Cup place in January 2007 when the lure of a return to take charge at Rangers was too great and he quit Scotland for a second spell in charge of the Ibrox side.

1967-68 Player Profiles

Iain Brown signed for United on a provisional form from Lochee Renton in July 1967. He was a full back and played in the reserves before making his first team debut, coming on as a substitute for Dennis Gillespie against Kilmarnock in a Scottish League match on 17th April 1968. Ian played from the start the following week and made another substitute appearance the next, but that was the end of his first team career with United. He continued in the reserves, making around 80 appearances in total, before he was released in May 1970.

Kenny Cameron

Kenny Cameron was a centre forward with a natural goal scoring talent. He had been with Dundee for five years and then Kilmarnock for a season, before he joined United in May 1968 for £7,500, a fee that turned out to be a bargain. Kenny made his debut for United on 8th May 1968 in a Forfarshire Cup tie against Forfar Athletic, scoring a hat-trick. Astonishingly, he recorded a total of 15 goals, including three more hat-tricks in Forfarshire Cup ties and friendlies, before the new season got under way. He opened his United account in major competition with a goal in a League Cup tie against Dunfermline Athletic on 10th August 1968. Kenny continued in great scoring form, hitting all four goals in a Forfarshire Cup win over Arbroath. An instant hero with the fans, Kenny ended the campaign as top scorer with 36 goals in major competition, including hat-tricks against Hearts and Ayr United. Competition for the centre forward position over the next two seasons meant fewer appearances for Kenny and his scoring rate did not hit the heights of that first season. However, he still had a knack of hitting them in the Forfarshire Cup where he netted five in one game against Brechin City. With Kenny still very much in the frame at Tannadice and still finding the net, a cash bid from Dunfermline Athletic was rejected in November 1971 and he had two more good seasons with United. During that time, Kenny graduated as a coach and when he was released in May 1974, he joined Montrose as player/coach, later becoming their manager. After he left Montrose, he used his football knowledge as a scout and helped United find many of the young players who would emerge over the years. He was also a coach at Tannadice for fifteen years, leaving to become manager of St Joseph's in February 1996. Eighteen months later, he returned to Dens Park as a coach, remaining there for several years.

Tommy Dunne had started his senior football career at Celtic before moving south to join Leyton Orient. He signed for Dumbarton in the Spring of 1965 before joining Albion Rovers for season 1967-68. Tommy came to United for a fee of £5,000 in April 1968. He was an inside forward and made his debut on 27th April 1968 against Stirling Albion in a Scottish League match. Never able to establish himself in the first team, Tommy made just fleeting appearances until the end of 1969-70 when he was in the side for a short run. He played almost 70 times for the reserves and eventually requested a transfer in August 1970 but there were no offers. After just one more first team appearance that season, he was released in March 1971.

Davie Hogg joined United in June 1968 on a free transfer, after four seasons with Hibs. He was a right winger and made his first appearance against Viking Stavanger on 19th June 1968, during United's summer tour of Norway. His debut in major competition followed on 10th August 1968 against Dunfermline Athletic in a League Cup tie. Davie settled into the right wing berth and was a regular in the line up that season. He played in the first team in the early part of the next season but in January, he lost his place and ended his two years at United in the reserves. Davie was transfer listed in March 1970 but with no offers received, he was released two months later. He then joined Berwick Rangers and later played for Hamilton Academical and Alloa Athletic.

Jimmy Millar had been with Dunfermline Athletic and then spent 12 highly successful years with Rangers before he was released at the end of 1966-67. He then signed for United where he joined his brother Tommy. United had tried to sign the player a year earlier but that deal had fallen through. Jimmy began his senior football career as a forward and had a great goal scoring record with Rangers. He had gained two international caps for Scotland in 1963. At United, he initially played in the half back line, making his first appearance on 5th August 1967 in a friendly against Sheffield United. His debut in major competition for United followed a week

Jimmy Millar

later against Celtic in a League Cup tie. He was soon playing in the front line but was out of the first team for two lengthy periods before leaving to join Raith Rovers as player/manager in February 1969.

Pat Purcell was an attacking player in the youth team at Chelsea but he was released in the summer of 1967. He was still just nineteen years old when he joined United and made his debut in a friendly against Sheffield United on 5th August 1967, coming on as a second half substitute. He made just one appearance in major competition, against St Johnstone in a Scottish League match on 9th September 1967, spending the rest of the season in the reserves, where he played around 30 times. Pat was released in April 1968, joining Raith Rovers, where he remained for two years before returning to the junior ranks with Newtongrange Star.

Andy Rolland began his senior football career with Cowdenbeath. In February 1967 United were keen to sign him and there was also interest from Rangers and Clyde at the time. He finally arrived at Tannadice in September 1967 for a fee reported at £10,000 and made his debut at left back on 30th September 1967 against Airdrieonians in a Scottish League match. The following week he moved to an attacking position. Over the next few months, Andy played in both inside forward slots but by March 1968, he was at right back. From that point on, he was a recognised defender but was

Andy Rolland

frequently pitched into the forward line. Nicknamed 'The Major', his strong running and tough tackling made him a huge favourite with the fans. In eleven seasons at Tannadice, he did not miss many games but his time at United had its ups and downs. In February 1970 he requested a transfer because he was unsettled following publicity received due to his disciplinary record but he withdrew his request soon after. The high point of his United career was most likely the run to the Scottish Cup final in 1974, in which he came on as a second half substitute. Andy also took part in many other memorable games, including several European ties. In November 1975, he broke Club rules by moving out of Dundee with his family and he was briefly suspended until a compromise agreement was reached. He then continued, as he always had, to play a big part in the United story. In March 1976, he received international recognition as part of the Scottish League side that played their English counterparts in the last of the inter league internationals. In April 1978 after a long career with United, in which he was a consistent performer, he was released. He played 440 times for United and is regarded as a Club legend, ranked eighth equal with Eamonn Bannon in the all time appearances chart. Andy went to America for a short time, but returned to Scotland and was with Dunfermline Athletic before re-signing for Cowdenbeath in December 1979. He took over as manager there a year later but in February 1982, he resigned and went into management in the junior ranks. Andy was inducted into the Dundee United Hall of Fame in January 2009.

Davie Wilson

Davie Wilson joined Rangers in 1956. In his ten years with the Glasgow side he had a tremendous scoring record, with over 100 goals to his credit as a left winger. He had also been capped 22 times for Scotland between 1960 and 1965, scoring 10 international goals. Davie came to United in July 1967 along with Wilson Wood, in part exchange for Orjan Persson. He made his first appearance in a friendly against Sheffield United on 5th August 1967 and made his debut in major competition a week later against Celtic in a League Cup tie. For four seasons, Davie was a regular in the line up as the first choice left winger but he could also play on the right and switched to that side for long periods during his time at United. In his final season, 1971-72, he was displaced by players such as Tommy Traynor and Ian Mitchell. In January 1972 he left United to join Dumbarton and he helped them win promotion just a few months later. He finished his playing career there, and became assistant manager with them and in 1977, he took over as their manager for three years. He then spent time with both Kilmarnock and Hamilton Academical before returning to Dumbarton for a second spell as manager, winning promotion in 1984. Less than two years later he resigned that post. Soon after, he took on his last job in football as manager at Queen of the South.

Wilson Wood began his senior career at Newcastle United and whilst he was there, United made an unsuccessful offer of £1,000 for his transfer in September 1960. He moved to Rangers in 1963 and in August 1967 finally landed at Tannadice along with Davie Wilson in part exchange for Orjan Persson. He was a left half and made his first appearance in a friendly against Sheffield United on 5th August 1967. His debut in major competition followed a week later in a League Cup tie against Celtic. Wilson became a regular in the line up for the next two years but in the summer of 1969, he became unsettled at United and requested a transfer. After unsuccessful trials at Nottingham Forest and Crystal Palace, he elected to remain at Tannadice, playing in the reserves. A proposed move to Hearts, in exchange for Tommy Traynor, fell through in December 1969. He almost joined Falkirk in exchange for Craig Watson soon after but that deal also collapsed. Finally, in April 1970, the swap deal to bring Traynor to United was completed, with Wilson moving to Hearts. He was with the Tynecastle side for three years before moving on to Raith Rovers.

1968-69 Player Profiles

Alan Gordon was a centre forward who joined Hearts in 1961. He left to play for Durban United in South Africa after six years at Tynecastle but eighteen months later, he was back with the Edinburgh side. Alan joined Dundee United for a fee of around £8,000, making his debut against Hibs on 31st March 1969 in a Scottish League match. Over the next two years, he became a regular in the United front line and in season 1970-71 he was the Club's top scorer with 20 goals in league and cup matches. Following the arrival of Jim McLean in December, there was a change of policy and

Alan Gordon

all players had to train in Dundee. In the case of Alan, that was impossible due to his work commitments and as no compromise was available, he was allowed to join Hibs for a fee of £12,000 in mid January 1972. After almost two years at Easter Road, he was transferred to Dundee to become the first player to turn out for both senior clubs in Dundee and Edinburgh. At the end of season 1975-76, Alan retired from football.

Jim Henry

Jim Henry signed from Carnoustie Panmure, initially on a provisional form in August 1967. He was an attacker who played in the reserve side before making his debut at first team level at inside left on 6th August 1968 against Hartlepools United in a friendly. By the time he made his debut in major competition against St Mirren on 25th October 1969 in a Scottish League match, Jim had been converted to left half, a position he retained for much of the remainder of that season and the next. In September 1970, he was in the Scottish League side against the League of Ireland. Two months later, he cited pressure from the fans as his reason for wanting to leave United but he changed his mind and withdrew his transfer request. Over the next two years, Jim was in the line up for around twenty games each season. On 6th March 1972, he left United, apparently to join Fulham, for a fee of £50,000. However, three days later, he returned to United after Fulham refused to complete the deal, stating that the player was not fully fit, a fact they were well aware of before Jim went to London. Subsequently, injury kept him out for the rest of the season. By the beginning of 1973-74, Jim was re-established in the side in a wide attacking role. He then accepted a move to Aberdeen in January 1974, with United receiving a fee of £20,000. Just over two years afterwards Jim left Aberdeen and went to America to play for San Antonio Thunders. He was soon back in Scotland with Forfar Athletic, where he spent most of the next four years, although he was also back in the USA during this period.

Hamish McAlpine

Hamish McAlpine signed provisionally from Dundee North End in the spring of 1966. He became a regular in the reserve side in season 1968-69 and made his first team debut on 6th August 1968 against Hartlepools United in a friendly. His debut in major competition came against Hearts on 8th March 1969 following an injury to first choice keeper Donald Mackay. Hamish spent some time on loan at Montrose in 1967-68 and they were keen to sign him permanently. However, he was persuaded to turn full-time at United where he again featured in the reserves until injury prevented him playing during most of season 1969-70. He recovered to make a dramatic entry into the first team on a more permanent basis against Sparta Prague in October 1970, when he had to come on as substitute for the injured Mackay. From that point on, Hamish was a regular in the side and first choice for almost sixteen years, overcoming other serious injuries in 1974 and 1980. During a period in the mid 1970s, Hamish became the Club penalty taker and netted three times from the spot. As a young player, he kept out more experienced keepers such as Sandy Davie and Donald Mackay, and once he was established, the deputies, including Andy Graham and John Gardiner, could not oust him. Even the arrival of Peter Bonetti for a short time, when Hamish was involved in a dispute with the club, did not keep him out for long. It was only with the arrival of Billy Thomson in the summer of 1984 that Hamish's position was threatened and by the end of 1985-86, Hamish was out of the side. After a very short visit to Dunfermline Athletic on loan he was released in May 1986. During a long career, the player was involved in numerous important games, including an uninterrupted run of 46 European matches between 1970 and 1984. He played in two Scottish Cup finals but not on a winning side. He was also in four League Cup finals, collecting a winner's medal in 1979 against Aberdeen and again in 1980 against Dundee. The final against Dundee gave him one of his proudest moments when he was invited forward by captain Paul Hegarty to receive the trophy. However, the crowning achievement of his career was the Scottish League championship medal for season 1982-83. In August 1983, Hamish was awarded a testimonial match against Spurs and in 1985 he was the SFWA Player of the Year. Never recognised at full international level, the closest Hamish came was five Under-21 caps in the early 1980s as an over-age player, and in 1978, he was a travelling reserve with the Scottish League side that played against the Irish League. After he left United, Hamish played with Raith Rovers and Arbroath and on one occasion played for Celtic during their summer tour in 1988. Most certainly the best known of all United's goalkeepers, Hamish is rightly regarded as a Club legend. The charismatic keeper is ranked fourth in the all time appearances charts with a total of 688. In 1991, Hamish was back at United briefly, as the part-time commercial manager for the Club, and continued to assist the commercial department for many years. He was inducted into the Dundee United Hall of Fame in January 2009.

Stuart Markland was a centre half signed from Berwick Rangers on a free transfer in August 1968. Initially he was on trial for a month at United. After playing well in the reserves he made his debut on 28th August 1968 in a League Cup tie against Clyde. He was then signed for the rest of the season. Stuart was with United for five seasons, playing just a few times in his first season and then in around half of the games in each of the next four, spending the rest of his time in the reserves. In competition for the centre half role with the dependable Doug Smith, Stuart found himself in every other defensive position during his Tannadice career and even filled

Stuart Markland

in as inside forward on a few occasions. He was transfer listed in October 1972 but there was no interest. Consequently, he was released in April 1973. Stuart then joined Montrose until he went to Australia in 1978 to play with Sydney Olympic. Around two years later he went back to Montrose, where he finished his senior career. He then returned to Penicuik Athletic where he had started playing as a junior.

Alec Reid was an inside forward who joined United in the summer of 1968 after he was released by Rangers, where he had been unable to break into the side. At the time, he was attracting attention from Aberdeen, Kilmarnock, Fulham and Brighton & Hove Albion. He made his first appearance for United, scoring against Preston North End in a friendly on 2nd August 1968. His debut in major competition followed on 10th August 1968 against Dunfermline Athletic in a League Cup tie. Alec became a regular in the line up for three seasons but in

Alec Reid

March 1971, he was transfer listed following a disagreement with Manager Jerry Kerr. The player was however retained for the next season. In August 1971, he was the subject of a bid from Carlisle United who offered Tommy Murray in part exchange. That offer was rejected but a month later negotiations began to bring Ian Mitchell back from Newcastle United, with Alec going to the English side, in a straight swap. The transfer was concluded in October 1971. Alec spent two seasons at Newcastle United. Towards the end of his time with them, he went on loan to Morton who then signed him in the summer of 1973. In December 1975, United paid Morton £10,000 and transferred Tommy Traynor to the Greenock side in order to bring Alec back to Tannadice. However, less than a year later he moved to Ayr United for a fee of £7,000. Unfortunately, Alec sustained a serious injury shortly after joining the Ayrshire side and he was forced to retire from the game.

1969-70 Player Profiles

Billy Bremner was a defender with Aberdeenshire Summer League side Forrit Brae and signed for United in September 1967. He played in the reserves, becoming a regular in the line up from August 1968 and totalled more than 50 outings in the second string. Billy made his first team debut on 16th August 1969 against St Mirren in a League Cup tie. In competition with established defenders, he had few chances to shine, making just four first team appearances before he was released in May 1970.

Ian Letford joined United from Cambuslang Rangers as an eighteen-year-old part-timer. He was an inside forward, capable on either side of the attack. After just one game in the reserves, he made his first team debut on 16th August 1969 against St Mirren in a League Cup tie. Ian made just one more appearance in the first team and spent the rest of the season in the reserves. He was offered in part exchange for Jackie Copland's transfer from Stranraer in December 1970 but they wanted straight cash. However, two days later it appears that Ian went to Stranraer on loan initially, and then signed for them shortly after.

Ged Reilly

Gerald 'Ged' Reilly signed for United as a sixteen-year-old from Montrose. Primarily taken on as cover for the injured Hamish McAlpine, Ged had never even seen the first team in action when he was thrown in at the deep end for his only first team appearance, as substitute for the injured Donald Mackay, in the last twenty minutes of the Fairs Cities Cup tie against Newcastle United on 15th September 1969. He made over 20 reserve appearances and he was released in May 1970 when McAlpine was fully fit again. He returned to Montrose for season 1970-71 and moved to Forfar Athletic a year later. The following season was spent with Highland League, Inverness Thistle, before Ged signed for Brechin City. He left them and returned to the juniors with Dundee North End but in 1978-79 he returned to Brechin City for a short time.

Eric Rooney joined United's ground staff before becoming a reserve player in the summer of 1968. He was a versatile forward and over two years at Tannadice he made over 40 second eleven appearances. Eric had just one first team outing when he played in a Forfarshire Cup final win over Arbroath on 18th March 1970. He was released just a few weeks later and joined Stenhousemuir.

Morris Stevenson

Morris Stevenson began his senior career at Motherwell and he also played for Hibs and Morton before moving to Luton Town in November 1968. His family did not settle in England and they moved back north in January 1970 when Morris joined United on a free transfer. Injury delayed his debut until 11th February 1970, when he turned out against Kilmarnock in a Scottish League match. Morris was able to play in most attacking positions and was also frequently drafted into the half back line. He remained with United for just over two years but towards the end of his time at Tannadice he played mainly in the reserves. Morris was released at the end of season 1971-72 to join Berwick Rangers.

Alex Stuart

Alex Stuart was a left half who joined Dundee during season 1958-59. Ten years later, he was released by the Dens Park side and after an unsuccessful attempt to join a club in Switzerland he signed for United. He made his first appearance on 2nd August 1969 against Everton in a friendly. A week later, he made a scoring debut in his first match for United in major competition, against Hearts in a League Cup tie. Alex played just a handful of matches for United and in November 1969, he was allowed to leave to join Montrose as their player/manager and remained there for around six years. He took charge at Ayr United in 1975 and three years later he had a spell in charge at St Johnstone. When Jerry Kerr resigned as Manager at United, Alex was one of several names touted in the press for the job, before Jim McLean was confirmed as the new man in charge.

1970-71 Player Profiles

Ian Clyde was a half back who joined United from Melbourne Thistle in the late spring of 1970. He spent the next season as a regular at left half in the reserves, making just two first team appearances. Both were against Newcastle United from the substitute's bench in friendlies, the first of which was on 1st August 1970 and the second four days later. He was released in May 1971.

Jackie Copland spent the first season of his professional career at St Mirren in 1967-68 before moving back to the junior ranks with Beith. He signed for Stranraer in 1969 and from there he joined United for a fee of £10,000. Initially signed as a centre forward, he made his debut on 19th December 1970 in a Scottish League match against St Mirren. In competition with Kenny Cameron and Alan Gordon for the No. 9 shirt, he played just a dozen times over the remainder of that season. In 1971-72, he was a regular in the line up and topped the goal scoring table at United despite netting just 11 times, including a hat-trick against Airdrieonians. The arrival of Pat Gardner

Jackie Copeland

in January 1972 resulted in a move to convert Jackie to right half, a position he then retained for the rest of his time at United, forming a formidable partnership with centre half Doug Smith. Jackie was one of the players who turned out for United in their first Scottish Cup final appearance against Celtic in May 1974. By that time it was rumoured he had attracted an unsuccessful £50,000 bid by Newcastle United. He had also been named as one of the initial squad of forty players for the World Cup in 1974 but was not in the final selection to travel to West Germany. In July 1974, he signed a new contract but also indicated that he would like to move elsewhere if the opportunity arose. Jackie continued in his regular right half berth for the next eighteen months and then gradually slipped out of contention for a first team slot. In September 1976, United turned down an offer of £17,000 from Partick Thistle for the player but two months later, he joined St Mirren for a similar fee. He remained with the Paisley side until he retired in 1983.

Alan Devlin joined United reserves from Tynecastle Boys Club at the beginning of season 1969-70. He was normally an attacking player, but played in the half back line in the latter part of his career at Tannadice. Alan made over 50 reserve appearances but featured only rarely in the first team after a scoring debut as a substitute for Jim Henry, early in the second half against Morton on 9th January 1971. In two seasons at United, Alan never made the breakthrough and accepted a free transfer in September 1972. He later played in one game for Exeter City.

George Hill was released by Dundee in the summer of 1970 and he then joined United. A versatile forward, he spent the season as a regular in United reserves, making just one first team appearance, as a substitute against Raith Rovers in a friendly on 2nd March 1971. He was released in May 1971.

George Hill

Alan Liddle joined United from Easthouses Boys Club in the summer of 1969. He turned out regularly in the reserve side for two seasons, making more than 70 appearances in the second string, but competing with Doug Smith for the centre half slot, he was unlikely to get a regular first team start. Alan made his first team debut as a late substitute for Andy Rolland against Hearts on 14th November 1970 in a Scottish League match. He also played in a friendly in March 1971 against Raith Rovers but he was released two months later.

Alan Liddle

Gordon McDonald came to United as an 'S' signing in April 1970 and joined the ground staff in May 1971. He could fill most defensive positions and played frequently for two seasons in the reserves, where he joined his brother Ian. Gordon made just one first team appearance, against Raith Rovers in a friendly on 2nd March 1971. He was released in May 1972.

Ian Reid had joined Nottingham Forest as a teenager but they released him, still aged just seventeen, in July 1970. A centre forward, he then signed for United and made a scoring first appearance against Newcastle United in a friendly on 1st August 1970. A week later, he made his debut in major competition against Clyde in a League Cup tie. Ian made an impressive initial impact and scored United's first goal against Grasshoppers of Zurich in the home leg of an important Fairs Cities Cup tie. Shortly afterwards he was relegated to

Ian Reid

the reserves where he eventually made a total of more than 70 appearances. He made just fleeting appearances in the first team during his three years at Tannadice and finally left United to join Queen of the South in September 1973. After five years with the Dumfries side he moved to Airdrieonians and then to Forfar Athletic.

Tommy Traynor joined Hearts in 1962 as a teenager and spent almost eight years there before he came to United. After an unsuccessful bid to bring him to Tannadice in 1969, he arrived in April 1970 in a swap deal that took Wilson Wood to Hearts. Tommy was generally considered a left winger but he could also play on the right. He made his first appearance for United on 5th August 1970 in a friendly against Newcastle United. That was followed by his debut in major competition three days later against Clyde in a League Cup tie. For the next five seasons, he was a regular in the side and occasionally

Tommy Traynor

found the net. He was listed for transfer in December 1972 but did not move at that time. Tommy played in United's first Scottish Cup final, coming on against Celtic as a late substitute for Doug Smith. One other highlight he would be particularly proud of, was a hat-trick against former club Hearts in October 1974. In December 1975, he went part-time and was then transferred to Morton in a swap deal for Alec Reid. His new club also received a fee of £10,000. After just one season with the Greenock side, he moved to Falkirk. He went into coaching for a while at Cowdenbeath and later emigrated to Australia.

Joe Watson

Joe Watson was a right winger who joined United on a free transfer from Nottingham Forest, where he had never really settled. He had also suffered a broken leg whilst with the English club. Joe made a spectacular debut on 5th April 1971 against Dundee in a Scottish League match, having a part to play in all three United goals in a 3-2 win. He then became an ever present in the side until late September 1971 when a back injury sidelined him for several weeks. When he returned, Joe played mainly in the reserves for the rest of the season but in March 1972 he made a brief come back into the first eleven. There is little doubt that the injury ended Joe's United career prematurely and he was unable to re-establish himself in the first team. At the end of 1971-72, he was released and joined Forfar Athletic. Joe had a relatively successful time there but at the end of the season, he emigrated to Australia where he signed for Hakoah. He later played for Sydney City and several other Australian sides. He became established in the Australian national side, and played in all three friendlies against England in 1983. He gained six caps in the 1986 World Cup qualifiers, helping his adopted country win the Oceanic sub group, and playing in the first leg of the play-off against Scotland in November 1985. In total he played 41 times for Australia and scored 2 goals.

Sandy White

Sandy White was a left winger who joined United from junior side Glenrothes, along with his twin brother Joe in February 1971. They both made their debuts on 2nd March 1971 against Raith Rovers in a friendly. Sandy's debut in major competition came on 29th September 1971 against Derby County in a Texaco Cup match. Three days later he made his Scottish League debut against Airdrieonians. The twins' first game together in major competition was on 18th December 1971 against Aberdeen, in a Scottish League match. The more successful of the White twins at Tannadice, Sandy was a regular in the reserves and made the breakthrough into the first team in season 1972-73. Towards the end of that campaign, he dropped out of contention and back into the second eleven, where he played more than 80 times in total. He left United near the end of season 1974-75 and then joined Forfar Athletic. Around four years later, he returned to the junior ranks with Glenrothes.

Joe White and twin brother Sandy were provisionally signed from Glenrothes in October 1970 and were called up to the United squad four months later. Both made their first appearance for United on 2nd March 1971 against Raith Rovers in a friendly. Joe was a defender and made his debut in major competition on 18th December 1971 against Aberdeen, in a Scottish League match. In that game, he was joined by his twin brother in the line up for their first time together in a major competition. He played a few more times before going back to the reserves where he eventually totalled more than 50

Joe White

appearances. Joe spent most of his time with United in the reserves and he was released in May 1973. He then played for Cowdenbeath briefly, before returning to the juniors with Glenrothes.

1971-72 Player Profiles

Brian Eddie had been for trials with Burnley and Everton before he signed for United from Whitburn Juniors in March 1972. He made his first team debut on 3rd May 1972 against Forfar Athletic in a Forfarshire Cup tie. Then, in the reserve side, he played in various positions over the season before making his first appearance in major competition at right back against Celtic on 10th March 1973, in a Scottish League match. He played in the next two matches but he was released in May 1973.

George Fleming

George Fleming was one of a group of experienced players brought in by new Manager Jim McLean with the primary aim of improving the team, but it was also intended that they would assist the development of the young players. George was an attacking midfield player who had started his senior career at Hearts and came to United in January 1972 for a fee of around £7,000. He made his debut in a Scottish League match against Rangers on 12th February 1972, becoming a regular in the line up for the rest of that campaign and for the next eight years. During his time at United, George played an important part in the Scottish Cup run in 1974, with two goals against Dunfermline Athletic in the quarter final replay. He was one of the players in the side that took part in United's first Scottish Cup final against Celtic that season. He collected a winner's medal in the League Cup final against Aberdeen in 1979. After a successful career at United, George joined St Johnstone in July 1980 for a fee of around £10,000 and he also began coaching at the Perth club. In December 1983, he became player/manager at Arbroath for just over a year, after which he left the game. With 340 games played for United, George is ranked seventeenth in the all time appearances chart and is regarded as a Club legend.

Pat Gardner

Pat Gardner was an attacking player who had spent time with Queen of the South, Airdrieonians and Raith Rovers before he joined Dunfermline Athletic. He helped the Pars lift the Scottish Cup in 1968, scoring twice in their 3-1 win over Hearts. Pat was signed by United for a fee reported at £6,500 in January 1972. He was one of a group of experienced players brought in by new Manager Jim McLean to stabilise the team and to assist the development of the young players. He made his debut on 29th January 1972 against Morton in a Scottish League match and soon settled into a regular first team berth. In each of his next two seasons, he made over forty appearances and was top scorer in 1972-73 with 15 league and cup goals. Pat scored a vital equaliser against Hearts in the Scottish Cup semi final in 1974 to earn United a replay, on the way to the Club's first ever Scottish Cup final against Celtic. He left United in October 1974 to join Motherwell for a fee of around £10,000 and later played for Arbroath. He was also with Airdrieonians as a coach and then undertook the same role at Motherwell and Celtic.

Billy Gray was a versatile half back who started his senior career at St Mirren in 1962 and then joined Morton in 1965. After six years there, Billy signed for United. He made his first appearance on 2nd August 1971 in a friendly against Blackpool. On 14th August 1971, he made his debut in major competition against Kilmarnock in a League Cup tie and during season 1971-72, Billy played in almost every defensive position. In October 1972 the player was transfer listed and left to join Raith Rovers shortly afterwards. Within a few months he moved to Stranraer, after which it appears he retired from the game.

Billy Gray

Archie Knox

Archie Knox started his senior career at Alloa Athletic and then played for Forfar Athletic and St Mirren before he joined United, for a fee reported at £3,000. The experienced midfielder made his debut on 8th January 1972 against Hibs in a Scottish League match and was in the side for much of the remainder of that season. In the next campaign, he made just over a dozen first team appearances. In 1973-74 he had his best season at Tannadice with over 40 appearances, scoring 10 goals. Archie was in the United line up for their first Scottish Cup final against Celtic in 1974. He played just occasionally in the first team over the next two seasons but was a regular in the reserves, where he employed his experience to further the development of United's emerging band of talented young players. In July 1976, he joined Montrose and later went to Forfar Athletic as player/manager, to begin a career in management that has seen him as assistant to Alex Ferguson at Aberdeen, manager at Dundee and then back to Aberdeen briefly, again as assistant manager. In late 1986, he joined Alex Ferguson at Manchester United. Just over four years later, he became assistant to Walter Smith at Rangers, following Smith to Everton, when he took charge there seven years later. He became assistant manager of the Scotland national side, and then spent some time at Millwall and Coventry City before teaming up with Richard Gough at Livingston. In 2005, he was back with the national squad, then managed by Walter Smith and in 2006, Archie was appointed coach of the Scotland Under-21 side. In August 2007, he became assistant manager at Bolton Wanderers. Just a few weeks later, he was appointed caretaker manager until a new manager took over. Archie remained as a coach until the end of that season.

Frank Kopel was a full back who started his senior career at Manchester United in 1967. He played just ten times in two seasons at Old Trafford before moving to Blackburn Rovers, who released him in December 1971. On the recommendation of Ian Mitchell, he was signed by United in early January 1972 and made his debut in midfield against Morton in a Scottish League match on 29th January 1972. Frank played just occasionally over the rest of the season but managed to record a hat-trick in a Forfarshire Cup tie in

Frank Kopel

April. Season 1972-73 was the first full season for Frank and in it, he made over 40 appearances, playing in either midfield or defence. In the following campaign, he became the first choice left back and held that position in the side for nine seasons, hardly missing a game. His most prized possessions would surely be his League Cup winner's medals, gained in 1979 against Aberdeen and 1980 against Dundee. He was also in the line up when United played and lost the Scottish Cup finals of 1974 and 1981. In 1979-80, he cemented his legendary status, with a stunning late goal in a UEFA Cup tie against Anderlecht in Belgium, to take United into the next round on the away goals rule. In February 1982, Frank was released by United and was quickly appointed player/coach at Arbroath. With 407 appearances, he ranks eleventh in the all time list. He returned to United in December 1983 to fill the need for an experienced defender in the reserves and retired at the end of the season. When United were short of reserve defenders in April 1985, Frank briefly signed for United for a third time. Eighteen months later, he was back at Tannadice as Promotions Manager. Amazingly, in August 1988, at the age of 39, he signed as a player for the fourth time, on a short-term basis to help out in the reserves once more. In February 1989, he joined Forfar Athletic as a coach, working with former United players Henry Hall and then Paul Hegarty. In January 1992, he ended his time there and left the game.

Harry Mollison was a defender who joined United on an 'S' form in October 1970 whilst with local side St Francis. He began playing in the reserves regularly at the beginning of 1971-72 and made his first team debut on 27ᵗʰ November 1971, against Motherwell in a Scottish League match. His next game followed against Hearts a week later, on the same day that new Manager Jim McLean took his place in the dug-out. Unfortunately for Harry, he scored an own goal and it was his last outing. He finished the season in the reserves and he was released in May 1972 to join Forfar Athletic.

1972-73 Player Profiles

Brian Cooper was an inside forward who spent three years at Brechin City before he signed for United in December 1972, for a fee of around £3,000. He made several reserve appearances before his first team debut as a substitute for Sandy White against Hearts in a Scottish League match on 10th February 1973. Although he was retained for the next campaign, he lasted just two months before joining Forfar Athletic in September 1973.

Brain Cooper

Joe Fascione was a wide attacking player who had been five seasons with Chelsea without making any real impact there and left to play with Durban City in South Africa in 1969. In late 1971, he returned to the UK but had difficulty getting his registration released to allow him to play here. In July 1972, he was finally released and signed with United for trials. He made his debut as a late substitute against Crystal Palace in a friendly on 29th July 1972 but after two more pre-season outings, he was released. He then joined Charlton Athletic and later played for non league sides Romford and Barking.

Duncan MacLeod

Duncan MacLeod was a midfield player who had been with Dundee for almost eighteen months but had failed to break into their first eleven. He joined United after he was released and made his first appearance on 23rd April 1973 against his former club in a Forfarshire Cup tie. His debut in major competition followed on 11th August 1973 against East Fife in a League Cup tie. He was with United for two seasons, spending more time in the reserves than he did in the first team. Never noted as a goal scorer, Duncan netted just three league goals, a hat-trick against Morton in the final game of season 1973-74. He left United to join St Johnstone in June 1975 in a deal that saw Henry Hall move in the opposite direction. In 1976, he joined Brechin City where he played for five years.

Ian Steen

(John) Ian Steen was a midfielder who joined United in July 1972 as an eighteen-year-old. He had spent 15 months at Blackpool without making a breakthrough there. Ian spent his first season at Tannadice in the reserves, making a first team debut in a Forfarshire Cup tie on 23rd April 1973 against Dundee. Five days later, he made his first Scottish League appearance against Dumbarton. He spent the next two seasons with United, playing in the reserves where he made around 80 appearances in all, but just three more games in the first team as a substitute. In May 1975, he was released and joined Forfar Athletic. From there he went to Stranraer before moving to Raith Rovers and later to East Stirlingshire.

1973-74 Player Profiles

Derek Addison was a former Hibs 'S' signing and he had trials with Aberdeen. Other clubs, including Manchester City and Dundee, were also showing an interest in the player before he signed from Lochee United in May 1973. He had played in the reserves in the previous season and after another few months there, he made his first team debut on 12th January 1974 against Hibs in a Scottish League match. A midfield player, Derek made barely 30 appearances in his first four seasons with United but he turned out regularly in the reserves. In 1977-78, he broke into the first team and was

Derek Addison

a regular in the line ups over the next four years. In September 1981, Derek left United for Hearts, along with Willie Pettigrew, for a joint fee said to be in the region of £180,000. Derek was on the move again soon after, joining St Johnstone in the summer of 1982. Three years later he added coaching responsibilities to his playing role at the Perth side. Shortly afterwards he joined Brechin City but after just one league game there he retired from the game.

Rodney Bush had been with South African side East London before joining United in October 1973, on the recommendation of former Dundee player Alec Hamilton. Rodney spent the season in the reserves, making just one first team appearance, as a substitute for George Fleming, against Dumbarton on 29th December 1973 in a Scottish League match. In April 1974, he was released and returned to South Africa.

Andy Gray joined United in May 1973 from Clydebank Strollers. At the time, the player was being tracked by several clubs including Falkirk, Clyde, Clydebank and Blackpool. He was quickly in the first team, making his debut, still aged just seventeen, on 18th August 1973 as a substitute for Jim Henry against Motherwell in a League Cup tie. Andy was the regular centre forward in the side from that

Andy Gray

point on and was part of the Scotland professional youth squad by October. He ended his first season with United as top scorer with 19 goals in 39 appearances, including four in one game against Dumbarton. It might have been five but he missed from a penalty kick! He played a major role in the run up to the Club's first Scottish Cup final in 1974, scoring a vital third goal against Hearts in the semi final replay. The young striker topped the United scoring charts in his second season with 26 goals from 46 games and Dumbarton suffered again as Andy netted a hat-trick against them. During his short career at Tannadice, there were several enquiries from other clubs including an offer of £75,000 from Nottingham Forest. Spurs, Manchester City, Manchester United and Birmingham City were also linked with the player. Sheffield United, Liverpool and Bristol City also had him watched and by December 1974 interest intensified as Andy played for Scotland for the first of three Under-23 caps while he was at Tannadice. Leeds United and Schalke 04 joined the chase in the early part of season 1975-76 and it was obvious that there would soon be an offer. It came from Aston Villa in late September 1975 and the player moved south for a fee reported at £110,000, then a United record, and an offer they could not refuse. Andy went on to play four seasons with Aston Villa, winning both the PFA Player of the Year and Young Player of the Year in 1977. He joined Wolverhampton Wanderers in 1979 and scored the winning goal for them in the League Cup final in 1980. In late 1983, he moved to Everton, where he won an FA Cup winner's medal, the English League Championship and a European Cup Winners' Cup medal. Andy returned to Aston Villa in July 1985 and had a spell on loan at Notts County before transferring to West Bromwich Albion in 1987. During his time in England Andy was twice linked with moves back to Dundee United. In 1982, his return was merely rumour but in 1986, United made a bid which was rejected by Aston Villa. When Andy moved back to Scotland, it was to join Rangers during 1988-89. He then progressed to a career as a football commentator and presenter on television. During his long career, he scored seven international goals in his 20 games for Scotland over a ten-year period, making his first appearance in December 1975 against Romania.

John Holt was a versatile defender who was just as capable in a midfield role. He first signed for United on an 'S' form in February 1972 when he was still at school and playing with Invergowrie Boys Club. By April 1973, John was playing in the reserves and after showing potential, he made a first team debut for United against Motherwell on 19th January 1974 in a Scottish League match. His early introduction to the senior side also propelled him into the Scotland professional youth squad. In his first few seasons at Tannadice, John had some tough competition for a full back berth and often played in midfield but gradually became established in the side from 1977 onwards. He continued to fulfil a variety of roles in a successful side, collecting League Cup winners' medals in 1979 against Aberdeen and in 1980 against Dundee. United lost the final of 1981 and John was in the side. In the same season, he collected the first of three Scottish Cup runners-up medals. John was a regular in the side for the best part of ten years, during which he played in numerous high profile matches, both in domestic and European competition. In

John Holt

season 1982-83 he played his part as United won the Scottish Premier League championship. Although never renowned as a goal scorer, it was in that season that John recorded his only hat-trick for United, against Kilmarnock in February 1983. He collected yet another League Cup runners-up medal in 1984. In a playing career studded with highlights, he took part in the Club's run to the European Cup semi final in 1984 and played against Gothenburg in both legs of the UEFA Cup final in 1987, collecting a runners-up medal yet again. John left United to join Dunfermline Athletic for £50,000 early in the next season and then joined Dundee a year later. His next move was to Forfar Athletic where he became player/manager. He then took on the same role at Deveronvale in the Highland League. In 1993, he was appointed manager at Montrose, still aged just 35. He later returned to United as SFA Community Development Officer and became part of the management team during Paul Hegarty's brief period in charge of United in 2003. He then turned his talent to scouting for Celtic, before returning to Dundee as a coach. With 405 appearances, John ranks twelfth in the all time list and is regarded as a Club legend.

Doug Houston

Doug Houston was a midfielder who began his football career at Queen's Park, signing professionally for the first time when he joined Dundee in May 1962. He was with the Dens Park side for eleven years. Well aware of the player's experience and ability, Jim McLean made a bid for him in January 1972. The amount was not disclosed but press reports indicated that a United record would have been set had he signed. Doug did not join United at that point and instead, signed for Rangers. After almost a full season there he had made just ten league appearances and jumped at a second chance to join United. The fee was around £10,000 and he made his debut on 30th March 1974 in a Scottish League match against Ayr United. Soon after, he played in the United side that took part in the Club's first Scottish Cup final. Doug went on to become a regular in the line up over the next three years, whilst assisting the development of the emerging young players. He left United in July 1977 to join St Johnstone, for a fee of around £4,000 and later became their reserve team coach. Doug was later the manager of Brechin City and then Forfar Athletic before returning to United in a coaching role in 1986.

Dave Narey

Dave Narey is a Club legend, and in the opinion of many, Dundee United's greatest ever player. In over two decades with United, he topped the appearances chart at 872 and scored 36 goals in major competition. He began his career as an 'S' signing in January 1972 whilst with St Columba's Boys Club and had briefly been the guest of Chelsea. Dave soon joined the ground staff and in season 1973-74 signed professionally, initially playing in the reserves as a central defender. On 21st November 1973, he made his first team debut against Falkirk in a Scottish League match as an attacking midfielder. Dave went on to play 14 times before the end of that season. He quickly reverted to a central defensive role and for the next sixteen years, he was a mainstay in the United rearguard. For a number of years he played alongside Paul Hegarty at the back and they made a formidable partnership that propelled United to some great achievements. Along the way, Dave took part in four Scottish Cup finals on the losing side, missing out on the 1994 success through injury, after playing twice in the earlier rounds. He also took part in four League Cup finals with United, collecting a winner's medal in 1979 against Aberdeen and 1980 against Dundee. In European matches, he played in a record 76 games, including a European Cup semi final in 1984 against AS Roma and the two leg 1987 UEFA Cup final against Gothenburg, as team captain. That was one of many career highlights, despite the 2-1 aggregate defeat. Dave's greatest achievement at Club level was a Scottish League championship medal in season 1982-83. After playing for Scotland at youth, Under-21 and Under-23 levels, Dave had a distinguished full international career spanning eleven years, winning the first of his 35 caps as a substitute against Sweden in April 1977. He was the first Dundee United player to be honoured at that level for Scotland. His famous goal against Brazil in the World Cup finals of 1982 in Spain, was his only one at international level but is one of the most memorable goals of that tournament. He also turned out once for the Scottish League side in November 1978. Over the years, several other clubs tried to lure Dave away from United but he remained at Tannadice despite some tempting offers. Dave was the supporters' Player of the Year in 1980 and received a testimonial match against Spurs in August 1988. In 1992, he received an MBE for his services to football. In season 1990-91 Dave was hampered by a back injury but returned to the side frequently in the two seasons that followed. At the end of 1993-94 it was announced that he had been released. He was offered a coaching role but he preferred to keep playing and spent a year with Raith Rovers, helping them to win promotion to the Premier League in 1994-95, ironically replacing United, who were relegated. Whilst with the Kirkcaldy side he also collected a third League Cup winner's medal, as Raith Rovers beat Celtic in a penalty shoot-out. Dave then retired from the game but re-signed for United in 1996 to help out in the reserves and was briefly back again two years later in a coaching capacity. In January 2008, Dave was one of the first players inducted into the Dundee United Hall of Fame.

Graeme Payne was one of the first players to benefit from the youth development system under the guidance of Jim McLean, although he was on an 'S' form with United as early as May 1971. He was called up for reserve duties from St Columba's Boys Club early in season 1972-73, making his first team debut at the start of the next campaign, still aged just seventeen, against East Fife in a League Cup tie on 11th August 1973. Graeme missed the wedding of his brother Kenny to make his United debut. He was a regular in the midfield for United over the rest of that season and played against Celtic when United turned out at Hampden Park for

Graeme Payne

their first Scottish Cup final. On route to the final, Graeme scored an important second goal against Hearts in the semi final replay. That season also saw Graeme involved in the Scotland youth team. In the next campaign, his appearances were limited due to injury but by 1975-76, he was an established first team player again, contributing in an attacking midfield role for six years. During that time, he collected a winner's medal for his part in the League Cup final against Aberdeen in 1979. He then collected a second winner's medal against Dundee a year later. Graeme played for Scotland at youth and Under-21 level. He was also named in the initial squad of forty players for the World Cup in Argentina 1978 but he did not make it into the final selection. In the same year he was the SPFA Young Player of the Year. His talent attracted attention from a few English clubs with Queen's Park Rangers, Liverpool and Newcastle United all keeping a close eye on him at various stages in the late 1970s. By the beginning of the next decade, Graeme began to feature less in the side and during the championship season of 1982-83, he played just three times in the league and spent the second half of that season on loan at Morton. In May 1984 Graeme joined Arbroath for a nominal fee. He later moved to Brechin City and also played for St Johnstone, before leaving football for a career in the insurance industry.

Brian Rankin was a nephew of former United favourite Dennis Gillespie. An attacking player, Brian signed for United in November 1971 from Vale of Clyde

Brian Rankin

and then spent three years in the reserves, where he racked up a total of over 70 appearances. He made his first team debut in a Scottish Cup tie against Airdrieonians on 26th January 1974, and had just a short run in the side. He scored a vital goal against Morton in a Scottish Cup tie to ensure United progressed, ultimately, to the final of that season's competition. Brian was unable to command a first team slot and in November 1974, he was offered to Hamilton Academical as part of the deal to bring Paul Hegarty to United. The Accies declined but signed Brian a week later and he was with them for the rest of that season. He then played with East Fife and Alloa Athletic before spending six years with Forfar Athletic, leaving them at the end of 1981-82.

Sean Sheehy was an attacking player who joined United on a free transfer from Preston North End in September 1973. He scored a hat-trick on his reserve debut and played several times in the second eleven before he was sidelined by injury. He recovered to make his first team debut as a substitute for Brian Rankin against Clyde in a Scottish League match on 2nd February 1974 but made just two more first team appearances. At the end of the season he was released and joined Irish side Dundalk.

1974-75 Player Profiles

Davie Dodds was a striker with Sporting Club and first joined United on an 'S' form in December 1972. In 1974-75 he played in the second eleven and was then added to the United party for the summer trip to Spain. Special permission was required because he was still just sixteen years old. He made his first appearance on 22nd June 1975 against Salamanca. Davie then played a second season in the reserves before making his debut in major competition on 18th August 1976, scoring twice against Arbroath in a League Cup tie. He continued to star in the second string, playing only four first team games that season.

Davie Dodds

Gradually introduced to the side over the following two years, he spent a short time at Arbroath on loan, in October 1977. By 1979-80 he was full-time and well established as a first team player. Forming an effective striking partnership with Paul Sturrock in 1980-81, Davie was joint top scorer with 23 goals in league and cup matches, including hat-tricks against Airdrieonians and Motherwell. He was by then an automatic first choice for the side and in season 1981-82 recorded two hat-tricks in matches against Partick Thistle. He topped the scoring charts in 1982-83 with 28 goals, including a hat-trick against Morton. The player also collected a Premier League championship medal that year to add to the League Cup winner's medal he won in December 1980 against Dundee. He also collected runners-up medals in two other League Cup finals and two Scottish Cup finals. In European competition, Davie played 40 times, including the European Cup run to the semi final in 1984. In 1983-84 he was United's top scorer again with 26 goals in 54 games. By the time his career at Tannadice ended, with a move to Neuchatel Xamax of Switzerland for £175,000 in July 1986, he had scored 102 Premier League goals in his total of 150 goals in major competitions. He is United's third top scorer of all time and in terms of games played, with 369 he is ranked at sixteenth in the all time appearances chart. Davie returned to

Scotland to join Aberdeen after just two months with the Swiss club and three years later moved to Rangers, where he later spent several years coaching, before leaving the game. Davie is considered a Tannadice legend. He represented Scotland at schoolboy, youth and Under-21 level before he won the first of just two full international caps against Uruguay in 1983, coming on as a substitute and scoring.

Allan Forsyth was a versatile defender who joined United from Larkhall Thistle in March 1972. He was a regular in the reserve side for almost three years before he made his first team debut on 11th January 1975, against Hibs in a Scottish League match. Alan had a tough time getting into a side that contained several good defenders but by the end of 1975-76, he was holding on to a regular place. However, following an injury late in 1976 he was sidelined for several months and after that he could not re-established himself in the line up. When he returned, it was to the reserve side in which he eventually racked up a total of more than 130 games. He left United in July 1978, joining Raith Rovers for a fee of around £15,000. Alan had six years with the Kirkcaldy club before joining Dunfermline Athletic for a couple of years and then returning to the junior ranks.

Allan Forsyth   *Brian Goodall*   *Paul Hegarty*

Brian Goodall of Lochee Harp was attracting the interest of Manchester United, Manchester City and Dundee before he signed for Dundee United on a provisional form in November 1972. He was an attacker and in season 1973-74, he began playing in the reserves where he made almost 60 appearances in his two years with United. Brian had just one game at first team level when he turned out against Inverness Clachnacuddin in a friendly on 29th July 1974. He was released in May 1975.

Paul Hegarty began his senior career as a striker at Hamilton Academical where he spent around three years. Still just twenty years old, he joined United for a reported club record fee of £40,000 and made his debut on 16th November 1974, coming on as a substitute for Andy Gray against Partick Thistle in a Scottish

League match. Over the remainder of the season he was gradually bedded in to the attack and in the next campaign, he was a regular in the front line after Gray vacated the centre forward position. In November 1976, in a friendly against Everton, he took on a central defensive role as an experiment. Within a few months that position became his for the rest of his United career. He quickly formed a partnership with Dave Narey on which the foundation of United's successes were built over the next decade. Paul was rarely out of the side for the next thirteen years, captaining United from 1978 to 1986, and he was named the SPFA Player of the Year in 1979. He collected a winner's medal in the League Cup in 1979 against Aberdeen, as United won a national trophy for the first time. He was in the side again a year later as United beat Dundee in the final of the same competition. Paul also collected two League Cup runners-up medals and appeared in four Scottish Cup finals, unfortunately always on the losing side. In European competition, Paul played 68 times for United, including the European Cup semi final against AS Roma and the UEFA Cup final that United lost 2-1 on aggregate to Gothenburg. It was also against Gothenburg that United arranged a testimonial match for Paul in November 1989. His crowning achievement was most likely leading the side through the 1982-83 season, collecting the Premier League championship trophy at the end of it. Despite some stiff competition at the time, he achieved international recognition, collecting the first of his eight caps against Wales in May 1979 and he became the first United player to captain the national side in May 1983, against Northern Ireland. Paul also played for the national Under-21 side as an over-age player and once represented the Scottish League side against the Irish League. His 707 appearances in major competition are bettered by only Maurice Malpas and Dave Narey, the latter being alone in representing United more often in Europe. After a long career with United, he was released to join St Johnstone in January 1990 and after helping them win promotion to the Premier League, Paul became player/manager at Forfar Athletic. He joined the coaching staff at United in 1992 and also had spells in a similar role at Hearts and Aberdeen, where he was appointed interim manager in January 1999. His contract was not extended at the end of that season and once again he returned to United. In October 2002, he was appointed caretaker manager but that lasted just three months until he was replaced by Ian McCall. Since leaving United in January 2003, he has been at Livingston, Dunfermline Athletic and Motherwell. His status remains undiminished at the Club, where he is quite rightly regarded as a legend. In January 2008, he was one of the first players inducted into the Dundee United Hall of Fame.

Iain McDonald signed for United on a free transfer from Rangers in the summer of 1974. He had been with the Ibrox side for three seasons but had played just a dozen or so first team games. A speedy left winger, Iain made his first

Iain McDonald

appearance for United, scoring a goal in a friendly against Inverness Clachnacuddin on 29th July 1974. He made his debut in major competition in the opening match of the season, coming on as a substitute for Andy Rolland against Ayr United in a League Cup tie on 10th August 1974. Iain rarely missed a game over the rest of the season and was in the Scotland Under-23 squad against Romania but was an unused substitute. He suffered a serious injury and missed most of the next season and in February 1976, the player was forced to retire from the game, still aged just 23. A benefit match was arranged for him in October 1976 against Dundee and it ended 7-7. Several guest players turned out, including John Greig and Ronnie Glavin.

Alan Munro was a surprise signing from Partick Thistle and made his debut on the right wing on the same day that he signed, 14th September 1974, scoring the opening goal against Dundee in a Scottish League match. He had started his senior career in 1967 at Clydebank where he had spent six years. Alan had a lean time with just one appearance at Partick Thistle and with United he fared little better, playing just twice. Two months after he was signed, he left to join St Mirren. Following two relatively successful years with the Paisley side, he returned to Clydebank in 1976 for a year, before moving on to end his career at Queen of the South.

Kenny Murphy was an attacking player who joined United from St Columba's Boys Club on an 'S' form in August 1973. He began playing in the reserves later that year, joining the squad permanently in 1974-75. Kenny was with United for two years but played exclusively in the reserves, apart from one appearance in the first eleven against Morton, as a substitute for Dave Narey in the final minutes of a Scottish League match on 14th December 1974. He then joined Forfar Athletic for a brief period before emigrating to Australia where he played for South Melbourne. Kenny became an Australian international, winning four caps in the 1986 World Cup qualifiers, whilst helping the national side to win the Oceanic sub group. He won another two caps, appearing in both legs against Scotland, in the play-off in November 1985. In total he played 40 times for his adopted country, scoring two goals.

Paul Sturrock was one of the finest attacking players ever to take the field for United and achieved the status of Club legend. He signed as a sixteen-year-old from Bankfoot Juniors in the summer of 1974. After making an early impact in the reserves, he came on as a substitute for Doug Houston against Jiul Petrosani of Romania in a European Cup Winners' Cup tie on 18th September 1974, to make his debut. By the end of 1975-76, his was a frequent name on the team sheet. In the next season, he was top scorer with 17 league and cup goals and from that point on he was rarely out of the side. He had a lower goals tally over the next three seasons but in the League Cup in 1979, he netted a double against Hamilton Academical in the semi final and then scored the clinching third against Aberdeen in the final to pick up a winner's medal, as United collected their first national trophy. Paul also hit a double against Dundee, winning his second League Cup winner's medal a year later, in a season that saw him joint top scorer alongside Davie Dodds, with 23 goals. Paul went one better in 1981-82 with 24 goals, to top the scoring charts again, including a hat-trick against Morton. In 1982 he was voted the SFWA Player of the Year. He missed out on a third League Cup winner's medal as United lost to Rangers after his potentially match winning 'goal', was controversially ruled offside. Season 1982-83 brought Paul the top national prize of a Premier League championship medal. Another League Cup runners-up medal followed in 1984. In that season Paul was again top scorer for United, with 20 goals. Morton suffered again, as Paul became the first Premier League player to net five goals in one game. Of course, 'Luggy' as he was known, was not just a goal scorer but also a provider, particularly when he partnered Davie Dodds. His record in European competition is remarkable, with 60 appearances over a thirteen-year period. The highlights of his European travels would surely include the European Cup semi final against AS Roma in 1984, a hat-trick against Bohemians of Dublin in 1985 in a UEFA Cup match, and stunning performances against Barcelona and Borussia Moenchengladbach leading to the two-leg UEFA Cup final against Gothenburg. A UEFA Cup runners-up medal seems scant reward for such talented displays. He also has four Scottish Cup runners-up medals, including one as an unused substitute. International honour also came his way, with professional youth appearances and nine Under-21 caps. After making his debut at full international level in May 1981 against Wales, Paul went on to win a total of 20 full caps, including two in the World Cup finals of 1986. He scored three international goals. His playing career wound down in the summer of 1989, by which time he had set the record for a Dundee United attacking player, with 576 appearances in major competition. Only five players have more appearances and they are all defenders. In goals scored, only Peter McKay has exceeded Paul's total of 171, all scored at a higher level than Peter. After his playing career ended in June 1989, he became a coach at United and then moved into management at St Johnstone in November 1993. One of the most qualified coaches in Europe, he took charge at Tannadice in September 1998 but resigned after two years. Since then he has managed Plymouth Argyle (twice), Southampton, Sheffield Wednesday and Swindon Town with varying degrees of success.

Paul Sturrock

1975-76 Player Profiles

David Cooper was a goalkeeper with junior side Glenrothes and had two spells with Alloa Athletic before he signed for United in the summer of 1975 from the juniors. He was the regular keeper in the reserves in season 1975-76, with over 30 appearances but he made just one first team appearance, on 30th July 1975 against Golspie Sutherland in a friendly. David was released in May 1976 and returned to Alloa Athletic for a third time before joining Cowdenbeath in 1978. Two years later he left them and returned to the juniors with Glenrothes.

Henry Hall

Henry Hall was an attacking player who joined St Johnstone in 1969 after spending four years with Stirling Albion. He had been capped for the Scottish League twice. After a highly successful career at Muirton Park, he signed for United in the summer of 1975. The deal took Duncan MacLeod in the opposite direction, along with a nominal cash adjustment to the Perth side. Henry made his first appearance for United on 2nd August 1975 in a Forfarshire Cup tie against Brechin City, when he came on as a substitute. His first match in major competition was against former club St Johnstone in a League Cup tie a week later. In his first season, Henry was a regular in the side and was joint top scorer with Tom McAdam on 13 goals. He had arrived at United as a full-time player but went part-time in May 1976, to pursue his career as a physical education teacher. As a result his first team appearances were far fewer and he spent much of 1976-77 in the reserves, before he was released in May 1977. He then signed for Forfar Athletic and began coaching there before becoming assistant manager at Brechin City and then at Forfar Athletic, where he took over as manager in July 1986. Henry went back into coaching with Dundee in 1991. He returned to St Johnstone as youth coach in 2000 and became manager at Montrose three years later. In 2008 he was appointed by the SFA as East Region Coach Mentor.

Tom McAdam was a striker with Dumbarton, a side he had joined in 1970 on an 'S' form. He came to United in October 1975 for around £37,000, as a replacement for Andy Gray. Tom made his debut on 1st November 1975 against St Johnstone in a Scottish League match, scoring twice. In his first season he netted 13 league and cup goals, including a hat-trick against Ayr United, to make him joint top scorer with Henry Hall. However, in the following season he scored just 11 times in 41 appearances. Although he had not achieved

Tom McAdam

what was expected, it still came as a surprise when he was transferred to Celtic in September 1977 for £60,000. Tom was with Celtic for nine successful years before he was released. He then joined Stockport County and had a spell at Hamilton Academical before signing for Motherwell during season 1986-87. He left them around three years later and played with Airdrieonians where he later became a coach.

Alex Rennie

Alex Rennie had started his senior career at Rangers without making it into the first eleven and then played briefly with Stirling Albion before he signed for St Johnstone in 1967. He was released by the Perth club in April 1975 and was offered terms by Hong Kong Rangers but then accepted an offer to sign for United in June 1975. A defensive midfielder, Alex made his first appearance for United in a testimonial for Brian McCann at Fraserburgh on 28th July 1975. He then made his debut in major competition on 23rd August 1975 against Kilmarnock in a League Cup tie. He was a regular in the United side for three seasons but his career ended prematurely following an eye injury in April 1978. A year later, he was advised to give up the game. He was a coach at Hearts before becoming manager at St Johnstone in April 1980. He later managed Stenhousemuir.

Billy Steele was released by Rangers after four seasons there without making it into the first team. He joined United in May 1975 and made a scoring debut as a substitute in a testimonial match for Brian McCann at Fraserburgh on 28th July 1975. On 9th August 1975, he scored in his first game in major competition, coming on as a substitute for George Fleming against St Johnstone in a League Cup tie. With intense competition for first team places, Billy spent more than half of season 1975-76 in the reserves, making most of his first team appearances that year from the bench. In

Billy Steele

September 1976, he joined Dumbarton for a fee of £5,000, staying for just one season before moving to Cowdenbeath, where he spent the next five years. He finished his senior career at Arbroath before joining the junior ranks in 1984.

1976-77 Player Profiles

Billy Kirkwood began his career at United as an attacker but he was later regarded very much as a utility player, filling midfield and defensive positions. Considered a Club legend, he was signed provisionally in May 1975 from Cornbank Boys Club and he started playing in United reserves in August 1976. Billy played for the first team, as a substitute, in Iain McDonald's testimonial match on 11th October 1976. He then made a scoring debut in his first match in major competition, against Hearts in a Scottish League match on 20th April 1977. In the next season, he made the breakthrough into the first team and for the next eight years

Billy Kirkwood

Billy was a regular in the line up. In his first two seasons, he was top scorer with just 11 goals each time, recording a hat-trick against Arbroath in October 1977. Although his goal tally then dropped, he still reached double figures in 1980-81 and 1983-84. Billy was a very dependable player and he collected winner's medals in the League Cup finals of 1979 and 1980, although in the latter match, he remained on the bench. He also has runners-up medals from two other League Cup finals and two in the Scottish Cup. In 1982-83 Billy played a big part in the United side that won the Scottish League championship. In Europe, he played regularly for United, appearing 44 times, including a run to the European Cup semi final against AS Roma in 1984. After returning to United in December 1986, following a six-month spell at Hibs, he played in the latter stages of the UEFA Cup run of 1986-87, where unfortunately, he collected a runners-up medal again. During his two stints with United, Billy played 399 times and is ranked fourteenth in the all time appearances chart. He joined Dunfermline Athletic in September 1987 and a year later signed for Dundee where he began a coaching career. His next move was as a coach at Rangers and in March 1995, he returned to United as Manager. In a short managerial career at Tannadice, he successfully took the Club back into the Premier League after they had spent a year in the

First Division. In the early weeks of the 1996-97 campaign, he was replaced by Tommy McLean. Billy then went to Hong Kong for a short time but returned in July 1997 to become assistant manager at Hull City. He had a brief spell as caretaker manager at St Johnstone and was also involved at Dundee, Dunfermline Athletic and Livingston. He later returned to Rangers as youth team coach.

Dave McKellar was signed in May 1976 after he was released by Ipswich Town. He had also been on loan at Peterborough United and Colchester United. During his one full season at Tannadice, he was the regular keeper in the reserves and played over 25 times, making the first of only two appearances in the first eleven on 2nd August 1976 against St Mirren in a friendly. His only other outing at first team level was in the testimonial for Iain McDonald two months later. He was released in May 1977, but after a couple of years in junior football, he signed for Derby County. He joined Brentford in 1980 and later played in Hong Kong before spells at Carlisle United and Hibs. Whilst with the Edinburgh side he went on loan to Manchester City and Newcastle United. Dave joined Hamilton Academical in 1986 and then went to Dunfermline Athletic and had a short stay on loan at Hartlepool United before going back to join Carlisle United. Late in his career, he turned out with Kilmarnock and ended his senior career at Rangers in 1992.

Ray Stewart signed an 'S' form with United in May 1973 when he was just thirteen years old and still a pupil at Perth Grammar School. He was with Errol Rovers in 1975, and captained the Scottish Schoolboys team. At the end of that year, he was playing in United's reserves. By early 1976 he was established in the Scotland professional youth side, eventually becoming captain and by May 1977 he was involved at Under-21 level. After playing regularly in United reserves, he made a first team debut on 1st September 1976 against Celtic in a League Cup tie but it was another year

Ray Stewart

before he became a first team regular. He was voted Young Player of the Year at the SPFA awards in 1979. Ray's talent attracted interest from south of the border and rumours of a move were confirmed when West Ham United bought him for around £400,000 at the end of August 1979, just days before his twentieth birthday. Part of the fee received was reinvested in the construction of the covering for the north terracing. Ray won an FA Cup medal with the London club, where he was the regular penalty taker, missing only ten times from almost ninety attempts. He earned full international recognition with a debut for Scotland in May 1981 against Wales, for the first of ten caps. In 1991 he left West Ham United to join St Johnstone and later played with Stirling Albion. Ray went into management at Forfar Athletic, Livingston and Stirling Albion.

Gordon G Wallace was a striker who began his career at Montrose in 1961, moving to Raith Rovers five years later. Winner of the SFWA Player of the Year award in 1967-68, he then played with Dundee and Seattle Sounders before joining United in August 1976. Gordon had a good goal scoring record and he had won a League Cup medal with Dundee in 1973. He made his United debut on 1st September 1976 against Celtic in a League Cup tie and went on to form a productive attacking partnership with Paul Sturrock over the next two years. He left United in February 1978 for a

Gordon Wallace

small fee, to become player/manager at Raith Rovers but returned to Tannadice three years later as a coach. In February 1989 he became manager at Dundee but left them in October 1991 to take the post of assistant manager at Dunfermline Athletic. Gordon remained there until 1993 when he returned to coach at United once again. Aged almost 51 years, Gordon actually played for United once more, in the summer of 1994 during the tour of Trinidad & Tobago. In 1998 he left Tannadice and became involved in broadcasting, as a football commentator and later returned to Dundee, again in a coaching role.

Billy Williamson

Billy Williamson was a midfield player who joined Aberdeen from the junior ranks in 1970. He initially turned down a move to United in early February 1977 but two weeks later, he signed for a fee reported at £14,000. Billy made his debut on 1st March 1977, coming on as a substitute for Tom McAdam against Partick Thistle in a Scottish League match. Used more in defence at Tannadice, he did not stay long and within six months he was transferred to Dundee in exchange for Bobby Robinson. Dundee also received a nominal cash adjustment. Billy spent four years at Dens Park and then moved to Australia where he played for Brisbane Lions, returning to Scotland in 1984.

1977-78 Player Profiles

John Bourke

John Bourke arrived at United to replace striker Tom McAdam. The initial offer to Dumbarton on 7th September 1977 for John was rejected but a bid of £60,000 was accepted a week later. He had joined Dumbarton in 1973 and netted an average of a goal every other game for them. After making a scoring debut for United against Clydebank in a Scottish League match on 17th September 1977, his season was hampered by a series of niggling injuries and he found the net just six times all season. In July 1978 he failed to return to Tannadice for pre-season training and was suspended by the Club. At the beginning of October 1978 he joined Kilmarnock for a fee of around £40,000. John returned to Dumbarton in 1983 and went to Brechin City in 1986 before signing for Kilmarnock for a second time. In 1989 he ended his senior career and moved to junior side Lesmahagow.

Andy Graham signed for United from Johnstone Burgh in December 1977. As deputy to goalkeeper Hamish McAlpine, he had few opportunities to get into the first team at United. Andy made his debut on 2nd May 1978 against Clydebank in a Scottish League match, but had just a few more first team appearances in his seven years at Tannadice. However, he played for the reserve side well over 100 times. During 1982-83 he was on loan at Forfar Athletic and Stirling Albion and during 1983-84 he was loaned out to Raith Rovers and Stirling Albion. He signed for the latter club on a permanent basis in the summer of 1984 and was with them for six years before joining Kilmarnock. In 1992 he joined Irish side Sligo Rovers.

Andy Graham

Tommy Hughes was a very experienced former Scotland Under-23 goalkeeper who had been with Chelsea, Aston Villa and Brighton & Hove Albion before joining Hereford Town in 1973, remaining with them for eight years. He arrived at Tannadice on loan for a month for trials in January 1978. However, the weather conspired to restrict him to just one first team outing, as a substitute for the second half against Raith Rovers in a friendly on 24th January 1978. He also played in a couple of reserve games before returning to his own club.

Jim McIntosh was an attacking player who had started his career at Montrose before joining Nottingham Forest in October 1970. He had been on loan at Chesterfield before moving to Hull City in March 1976 but was released by them in the summer of 1977 and signed for United. He made his first appearance against Alloa Athletic in a friendly on 1st August 1977 and played in one more friendly and a few reserve matches before he was released in November 1977, returning to Montrose, where he spent the next two seasons.

Ralph Milne was a Dundee United 'S' signing from Celtic Boys Club in early 1976. By 1977-78, he was an established reserve player and turned out for his first team debut against Alloa Athletic in a friendly on 1st August 1977. By March 1978 he was part of the Scotland Under-18 squad. Ralph made his debut in major competition against Dunfermline Athletic on 28th July 1979, in a Dryburgh Cup match, scoring one of the goals. During that season his name appeared frequently in the line ups. By 1980-81, he was firmly established in the first team and he collected a runners-up medal in the Scottish Cup final against Rangers at the end of

Ralph Milne

the season. Six months later Ralph picked up another runners-up medal against Rangers, this time in the League Cup final. His best season came in 1982-83, when his 16 league goals helped United win the Premier League championship. The goal he scored against Dundee in the final match of the league campaign is enough on its own, to warrant his status as a Club legend. In season 1984-85, he again collected runners-up medals in both the League Cup and Scottish Cup. Ralph was a wide attacking player with a flare for scoring spectacular goals and always saved his best for the big stage in Europe. He played in 41 European matches and holds the Dundee United record of 15 European goals, four of which he scored in the European Cup run to the semi final against AS Roma in 1983-84. In the opinion of many fans, Ralph never achieved his full potential. He was capped for Scotland three times at Under-21 level but had the ability to go much further in the international arena. He left United at the end of January 1987 to join Charlton Athletic and a year later went to Bristol City. He signed for Manchester United in November 1988 and spent some time on loan at West Ham United in 1989 before moving to Hong Kong to join Sing Tao. Ralph was inducted into the Dundee United Hall of Fame in January 2009.

Derek Murray

Derek Murray signed provisionally for Dundee United from Oakley United in March 1977. At the beginning of 1977-78 he was drafted into the second eleven, making a first team debut on 8th August 1977 in a friendly against East Fife. He was the regular left back in the reserve line up and made around 230 appearances in the second string in his seven years at United. Derek did not make his first team debut in major competition until 20th August 1980 against East Fife in a League Cup tie. In season 1981-82, he had an extended run in the side but that apart, he never broke into the first team and was released in the summer of 1984. He then joined Motherwell for a successful four seasons and had three years at Raith Rovers before returning to Oakley United as assistant manager.

Bobby Robinson joined United from neighbours Dundee in August 1977, in a deal that saw Billy Williamson and a nominal cash sum going in the opposite direction. A midfielder, Bobby had joined the Dark Blues from Falkirk in 1972 on a free transfer and won a League Cup winner's medal with Dundee in 1973. Whilst at Dens Park he had collected four international caps. He made a scoring debut for United against Albion Rovers on 17th August 1977 in a League Cup tie. Bobby was a regular in the side for the rest of the season but only played a dozen games in 1978-79, although he turned out frequently in

Bobby Robinson

the reserves. He joined Hearts early in August 1979 and later played for Raith Rovers before joining junior side Forfar Albion. Sadly, Bobby died in 1996 as a result of illness, aged just 46.

Derek Stark

Derek Stark was a schoolboy international who joined United on a provisional form from Glenrothes in 1975. A cultured defender who was just as capable in midfield, he was drafted into the squad for season 1976-77 and became a regular in the reserve line up. He made his first team debut a year later on 8th August 1977 against East Fife in a friendly. Another season developing in the reserves brought a first appearance in major competition on 2nd May 1978, against Clydebank in a Scottish League match. From the start of the next season, Derek was established in the defence and for six years he was a regular in the side. In December 1979, Derek collected a League Cup winner's medal against Aberdeen and was an unused substitute against

Dundee a year later. Derek also collected a runners-up medal in the Scottish Cup and League Cup. He was also a vital member of the side that won the Premier League Championship in 1982-83. Derek was not known for his goal scoring, but when he did find the net, it was often spectacular; like his long range effort against AS Roma, to give United a 2-0 win in the first leg of the European Cup semi final in 1984. Unfortunately that was to be his last season in senior football, as a recurring injury forced him to retire from the game aged just 26. He then became a police officer with Fife Constabulary. For his contribution to the 1982-83 championship success, he ranks amongst the Club legends.

Sandy Thomson was a goalkeeper who had been with Alyth United, Dunfermline Athletic and Blairgowrie. He then joined Alloa Athletic and after three seasons there, he signed for United in the summer of 1977. His first team debut was on 1st August 1977 against his former club in a friendly but after one other friendly, he was released in October 1977. Sandy then spent a short time at Brechin City before returning to the junior ranks with Blairgowrie.

Norman Vannart joined United reserves at the start of season 1976-77 after signing in the previous summer on an 'S' form. He was a left-sided attacking player and after a good season in the second string, he was given a first team debut as a substitute against Alloa Athletic in a friendly on 1st August 1977. Norman went no further with United and signed for Forfar Athletic two months later, joining a growing contingent of former United players. He appears to have been released by the Angus club at the end of the season and joined junior side Broughty Athletic.

Gordon Wallace was an attacking player who joined Raith Rovers in 1970. He had played well over 200 games for the Fife club before he signed for United in October 1977, for a fee reported at £12,000. Gordon made his debut when he came on as a substitute for John Bourke against Celtic, on 22nd October 1977 in a Scottish League match. He struggled with injury during his time at Tannadice and following a knee operation in August 1978, he was unable to re-establish himself in the first team, completing his career with United in the reserves. In the summer of 1979, he moved to Berwick Rangers where he spent eighteen months before signing for Cowdenbeath. In 1981, he moved to Australia where he joined Green Gully and played there for several years.

1978-79 Player Profiles

Ian Ballantyne

Ian Ballantyne was an attacking player who spent two years with Queen's Park where he earned the reputation of a penalty kick expert. He joined United in April 1979, making his first appearance when he came on as a substitute and scored, in a Forfarshire Cup tie against Dundee on 14th May 1979. His debut in major competition followed on 25th August 1979, when he came off the bench to replace Davie Dodds in a Scottish League match against Aberdeen. Ian did not stay long with United, leaving to join Raith Rovers for £12,500 in November 1979. He was with the Kirkcaldy side for four seasons and then went to East Stirlingshire. A year later, he was playing for Zindabad in Hong Kong.

Derek Frye began his senior career at Kilmarnock in 1972 and then moved to Queen of the South before joining Stranraer, where he became top scorer in the Second Division. He was then signed by United for a fee estimated at £15,000, making his debut on 12th August 1978, as a substitute for George Fleming against Hibs in a Scottish League match. He did not have the desired impact at Tannadice and was soon out of the running for a first team place, spending much of the remainder of the season in the reserves. In August 1979, Derek was transferred to Ayr United. After around five years there, he moved to Clyde

Derek Frye

for three years and then had a season at Airdrieonians before returning to Queen of the South and then back to Stranraer. In 1992, he was coaching at Queen of the South and later he managed non league Annan Athletic.

Graham Honeyman joined United for a one month trial in November 1978 after a short time playing in Australia with Hakoah and West Adelaide. Prior to that, he had been with East Fife for seven years. A midfield player, he made his debut for United as a substitute for Graeme Payne against Morton on 11th November 1978 in a Scottish League match. After two more games he was released and returned to West Adelaide.

Iain Phillip was a defensive player who began his senior career with Dundee in 1970. He moved to Crystal Palace in 1972 but a year later was back at Dens Park. He won his first League Cup medal with Dundee in December 1973. After four more years with Dundee, he crossed Tannadice Street for a fee of £25,000. Iain made his debut for United in a Scottish League match as a substitute for Davie Dodds against Celtic on 16th December 1978. He was a regular in the side for the next four years and collected League Cup winners' medals in 1979 against Aberdeen and in 1980 against Dundee. He

Iain Phillip

played in the losing final of 1981 against Rangers and also collected a runners-up medal in the Scottish Cup final in 1981. His last season with United was 1982-83 and he played five times in the Premier League championship winning campaign. Iain joined Raith Rovers midway through season 1983-84 and after three years there, moved to Arbroath before retiring from football.

The Statistics

The following chart lists the appearances and goals scored by Dundee United players signed from August 1945 – May 1979.

The total appearances in Scottish League, Scottish Cup, League Cup, European matches and in the Forfarshire Cup are self evident.

Matches grouped as 'Other Competitions' include all major national competitions other than the above.

Matches in local competitions, friendlies, testimonials, benefits, charity matches, tour games and abandoned matches have been excluded due to limitation of space. However, included in the chart are players who turned out for United in these types of matches only.

Debut	Name	League		Scottish Cup		League Cup		Europe		Other Comp		Forfarshire Cup	
		App	Gls	App	Gls	App	Gls	App	Gls	App	Gls	App	Gls
12-Jan-74	Addison D	105	9	5	4	17	2	8		2		9	
23-Aug-58	Adie J	5				3							
05-Feb-55	Aikman A	55	19	4	1	11	4					2	3
18-Aug-54	Anderson A	4				2							
16-Aug-52	Arnold A	109		10		21						7	
14-May-79	Ballantyne I	2				1						1	1
20-Aug-55	Barclay F	2				1							
13-Dec-47	Barr J	2											
10-Apr-46	Barron G	Took part in Miscellaneous/Other matches only											
14-Aug-54	Bell D	7	1	1		6						1	1
14-Nov-59	Bell J	4											
12-Dec-64	Berg M	43	8	2		6				10	8	4	2
14-Dec-46	Berrie D	144		13		23				5		18	
13-Apr-57	Berry A	3	2										
18-Mar-61	Boner D	21	4			6						1	
17-Sep-77	Bourke J	26	5	4	1							1	
16-Aug-47	Boyd J	48		1		12				1		4	
30-Apr-47	Brannan J	1				1						1	
16-Aug-69	Bremner W			1		3							
24-Aug-55	Briggs J	299	25	22	2	59	4	5		16	2	17	4
18-Nov-61	Brodie E	17	3	4	1	5	1					2	
10-Sep-58	Brown A	76		3		11						4	
17-Apr-68	Brown I	3											
22-Apr-57	Brown J	23	6			4						1	
19-Jan-46	Brown J	7	2			6	1			15	7	2	
29-Dec-73	Bush R	1											
10-Sep-60	Cairns K	22		1								1	
21-Nov-53	Callaghan F	76	2	2		16						7	2
23-Nov-57	Cameron A	13	4	2									
22-Apr-67	Cameron J	159	1	11		29		6		3		10	
26-Feb-49	Cameron J F	12				4				1		3	
08-May-68	Cameron K	133	64	7	5	28	13	1		1	1	11	16
23-Sep-50	Campbell C	3											
05-Mar-60	Campbell T	19	14			2						1	

Debut	Name	League App	League Gls	Scottish Cup App	Scottish Cup Gls	League Cup App	League Cup Gls	Europe App	Europe Gls	Other Comp App	Other Comp Gls	Forfarshire Cup App	Forfarshire Cup Gls
04-May-60	Carlyle W	78	39	8	2	17	4					5	2
14-Aug-65	Carroll R	2				4	1						
30-Oct-63	Clark J	2											
01-Aug-70	Clyde I	Took part in Miscellaneous/Other matches only											
16-Mar-57	Coats A	1											
17-Aug-49	Colgan J					2	1						
12-Aug-59	Collins P	1				1							
03-Apr-46	Collins R									1			
10-Feb-73	Cooper B	3											
30-Jul-75	Cooper D	Took part in Miscellaneous/Other matches only											
19-Dec-70	Copland J	144	18	14	1	19		5	1	10	2	5	
24-Aug-55	Coyle Jimmy	27	7	2		6	1					1	
30-Apr-51	Coyle John	96	78	9	9	27	25					3	2
05-Oct-59	Crabb D	1		1		1						2	
14-Feb-48	Craig J	3	1									2	1
18-Apr-59	Craig R	14	1			5						1	
14-Aug-54	Cross D	102	2	9	2	26	1			1		4	
11-Jan-47	Crothers W	33	26	2	2	8						6	7
04-Sep-48	Cruickshank G	134	23	14	2	35	7			3		12	
19-Jan-46	Cruickshanks J									12		1	
16-Aug-47	Dalling W			1		2							
10-Aug-46	Davidson J	11	2			4	1			3	3	2	
30-Oct-63	Davidson N	8	3	1									
02-Oct-61	Davie A	142		19		13		4		6		7	
09-Jan-71	Devlin A	8	3	1						2	1		
20-Mar-48	Dewar J	47	9	2	1	8	1			2		3	
14-Nov-64	Dick K	7	4	1									
26-Jun-63	Dick S	8				12							
18-Apr-59	Dickie W	10		1		2						1	
27-Dec-47	Dickson J	37	5	4	2	6				2		4	1
22-Jun-75	Dodds D	243	102	31	12	53	25	40	11	2		14	7
31-Oct-53	Doig E	1											
06-Sep-49	Donaldson A	8								1		1	

Debut	Name	League App	League Gls	Scottish Cup App	Scottish Cup Gls	League Cup App	League Cup Gls	Europe App	Europe Gls	Other Comp App	Other Comp Gls	Forfarshire Cup App	Forfarshire Cup Gls
05-Dec-64	Dossing F	86	60	8	5	11	1	1	1	9	9	3	2
02-Jul-63	Dougan R	Took part in Miscellaneous/Other matches only											
20-Aug-58	Douglas I	16		4		2						2	
15-Oct-49	Downie E	67	1	9		10				1		6	
10-Aug-57	Duncan J	11				6	2						
10-Nov-51	Dunlop T	2											
13-Nov-54	Dunlop W	20	8			1						1	1
27-Apr-68	Dunne T	11				1						6	5
12-Mar-49	Dunsmore A	75	16	9	3	17	8			3		12	
03-May-72	Eddie B	3										1	
08-Jan-49	Edmiston A	142		12		21				3		17	
27-Aug-49	Elliot J	6	6			3				1			
15-Nov-52	English S	38		3		8						9	
22-Aug-56	Evans A	1											
29-Jul-72	Fascione J	Took part in Miscellaneous/Other matches only											
12-Oct-55	Fenton E	Took part in Miscellaneous/Other matches only											
01-Sep-45	Ferguson C									9	4		
22-Sep-51	Fleck N	11	1	1	1							1	
12-Feb-72	Fleming G	259	31	19	3	40	2	11		11	1	9	
08-Aug-53	Forbes J	69	6	6		18	1					2	
22-Feb-58	Forrester G	9				1							
11-Jan-75	Forsyth A	27	2	2				1		2		2	1
21-Sep-57	Fox G	1											
14-Apr-47	France L	1											
18-Sep-57	Fraser S	193	11	16		31	2	1		6	2	8	1
12-Aug-78	Frye D	9	1			2		1		1		2	
29-Jan-72	Gardner P	76	18	9	3	18	2	2	1	8		5	5
14-Dec-57	Garvie A	10	3	3		10						1	
10-Aug-57	Gibson A	53										1	
05-Sep-59	Gillespie D	348	94	28	5	55	14	8		16	2	20	9
12-Aug-59	Goldie J	2				2							
29-Jul-74	Goodall B	Took part in Miscellaneous/Other matches only											
31-Mar-69	Gordon A	79	34	6	1	13	4	5	1	1	1	3	
18-Feb-61	Gordon H A	80	1	7		13				6		6	3

		League		Scottish Cup		League Cup		Europe		Other Comp		Forfarshire Cup	
Debut	Name	App	Gls	App	Gls	App	Gls	App	Gls	App	Gls	App	Gls
08-Aug-53	Gormley P	4				4							
02-May-78	Graham A	24	10			1				2		1	
27-Aug-66	Graham Jackie	15	1	1		5						1	1
08-Aug-64	Graham Johnny	52		2		8	3					1	
05-Sep-59	Graham T					7						3	
07-Dec-46	Grant G D	186	42	17	3	36	5			5	1	20	5
21-Jan-56	Grant G	7		2									
18-Aug-73	Gray A	62	36	8	3	14	7	5		6	1	2	2
15-Sep-56	Gray D	35		2		3							
02-Aug-71	Gray W	29	1			11				3		3	
03-Feb-51	Grieve R	1											
18-Apr-56	Grubb F												
06-Sep-49	Guthrie W	4	2										
12-May-52	Guy J	2				4							
16-Mar-66	Hainey W	47	8	2	1	12	5	4	2			1	1
02-Aug-75	Hall H	35	8	3	2	6	1	2	2	2	1	2	1
16-Oct-54	Halpin V	1											
13-Apr-57	Hamilton A	Took part in Miscellaneous/Other matches only											
12-Oct-55	Hamilton I	8										5	
17-Oct-53	Hamilton J	26		1		4						1	
29-Dec-45	Harrow W	15	3							8			
09-Aug-58	Hay H			3	1	3	1					1	1
16-Nov-74	Hegarty P	493	51	58	7	86	12	68	12	2		16	2
20-Mar-48	Henderson G	5								1	2	1	
11-Aug-56	Henderson R	2				8							
06-Aug-68	Henry J	93	7	4	2	22	1	4		7	2	3	
12-Apr-67	Hernon G	1	1										
11-Sep-54	Higgins L	5											
02-Mar-71	Hill G	Took part in Miscellaneous/Other matches only											
19-Jun-68	Hogg D	41	6	4	1	8	1	1				2	
19-Jan-74	Holt J	272	16	38	3	52	5	43				18	2
11-Nov-78	Honeyman G	3				1							
13-Aug-49	Hood A												
30-Mar-74	Houston D	86	5	8		6		7				4	

Debut	Name	League		Scottish Cup		League Cup		Europe		Other Comp		Forfarshire Cup	
		App	Gls	App	Gls	App	Gls	App	Gls	App	Gls	App	Gls
19-Nov-60	Howieson R	66	5	5	2	2						1	4
24-Jan-78	Hughes T	Took part in Miscellaneous/Other matches only											
23-Mar-46	Hull L												
14-Aug-48	Hume W	9								4		1	
10-Aug-57	Humphries W	54	32	5		10	6					1	
09-Aug-58	Hunter Jackie	19	9	4		6	3					2	1
25-Aug-45	Hunter John									5	2		
27-Oct-56	Hutton C	3											
29-Dec-56	Inglis I	1											
01-Nov-58	Irvine A	8											
14-Aug-54	Irvine I					1						1	
19-Aug-59	Irvine J	125	62	11	6	21	7			3	1	8	6
19-Apr-52	Irving J	7				4	1					1	
03-Oct-60	Jackson J	1											
09-Mar-46	Jardine A	67	2	4		24	14			13		7	2
28-Aug-46	Jeffrey G	3	1							2			
18-Dec-54	Johnston R	6	2										
30-Sep-50	Johnstone D	4											
13-Sep-47	Jones J					1							
18-Aug-45	Kelly W									20			
13-Aug-47	Kerr J	5	2			4	1					2	2
23-Sep-59	Kidd D	15		1								1	
28-Sep-59	King J	3	1			1							
03-May-47	Kinloch T	3				2				1		2	
14-Oct-50	Kinnell D	4	1			3				1		1	
11-Oct-76	Kirkwood W	261	46	34	5	59	14	44	5	1		11	2
15-Sep-51	Knight J	2											
08-Jan-72	Knox A	57	12	9	1	9	2	5		3	1	2	
29-Jan-72	Kopel F	284	7	28		61	1	22	2	12	3	11	6
29-Nov-52	Laird J	15		1	1								
16-Aug-69	Letford I					2							
06-Sep-49	Leven E	Took part in Miscellaneous/Other matches only											
14-Nov-70	Liddle A	1											
19-Oct-46	Lister A	23	16	1		6	5						

Debut	Name	League App	League Gls	Scottish Cup App	Scottish Cup Gls	League Cup App	League Cup Gls	Europe App	Europe Gls	Other Comp App	Other Comp Gls	Forfarshire Cup App	Forfarshire Cup Gls
23-Jan-54	Locherty J	1											
10-Sep-55	Lornie I	2											
28-Feb-53	Lovie J	6										3	
08-Apr-57	Lucas W	57		6		12						2	
08-Aug-59	MacFadyen I	13		1		6						1	
01-Sep-45	MacFarlane A	5				2				11	1	2	
11-Aug-62	Mackay D	171		12		44		5		11		12	
04-Sep-46	Mackay P									1			
23-Apr-73	MacLeod D	25	3	2		7	1	1		1		3	
27-Aug-47	Malcolm A	3	1			3							
29-Dec-56	Markie J	Took part in Miscellaneous/Other matches only											
28-Aug-68	Markland S	78	2	6		13		6	1	3		3	
06-Sep-58	Martin T	11	3										
17-Nov-45	Martin W									4	1		
20-Nov-54	Massie A	40	3	1		5						2	
01-Nov-75	McAdam T	61	21	4	1	7				2	1	2	
06-Aug-68	McAlpine H	477	3	45		103	1	52		11		20	
08-Jan-55	McBain J	45	1	3		4						2	
05-Sep-53	McCann R	27	4	1								5	
06-Mar-48	McCormack J	7								1		2	1
02-Mar-71	McDonald G	Took part in Miscellaneous/Other matches only											
29-Jul-74	McDonald I	30	6	2		9		5				2	
09-Feb-57	McDonald W	70	28	6	1	13	4					4	2
01-Jun-66	McFall R	Took part in Miscellaneous/Other matches only											
04-Dec-54	McGairy T	28	13			5	1			6		2	
11-Aug-45	McGowan J												
08-Aug-59	McGrory F	1				1							
26-Jan-57	McGuinness J	5	2	3									
07-Oct-50	McIlwain M	4	1										
29-Dec-45	McInally E									5	1		
12-Aug-50	McIndewar A					2	1						
01-Aug-77	McIntosh J	Took part in Miscellaneous/Other matches only											
10-Nov-51	McIvor J	4	1			5						3	
13-Sep-47	McKay P	185	157	15	12	37	30	4	4	4		20	27

Debut	Name	League App	League Gls	Scottish Cup App	Scottish Cup Gls	League Cup App	League Cup Gls	Europe App	Europe Gls	Other Comp App	Other Comp Gls	Forfarshire Cup App	Forfarshire Cup Gls
30-Aug-47	McKee F	14		1		3							
19-Sep-53	McKee J	1											
02-Aug-76	McKellar D	Took part in Miscellaneous/Other matches only											
31-Jan-48	McKenzie G	13		1						1		1	
20-Mar-48	McKenzie R	5								1		1	
04-Sep-57	McKillop R	1											
23-Mar-63	McKinlay H	2	1										
24-Nov-45	McKinnon N	6	1			6	4			18	7	1	
24-Dec-55	McKinven N	3											
20-Nov-54	McLaren A	10				4							
08-Aug-53	McLean D					3							
04-Apr-66	McLeish H	Took part in Miscellaneous/Other matches only											
14-Aug-54	McLeod T S					2	1						
20-Aug-60	McLeod T	7	2			3	3						
24-Aug-63	McManus J	11	2	2		4	2			4		1	
31-Dec-60	McMichael J	9	1	1		1							
27-Nov-54	McMillan D	1											
25-Aug-51	McMillan G	11				5						1	
19-Apr-52	McMillan J	5				5							
13-Aug-52	McMullen C					3	1						
23-Apr-52	Melville J	Took part in Miscellaneous/Other matches only											
05-Aug-67	Millar J	16	3			6						4	1
17-Mar-62	Millar T	207	8	21	1	34	1	4		16		10	1
10-Aug-46	Miller A	25	18	1		14				4			
16-Apr-55	Milne M	62		7	5	15	8					1	
01-Aug-77	Milne R	179	45	22		43	14	41	15	1	1	13	6
01-Jan-49	Mitchell G	71	9	9	1	19				2		7	1
29-Sep-62	Mitchell I	239	101	23	9	34	16	5	1	13	6	12	6
19-Nov-60	Mochan N	70	31	4		11	4					3	1
27-Nov-71	Mollison H	2											
28-Aug-63	Moore J	5		1		1							
08-Aug-64	Moran D	3	1			7	2						
08-Aug-53	Morris H					2							
25-Mar-50	Morrison G	17	5	1		2						1	

359

Debut	Name	League		Scottish Cup		League Cup		Europe		Other Comp		Forfarshire Cup	
		App	Gls	App	Gls	App	Gls	App	Gls	App	Gls	App	Gls
02-Apr-60	Morrison S	2											
24-Nov-45	Mudie G									1			
01-Mar-47	Muir T	6				3						1	
14-Sep-74	Munro A	2	1										
08-Aug-64	Munro F	50	14	3		17	8			10	1	1	
13-Aug-52	Munro G	20	1	2		3							
14-Mar-53	Murphy J	19	5	1		7	1					2	
14-Dec-74	Murphy K	1											
08-Aug-77	Murray D	16		1		3		3				1	
03-Jan-59	Napier A	10	2	2								1	
21-Nov-73	Narey D	612	23	70	1	108	6	76	6	6		21	1
24-Oct-59	Neilson T	235	9	23	1	38	6	4		16	1	12	3
25-Apr-59	Newton W	13	8			6							
04-Apr-59	Norris R	29	5	2	1	5						1	
14-Aug-48	Ogilvie D	18		3		6				1		2	
27-Feb-60	Ormond G	44	7	2		10	1					3	
09-Dec-50	Ormond H	7				4							
20-Oct-45	Pacione E	53	13	2	1	12	6			22	15	10	5
23-Apr-62	Pattie G	7	1			1						1	
11-Aug-73	Payne G	201	11	17	3	50	5	21	1	4	1	8	1
17-Aug-55	Penman R	8				1							
17-Dec-55	Penman W	5	1										
05-Dec-64	Persson O	77	15	8	1	12	1	4				3	
16-Dec-78	Phillip I	88	1	11		33		15		2		3	
12-Dec-59	Prior P	5	2										
05-Aug-67	Purcell P	1										1	1
01-Sep-48	Quinn F	156	89	14	5	26	13			4	2	13	5
22-Mar-58	Rae A	10		1		3				3			
23-Mar-46	Rae L	26				3						4	
26-Jan-74	Rankin B	2		3	1	3							
02-Aug-68	Reid A	101	14	8	1	29	4	6	1	3		2	
15-Oct-60	Reid Dave	2	1										
02-Jan-46	Reid Devon									3			
01-Aug-70	Reid I	13	3	2		7	2	1	1			1	2

Debut	Name	League		Scottish Cup		League Cup		Europe		Other Comp		Forfarshire Cup	
		App	Gls	App	Gls	App	Gls	App	Gls	App	Gls	App	Gls
26-Mar-55	Reid J	52	16	4	1	20	10					1	
15-Sep-69	Reilly G												
28-Jul-75	Rennie A	63		7		11		1		2		4	
25-Aug-62	Riddle A	4	1			3		5	1				
27-Sep-58	Robertson C	27		4		1						2	
18-Aug-54	Robertson J	2				3							
13-Nov-54	Robertson T	3											
17-Aug-77	Robinson R	30		1		5	1	3				2	
31-Aug-60	Roe J	10				2							
30-Sep-67	Rolland A	327	29	27	2	60	5	14	1	12	1	18	3
19-Jun-63	Rooney B	22	4	2		9	3			5	1	3	3
18-Mar-70	Rooney E											1	
10-Aug-46	Ross S	28	2	1		14	1			4		3	1
28-Sep-57	Roy J	14	1										
17-Aug-46	Salmond J	1	1										
08-Aug-53	Samuel J	4	1			5						1	
20-Sep-58	Scott A I	27	9	2	1							1	
06-May-67	Scott I	63	14	4	3	5	1	3	1	1		4	
29-Mar-52	Scott John												
25-Nov-59	Scott Jack												
04-Jan-54	Scrimgeour A	2	1			2						1	
27-Oct-65	Seemann F	52	12	6		5	4	4	1			1	
18-Feb-50	Shaw A	12	5									1	
12-Dec-53	Shearer J	16		1								5	
02-Feb-74	Sheehy S	3											
17-Aug-49	Sherry R	6				4							
08-Sep-45	Shufflebottom F									28	1	1	
26-Apr-61	Sievewright G	8										1	
10-Aug-46	Simpson Robert	46	1	2		12				4		3	
05-Oct-63	Simpson Ronnie	3											
11-Dec-54	Simpson T	5	1										
18-Oct-47	Sinclair M	16	2										
22-Aug-53	Smith A	10										1	
22-Apr-59	Smith D	456	18	42	3	91	5	16		23	1	27	2

Debut	Name	League App	League Gls	Scottish Cup App	Scottish Cup Gls	League Cup App	League Cup Gls	Europe App	Europe Gls	Other Comp App	Other Comp Gls	Forfarshire Cup App	Forfarshire Cup Gls
01-Feb-64	Smith G	6	1									1	
22-Dec-45	Smith H									9	1	1	
08-Aug-59	Smith P	18	2	1		5	1			2		1	
29-Aug-62	Smith R	7	1			3				9			
20-Mar-67	Smith Walter	134	2	17		18	1	5		3		10	2
11-Aug-45	Smith William												
22-Sep-51	Sneddon R	1											
27-Apr-63	Soutar D	4	1			1						1	1
07-Mar-59	Stalker J	15	5			1						2	1
08-Aug-77	Stark D	164	7	15		40		26	4	2		8	
01-Jan-46	Steele P									5	5		
28-Jul-75	Steele W	10		1		5	3	1				1	
23-Apr-73	Steen I	4											
16-Jan-54	Stenhouse A	27	3	2		5						4	2
06-Nov-54	Stephen A	25	6	2		3	4					1	
11-Feb-70	Stevenson M	32	3	4		2		3		2			
10-Nov-45	Stewart Alec												
30-Aug-61	Stewart Alex					1							
11-Sep-54	Stewart E	71	2	3		14						2	
09-Nov-46	Stewart G	7	4										
02-Nov-65	Stewart I	1	1										
28-Apr-65	Stewart J	Took part in Miscellaneous/Other matches only											
01-Sep-76	Stewart R	44	5	1		4		1		2	1	4	2
02-Oct-50	Stratton D	43	2	2		4				3		2	1
02-Aug-69	Stuart A	1				2	1						
12-Oct-55	Sturrock D	83	20	10	2	17	4			2		2	
18-Sep-74	Sturrock P	386	109	48	12	79	38	60	11	3	1	15	4
24-Mar-51	Swan R	31		6		3				1		3	
19-Sep-53	Tait A	21	2	1								3	
06-Dec-52	Temple J	29	4	1		1						4	4
09-May-64	Thom L	11	2			9	4			13	2	1	
04-Apr-66	Thompson I	Took part in Miscellaneous/Other matches only											
01-Aug-77	Thomson A	Took part in Miscellaneous/Other matches only											
11-Oct-52	Timmins J	1											

Debut	Name	League		Scottish Cup		League Cup		Europe		Other Comp		Forfarshire Cup	
		App	Gls	App	Gls	App	Gls	App	Gls	App	Gls	App	Gls
27-Oct-45	Tivendale J	1											
06-Oct-58	Tosh G												
05-Aug-70	Traynor T	122	15	13	3	26	4	8	1	7		5	
13-Aug-60	Ugolini R	44		1		7				7		1	
01-Aug-77	Vannart N	Took part in Miscellaneous/Other matches only											
09-Jan-60	Walker E	8	2	2		3	2						
02-Oct-56	Wallace C	7	3			5							
22-Oct-77	Wallace G	15	3	1									
01-Sep-76	Wallace G G	38	16	1		9	3					1	
09-Aug-58	Wallace J	20	3	1		5		2				1	
22-Aug-56	Wannan N	6				1							
22-Aug-53	Ward J					3							
18-Aug-48	Watson A	6				3				1		1	
05-Apr-71	Watson J	8				6				1		1	
24-Nov-56	Watt D	17	8	3									
28-Mar-59	Welsh J	3											
02-Mar-71	White A	47	11			10	2			3	1	3	1
02-Mar-71	White J	5											
26-Dec-59	Whytock D	8	6	1									
24-Aug-55	Will A	18		4		11							
01-Mar-77	Williamson W	11	1										
05-Aug-67	Wilson D	129	20	11	3	24	4	5				6	3
16-Feb-46	Wilson Jack											1	
04-Sep-57	Wilson Jimmy	2											
23-Jan-65	Wing L	68	9	7		7						3	
05-Aug-67	Wood W	67	5	5		10	1			1		7	1
19-Nov-49	Wyllie R	86		9		13	1					5	
02-Jan-47	Wyllie T	3				2							
02-Jan-58	Yeats R	95	1	9		14				1		3	
24-Nov-45	Yorston B												
03-Sep-58	Young A	35		4		5		4				2	
12-Oct-55	Young D	29		3		12						1	
11-Aug-45	Young H									6			
20-Oct-45	Young L									8	3		
11-Mar-64	Young R	7	3							1		3	

Bibliography

My main information sources were periodicals produced by D C Thomson & Co Ltd.

The Dundee Courier & Advertiser
The Evening Telegraph & Post
The Saturday Evening Post
The Sporting Post
The Sunday Post
The People's Journal

Amongst countless internet sites the following were most useful:-
www.since1888.com
www.neilbrown.newcastlefans.com
http://geocities.com/br1anmccoll/
www.scottishfa.co.uk
www.soccerbase.com
www.wikipedia.com
www.dutchplayers.nl
www.ozfootball.net
www.rsssf.com
www.dbu.dk
www.fifa.com
www.dallasnews.com

Other websites of interest to Dundee United fans include:-
www.dundeeunitedfc.co.uk
www.youthatunited.com
www.feddusc.com
www.a90arabs.net
www.weejimsta.co.uk

www.glenrothesarabs.co.uk
www.eastangusarabs.co.uk
www.ediarabs.co.uk
www.glsarabs.co.uk
www.southlondontangerines.co.uk
www.arabtrust.org.uk

Other sources of information.
Dundee United Who's Who by Pat Kelly, John Donald Publishers Ltd.
Rags To Riches by Mike Watson, David Winter & Son Ltd.